Absent the Archive
Cultural Traces of a Massacre in Paris
17 October 1961

Contemporary French and Francophone Cultures, 73

Contemporary French and Francophone Cultures

Series Editor

CHARLES FORSDICK
University of Liverpool

Editorial Board

TOM CONLEY
Harvard University

JACQUELINE DUTTON
University of Melbourne

LYNN A. HIGGINS
Dartmouth College

MIREILLE ROSELLO
University of Amsterdam

DEREK SCHILLING
Johns Hopkins University

This series aims to provide a forum for new research on modern and contemporary French and francophone cultures and writing. The books published in *Contemporary French and Francophone Cultures* reflect a wide variety of critical practices and theoretical approaches, in harmony with the intellectual, cultural and social developments which have taken place over the past few decades. All manifestations of contemporary French and francophone culture and expression are considered, including literature, cinema, popular culture, theory. The volumes in the series will participate in the wider debate on key aspects of contemporary culture.

Recent titles in the series:

60 Nicholas Harrison, *Our Civilizing Mission: The Lessons of Colonial Education*

61 Joshua Armstrong, *Maps and Territories: Global Positioning in the Contemporary French Novel*

62 Thomas Baldwin, *Roland Barthes: The Proust Variations*

63 Lucas Hollister, *Beyond Return: Genre and Cultural Politics in Contemporary French Fiction*

64 Naïma Hachad, *Revisionary Narratives: Moroccan Women's Auto/Biographical and Testimonial Acts*

65 Emma Wilson, *The Reclining Nude: Agnès Varda, Catherine Breillat, and Nan Goldin*

66 Margaret Atack, Alison S. Fell, Diana Holmes, Imogen Long, *Making Waves: French Feminisms and their Legacies 1975–2015*

67 Ruth Cruickshank, *Leftovers: Eating, Drinking and Re-thinking with Case Studies from Post-war French Fiction*

68 Etienne Achille, Charles Forsdick, Lydie Moudileno, *Postcolonial Realms of Memory: Sites and Symbols in Modern France*

69 Patrick Crowley and Shirley Jordan, *What Forms Can Do: The Work of Form in 20th and 21st-century French Literature and Thought*

70 Erin Twohig, *Contesting the Classroom: Reimagining Education in Moroccan and Algerian Literatures*

71 Keith Reader, *The Marais: The Story of a Quartier*

72 Jane Hiddleston and Khalid Lyamlahy, *Abdelkébir Khatibi: Postcolonialism, Transnationalism and Culture in the Maghreb and Beyond*

LIA BROZGAL

Absent the Archive

Cultural Traces of a Massacre in Paris
17 October 1961

LIVERPOOL UNIVERSITY PRESS

First published 2020 by
Liverpool University Press
4 Cambridge Street
Liverpool
L69 7ZU

British Library Cataloguing-in-Publication data
A British Library CIP record is available

ISBN 978-1-78962-238-6 cased
ISBN 978-1-80034-819-6 limp

Typeset by Carnegie Book Production, Lancaster
Printed and bound by CPI Group (UK) Ltd, Croydon CR0 4YY

Pour tous ceux qui militent contre l'oubli.

For Alice !
for the inspiration !
for the friendship !
for the fabulous conversations !
With fondness + admiration, always.
— Lu

LA, 20 avril 2020

Contents

List of Figures   ix

Acknowledgments   xi

Introduction: The Scene of the Crime, The Crime of the Seen   1

1   Excavating the Anarchive: An Archeology of the Corpus   31

2   Archive Stories: From Politics to Romances   71

3   *Non-lieux de mémoire*: Maps and Graffiti in the Scriptable City   115

4   The Seine's Exceptional Bodies   163

5   "How Lucky Were the Blond Kabyles": Reading Race in the Anarchive   213

6   The Entangled Stories of October 17, Vichy, the Jews, and the Holocaust   265

Epilogue: The Ends of the Anarchive   311

Bibliography   319

Index   337

Figures

Fig. 1. Graffiti inscribed on the Quai de Conti, across from
the Institut de France (Paris 6th *arrondissement*).
Photo © Jean Texier. October–November 1961.   18

Fig. 2. "50th Anniversary of the Day of Emigration."
Commemorative stamp issued by Algérie Poste
(the Algerian postal service) in 2011.   23

Fig. 3. Cover of play by Marie-Christine Prati-Belmokhtar.
Inset: painting by Afif Cherfaoui, "Enfants d'octobre"
(Children of October).   62

Fig. 4. "Paris, le 17 octobre 1961."
Graphics © Mustapha Boutadjine.   63

Fig. 5. "Three starting points in the suburbs."
Graphic by *France-Soir*. October 19, 1961.   125

Fig. 6. Graphic representations of colonial incursions in
La France est un empire (France is an Empire).
Documentary. Dir. Jean D'Agraives. France, 1939.   129

Fig. 7. Hand-drawn map of the demonstration on
October 17, 1961, in *Mémoires du 17 octobre*.
Documentary short. Dir. Faïza Guène. France, 2002.   133

Fig. 8. Inside "les RG," the intelligence service of the French
Police. *Ici on noie les Algériens* (Here we drown Algerians).
Documentary. Dir. Yasmina Adi. France, 2011.   134

Fig. 9. Mapping the October 17 graffiti. Map created by
Yann Potin and Vincent Lemire. © 2002.   155

Fig. 10. "Résister à l'oublis" [*sic*]. (Resist forgetting.) "Fresco"
created during street performance by Komplex Kapharnaüm.
Marseille, October 17, 2014. Photo: Lia Brozgal.   161

Fig. 11. A foreign body in the Seine? *Octobre à Paris.*
Documentary. Dir. Jacques Panijel. France, 1962.   185

Fig. 12. The scars of October 17. *Octobre à Paris.*
Documentary. Dir. Jacques Panijel. France, 1962.   187

Fig. 13. Beneath the surface; last images of
Ici on noie les Algériens. Documentary.
Dir. Yasmina Adi. France, 2011.   199

Fig. 14. Two commemorative posters: "17 octobre 1961.
Bleu, blanc, rouge" and "17 octobre 1961. Noir et blanc."
Graphics © Miloud Kerzazi.   200

Fig. 15. Juliette Binoche and Daniel Auteuil in *Caché.*
Feature film. Dir. Michael Haneke, 2005.   210

Fig. 16. "On a appris à nager" (We've learned to swim).
Final image of music video by Zik Zitoun (2017).   317

Acknowledgments

In the fall of 2005, when I was supposed to be writing a thesis on Albert Memmi, two unrelated texts drew my focus and have been distracting me ever since: one was the novel *Vivre me tue*, which I just happened to pluck off the bookshelf at L'Harmattan. Improbably, I opened the book to a passage where the narrator mentions his Uncle Mehdi, a gentleman who was killed by the police on October 17, 1961—*even though he was not Algerian*. That afternoon, I went to a café instead of the BnF, and read the novel in a single go. The second distraction came shortly thereafter: a new Haneke film was playing in the neighborhood, so I went along to see *Caché*. October 17 is one of many things hidden in this film: "Je te fais pas un dessin," Daniel Auteuil's character explains to his wife, played by Binoche—in other words, "I don't have to spell it out for you..." And yet, maybe he did? That year, in moments of distraction (or perhaps we should call it creation), I often found myself gazing away from the pages of my dissertation only to write, in my mind, a different story: one about a seemingly unknown event with no name other than a date, that I had just learned about in a novel and in a fleeting mention in a film.

So began a years-long (and ongoing) process of seeking out the cultural traces of October 17. Support in this endeavor has taken so many forms that I fear I won't be able to account for them all. This project was underwritten, at various stages, by several University of California, Los Angeles (UCLA) Academic Senate Faculty Research Grants; a University of California (UC) Presidential Fellowship in the Humanities (2012–13); the Camargo Foundation's Scholar in Residency program (2014); and a grant from the American Council of Learned Societies (ACLS) (2015–16). I am grateful to the Office of the Dean of Humanities and the Department of French and Francophone Studies at UCLA for making it possible for me to take full advantage of the resources and time these awards provided. Infinite thanks to Dean David Schaberg for making possible this book's existence in paperback. I am also grateful to Dominic Thomas and Françoise Lionnet for their intellectual support.

Numerous scholars have given me opportunities to share my work at their home departments or at conferences they hosted. This project has thus been shaped, at every turn, by stimulating conversations with students and faculty at the University of Notre Dame, King's College London, Stanford University, The University of Texas at Austin, Yale University, the University of Southern California (USC), the Universities of California at Irvine and Berkeley, and l'EHESS-Marseille. Presentations at Texas A&M's Glasscock Center for Humanities Research ("Foreigners and Outsiders in Modern European Culture" conference) and at the University of Kentucky's Bale Boone Symposium ("Europe Today and the Memory of Violence"), also provided a lively context for exchange. I have also had opportunities to workshop parts of this book thanks to the exceptional scholars who came together for 2017 The Maghrib Workshop (organized by Camilo Gómez-Rivas, UC, Santa Cruz) and for the ongoing meetings of the California Working Group on Jews in the Maghrib and the Middle East, or CalJEMM (organized by Jessica Marglin (USC) and Emily Gottreich (UC, Berkeley)).

No matter where his future research takes him, Jim House will forever be associated with his work on October 17. I have benefited immensely not only from his masterful account of the event and its afterlives (co-written with Neal MacMaster), but also from his unparalleled generosity. Jim has shared his time, his expertise, and his archives; he has responded to countless emails about details and big questions. Conversations with other October 17 scholars—notably Gilles Manceron and Alexandra Weik Van Mossner—have also been invaluable.

Access to documentation held at the Archives de la police de Paris (when it was still located in Paris' 5th *arrondissement*) and at the Centre culturel algérien à Paris has been critical to telling this story. I have also had the privilege to meet (sometimes in person, sometimes only virtually) a number of the cultural agents whose work forms the bedrock of this book. Je remercie très chaleureusement Leïla Sebbar, Mehdi Lallaoui, et Alexandra Badea, ainsi que les artistes Miloud Kerzazi et Mustapha Boutadjine, et les musiciens du groupe « Zik Zitoun » (surtout Brahim, alias Mess B, qui a patiemment répondu à une flopée de questions). Votre générosité et votre esprit de partage me touchent et me motivent. Sachez que l'on s'érige contre l'oubli du 17 octobre depuis Los Angeles, aussi.

Several cohorts of graduate students and undergraduates in UCLA's Department of French and Francophone Studies have been my (mostly) witting guinea pigs in seminars on October 17. The group of young scholars who came together for the 2019 edition of Bryn Mawr's *Institut d'Avignon* also gamely took on some of this material. My students' enthusiasm continually reinforces my conviction that this project models a way of thinking, a toolkit that can be carried into other territories and used to read other texts.

I have benefited from the support of Charles Forsdick and his amazing team at Liverpool University Press—a group that has emerged as a standard-bearer for professionalism in academic publishing. My editor, Chloé Johnson, is a pleasure to work with; I am grateful to her for calling on expert peer-reviewers whose reports have improved this manuscript immensely. In addition to the press's official, anonymous reviewers, I would like to thank the squadron of unofficial reviewers who have read and offered generous comments on book proposals, chapters, and the thorny question of the title: Susan Rubin Suleiman, Alice Kaplan, Sara Kippur, Patrick Bray, and Sarah Stein. Greg Cohen and Nick Harrison read the entire manuscript cover to cover, pointing out gaps and problems, but also offering so many refinements. Although this project was nearly complete when I joined the "USC writing group," Olivia Harrison, Jessica Marglin, and Neetu Khanna were catalysts in the choice of the book's ultimate title.

I'm indebted to numerous others: Alison Rice, whose talk at UCLA in 2009 gave me the inspiration to pursue this work; Kareem James Abu-Zeid for his astute editing; Rebecca Glasberg for her eleventh-hour bibliography interventions; Maya Boutaghou for the opportunity to publish an early version of the material on documentary film; David Hirsch for his research expertise; Tom Garbelotti, for his assistance in preparing the images featured in this book; Susan Johnson, for her keen eye, her mastery of style, and her indexing acumen; Julie Chenot for her welcome at the Camargo Foundation; Carrie Noland for her generous commentary on a grant proposal; and to Susan, Alice, Sarah, Nick, Michael Rothberg, Max Silverman, Gil Hochberg, Françoise Lionnet, and Dominic Thomas, for modeling the types of engagement with culture and politics that I strive to emulate.

And for all the kinds of support too capacious to be articulated properly: Jean-Claude Carron, Erin Cooney, Amy Cooper, Laurence Denié-Higney, Maggie Flinn, Nicolas Gorodetska, Laura Hartson, Sara Kippur, Josh Lambert, Andrea Moudarres, Angela Sarno, Malina

Stefanovska, Bess Whitesel, and Loren Wolfe. With gratitude to Dinah Diwan and Marc Sounigo. And to my stepfather David Urbanski, and to my mother, Toni Urbanski, who raised me under a sign—a poster featuring the Jedi Master Yoda—that ordered: "READ. And the force will be with you." This book is for her; may she read it, and may the force be with her.

Introduction

The Scene of the Crime,
The Crime of the Seen

> Politics revolves around what is seen and what can be said about it, around who has the ability to see and the talent to speak, around the properties of spaces and the possibilities of time.[1]
>
> —Jacques Rancière

> Literature is not evidence but an instrument for imaginative thinking.[2]
>
> —Gayatri Spivak

On the night of October 17, 1961, it was drizzling in Paris. The Shah of Iran, Mohammad Reza Pahlavi, was in town for a three-day state visit, accompanied by his wife, the Empress Farah. Near the Porte de Versailles, in the southwestern corner of the city, workers prepared the brand new Palais des Sports (built on the location of the former Vélodrome d'Hiver) for a series of concerts by the American jazzman

---

Note on translation: Wherever possible, I have used published English-language translations (for all text) and English subtitles (for film). All unattributed translations are my own.

1   Jacques Rancière, *The Politics of Aesthetics*, trans. Gabriel Rockhill (London: Continuum, 2004), 13.

2   Gayatri Spivak, "Afterword," in *Approaches to Teaching the Works of Assia Djebar*, ed. Anne Donadey (New York: Modern Language Association of America, 2017), 158.

Ray Charles.[3] In the center of the capital, at the storied Olympia concert hall, Belgian crooner Jacques Brel wooed a star-studded crowd. A few blocks away, along the *grands boulevards*, posters at the Rex announced an extended run for John Huston's 1960 Western *The Unforgiven* and the marquee of the Berlitz touted Jean Gabin's star turn in *Le cave se rebiffe* (The Counterfeiters of Paris).[4]

On October 17, 1961, Paris went about its business, while beneath the gazes of Lancaster, Hepburn, and Gabin, in the streets of the capital from the Garnier opera house to the literati headquarters of Saint-Germain-des-Prés, and from the Latin Quarter to the tony suburb of Neuilly-sur-Seine, Algerians were being bludgeoned en masse by the police.

————

Although France had been at war with Algeria for nearly seven years, on that autumnal Tuesday night, in the ordinary hustle and bustle of the capital, the conflict must have seemed only a distant reality. Yet after nightfall, when some 20,000 Algerians took to the streets in a peaceful demonstration against the repressive measures to which they had been subjected by the French state, Algeria and all it symbolized was thrust onto center stage. Rigorously orchestrated by the Front de libération nationale (FLN) (National Liberation Front), the demonstration was peaceful and dignified: marchers were given strict orders to turn out in their best clothes and with their families; weapons of any kind were forbidden.

Notwithstanding these precautions, the protest was met with disproportionate brutality: following the government's order to defend the capital, Chief of Police Maurice Papon gave free rein to his men; unprovoked, the police fired into crowds and bludgeoned with impunity. When the sun came up on October 18, some 10,000 Algerian men had

3   For more on the Ray Charles concert in the context of the Algerian War, see Celeste Day Moore, "Ray Charles in Paris: Race, Protest, and the Soundscape of the Algerian War," *American Quarterly* 71, no. 2 (2019): 449–72.

4   Released in 1960, John Huston's *The Unforgiven* (in French: *Le vent de la plaine*; with Burt Lancaster and Audrey Hepburn) deals with racism against Native Americans in the Old West. *Le cave se rebiffe*, directed by Gilles Grangier, opened in Paris in September 1961. Jean Gabin's presence recalls his role as Pépé le moko (in Julien Duvivier's 1939 eponymous film), in which he plays a jewel thief on the lam, hiding from the French police in the casbah of colonial Algiers.

been arrested, countless beaten and injured, and 200 were dead.[5] Some had been shot to death, some succumbed to traumatic injury; others, in one of the more grisly details in modern French history, had been handcuffed and thrown into the river to drown, transforming the iconic Seine into a watery tomb. The death toll among the police that night was zero.

Within a matter of days, official narratives minimized the violence, citing only three Algerian deaths and pinning the blame on internecine vendettas.[6] This muted version of events was propped up by a variety of authoritarian measures: the government censored the press and publishing houses, ordered cameras and film rolls seized and destroyed, and quickly deployed crews to whitewash accusatory graffiti spray painted along the riverbanks, claiming, "Ici on noie les Algériens" (Here we drown Algerians). The police archives were sealed and would remain classified for the next five decades. The coroner's office, faced with undeniable physical evidence of the crimes, grimly and euphemistically recorded the cause of death as "noyade par balles" (drowning by

---

5   The actual death toll among Algerians on October 17 is a point of contention. Jim House and Neil MacMaster provide an excellent overview of what they have dubbed "the numbers battle" in official reports and historical accounts. See Chapter 6, "Counting the Victims and Identifying the Killers," in *Paris 1961: Algerians, State Terror and Memory* (Oxford: Oxford University Press, 2006), 161–79. Hélène Jaccomard has observed, in the context of other massacres, that counting the dead is often fraught; in the case of October 17, however, "the discrepancy is so wide that the magnitude of the massacre, and therefore its fundamental meaning, is at stake." See "The Algerian War on French Soil: The Paris Massacre of 17 October, 1961," in *Theatres of Violence: Massacre, Mass Violence and Atrocity throughout History*, ed. Philip G. Dwyer and Lyndall Ryan (New York: Berghahn Books, 2012), 258–70.

6   In the immediate aftermath of October 17, Papon and others claimed that Algerian deaths were the result of retaliations between the FLN and its rival group, the MNA (le Mouvement national algérien) led by Messali Hadj. This explanation has been discounted by most historians, including Jean-Luc Einaudi, author of several influential works on October 17, including *La Bataille de Paris, le 17 octobre 1961* (Paris: Seuil, 1991). In an interview with *L'Humanité* in 2001, Einaudi states that the FLN–MNA conflict in Paris had been resolved in 1958. "Un crime toujours pas condamné," October 13, 2001, http://www.humanite.fr/node/253802. One of the few victims named in the press at the time was in fact a French man killed by the police. Guy Chevalier was standing front of the Rex cinema when he was felled by a fatal blow to the head. Somewhat ironically, Chevalier, a sailor, had just arrived in Paris aboard a barge named "L'Algérie" (Einaudi, *Bataille*, 154–55).

bullets). Then-president Charles de Gaulle reputedly called the events "unacceptable, but secondary."

In the first weeks after the massacre, notwithstanding the government's attempts to repress physical evidence, silence eyewitnesses, and gag the press, oppositional voices emerged: on October 20, Algerian women staged their own peaceful protest march to demand the release of their husbands and brothers; on October 23, more than 200 scholars and public intellectuals signed a petition denouncing the police violence; and certain daily newspapers published damning photos with unequivocal headlines such as, "Beatings that Went on for Hours: Proof of Abuse Suffered by Algerians." Yet, by the end of November, the proverbial dust, thick and seemingly impenetrable, had settled: newspapers ceased reporting on the events, politicians and private citizens gave up on obtaining answers, and complaints filed on behalf of Algerian victims were consigned to the archives, only to be destroyed later. Knowledge about "October 17"—the only name given to the event and a convenient sobriquet that handily captures the massacre's failure to gain traction in the national narrative—retreated to the dark corners of French collective memory.[7]

Yet October 17 has in fact been recounted, albeit in forms and venues far removed from official accounts and state archives. During decades of governmental silence, intermittent or biased scholarly attention, and archival inaccessibility, the stories of October 17 and its putative disappearance from memory were smuggled into the world in the form of cultural texts—novels, film, poetry, songs, and visual and performance art. As early as 1963, the massacre that would later be qualified as an "occluded" or "repressed" event had already been the subject of a French documentary, an Algerian poem, and an American novel.[8] And as recently as 2016, Zik Zitoun, an alternative Mediterranean rap collective, released an original track and music video whose title, "On a appris à nager" (We've learned to swim), seems to be an answer to an unspoken question: What has changed for Algerians in France since 1961?

---

7 Georges Bouvard, "Bastonnades des heures durant: voici des preuves des sévices infligés aux Algériens révélées par le Secours populaire," *L'Humanité*, November 4, 1961, p. 4. Einaudi's account of the massacre, "The Battle of Paris," attempted to name the event (with obvious reference to the battle of Algiers). The label has not stuck.

8 Jacques Panijel, *Octobre à Paris* (October in Paris) (documentary film, 1962); Kateb Yacine, "Dans la gueule du loup" (In the jaws of the wolf) (poem, 1962); and William Gardner Smith, *The Stone Face* (novel, 1963), respectively.

Indeed, the past half-century has seen the emergence of a corpus of cultural productions whose formal, diegetic, and discursive strategies represent the massacre and its subsequent erasure. Obliquely or directly, all of these works produce knowledge about October 17 by narrativizing and contextualizing the massacre, registering its existence, its scale, and the role of the state, while also providing access to the subjective experiences of violence and trauma. Sometimes, the events of October 17 provide the primary narrative material; at other times, October 17 is a small detail or a passing mention—a textual economy that embodies the event's shadowy presence in history.

————

Absent the Archive: Cultural Traces of a Massacre in Paris (17 October 1961) is about these stories, the way they have been told, and their function as both aesthetic and documentary objects. In this *anarchive*—this rogue collection of cultural texts—we find stories that run the gambit from internationally acclaimed works of cinema (Michael Haneke's feature film *Caché*) to popular pulp fiction (the police procedural novel *Murder in Memoriam* by Didier Daeninckx), to a raft of lesser-known and often unsung novels, short fiction, and films. The stories of October 17 have been captured in works of theatre, some of which exist only as scripts and have never been performed, some of which have been recorded as dramatic readings, and one of which—Alexandra Badea's *Points de non-retour: Quais de Seine*—made its world premiere at the prestigious Avignon Theatre Festival in 2019.

While the events of October 17 are embedded in the DNA of this book, *Absent the Archive* is neither a work of historical scholarship nor an analysis of the massacre per se. While an engagement with history is critical to an appreciation of the texts under consideration in this study, my goal is neither to contest existing historical accounts nor to mount an attack on historical work. In telling the story of these stories, this book accounts for their referential, sometimes indexical nature, but it is also interested in something other than the mimetic qualities of fiction and in something beyond the use of fiction to prove or disprove contested histories. It is invested in exploring how literature and culture may "do history" differently by complicating it; by functioning as first responders and persistent witnesses; by reverberating against reality but also speculating on what might have been; by activating networks of signs and meanings; and, sometimes, by showing us things that otherwise cannot be seen. This is, ultimately, a book about the value and function of literature and cultural production, about how they make the silences of history speak, and to what ends.

But this is also necessarily a book about a massacre, its disappearance from history, and its afterlives as a trace, a memory, and even a sign. It argues, on one level, that October 17 was neither the paroxysm of a dying colonialism, nor just another bump in the turbulent era of decolonization, but a signal event with ramifications for our understanding of France and Algeria's historical entanglements and for ongoing negotiations of multiculturalism within contemporary France. As the deadliest episode of colonial violence to take place on metropolitan soil, the massacre lays claim to a superlative status charged with meaning. Yet, unlike other significant moments such as Vichy or May 1968, in France the mention of October 17 does not immediately conjure a set of political problems, a historical conjuncture, a zeitgeist. Notwithstanding a handful of historiographical works, politically active victims' organizations, and periodic mentions in the press, there is no consensus on the event's nature or significance. The hallmark of October 17, then, is its intractable ambivalence: the massacre and its memory are—and I would argue that they have always been—at once visible and invisible, known and unknown, remembered and forgotten.

Becoming Invisible

The events of October 17 and their eventual eclipse must be understood within the political context of early 1960s France and the history of the Algerian War of Independence, which ran from 1954 to 1962 and stands as one of the bloodiest and most protracted third-world liberation struggles.[9] When Algeria gained its independence in 1962, it had been

9   The Algerian War of Independence lasted from 1954 to 1962. There is an extensive bibliography on this topic; see, for example: Matthew James Connelly, *A Diplomatic Revolution: Algeria's Fight for Independence and the Origins of the Post-Cold War Era* (Oxford: Oxford University Press, 2002); Mohammed Harbi and Benjamin Stora, *La guerre d'Algérie* (Paris: Fayard, 2010); Alistair Horne, *A Savage War of Peace: Algeria 1954–1962* (New York: Macmillan, 1977; NYRB, 2006); Ali Haroun, *La 7e wilaya: la guerre du FLN en France, 1964–1962* (Paris: Seuil, 1986); Todd Shepard, *The Invention of Decolonization: The Algerian War and the Remaking of France* (Ithaca, NY: Cornell University Press, 2006).

under the yoke of French rule for 130 years, longer than any other territory of the empire. The story of Algeria and its decolonization constitutes a site of particular rancor in France, a fact that is often but only partly explained by the North African country's exceptional status in the landscape of French imperialism and the particular attachments this produced. As the only settler colony of the French empire, Algeria was a constitutive part of the Republic from 1870 to 1962; it was not only *French*, by virtue of possession, but *France*—an administratively and even mythically, if not geographically, contiguous extension of the *métropole*.[10] This complex politics of colonial administration produced an imperial space with an unusually high proportion of historically embedded French citizens (so-called *pieds noirs* and Algerian Jews), who laid claim to a strong trans-Mediterranean affective bond while being deeply attached to the idea of an *Algérie française*. French political, economic, but also emotional connections to Algeria made disentanglement, when the time came, significantly more difficult than was the case for Morocco and Tunisia.[11]

For the rank-and-file French back at home, the war in Algeria, in its early years, would have been dim yet persistent ambient noise. Considered by many to be a "police action," and often referred to euphemistically as "the events" in Algeria, the war appeared to have little impact on metropolitan France at first, when only 5 percent of French surveyed reported having any interest in Algeria or reading about "the events" in the newspaper.[12] This would change, however, beginning

10 The French invaded Algeria in 1830, but the conquest was uneven, and the status of the territory and its various populations evolved over time. Beginning in 1870 and in parallel with the founding of the Third Republic in France, the military governance of Algeria was replaced by a civil administration. In 1881, Algeria became an official, administrative part of France. Martin Evans notes that during debates in the National Assembly, "no doubts were expressed about the legal or moral legitimacy of this action. The consensus from right to left was that France had a right to be there. Algeria was declared to be French in the same way as Normandy, Brittany, or the Savoy." Martin Evans, *Algeria: France's Undeclared War* (Oxford: Oxford University Press, 2012), 19.

11 Considered protectorates rather than administrative outposts of France, Morocco and Tunisia gained their independence in 1956, with significantly less bloodshed. Algerian Jews were granted French citizenship in 1870 under the Crémieux Decree. This was not the case for the Jews of Morocco and Tunisia.

12 Charles-Robert Ageron, "L'Opinion française devant la guerre d'Algérie," *Revue française d'histoire d'outre-mer* 63, no. 231 (1976): 259.

in 1958, when the FLN (the revolution's political and military party), opened a second theatre of operations in mainland France, administered locally by the Fédération de France du FLN (FF-FLN).[13] Because of its high concentration of government buildings and personnel, and the symbolic value of guerilla attacks carried out in the capital, Paris was the nerve center of this putative "second front."[14] It was also, not coincidentally, the site of the biggest Algerian population outside of Algiers, a community largely made up of unskilled male workers and their families, who lived in dense concentrations in the outer districts of Paris and in shantytowns like Nanterre (a commune northwest of Paris and, at the time, the site of the largest slum in Europe).[15] The FF-FLN exercised near-total control over this population, which was organized into a clandestine network of cells and pressed into the service of the revolution both operationally and financially.[16]

From 1958 to 1961, the rhythm of FF-FLN attacks in France ebbed and flowed, often following the vagaries of political negotiations between the FLN and delegates of the French government. August and September of 1961 saw a significant uptick in coordinated armed attacks by FF-FLN

13   The establishment of the FLN in France came to be known as the seventh *wilaya*, an Algerian Arabic term designating an administrative region. See Haroun, *La 7e wilaya*.

14   House and MacMaster, 65.

15   Algerians at the time held an administrative status known as FMA (Français musulmans d'Algérie or French Muslims of Algeria)—a distinction that made them French subjects but not fully enfranchised French citizens. For a thorough review of the complexities of civil status and nationality in colonial Algeria, see Patrick Weil, "Le Statut des musulmans en Algérie coloniale: une nationalité française dénaturée," in *La Justice en Algérie, 1830–1962* (Paris: La Documentation française, 2005), 95–109. For detailed accounts of the Nanterre *bidonville*, see Abelamalek Sayed and Eliane Dupuy, *Un Nanterre algérien: terre de bidonvilles* (Paris: Éditions Autrement, 1995) and Neil MacMaster, "Shantytown Republics: Algerian Migrants and the Culture of Space in the Bidonvilles," in *Transnational Spaces and Identities in the Francophone World*, ed. Hafid Gafaïti, Patrica Lorcin, and David G. Troyansky (Lincoln: University of Nebraska Press, 2009), 74–93.

16   FLN fundraising among the population both in Algeria and in France is well documented. The Paris police archives contain specific information on the sliding scale used to assess contributions, noting that the Paris sector alone was worth 66 million francs (in 1961 currency). Police archives, HA 110/111; see "Présentation Générale du fonds." See also Gilles Manceron, "La Triple occultation d'un massacre," afterword to *Le 17 octobre des Algériens* by Marcel and Paulette Péju (Paris: La Découverte, 2011), 125–26.

operatives, particularly against police headquarters and individual police officers suspected of being involved in the torture of Algerian revolutionaries, as well as random assassinations of ordinary policemen.[17] At the same time, rank-and-file Algerians were hassled on a daily basis by both regular police and *Harkis*.[18] They were subjected to random identity checks (which often entailed spending hours or days in a communal cell at a local police headquarters or at the Vincennes "identification center"), but also to beatings, humiliations, and, in the case of individuals perceived as having strategic information, torture.[19] In response to the climate of terror and tension generated by the FLN's surprise attacks, on October 5, 1961, Paris Police Chief Maurice Papon issued a curfew that prohibited Algerians from circulating in public from 8:30pm to 5:30am, forced the early closure of Algerian-run cafés and restaurants, and made it illegal for Algerian men to congregate in groups of more than two.[20]

The FLN, who excelled at propaganda as well as guerilla warfare, saw in the curfew a unique opportunity to garner support for the Algerian cause. With its explicit discrimination against a particular group based on ethnicity or religion, the curfew ran counter to French Republican ideology, and FLN manifestos targeting sympathetic French communists, workers, and left-wing intellectuals were quick to underscore this point. Rather than continue the cycle of attacks and reprisals, FLN leaders decided to stage a peaceful demonstration, one whose ostensible goal

17 House and MacMaster, 89–95. The table on page 90 suggests that violence against police more than doubled from 1958 to 1961.

18 In order to maintain a police presence in the capital, Papon employed what he called "auxiliary" and "special" forces. The FPA (*Force de police auxiliaire*, or Auxiliary Police Force), was made up, in large part, of *Harkis*, or Algerian soldiers who fought for and with the French. See Chapter 2, n. 62; Manceron, "Triple occultation," 123–31; and House and MacMaster, 77–80.

19 See House and MacMaster, 83–87. The address 28 rue de la Goutte d'or in the 18th *arrondissement* was a notorious torture site; see Emmanuel Blanchard, "Police judiciaire et pratiques d'exception pendant la guerre d'Algérie," *Vingtième Siècle. Revue d'Histoire* 2, no. 90 (2006): 61–72.

20 The full text of the curfew and its ancillary documents can be found in Gilles Manceron and Sortir du colonialisme, *Le 17 octobre 1961 par les textes de l'époque* (Paris: Les Petits matins, 2011), 35–41. It is important to note that, in keeping with republican values, the order in question was not technically considered a curfew and did not explicitly prohibit any of the acts it mentioned; given the context and the power differential, however, the "strong suggestion" can be considered tantamount to an official curfew.

was to compel the revocation of the curfew, but whose more strategic objective was to show France and the world that the Algerians were a dignified people whose human rights were under attack—in the very capital of the nation synonymous with "the rights of man." That the United Nations General Assembly was scheduled to issue a resolution on Algerian self-determination at its December 1961 meeting was certainly not lost on anyone.[21]

The protest itself was highly orchestrated by FF-FLN cadres: beginning at 8pm on October 17, organized columns converged on strategic areas in Paris (the Place de la République, the Pont Saint-Michel, the *grands boulevards*, the Place de l'Étoile). Participation was compulsory for all Algerian men, who were to be accompanied by their wives, sisters, and children; marchers had orders to turn out in their best clothes and to comport themselves calmly and peacefully. Weapons of any kind were strictly forbidden, and this measure was enforced by FF-FLN strongmen who frisked participants as they left their homes in the Nanterre shantytown or their lodgings in Paris.

If at least one account describes October 17 as a pitched battle, the most authoritative research indicates that no weapons were found on the Algerians killed or arrested, and thus favors the theory of an anxious, trigger-happy police force desperate for revenge and easily influenced by rumors circulating over police radios and reporting that Algerians had fired first.[22] There is, however, ample evidence of a brutal repression:

---

21   Resolution 1742 (XVI), "The Question of Algeria," regrets the breakdown in peace negotiations and encourages the two parties to return to the bargaining table with an eye to Algerian independence. Full text available online at https://research. un.org/en/docs/ga/quick/regular/16.

22   An article appearing in *Le Monde* on November 14, 1962, mentions rumors circulating on the radio waves about policemen "éventrés à coups de couteau" (gutted with knives). Cited in Sylvie Thenault, "Le fantasme du secret d'Etat autour du 17 octobre 1961," *Matériaux pour l'histoire de notre temps* 58 (2000): 73. A discussion of the "false reports" circulating on the police short-wave radio frequencies can be found in Jean-Paul Brunet, *Police contre FLN: le drame d'octobre 1961* (Paris: Flammarion, 1999), 185–90. Brunet refers to audio recordings of the orders given over the police radio and incorporated into Hayling and Brooks' documentary *Drowning by Bullets*. These same recordings can be found in Yasmina Adi's documentary *Ici on noie les Algériens* (Here We Drown Algerians, 2011). All historians concur that reports of Algerians firing first, or at all, are indeed false; however, there does not seem to be a consensus on the origin of these rumors, nor, according to Brunet, is it clear why these inflammatory statements were not immediately retracted.

with the support of Interior Minister Roger Frey (who would later be instrumental in the cover up), Papon rallied his troops, having declared only a few days earlier, "for every blow we receive, we will dole out 10" and ordering officers to "deal with the Algerians as you see fit; you will be covered."[23] Despite receiving no blows, the police, angry and unfettered, bludgeoned with impunity and fired into crowds. In addition to the thousands of injured and the still-contentious death toll of 200, an unknown number of men were summarily deported to their *douars d'origine*—a euphemism for detention camps in Algeria.[24]

Little is known about the government's statements regarding the events of October 17, and Charles de Gaulle's purported comment that the outcome was "secondaire mais inacceptable" (secondary but unacceptable) does little to shed light on the matter. This baffling and ambiguous declaration has been widely reproduced but never fully documented, in part because de Gaulle's presidential archives remain classified; one source, however, claims it was made at a cabinet meeting on October 25, 1961.[25] Unsurprisingly, then, the statement ascribed to de Gaulle has known various iterations: sometimes it is rendered "secondaire mais inacceptable" (secondary but unacceptable), at other times as "inadmissible mais secondaire" (inadmissible but secondary). More often than not, it is reported using the conditional tense ("de Gaulle aurait dit…" or de Gaulle supposedly said…)—as if to hedge against accusations of misrepresentation. Notwithstanding these ambiguities, the profoundly contradictory assessment has to be

---

23 Papon is widely reported to have uttered this retaliatory statement on October 2, 1961, in the courtyard of the prefecture, at the funeral service for Brigadier Demoën, who had been killed by the FLN. The second statement was reported by police officers who banded together to denounce Papon in an anonymous tract dated October 31, 1961. The full text of their tract is available in Police archives, HA 110/111, document titled "Un groupe de policiers républicains déclarent…," dated October 31, 1961. The tract has also circulated widely in various venues; see Chapter 2.

24 According to the Mandelkern Report, 5,887 Algerians were deported from Paris and environs from September 1961 to March 1962; of these, some 2,299 were deported immediately after October 17. See Rapport Mandelkern, section 2.3.4, "Le nombre de manifestants transférés en Algérie," http://17octobre1961.free.fr/pages/dossiers/Rapport.htm.

25 See House and MacMaster, 141; and "Autopsie du 17 octobre 1961: un Papon peut en cacher un autre," http://interdits.net/interdits/index.php/Autopsie-du-17-octobre-1961-un-Papon-peut-en-cacher-un-autre.html.

understood as a function of de Gaulle's broader Algerian strategy, in which October 17 was certainly "secondary" to the primary objective of ending the war. The president's comment is often thought to imply that the peace process should not (and, in fact, *could* not) be thwarted by the events. If this is indeed what de Gaulle intended, his remark turned out to be prescient: however devastating for the Algerian community, October 17 and its fallout barely registered on the seismograph of Franco-Algerian peace talks, which marched inexorably forward to their ultimate conclusion with the Évian Accords of March 1962.

Regardless of how de Gaulle's minimizing gesture might be glossed, it is impossible to deny that October 17 has occupied a decidedly "secondary" status in scholarly and political narratives from both sides of the Mediterranean: it represents a slender chapter in the story of the Algerian War, and a minor installment in the history of French imperialism.[26] The status of knowledge about October 17 is both unclear and unstable; paradoxically, this condition may be produced, and is certainly reinforced, by a proliferation of discourses about the event that rely on tropes of invisibility, silence, and pathologies of "blockage," such as occlusion, amnesia, and aphasia.[27] Even when it comes to the realm of representation, that is, to the matter at the heart of this book, it is also the case that the October 17 anarchive is a modest corpus in the context of the large number of cultural productions that reenact or remember the Algerian struggle for independence.[28]

26 Other significant colonial massacres include: Diên Biên Phu, Indochina (1953–54); Sétif, Algeria (1945); Thiaroye, Senegal (1944). Studies of colonial massacres have garnered serious scholarly attention in recent years. For a theoretical approach and comparative study of Thiaroye and October 17, see Charles Forsdick, "'Ceci n'est pas un conte, mais une histoire de chair et de sang': Representing the Colonial Massacre in Francophone Literature and Culture," in *Postcolonial Violence, Culture, and Identity in Francophone African and the Antilles*, ed. Lorna Milne (Bern: Peter Lang, 2007), 31–57. For a study of another colonial massacre in mainland France, see Daniel Kupferstein, *Les balles du 14 juillet 1953. Le massacre policier oublié de nationalistes algériens à Paris* (Paris: La Découverte, 2017).

27 Titles of works of scholarship and journalism alike are evocative of this; see, for example, Manceron's "La triple occulation d'un massacre," which refers to a "triple suppression," and Claude Liauzu's "Voyage à travers la mémoire et l'amnésie: le 17 octobre 1961," *Hommes et migrations* 1219 (May–June 1999): 56–61, which refers to a journey through "memory and amnesia."

28 These are far too numerous to list, but I would mention a few of the best-known and most widely circulated works: films such as Gillo Pontecorvo's *The*

Persistent In/Visibility

Certainly, as part of a broader set of historical and cultural phenomena, October 17 and its erasure could be understood as paradigmatic rather than exceptional, as a not-uncommon by-product of liberation struggles, and as part and parcel of the fate of colonial memory. After all, what might be said of October 17 and its failure to signify can also be said of the memory of the Algerian War and of France's colonial past more generally, which the Fifth Republic has been slow to recognize and reluctant to incorporate into the national narrative.[29] Notwithstanding recent institutional gestures—a call, however clumsily conceived and worded, to promote the teaching of colonial history (2005); the creation of a museum of immigration (2012); a flurry of activities commemorating the 50th anniversary of the end of the Algerian War (2012)—France has been slow to come to terms with its Algerian entanglements, and here we can understand "coming to terms" quite literally: it was only in 1999, that is, 37 years after independence, that the "police operations" or "events" in Algeria were officially recognized as a "war."[30]

Battle of Algiers (1966); Jean-Luc Godard's *Le petit soldat* (1960); André Téchiné's *Les roseaux sauvages* (1994); and novels like Kateb Yacine's *Nedjma* (1956), or, more recently, Yasmina Khadra's *Ce que le jour doit à la nuit* (2008).

29 See Kristen Ross's *Fast Cars, Clean Bodies* (Cambridge, MA: MIT Press, 1995). The creation of associations and the publication of collected volumes attest, in the 2000s, to a desire to come to terms with what has been called "l'oubli colonial." Groups include ACHAC; Indigènes de la République; and the more modest Les Oranges. Major works include: Benjamin Stora's *La gangrène et l'oubli* (Paris: La Découverte, 1991); *Les guerres des mémoires*, ed. Isabelle Veyrat-Masson and Pascal Blanchard (Paris: La Découverte, 2008); and *La fracture coloniale: la société française au prisme de l'héritage colonial,* ed. Nicolas Bancel, Pascal Blanchard, and Sandrine Lemaire (Paris: La Découverte, 2006).

30 See Evans, *Algeria: France's Undeclared War,* 364. Slavery was officially recognized as a crime against humanity in France in 2001. Even official gestures that suggest a willingness to recognize the colonial past may contain a disturbing whiff of revisionism: in 2005, Jacques Chirac's government passed a highly contested law mandating that the teaching of colonial history focus on "the positive role of colonization." Several years prior, *Le Monde diplomatique* published a study of how the history of the Algerian War had been taught in public schools over the course of four decades. The essay argued that "colonial history itself, and the resistances it created [...] were expurgated from school curriculums," producing a generation with a warped knowledge of Algeria and an "expunged, bowdlerized history" of the Algerian War. See Maurice T. Maschino, "L'histoire expurgée de

In this regard, what is known about the representation of Algerian and colonial history may seem to obviate the need for special consideration of October 17: like any of the numerous bloody confrontations of decolonization, and like the details of the decline of empire more generally, it reads as an unpleasant memory that has been largely edited out of national history, only to return to consciousness from time to time when anniversaries or other significant cultural-political moments stimulate a passing awareness.

It is my contention, however, that certain exceptional aspects of October 17—its particular material conditions and the complex discourse it has produced—compel us to read it as marking a significant rupture in established narratives about the memory of France's colonial past. When October 17 is described in superlative terms as the only episode of colonial violence to take place on metropolitan soil, or as the largest repression of a street protest in the modern history of Western Europe, these statements of exceptionalism are predicated upon the event's having taken place in *Paris*.[31] Unlike the Algerian massacres in Sétif and Guelma, or the battle of Diên Biên Phu in Indochina, for example, October 17 happened not in the hinterlands of the empire but in its capital, marking the first moment the colonized subject emerged—embodied, and imbued with agency—in the geographical (that is, literal), political, and affective center. It also marked the first time the colonized subject made himself visible "in a space that was not the very site and object" of his revolution.[32] Moreover,

la guerre d'Algérie," *Le Monde diplomatique* (February 2001), 8–9; translated by Ann Laura Stoler in "Colonial Aphasia: Race and Disabled Histories in France," *Public Culture* 23, no. 1 (2011): 143. Chirac's law undoubtedly intended to redress this imbalance by requiring the teaching of colonial history, yet its crafty editing of the language of imperialism and its focus on both the "Nation" (France) and the "positive" were certainly not neutral. It is worth noting, moreover, that the official text of the legislation uses the euphemism "the role of French presence abroad" rather than "colonization," the latter being the term the press used widely in its discussions of the legislation in order to clarify the stakes of the law.

31   House and MacMaster, 1. Historians remain divided over the question of October 17's status within narratives of colonial violence and decolonization. See Jim House, "October 17: On the Past and Its Presence," *Bulletin of Francophone Postcolonial Studies* 3, no. 2 (Autumn 2012): 2–9; E. Blanchard, *La police parisienne et les Algériens: 1944–1962* (Paris: Nouveau Monde éditions, 2011); and Daniel Gordon, *Immigrants and Intellectuals: May '68 and the Rise of Anti-Racism in France* (London: Merlin Press, 2012).

32   Hannah Feldman, *From a Nation Torn: Decolonizing Art and Representation in France, 1945–1962* (Durham, NC: Duke University Press, 2014), 170.

this embodied subject emerged as a *political* subject with a specific demand: sovereignty. The demand itself makes visible the *absence* of that very sovereignty, and the heightened nature of Algerian visibility on October 17—the spectacular aspect of the demonstration—could not but underscore the desperate invisibility to which human beings, French subjects, had been relegated.

Historian Pascal Blanchard has suggested that France's difficult recognition of its imperial past is rooted in the impossible cohabitation of French universalism and the colonial project. For Blanchard, a double investment in the rights of man in the absolute, and in the rights of man as a justification for colonial expansion and domination, is ethically and practically unmanageable, resulting in an excruciating double bind.[33] This quandary, however abstract, would have crystallized on October 17, at a moment when it became undeniable that the philosophical and physical violence of the colonial project was no longer something that happened elsewhere. Rather, it took place at home, in full view of the polis and on the *place publique*, in the symbolic heart of the very country that conceived the rights of man and citizen.

Compared to knowledge about the Algerian War writ large, knowledge about October 17 has been subject to unique pressures, and as such it is often figured in paradoxical terms as both known and unknown, as both visible and invisible. Some facts of colonial history and the processes of decolonization may be the source of lively polemics and even dispute, but few other moments of French colonialism or decolonization continue to occupy such diametrically opposed positions within the episteme. Even as October 17 becomes increasingly established as a known

---

33 Pascal Blanchard specifically refers to the "paradox" of human rights originating from a colonial republic in his interview with Mouâd Salhi, "La mémoire sans histoire c'est une catastrophe," November 15, 2015, http://alohanews. be/politique/pascal-blanchard-la-memoire-sans-histoire-cest-une-catastrophe. This notion of a paradox is at the heart of the book co-written by Blanchard, Bancel, and Françoise Vergès, *La République coloniale* (Paris: Hachette, 2003), in which the authors maintain that the very notion of race was antithetical to the founding fathers of France, calling it the "unthought" of the Republic and a major constituent of the "fracture of republican universalism," iv. This position has been complicated, or indirectly challenged, by thinkers who view Enlightenment philosophy and universalism as having paved the way for racial categories. See, for example, Natalya Vince, "Transgressing Boundaries: Gender, Race, Religion and 'Françaises Musulmanes' during the Algerian War for Independence," *French Historical Studies* 33, no. 3 (2010): 448.

historical quantity, uncertainty persists as to its importance, and as to the relative weight and significance it should occupy in both national and scholarly narratives.[34] It is this discursive and epistemological instability, amply rendered in the anarchive, that makes October 17 an especially instructive and evocative text.

Given the eminently visual and sited qualities of October 17, the persistence of the trope of invisibility is a fascinating phenomenon. Of course, this invisibility is metaphorical—it is impossible to imagine that Parisians would have failed to see what was happening in their streets. But metaphors are not just descriptors; they also generate meaning. So in the case of October 17, if we can take for granted that the demonstration and its repression would have been largely seen, it is worth trying to understand how these events came to be figured as invisible, and how the ambivalent pairing of visible-invisible has come to characterize the massacre and its traces.

Jacques Rancière, whose work has been devoted to thinking through the relationship between aesthetics and power, and who has argued that only the "mise-en-scène of words" is capable of revealing the "visible behind the invisible," reads the scene on October 17 in the following manner:[35]

> That day, with its twofold aspect (manifest and hidden), was a turning point [...]. The crucial thing about the effect of that day was the way in which the questions of the visibility and invisibility of repression became interwoven [...]. In a word, the police cleared the public space and, thanks to a news blackout, made its own operations invisible. [...] A phrase used by Sartre in his preface to *Les Damnés de la terre* helps us to understand, *a contrario*, the meaning of that twofold disappearance: "The blinding sun of torture has now reached its zenith, and it is lighting up the whole country." Now, the truth is that this blinding sun never lit up anything. Marked and tortured bodies do not light up anything. [...]

34   According to a CSA poll done for *l'Humanité hebdo* (*L'Humanité*'s weekly magazine) in 2001, 47 percent of French people surveyed said that they had "heard about the event" (that is, October 17, 1961), while 21 percent stated that they knew exactly what had happened on the date in question. According to the article, results such as these were unimaginable ten years ago, when, presumably, the numbers would have been much lower. See Jean-Paul Monferran, "Le 17 octobre: le crime enfin reconnu," *L'Humanité*, October 17, 2001, https://www.humanite.fr/node/253988.

35   Jacques Rancière, *Figures of History*, trans. Julie Rose (New York: John Wiley and Sons, 2014), 44.

It was not the blinding sun that lit up the political scene in 1961. On the contrary, it was an invisibility, the removal of something by the action of the police. And the police are not primarily a strong-arm repressive force, but a form of intervention which prescribes what can be seen and what cannot be seen.[36]

This canny reading of the reversals of visibility and invisibility underscores the event's inherent paradox and turns it into a heuristic tool. While Rancière recognizes the police's prescriptive powers and their domain over what is seen (or not), he also argues for the capacity of invisibility to produce knowledge, to "illuminate" in the various connotations of the term. This critical maneuver also positions visibility-invisibility as something both intrinsic to and generated by October 17, as more than a discourse simply imposed on the events *post facto*.

Rancière's abstractions are anchored in the concrete, material ways in which October 17 was made at once visible and invisible. There was, in the immediate aftermath of the repression, ample production of visual evidence—wounded bodies, dead bodies, bloodstained sidewalks and parapets, and damaged personal property. And, for a time, traces of this visibility were in circulation, primarily in the mainstream press (with feature articles often accompanied by photographs), but also in the form of letters to the police, political debate, street protests, and denunciatory graffiti. In certain cases, even very early on, evidence of visibility was produced in layers: Jacques Panijel's documentary *Octobre à Paris* (1962) uses photographs taken by Élie Kagan on October 17 to depict the protest and its repression; the graffito "Ici on noie les Algériens" (Here we drown Algerians), which appeared on Parisian bridges in the weeks after the event, has become a "militant icon" of the massacre only because it lives on in a photograph taken on the fly by an amateur photographer.[37] (See Fig. 1.) The proliferation and densification of the visual signs is worthy of note in the context of a war often called "la guerre sans images" (the war without images), and particularly so given October 17's purported "invisibility."[38]

36 Rancière, "The Cause of the Other," *Parallax* 4, no. 2 (1998): 28.

37 For an excellent investigation of the 1961 graffiti and the photo that made it famous, see Vincent Lemire et Yann Potin, "'Ici on noie les Algériens': Fabriques documentaires, avatars politiques et mémoires partagées d'une icône militante (1961–2001)," *Genèses* 49 (December 2002): 140–62.

38 Stora, *Les guerres sans fin: un historien, la France et l'Algérie* (Paris: Stock, 2008), 130–33. Although he uses the expression "une guerre sans images" (a war

Fig. 1. Graffiti inscribed on the Quai de Conti, across from the Institut de France (Paris 6th *arrondissement*). Photo © Jean Texier. October–November 1961.

But just as the police intervention would have "prescribed" what could and could not be seen, the state had other tools at its disposal, most notably its ability to censor the press and publishing houses, seize images, and secret away most traces of October 17 into archives that would be sealed for decades. These operations, however, like those of the police, worked to ambivalent effect. Although the gag order was decreed almost immediately after the massacre, it would take the censors several weeks to fully halt the presses and to seize issues already in circulation (as well as photographs and film reels). In the case of images or testimonial evidence produced or captured but not immediately published (by free agents such as Kagan, fellow photographer Georges Azenstarck, Panijel, or engaged intellectuals like Marcel and Paulette Péju), the announced repression of material evidence allowed for time

without images) in reference to the Algerian Civil War of the 1990s, Stora views the lack of visual images as the continuation of processes of "making invisible" that began with the Algerian War of Independence. Philip Dine's excellent book *Images of the Algerian War: French Fiction and Film, 1954–1962* (Oxford: Clarendon Press, 1994) offers an intriguing look at how the war was made visible through means other than state-sanctioned images.

to prepare, that is, to make and hide duplicates, but also to share images and information.[39] This lapse produced a window of visibility, a period of just over a month during which photos, interviews, and testimonials found their way onto newsstands and into homes.[40] As a result, and to a degree impossible to measure, October 17 would have penetrated individual, if not collective, consciousness. Although censorship would eventually produce its desired effect—a total blackout—the invisibility that cloaked October 17 would only ever be partial. It has been haunted by the metaphorical after-images and psychic traces of actual visual evidence deleted from the public record but scrupulously saved in the police archives.

Like the scene on October 17, rendered invisible by police operations that hid the traces of the violence they had committed, complex state archival regulations have hidden knowledge of that violence. Originally subject to legislation governing the consultation of "sensitive" archival material (dossiers containing state secrets, including those related to the

---

39 Kagan's photos are featured in Panijel's documentary (1962) and are the subject of a small book prefaced by Jean-Luc Einaudi, titled *17 octobre 1961* (Arles: Actes Sud, 2001). Azenstarck, who worked for *L'Humanité*, shows the photos he preserved in Faïza Guène's documentary *Mémoires du 17 octobre* (2002). Marcel Péju was general secretary of the journal *Temps modernes* and personal secretary to Sartre. He and his wife, Paulette Péju (a journalist with *Libération*), collected photos, eyewitness and victim accounts, and official complaints made by Algerian victims and their families, which were published in November 1961 by François Maspero under the title *Ratonnades à Paris*. The book was censured and seized, circulating only illegally until it was republished in 2000 by La Découverte with a preface by Pierre Vidal-Naquet, an introduction by Marcel Péju, and an afterword by François Maspero.

40 The demonstration garnered significant press coverage—photos and articles were published in the immediate aftermath, despite the censors and even though the FLN had waited until the last possible moment to announce the plan for the demonstration to the Algerian rank and file. The press had been informed and was present to cover the various sites within Paris, thanks to the intervention of Georges Mattei, an anticolonial activist who leaked the information to journalists (see Paul Thibaud, "Le 17 octobre 1961: un moment de notre histoire," *Esprit* 11, no. 278 (November 2001): 11). On October 27, 1961, journalist Claude Bourdet (*France Observateur*) questioned Papon at a city council meeting, and by the end of October debates in the National Assembly had taken up issues of excessive force and racial profiling. These are available in the official newsletter of the Senate. Transcripts of meetings on October 19 and November 17, 1961, are also preserved in the police archives.

Vichy period or the Algerian War), the October 17 police archives were destined to remain classified for 50 years following the events.[41] Now available for consultation by the general public (having been officially declassified by President Nicolas Sarkozy in 2011), the status of the police archives—and, most importantly, the political and public discourse surrounding the status of these archives—drives home October 17's dual visibility-invisibility. My own experience sifting through press clippings, teletexts announcing the discovery of bodies floating in the Seine, and letters from politicians, local captains of industry, and benevolent associations such as the Red Cross, was one of red-hot discovery tempered with a creeping feeling of belatedness. Because they have been "invisible" (and more precisely: censored) for so long and have been seen thus far by so few, these archival images feel contemporary, like new material for the present moment. And yet the reality of their true temporality—they belong, of course, to a moment in the past—provokes an eerie sense of déjà vu; here, again, is not just visual evidence of what happened on October 17, but evidence of how visible the events were, and of how a state produced invisibility to cover its own actions.

The invisibility of October 17 is of course not only a rhetorical or abstract construction. It is also the result of a specific historical conjuncture.[42] Immediately after the massacre, the FLN halted all terrorist activity in Paris, and by November the police had also ceased its practice of *ratonnades*.[43] Papon and Interior Minister Roger Frey obfuscated and deferred demands for inquests just long enough that by March 19, 1962, barely six months after the massacre, Franco-Algerian negotiations had reached a point where amnesty was declared, thus closing the curtain on the farce of due process that had been performed, up to that point, by police investigators and the public prosecutor's office.[44]

---

41   For more on the protection of state secrets and archival legislation in France, see https://francearchives.fr/fr/article/26287562.

42   This trifecta of factors—the silence of the French government, the screen memory of the Charonne massacre on February 8, 1962, and the reluctance of the new Algerian government (the first government of a free Algeria) to emphasize the event given that some of the protest's organizers were now the government's opposition—constitute what Manceron refers to as the event's triple suppression. See Manceron, "Triple occultation," 113–14.

43   Thibaud, 11–12. *Ratonnade*, derived from the word *raton* (rat), originated in French Algeria to describe the practice of targeting Algerians, and continues to be used to describe violence committed against persons of North African origin.

44   Thibaud, 12. Full text of the declaration of amnesty (decree no. 62-326

More potently, however, the massacre of Algerians on October 17 came to be obscured by, and continues to be confounded with, another episode of police brutality known simply as "Charonne." On February 8, 1962, in the Parisian metro station of the same name, nine French anti-war protesters were killed as they fled a police charge.[45] The public and political outcry over Charonne was immediate and considerable: On February 13, the victims were memorialized in a large-scale demonstration attended by thousands of protesters who marched from the Place de la République to the Père Lachaise cemetery where the victims were buried.[46] The intensity—and the intense visibility—of the response to Charonne is an instructive counterpoint to October 17, revealing a profound inequality in the symbolic capital of human life: the deaths of nine French citizens had permission to signify; the uncounted Algerian dead did not.[47]

Moreover, the name "Charonne" has been elevated to the status of a sign. Its mention not only refers to the injustices of this particular crime (peaceful anti-war protesters murdered by the state), but has also come to function metonymically, thus to describe any gratuitous violence against innocent protesters.[48] House and MacMaster have noted that while numerous scholars have posited the militants of the "Algerian generation" as ancestors to the student and worker protests of

---

dated March 16, 1962) is available in *Journal officiel de la République française*, March 23, 1962, p. 3143, https://www.legifrance.gouv.fr/affichTexte.do?cidTexte= JORFTEXT000000673799&dateTexte=.

45 For thoroughgoing analyses of the Charonne event, see Alain Dewerpe, *Charonne, 8 février 1962: Anthropologie historique d'un massacre d'État* (Paris: Gallimard, 2006); multiple authors, preface by Bertrand Delanoë, *Un crime d'État—Métro Charonne, 8 février 1962* (Paris: Le temps des cerises, 2017); and House and MacMaster, Chapter 9, "The Marginalization of 17 October 1961 (1961–1968)," 242–64.

46 Statistics on the number in attendance at the memorial march range from 125,000 (the number released by the prefecture) to 500,000 (estimated in *Le Monde* and *Paris-Jour*). Footage of the demonstration even features in Chris Marker's documentaries *Le Joli mai*—filmed during "the first springtime of peace" and released in the fall of 1962, and *Le Fond de l'air est rouge* (A Grin Without a Cat) (1977).

47 House and MacMaster, 185. "Charonne, both the event and the reaction to it, merely confirmed the relative disappearance of 17 October that had already occurred within most sectors of French society, and provided an event that, for political reasons, was far more 'worthy' of commemoration than 17 October."

48 House and MacMaster, 247–48.

May '68, the discourse of that movement tended to activate memories of Charonne far more readily than those of October 17, which appeared, if they appeared at all, as a "shadow trace."[49] One May '68 poster, for example, made ironic reference to a "sadistic police that can already boast of Charonne and torture in Algeria."[50] The similarities between the massacres of October 17 and Charonne (both took place in Paris during the Algerian War, and in both cases unarmed protesters were victims of a violent police acting with impunity) have come to outstrip their massive differences in the number and type of victim, and in their ideological implications. And so, notwithstanding the little they actually hold in common, Charonne (rather than, for example, the 1945 Sétif Massacre in Algeria) has emerged as a screen memory for October 17.[51]

The making invisible of October 17, however, was neither solely a product of the French government's machinations, nor a purely French phenomenon. Indeed, the third factor in what Manceron describes as the "triple occultation" of October 17 is the silence of Algerians themselves.[52] On the one hand, individual Algerians (victims and their families) were circumspect when speaking publicly about the massacre, either because they feared reprisals or because experience had taught them that nothing good would come of making an official complaint. On the other hand, for the FLN leadership, October 17, once in the past, served no political purpose. There was also a certain soft backlash against the FLN—various camps would speculate as to whether or not the FLN had thrown its sometimes-unwitting foot soldiers into the "jaws of the wolf" (as Kateb Yacine suggests in his eponymous 1962 poem).[53] Six months after the fact, when the FLN emerged as the ruling party of a free Algeria, they opted for a national genesis narrative that was resolutely forward looking. In Algeria today, October 17 is consecrated only as the "national day of emigration," a highly ambiguous designation that, like

49   House and MacMaster, 281.

50   House and MacMaster, 281.

51   First defined by Freud in 1899, the notion of "screen memory" refers to a memory that hides another, ostensibly related, memory. Kristen Ross observed, more specifically, the way memories of Charonne function as a screen for memories of October 17 in her reading of Jean-François Vilar's *Bastille Tango* (1986); see Ross, *May '68 and its Afterlives* (Chicago: University of Chicago Press, 2002), 40–42.

52   Manceron, "Triple occultation," 175–79.

53   Kateb Yacine, "Dans la gueule du loup," *Jeune Afrique* 90 (June 25, 1962): 22–23.

Fig. 2. "50th Anniversary of the Day of Emigration." Commemorative stamp issued by Algérie Poste (the Algerian postal service), in 2011.

so many other things, makes October 17 visible while also continuing to hide its significance.[54] (See Fig. 2.)

Becoming Visible: The October 17 Anarchive

Like the events they represent, the October 17 cultural productions have been variously visible and invisible—an ambivalence that might be attributed to political context; to qualities inherent to a given genre; to the vagaries of circulation; to a particular author's notoriety and cultural capital (or lack thereof); or, simply, to the zeitgeist. While all of these works represent the events of October 17 and/or their erasure, and while most were conceived during a period of time when the police archives were classified, they nonetheless constitute a heteroclite and idiosyncratic collection of works that would not, without critical intervention, organically coalesce as a corpus. The work of this book— indeed, its primary critical intervention—is to collect and to name this variegated body of primary material, to trace the contours of its borders, to articulate its internal divisions, and to speculate on its synergies, both internal and external. The work of this book, then, is to make the *anarchive* visible.

When I first began experimenting with the anarchive—both the word itself and the concept it would come to name—it was not a richly theorized concept. Derrida's notional flirtations with the term in *Mal d'archive: une impression freudienne* (1995) had more to do with identifying a kind of death drive inherent to the archive, or "the possibility of putting to death the very thing, whatever its name,

---

54   The first national "day of emigration" was celebrated in October 1968. Highly politicized, the gesture had less to do with the massacre on October 17 than with the marketing of national mythologies. For more information on Algerian activities memorializing emigration, see Jean-Charles Scagnetti, "Émigration représentée, une exception algérienne? Étude du timbre édité le 17 juin 1968," *Cahiers de la méditerranée* 91 (2015): 267–76. A postage stamp was issued in 1968 to consecrate the first national "day of emigration"; in 2001, to mark the 50th anniversary of the "day of emigration," the Algerian government issued a stamp whose text reads simply in French and in Arabic "50th Anniversary of the Day of Emigration," but whose imagery includes the Eiffel Tower, the Seine, and realistic renderings of men being beaten and drowning in the river. The irony here, of course, is that 2011 did not mark the 50th anniversary of the Day of Emigration (instituted in 1968), but the 50th anniversary of the October 17 massacre.

which carries the law in its tradition."[55] Indeed, Derrida spends more time discussing the "anarchivic" or "anarchiviolithic" (the bent to destroy the archive) than he does glossing his single use of the word "anarchive," which hangs suspended in the middle of his text, perhaps deliberately left without comment for the reader to invest with her own interpretation.[56] Nevertheless, his attention to the instability of the archive (as both term and site) at a time when the archival turn was nigh, and the core ambivalence embedded in the idea of "mal d'archive" (being archive "sick," that is, both desiring and being undone by the archive), are foundational to the concept of the October 17 anarchive. More than 20 years have passed since Derrida first called our attention to "archive fever"—a gesture that anticipated, or perhaps even provoked, a slew of archival "turns" in historical scholarship, but also in literary and visual studies. Since then, the term "anarchive" has been taken up and refigured, primarily within art- and practice-based research collectives, and perhaps nowhere more rigorously than by the Montreal-based SenseLab. Certain of the "Working Principles of the Anarchive" articulated by Brian Massumi in SenseLab's guide to anarchiving resonate strongly with my project's sensibilities: notably, the idea that the anarchive "pertains to the event" or can be understood as an "event derivative or surplus-value of the event"; that the anarchive is not a "documentation of past activity" but rather "needs documen-tation," in other words, it nonetheless requires the archive and is "a kind of supplement of the archive"; and, finally, that the anarchive "is never contained in an object."[57]

Reading the concept of the anarchive through Derrida's theoretical musings or through Massumi's more programmatic notions allows us to contextualize it within a recent tradition of pugnacious thinking about the archive and its limits. Nevertheless, as a word composed of the common noun "archive" and the polysemic prefix "an-"—signifying

---

55   Jacques Derrida, *Archive Fever: A Freudian Impression,* trans. Eric Prenowitz (Chicago: University of Chicago Press, 1996), 79.

56   Jean Birnbaum, in a brief editorial discussing the "allure of the archive" that draws so many to "Les rendez-vous de l'histoire" (an annual festival for historians held in Blois), offers the following gloss of Derrida's anarchive (used exactly once in *Archive Fever*): "Pour designer cette archive vouée à l'avenir, tout à la fois intempestif et explosive, le philosophe Jacques Derrida inventa un mot superbe: l'anarchive." "Le goût de l'anarchive," *Le Monde,* October 18, 2012.

57   Brian Massumi, "Working Principles," in *The Go-To How to Book of Anarchiving,* ed. Andrew Murphie (Montreal: SenseLab, 2016), 7.

"anti-archive," "not the archive," or "in opposition to the archive"—
anarchive's meaning also obtains through straightforward etymology.[58]
Anarchive, then, is a linguistic riff with conceptual and even political
implications. Negating the term to which it is annexed, the prefix an-
can mean both "without" or "not." Both meanings are germane to the
October 17 corpus, which came into existence during a period when
researchers were *without* an official state archive (and thus refers to
that very absence), and that is *not*, in any traditional sense, an archive
(despite the fact that it may function as one).

At the same time, anarchive can be understood as a portmanteau
word, or a *mot-valise*, a blending of "anarchy" and "archive." Beyond
the semantic conveniences afforded when we pack two meanings into
a single term (and unlike the portmanteau words bandied about in
popular culture), there are also etymological factors in play here, as both
words are based on the Greek *arkhê*, meaning power or hierarchy. In the
case of the October 17 anarchive, I would suggest that this particular
anarchy—this chaos, lack of order, and absence of authority—is highly
generative. Furthermore, insofar as anarchy connotes that which is
without place and without origin, and implies the absence of the state
or its representatives (*an-arkhos*), its implied presence within the notion
of the anarchive signals the lack of a common origin and the absence of
a physical site of collection for the heteroclite October 17 corpus, while
also gesturing to its conditions of production independent of the aegis
of the state.

To pursue analogies one step further, just as the archive has its
archon—its guardian or executor—the anarchive also has its *anarchon*—
the literary scholar. One can argue, of course, that the archon has
never been a mere gatekeeper; by virtue of filtering access and making
curatorial decisions about what materials are and are not seen, the
archon's role can also be understood as an exercise in interpretation. But
the anarchon's task is more deeply hermeneutical: Less guardian than
docent, translator, and reader, it is her job to actively "consign" (that is,
gather together and make signify) works relative to October 17. And it

---

58   This is the case for many (if not most) of the instances of anarchive or
anarchiving that now proliferate. Art critic, professor, and curator Anne-Marie
Duguet uses the term anarchive to describe "collections of interactive multi-media
projects that allow for the exploration of an artist's work through multiple different
archives." Here, the "an" of anarchive also stands for "archive numérique." See
http://www.anarchive.net/.

is this work that makes the anarchive visible, formulating and "lighting up" an essential epistemological scene.[59]

————

Absent the Archive focuses less on questions of fact and more on the function, aesthetics, and even the political stakes of representation, a gesture that acknowledges the crucial role played by cultural texts in the production and transmission of historical knowledge and subjective experience alike. Chapters One and Two revolve around questions specifically related to the long-sequestered police archives and the anarchive. Sensitive to the potential pitfalls of totalizing gestures, the first chapter, "Excavating the Anarchive: Notes on the History of the Corpus," nevertheless seeks to articulate the essential temporal and thematic structures of the October 17 corpus. My interest, here, is to establish a historicized model that functions as a touchstone for the chapters that follow, without imposing a single narrative on the corpus. At the same time, this exploration also probes the limits of the anarchive as a concept, speculating on its eventual exhaustion. The actual police archives and their representation in fiction form the center of gravity of the second chapter, "Archive Stories: From Politics to Romances." Through a blend of personal anecdote, discourse analysis, literary interpretation, and theoretical reflection on archives, I consider both the contents of the institutional documents and the reader's experience of consultation, discovery, and disappointment. "Archive Stories" is also very much about the role that archives have played in the anarchive—about the

59 Other models, unrelated to October 17 per se, may perform operations similar to that of the anarchive. Mireille Rosello has called for attention to what she terms the "missing archive," born of "the silence of ordinary people." James C. Scott's notion of "hidden transcripts" performs a similar critical move; for Scott, there is always a record of the relationships between the powerful and the powerless. The "hidden transcript" in question describes the narrative produced by a subordinate group to describe and critique its ordeal, as well as the narrative produced by the dominant group to claim the legitimacy of its practices. See Mireille Rosello, "Remembering the Incomprehensible: Hélène Cixous, Leïla Sebbar, Yamina Benguigui, and the War of Algeria," in *Remembering Africa*, ed. Elisabeth Mudimbé-Boyi (Portsmouth, NH: Heinemann, 2002), 191, and James C. Scott, *Domination and the Arts of Resistance: Hidden Transcripts* (New Haven, CT: Yale University Press, 1990), xii.

staging of imaginary truth-seekers, detectives, and historians as they search for a smoking gun, and about the use of real archival material in works of fiction and in documentary film.

The third and fourth chapters are both keenly invested in the way that October 17 has been represented as a sited, place-specific event. Chapter Three, "Non-lieux de mémoire: Maps and Graffiti in the Scriptable City," explores the ways in which the anarchive works to re-map the city and inscribe traces of October 17. Drawing on the evolution of the Parisian "memorialscape"—from activist slogans graffitied on bridges in the fall of 1961 to the contemporary politics of recognition—this chapter reads novels, maps, monuments, photographs, and street performance to consider the importance of city space and the way October 17 both is and is not made visible within the very physical ground that engendered it. The fourth chapter remains in Paris, training its gaze specifically on the capital's river. "The Seine's Exceptional Bodies" suggests that the anarchive compels us to imagine the iconic French river as an accomplice, a witness, a watery tomb, a haunting figure. Beginning with a short history of the capital's fluvial thoroughfare as a site emblematic not only of leisure and romance, but also of criminality and deviance, I explore the anarchive's representation of the Seine in poetry, novels, theatre, music and music video, and feature and documentary film.

The final two chapters wrestle, albeit in quite different ways, with the complex racial politics and questions of identity and identification that are at the heart of October 17. Chapter Five, "How Lucky Were the Blond Kabyles: Reading Race in the Anarchive," excavates discourses of race as they have been produced in more than 50 years' worth of cultural production. But even as I look to the ways in which literature and film have engaged, both explicitly and implicitly in "race talk"—talk about discrimination, passing, racial profiling, mistaken identity—I am also interested in how, prior to October 17 and in its immediate aftermath, politicians, social actors, and individual citizens manifested a keen awareness of the racialized nature of French government policies. In the final chapter, "The Entangled Histories of October 17, Vichy, the Jews, and the Holocaust," I examine the knot created when stories of Jews, Vichy, and the Holocaust become intertwined with representations of October 17, both in the anarchive and in archival materials: in the press, in statements by politicians, in the spontaneous discourse of private citizens who mused, in 1961, that the police actions and government politics bore an uncanny resemblance to a nightmare they believed to have ended some 15 years earlier.

Each chapter, then, evinces its own particular problematic, and each engages historical context, archival material, and a selection of primary (or anarchival) texts. Works that are well known and available in English—Michael Haneke's feature film *Caché* (*Hidden*) or Didier Daeninckx's novel *Meurtres pour mémoire* (*Murder in Memoriam*), for example, which have a popular following and are fixtures in university courses on postcolonial France—find their place alongside cultural productions that are less renowned, such as the noir thriller *Les caves de la Goutte d'or*, or the made-for-TV movie *Nuit noire*. Reading and valorizing lesser-known works is crucial insofar as October 17 representations have proliferated in cultural productions that have, themselves, often been "invisible" in popular or academic discourse. Some of these works have fallen prey to the vagaries of publishing, circulation, and translation: William Gardner Smith's novel, *The Stone Face*, is currently out of print and has never been translated into French; certain films are not subtitled in English; and some graphic representations can only be found on the internet, and thus sometimes cannot be found at all. Others, however—detective fiction, young adult literature, graphic novels, popular music, music videos, community theatre, street performances, graffiti—are still, even in the age of cultural studies and notwithstanding Derrida's declaration that "everything is a text," often considered unworthy of serious scholarship.[60]

The anarchive plays a capital role in embodying the uneasy position of October 17 between "secondary" and "exceptional," visible and invisible, and thus in representing its signal qualities. The anarchive is also a space in which the ambivalences of October 17 can be explored and even emphasized, unburdened by expectations of resolution. It is here, perhaps, that the anarchive is at its most instructive and illustrative: nearly all the works contained therein *represent* the massacre and/or its erasure—its visibility and its becoming invisible—and these representations often recreate the conditions of invisibility through literary,

---

60 Now more an aphorism than a well-understood concept, Derrida's original declaration in *De la grammatologie* 1967), "il n'y a pas de hors-texte," is usually translated as "there is nothing outside of the text," or "there is no outside-text," but is often glossed in English as "all is text" or "everything is a text." (Dinitia Smith, in an article on the philosopher in the *New York Times*, wrote of a dinner with Derrida in which he waved his arms at diners at the Polo Grill, stating, "Everything is a text; this is a text." See "Philosopher Gamely in Defense of His Ideas," *New York Times*, May 30, 1998.)

filmic, or visual strategies. But so many anarchival works also *embody* this "twofold aspect," having been rendered "invisible" by factors ranging from language to censorship, from conditions of production to conditions of performance. Among the many ways in which it makes details about October 17 visible, the anarchive is particularly attentive to questions of location, that is, in pressing Paris into service as a protagonist and in making the city signify in ways not found in archival documents and historical studies. The anarchive is also alive to the ambivalent status of knowledge, sometimes staging its fragmentary and partial nature, sometimes incarnating its aporias. It is in large part the anarchive—a proportionally large body of work devoted to a putatively secondary event—that makes October 17 *signal*.

CHAPTER ONE

Excavating the Anarchive
An Archeology of the Corpus

> The need for the anarchive is well and truly arrived.
> —Andrew Murphie
> The anarchive pertains to the event.
> —Brian Massumi[1]

An *anarchive*, by virtue of its name and its nature, should resist totalizing gestures, defy order, balk at containment. The October 17 corpus in principle is no different; no matter what pressures we apply, it resists coherence and denies the reader a master narrative of the event.

Yet the anarchive is not entirely elusive: it is possible to trace its contours and observe its inner workings. What follows in this chapter—a chapter whose goals are far more programmatic than those presented in the remainder of this book—is an attempt at an archeology, a bid to inventory, sort, and identify the contents of the anarchive. Through this excavation, I hope to label (however provisionally) not only objects but also the spaces in between them. I also take this process as an occasion to gesture to those critical paths that emerged over the course of my reading yet remain, for different reasons, roads not taken.

The anarchive in question is constituted by a variety of cultural productions representing October 17, and these include: text (novels, short stories, poetry, theatre, song, *bande dessinée*, and graphic novels); image (fiction and documentary feature films, photographs, posters, graphic art); and performance (ranging from staged theatrical drama

---

1 Andrew Murphie, "Not Quite an Anarchive" and Brian Massumi, "Working Principles" in *The Go-To How-To Book of Anarchiving*, ed. Andrew Murphie (Montreal: SenseLab, 2016), 5, 7.

to site-specific street shows). The authors are primarily of Algerian, Franco-Algerian, and French origin; the exceptions include an American novelist, an Austrian filmmaker, and a Romanian dramaturge. The works were created any time from the event itself to the present moment (2019). Resisting the temptations of totality, I have opted not to pin down an end date for the anarchive, despite the fact that 2011—the moment when the sealed police archives were ultimately declassified—would have provided an obvious temporal bookend. While analyses of October 17 works produced after 2011 may need to account for the shift in archival policy, and while there may be good reason to draw a distinction between cultural productions created prior to the opening of the police archives and those created after it, it is also true that the availability, status, and completeness of the official archives, even now that they are declassified, remain a topic of debate. If 2011 has symbolic importance as the moment when the putative final obstacle to knowledge about the massacre was removed, it behooves us to consider the year of declassification as a soft limit, a porous barrier, and a factor that complicates the notion of the anarchive in interesting ways. Moreover, if the influence of the archival material on cultural production is complicated to assess, it is imperative to point out that no significant new historical scholarship has been produced as a result of the opening of the police archives in 2011.[2]

In varying ways and to different degrees, the works of the anarchive are all *instructive*, but they are not all *didactic*; the works of the anarchive necessarily produce knowledge about October 17 and/or its subsequent erasure, but that knowledge may be implicit, analogic, or experiential. Across the corpus, however, the proportion and type of

---

2   Although there are too many accounts to mention, House and MacMaster's *Paris 1961: Algerians, State Terror, and Memory* bears special recognition for its detailed and scrupulously researched account of the complex historical and political factors leading up to the October 17 repression, and of the divergent and often contradictory responses to the repression in its aftermath. Also worthy of note are the previously mentioned works by Einaudi and E. Blanchard; Linda Amiri's *Les Fantômes du 17 octobre* (Paris: Éditions Mémoires génériques, 2001) and *La Bataille de France, la guerre d'Algérie en métropole* (Paris: Robert Laffont, 2004); and multiple works by Sylvie Thénault and Gilles Manceron. Interest in episodes of police violence, in general, also seems to be on the rise in the era of the third wave; see, for example, Kupferstein's aforementioned *Les balles du 14 juillet 1953*. Studies by Brunet, House and MacMaster, Dewerpe, and Amiri were all published prior to official declassification in 2011. These researchers, however, had all been given special permission to consult the police files.

representation devoted to the events of October 17 varies: In certain texts, October 17 constitutes the primary narrative material, sometimes including a recreation of the massacre itself and the subjective experiences of victims (and occasionally of perpetrators). In other works, October 17 is mentioned only briefly or even obliquely, a passing reference within a narrative that has otherwise little or nothing to do with the massacre. Still others represent the violence of the repression of knowledge, the breakdown of its transmission, and the occlusion of memory. Finally, the anarchive includes a small handful of works that, by accident or by design, misrepresent October 17 or include factual errors about the event.

This excavation also, although perhaps not unproblematically, includes a number of October 17 "activist works": nonfiction texts of various genres—pamphlets, photobooks, documentary shorts, websites, and interactive web platforms—generally produced by militant groups representing different milieus or fields of expertise. These works differ from the primary material of the anarchive in that they explicitly foreground the goal of disseminating information and nearly always seek to impact public opinion and policy through demands for archival access, official recognition of the massacre, and reparations. Including activist works stretches the boundaries of the anarchive and tests the limits of the term "cultural production"; it also provides an important supplementary layer of information about the nature and proportion of October 17 discourse in the public sphere.

Even the most successful archeologist is only as good as her sieve is fine; notwithstanding my desire for totality, this chapter cannot catalog *all* of the objects found in the anarchive without becoming an encyclopedia of itself and undermining its own mission. To that end, this chapter offers a periodization of primary works that places waves of cultural production in their historical and political contexts, thus permitting shifts in themes, genre, diegetic strategy, and political investment to emerge. At the same time, I am especially interested in exploring the paradoxes of periodization: although such a structured approach allows me to classify and name (both essential for interpretation), it also threatens to limit the potential for diachronic connections. By organizing the material into three periods and then tracing different paths through them, I both propose and complicate the rubrics that might be used to categorize the October 17 corpus. I am particularly interested in how the nature and proportion of October 17 representation changes over time, and to what degree representation can (or should) be imputed to political and cultural shifts related to the memory of the Algerian War. This analysis is also infused with a concern for epiphenomenal and metatextual matters, how issues of circulation, translation, marketing, authorial status, genre, and medium bear upon interpretation.

The Original Scene and the Fate of the First Wave (1961–63)

The first wave of anarchival texts is the only one whose start and end dates can be definitively anchored in time. The shortest of the three periods and the least prolific (featuring only three works), this wave corresponds to the early years of what Henry Rousso terms the "amnesty" phase in Algerian War memory—a moment that constitutes a "juridical fiction of forgetting."[3] All of the first-wave texts were directly inspired by the massacre, created in the immediate aftermath of the events, and published or disseminated within two years of the massacre. Unlike later texts, they all confront the physical violence of the repression (often in detail) and, in ways perhaps less direct, prefigure the event's erasure from the scene. Although their genres, aesthetic practices, political commitments, and authorial origins could not be more different, the three works share both a common temporality and a similar imperative to bear witness and to create a trace of an event that would later "disappear."

Jacques Panijel's hour-long documentary *Octobre à Paris* was filmed beginning in November 1961 and, as a result of government censure, was screened only a few times during the spring of 1962. A biologist by training and a researcher at the French National Centre for Scientific Research (CNRS), Panijel was politically engaged: he was active in the Resistance during World War II and a founding member of the Audin Committee—an organization named for Maurice Audin, a young French mathematician who was killed by French paratroopers in Algeria in 1957 and whose death became a *cause célèbre*.[4] Having witnessed

---

3 Henry Rousso, "Les raisins verts de la guerre d'Algérie," in *La Guerre d'Algérie (1954–1962)*, ed. Yves Michaud (Paris: Odile Jacob, 2004), 135. Rousso describes four stages of memory in the remembrance of the Algerian War (134–40): amnesty (1962–68); amnesia (1968–80); anamnesis (the 1980s); and hypermnesia, or obsessional memory (1999 and beyond).

4 The historian Pierre Vidal-Naquet was also a co-founder, and the most visible member of the Audin Committee. Vidal-Naquet is the author of *L'affaire Audin (1957–1978)* (Paris: Éditions de Minuit, 1989).

the repression on October 17, Panijel proposed that the Committee undertake a documentary film project to recreate the demonstration, its repression, and the social context of Algerians living in Paris at this particular moment in time. After numerous failed attempts to convince major directors like Jean Rouch or François Truffaut to take on the project, Panijel, who had only amateur film experience, opted to make the film himself with the financial backing of the Audin Committee.[5]

William Gardner Smith's novel *The Stone Face* (1963), set in Paris in 1961, is the very first work of fiction to represent October 17. (The first French-language novel would not appear until 1983.) Published by Farrar, Straus and Giroux, it tells the story of Simeon Brown, a black American artist who settles in Paris, having fled the racism of 1950s Philadelphia.[6] The temporal setting of the novel corresponds with the waning months of the Algerian War and with the beginning of the civil rights movement in the US, which Simeon follows from abroad. Unlike the rest of the expat community Simeon frequents, all of whom avoid French politics, Simeon befriends several Algerian men and is deeply touched by the story of their struggle for independence.

The third work of the first wave is the scathing poem "Dans la gueule du loup" (In the jaws of the wolf), penned shortly after the repression by the Algerian novelist, playwright, and poet Kateb Yacine. Considered one of the founding voices of Maghrebi literature in French (although he also wrote in Algerian dialect), Kateb was a staunch anti-colonialist who, as a young man, spent several months in prison after participating in the demonstration that led to the 1945 Sétif Massacre, an event considered to be the symbolic beginning of the Algerian War of Independence.[7]

---

5   Jacques Panijel, "Festivals d'un film maudit," interview with Jean-Philippe Renouard and Isabelle Saint-Saëns, *Vacarme* 13 (Fall 2000), https://vacarme.org/article221.html, (accessed August 27, 2020). Panijel notes that *Le Monde* helped with fundraising efforts. According to certain sources, the FLN also funneled money into the project.

6   For more on William Gardner Smith, see Alexa Weik von Mossner, "Cosmopolitan Sensitivities: Bystander Guilt and Interracial Solidarity in the Work of William Gardner Smith," chapter three, in *Cosmopolitan Minds: Literature, Emotion and the Transnational Imagination* (Austin: University of Texas Press, 2014), 89–119.

7   Known in French as *le massacre de Sétif, Guelma et Kherrata*, and in English as the Sétif and Guelma Massacre, this series of bloody reprisals began in Sétif on May 8, 1945 (the same day Germany capitulated, ending the Second World War). Initially both a celebration of the end of the war and an anti-colonial

Published for the first time in *Jeune Afrique* in June 1962, the poem
has been reprinted multiple times in various venues, including the 1986
special issue of *Actualité de l'émigration* commemorating the 25th
anniversary of October 17.[8] Concise at 18 brief lines, "Dans la gueule
du loup" is a razor-blade of a poem, a trenchant critique that cuts both
ways: Directly addressed to "le peuple français" (the people of France),
its final stanza asks whether or not the French nation will bear witness to
what it saw "with its own eyes." The poem, however, is also an implicit
critique of the FLN leadership, which, for Kateb, effectively threw the
Algerian proletariat into the "jaws of the wolf."[9]

What binds these works in spite of their differences (and above and
beyond their common subject and temporality) is their failure to signify,
either as cultural works in and of themselves, or collectively as the vanguard
of October 17 representation. Initially, Panijel's film was subject to the
same censorship that targeted all information related to October 17 (which
included the written press and all images made during the repression).
As a result, the first screenings, which took place at the ciné-club Action
in Paris and at the Cannes and Venice film festivals in May 1962, were
interrupted by police who confiscated the film.[10] In the 1970s, director-
activist René Vautier's request for an export visa (which would have
allowed his company to distribute *Octobre à Paris*) was denied. Political
censorship of cinema was a common practice in France at the time—nearly
all the *nouvelle vague* films had been refused visas as well—and Vautier
began a hunger strike in protest.[11] Thanks to Vautier's efforts, *Octobre*

protest, the gathering ultimately pitted French colonizers against rank-and-file
pro-Independence Algerians. French police officers fired on Algerian demonstrators,
touching off riots that would leave approximately one hundred dead on the French
side, and thousands dead among the Algerians. Although the War of Independence
would begin in earnest only nine years later, the Sétif incidents are seen as a
catalyst for anti-colonial sentiment. See Horne, *Savage War of Peace*.

8   Kateb, "Dans la gueule du loup," in "Hommage et témoignages," *Actualité
de l'émigration* 59 (October 1986), p. 30. *Actualité de l'émigration* was the official
news organ of L'Amicale des Algériens en Europe (the Fraternal Order of Algerians
in Europe).

9   This critique emerges in the commentary accompanying the 1986 reprint of
the poem in *Actualité*, where Kateb compares the FF-FLN action of October 17
to an FLN demonstration that had taken place in Algiers in December 1960. See
Chapter 4 for a longer discussion of this poem.

10   The ciné-club Action met at the now defunct cinema Studio Bertrand (Paris 7e).

11   Vautier was as famous for his political and anti-colonial engagement as he

à Paris was ultimately granted a visa in 1973; however, Panijel refused to release the film on the grounds that, so many years after the event, the film required a prologue to contextualize October 17 as a state crime. Whereas the state was responsible for the film's failure to signify in the first decade of its existence, it was the director himself who kept the film closeted (quite literally) for the following four decades.[12]

In 2011, on the 50th anniversary of the repression and thanks to a filmic preface made by Mehdi Lallaoui, *Octobre à Paris* was released on DVD and in theatres. At that moment, however, it shared the spotlight with a newer documentary by Yasmina Adi, *Ici on noie les Algériens*—a film that benefited from 50 years of hindsight, the availability of archival footage and documentation, and slick twenty-first-century production techniques.[13] *Octobre à Paris* has spent most of its life in the shadows and, ironically, its impact 50 years after its making has been somewhat mitigated by Adi's film, which has figured more prominently in the press and been more widely distributed.[14] Moreover, although its narrative approach and filmic techniques make Panijel's film arguably one of the most important works in the history of French documentary, it has been largely eclipsed by the films of Jean Rouch, Alain Resnais, and Chris Marker, and received little, if any, scholarly attention.[15]

---

was for his one major work of cinema, *Avoir vingt ans dans les Aurès* (1972). He is credited with having made the first anti-colonial French film, *Afrique 50*, a documentary short, in 1956. For more on Vautier, see Valentin Schaepelynck, "René Vautier: esthétique et politique de l'intervention," *Décadrages* 29–30 (2016): 45–59, and Vautier's own memoir, *Caméra citoyenne—Mémoires* (Rennes: Apogée, 1998).

12   Panijel apparently lacked the means to produce the preface himself. See his comments in "Festivals d'un film maudit."

13   Yasmina Adi is a French director of Algerian origin. Her filmography also includes a documentary on the Sétif Massacre, titled *L'Autre 8 mai 1945* (2008).

14   See Jacques Mandelbaum, "*Octobre à Paris* et *Ici on noie les Algériens*: le 17 octobre 1961, la justice se noya dans la Seine," *Le Monde*, October 14, 2011, and Brozgal, "Gros plan sur le 17 octobre 1961: violence coloniale, cinéma documentaire et le sujet algérien," in *Représentations de la guerre d'indépendance algérienne*, ed. Maya Boutaghou (Paris: Classiques Garnier, 2019), 99–114.

15   Key articles on *Octobre à Paris* include: Maria Flood, "(Un)Familiar Fictions: Documentary Aesthetics and the 17th October 1961 Massacre in Jacques Panijel's *Octobre à Paris* (1962)," *Forum for Modern Language Studies* 54, no. 2 (2018): 157–75; Mani Sharpe, "Visibility, Speech, and Disembodiment in Jacques Panijel's *Octobre à Paris*," *French Cultural Studies* 28, no. 4 (2017): 360–70; and Brozgal, "Gros plan sur le 17 octobre."

Like *Octobre à Paris*, *The Stone Face* is noteworthy for both its status as a vanguard representation of October 17 and its disappearance from the cultural radar. As the only English-language work in the anarchive, the novel's lack of traction is perhaps unsurprising; after all, *The Stone Face* has never been translated into French, despite the fact that in the 1960s the French appetite for new American fiction was particularly keen. Works by Nelson Algren and William Faulkner, along with those by James Baldwin, Richard Wright, and Chester Himes, quickly found translators and publishers, often with the patronage of major French intellectuals.[16] Moreover, two of Smith's other works were published in French.[17] More curiously, *The Stone Face* has also remained invisible to an American public likely more familiar, both then and now, with the names of Smith's comrades in arms. As of this writing, *The Stone Face* remains out of print and only rarely appears on syllabi for courses on American literature or on the civil rights era.[18] However, just as *Octobre à Paris* has been resuscitated thanks in part to the efforts of Lallaoui, there have been several recent attempts to shine a light on *The Stone Face* and its timely message. Critical attention by scholars such as Tyler Stovall, Paul Gilroy, and Alexa Weik von Mossner has contributed to the novel's modest renaissance.[19]

16   Sartre's *Les Temps modernes* played an active role in promoting and publishing American writers, including Wright, Algren, and others. See Anne Boschetti, *The Intellectual Enterprise: Sartre and* Les Temps modernes, trans. Richard McCleary (Chicago: Northwestern University Press, 1988).

17   Smith's novel *Anger at Innocence*, published in New York City in 1950, was published in French in 1952 under the title *Malheur aux justes*, trans. Jean Rosenthal (Paris: Club Français du livre, 1952), and his book-length essay recounting his temporary return to the US after 16 years of exile, *Return to Black America* (1970), also quickly appeared in French under the title *Retour à l'Amérique noire*, trans. Rosine Fitzgerald (Paris: Casterman, 1972).

18   According to several sources, the novel is slated for reissue in the NYRB Classics series. See Adam Schatz, "'How does it feel to be a white man?': William Gardner Smith's Exile in Paris," *New Yorker*, August 11, 2019, https://www.newyorker.com/books/page-turner/how-does-it-feel-to-be-a-white-man-william-gardner-smiths-exile-in-paris.

19   Tyler Stovall, who has long championed the novel, prefaced an excerpt translated into French by Mona de Pracontal. See Stovall, "Preface to *The Stone Face*," *Contemporary French and Francophone Studies* 8, no. 3 (2004): 305–27. See also Gilroy, *Against Race: Imagining Political Culture Beyond the Color Line* (Cambridge, MA: Harvard University Press, 2000); Weik von Mossner, "Cosmopolitan Sensitivities."

Finally, although it has arguably circulated more widely than the other two works, Kateb's rallying cry remains largely unknown, despite Kateb's status as one of the most important and prolific Algerian writers. Today, while the poem is frequently reproduced on internet sites (both specialized and general), it has not been reprinted in anthologies of Kateb's work. It is, however, one of the few October 17 texts to have a second life in adaptation: "Dans la gueule du loup" was set to music by the French rock group Têtes Raides (on their 1998 album *Chambouletou*) and produced as a music video, a development that may be responsible for the poem's greater visibility since 2000. In an evocation, perhaps, of Têtes Raides' political gesture, the poem is also featured in Didier Daeninckx's graphic novel *Octobre noir* (2011), which culminates on October 17, 1961, with the protagonist—a young Algerian musician whose sister has just been killed during the police violence—performing "Dans la gueule du loup" at a club. Kateb's accusatory lines (people of France, you saw it all…) thus become a powerful closing salvo to a "pulp" fiction dedicated to one of the few female victims of October 17, Fatima Bédar.[20]

More than in any other period of October 17 cultural production, the works of the first wave embody the essential ambivalence of the event itself. Their material existence alone would have made them visible; they should have signified by sheer dint of their encoded attempts to give an account of the massacre and its repression. Yet, regardless of the various processes that conspired to "disappear" them from the cultural scene, narratives of their various "comebacks" (*Octobre à Paris* through re-issue on DVD; *The Stone Face* by virtue of scholarship; "Dans la gueule du loup" through musical adaptation) produce lively metatexts suggesting that their invisibility has never been total. More to the point—and here we already begin to chip away at the boundaries of the periods, thanks to their reemergence in recent decades and to greater visibility in their

---

20 Daeninckx, *Octobre noir*, illustrations by Mako (Anthy-sur-Léman: Ad libris, 2011). The story of Fatima Bédar, one of the few female victims on October 17, and the youngest among them, has long fascinated Daeninckx. Prior to *Octobre noir* and along with Einaudi, he was the first to investigate the Bédar case and to discover proof that her death in the Canal Saint-Denis was not a suicide but a homicide. In 1986, Daeninckx published a damning article titled "Délphine pour mémoire" in *Actualité de l'émigration* (28–29). He also devoted a short story to her; see "Fatima pour mémoire," in *17 octobre 1961, 17 écrivains se souviennent*, ed. Samia Messaoudi and Mustapha Harzoune (Montigny-lès-Cormeilles: Au nom de la mémoire, 2011), 81–88.

afterlives than in their original iterations, these initial three works could just as plausibly be ascribed to the third wave of the anarchive.

Returning to the Scene: The Second Wave (1983–99)

The urgent cries of the first-wave works were ultimately un-sustained and unsustainable; 1963 marked the end of this first installment of committed cultural production, and the beginning of a nearly two-decades-long fallow period. In the immediate aftermath of the events, the fact of state censorship explains the limited number of works and their poor circulation, but it does not account for nearly 20 years of cultural silence. Processes of forgetting are undeniably complex, and Pierre Nora's now well-known comment—"dès que fermées les portes de la guerre, tout le monde a oublié, du moins, tout le monde a fait semblant" (as soon as the doors of the war slammed shut, everyone forgot or, at the very least, everyone pretended to have forgotten)[21]—with its suggestion that forgetting may be real or "performed," only amplifies this complexity. Regardless of whether various parties and actors "forgot" October 17, a deafening silence emerged, during the 1960s and 1970s, as both an official state posture and a "strategy" on the part of the Algerian community in France.[22] Echoing the political zeitgeist and absence of public discourse, cultural production went dormant, suggesting that memory itself had gone underground, and that October 17 had indeed been invisible.[23]

   The beginning of the end of forgetting (such as it was), and of the silences that accompanied and constituted it, can be indexed to two key moments of the early 1980s: first, the initial glimmers of what would become the two-decades-long Papon "affair"; and second, the emergence of the *beurs*, or second-generation Algerians, as political actors and cultural agents.[24]

---

21   Pierre Nora, "Algérie fantôme," *L'Histoire* 43 (March 1982): 9.
22   On "strategic silence," see Ronald L. Cohen, "Silencing Objections: Social Constructions of Indifference," *Journal of Human Rights* 1, no. 2 (June 2002): 187–206. Cited in House and MacMaster, 265. Even Algerians in France opted for a "strategic silence," preferring to discuss the events only within family circles, if at all.
23   See Stora, "Guerre d'Algérie, France, la mémoire retrouvée," *Hommes et migrations* 1158 (October 1992): 10–14; and Rousso, "Les raisins verts de la guerre d'Algérie," 134–40.
24   I borrow the concept of "cultural agents" from Doris Sommer, who defines "cultural agency" as "a range of social contributions through creative practices."

In 1981, the French satirical newsweekly *Le Canard enchaîné* published lightly redacted versions of classified documents from the Gironde prefecture that exposed Maurice Papon's role in the deportation of Jews from Bordeaux. The scathing article that accompanied the documents took the opportunity to suggest a cruel continuity in the career of the man who, barely 20 years after having sent French Jews to their death, found himself commanding the forces that would beat, kill, and drown Algerians in the Seine.[25] Shortly after the article appeared, there began a series of legal episodes that would become the longest-running courtroom drama in French history, culminating with a victory for the prosecution: In 1998, Papon was found guilty of complicity in crimes against humanity for his role in the fate of the Jews from Bordeaux.

Independent of the Papon affair, the emergence of the *beur* movement in the early 1980s provided another important catalyst for October 17 cultural production. The term *beur*, derived from the word *arabe* through the popular syllable-inversion slang known as *verlan*, refers to the generation of North Africans born in France (or having immigrated to France at a young age with their families) during and just after the Algerian War.[26] France had actively encouraged Algerians (and other former colonial subjects) to pursue work in the *métropole* during the economic boom known as *les trente glorieuses* (or the "Glorious Thirty"), when postwar rebuilding efforts meant that cheap labor was both welcome and essential. The last chapter of this story of cohabitation had, however, never been drafted: there was no script for integrating a large mass of culturally different foreigners, nor were there provisions for their return to an Algeria that was no longer French.[27] Housing,

Sommer, "Introduction: Wiggle Room," *Cultural Agency in the Americas*, ed. Doris Sommer (Durham, NC: Duke University Press, 2006), 1.

25   Nicolas Brimo, "Papon aide de camps: Quand un ministre de Giscard faisait déporter des Juifs," *Le Canard enchaîné*, May 6, 1981, p. 4.

26   Although originally coined by the very community it describes, the term *beur* (and its derivatives *beurette*, *bourgeois*(e)) is considered pejorative by some.

27   See in particular the groundbreaking work by Patrick Simon and his team of demographers at the INED (The National Institute for the Study of Demographics): Cris Beauchemin, Christelle Hamel, and Patrick Simon, *Trajectoires et origines. Enquête sur la diversité des populations en France* (Paris: INED, 2015). See also Sylvia Zappi, "Les 'beurs', acte III," *Le Monde*, October 10, 2013. Unlike, for example, the *Gastarbeiter* program in Germany, which provided for foreign workers' eventual return to their countries of origin, French immigration policy had no such provision.

education, and other services were thus improvised; most immigrant children were raised in shantytowns and, as they became available, in high-density, low-cost housing projects, or HLM, originally intended to house French workers.

Although the *beurs* were not the first generation of immigrants (or children of immigrants) to find themselves pulled between the traditional, sometimes rural culture of a distant parental homeland and the modern, urban, secular culture of their daily lives in France, they were the only ethnic minority group to challenge French republican ideology by pointing a collective finger at the structural inequalities affecting them.[28] They were also one of the first groups to protest en masse against racism and violence: In 1983, second-generation French citizens of immigrant backgrounds staged a cross-country march under the banner of *La marche pour l'égalité et contre le racisme* (The march for equality and against racism). Their success in drawing attention to police violence and everyday racism was somewhat mitigated by the media's rebranding of the multi-city demonstration as *La marche des beurs* (The Beurs' March), a slogan that effectively defanged the political gravitas of the movement. Culturally, however, the *beurs* would strike back with a series of novels and films about second-generation Algerians and Maghrebis and their experience of cultural in-betweenness; among these were several of the first French-language novels to evoke October 17.

In different ways, the Papon affair and the emergence of the *beurs* rekindled the memory of October 17 and, more importantly, reinvigorated practices of cultural representation. In 1983, Didier Daeninckx, who had witnessed the Charonne repression as a teenager and was fascinated by the emerging Papon scandal, published his second novel— the *noir* police procedural *Meurtres pour mémoire*.[29] *Meurtres* was the very first French-language novel to represent October 17, and if quantities of scholarship and republication are any measure, it remains

28   As Alec Hargreaves has noted in his pioneering study on *beur* literature and culture, "the *Beurs* are [not] unique in experiencing a divided sense of identity. What is distinctive [...] is the particular set of parameters within which these tensions arise [...], rooted in the juxtaposition of radically different cultural systems consequent upon large-scale international population movements." *Immigration and Identity in Beur Fiction: Voices from the North African Community in France* (London: Berg, 1991), 2–3.

29   Daeninckx, *Meurtres pour mémoire* (Paris: Gallimard, 1983). English translations are from *Murder in Memoriam*, trans. Liz Heron (New York: Melville House, 2012).

one of the best-known works in the anarchive, both in France and abroad. The plot of the "hard-boiled" detective novel weaves together the Vichy and Algerian war crimes of André Veillut, a fictional avatar of Papon. In the novel, Veillut's role in the deportation of Jews is tied to the murder of two historians, one killed on October 17, 1961, in Paris, the other in 1983 in Toulouse, after having consulted the municipal archives. These crimes turn out to be "hits," that is, executions ordered by the government in a bid to prevent the revelation of an embarrassing state secret: In 1942 Veillut had personally ordered the deportation of Jews from Toulouse (standing in for Papon's Bordeaux) to Drancy, from where they were transferred to Auschwitz. The two victims had consulted—20 years apart—the same set of incriminating documents held by the municipal archives of Toulouse.

Within the anarchive, the significance of *Meurtres* goes beyond its pioneering status as a "first." Daeninckx has argued that the conventions of the *polar* subgenre allow the novel to function as "a hypothesis about reality."[30] In spite of its pulpy trappings (or, perhaps, because of them), the detective novel is imbued with the power to "smuggle truth past the guardians."[31] Indeed, the putative contraband of *Meurtres* has been taken up and reworked in other October 17 texts. Although allusive links between October 17 and Vichy are present in several of the first-wave texts and continue to be leveraged in the second and third waves, *Meurtres* was the first fiction to mobilize actual historical figures and events to speculate on an institutional connection that would later be established in fact. Moreover, *Meurtres* has had significant afterlives: the novel has not only been translated into multiple languages, it was adapted as a graphic novel (see Jeanne Puchol, *Meurtres pour mémoire*, Futuropolis, 1991) and as a made-for-TV movie directed by Laurent Heynemann.[32] The author is often pressed into service as an expert on

30   Donald Reid, "Didier Daeninckx, Raconteur of History," *South Central Review* 27, no. 1–2 (2010): 57 n.25.

31   Reid, 24.

32   Scholarly works on *Meurtres* include: Margaret Atack, "From *Meurtres pour mémoire* to Missak: Literature and Historiography in Dialogue," *French Cultural Studies* 25, no. 3–4 (2014): 271–80; Catherine Dana, "Les enfants Antigone," *French Forum* 29, no. 1 (Winter 2004): 113–25; Charles Forsdick, "Direction les oubliettes de l'histoire: Witnessing the Past in the Contemporary French Polar," *French Cultural Studies* 12 (2001): 333–50; Richard J. Golsan, "Memory's *bombes à retardement*: Maurice Papon, Crimes Against Humanity, and 17 October 1961," *Journal of European Studies* 28, no. 1 (1998): 153–72; and Claire Gorrara,

October 17 and its historical context, and has written numerous prefaces and postfaces.[33] In 2008, *Meurtres* was reissued in Gallimard's "Classico collège" series. Intended for use in 3e in France (ninth grade in the US; year ten in Great Britain), this version comes with a pedagogical dossier, footnotes, and accessible essays on historical context.

If the resurgence of October 17 in the cultural sphere has a clear connection to the Papon affair, the *beurs'* role in catalyzing the "second wave" of October 17 representation is often overlooked. The *beurs* never considered themselves a formal political movement, nor have they ever coalesced as a unified literary entity. Yet their activism emerged in tandem with their first novels, suggesting a common source for *beur* political subjectivity and cultural agency.[34] The first *beur* novel, *Le thé au harem d'Archi Ahmed*, was written in 1983 by Mehdi Charef, and the next two years saw the publication, in rapid succession, of the first *beur* novels to represent October 17: Nacer Kettane's *Le Sourire de Brahim* (1985) and Mehdi Lallaoui's *Les Beurs de Seine* (1986).[35] Later *beur* works dealing with October 17 and its memory include: *Une fille sans histoire* (1989) by Tassadit Imache; the singer Mounsi's hybrid autobiographical treatise-text *Territoire d'outre-ville* (1995);[36] and the controversial novel *Vivre me tue* (1997) by Paul Smaïl.

"Reflections on Crime and Punishment: Memories of the Holocaust in Recent French Crime Fiction," *Yale French Studies* 108 (2005): 131–45.

33 See, for example, "Entretien avec Didier Daeninckx" at the end of Ahmed Kalouaz's novel *Les Fantômes d'octobre* (Paris: Oskar, 2011), 114–26.

34 "*Beur* literature and cinema" is more of an ad hoc category than this language would suggest; the *beur* writers and filmmakers did not band together to create a coherent corpus or cultural practice. If *beur* novels share similar thematics, this is a result of their realism and the common predicaments of many *beurs* (but also of many immigrants hailing from other ethnic backgrounds).

35 There is some dispute about the first *beur* novel. Hargreaves claims this distinction for Hocine Touabti's *L'Amour quand-même* (1981), but other critics suggest that the topic of Touabti's book does not represent *beur* concerns. Charef's novel is thus often considered the inaugural work, bolstered by the fact that he was the first mediatized *beur* (thanks to his appearance on Bernard Pivot's legendary literary talk show *Apostrophes,* on April 1, 1983), and that his *Thé au harem d'Archi Ahmed* was adapted for the cinema not long after its publication. (*Le thé au harem d'Archimède* (1985) was directed by Charef and underwritten by Michèle Costa-Gavras.) For more on *beur* writers in the French media, see Kathryn A. Kleppinger's thoroughgoing study *Branding the 'Beur' Author: Minority Writing and the Media in France* (Liverpool: Liverpool University Press, 2015).

36 As Laura Reeck observes, "Mounsi claims that (October 17) was the moment

Scholars of *beur* literature and cinema generally converge in reading these works (particularly the novel) as highly autobiographical documents that bear witness to a specific socio-cultural phenomenon; stated otherwise, they are often understood as "auto-ethnographies."[37] Frequently neglected, however, are the fundamental historical commitments of this literature. In *Le Sourire de Brahim*—the second novel in French to take up the October 17 repression—the first chapter moves contrapuntally between the protagonist's experience of the massacre in Paris and historical vignettes that recount the hardships of Kabylia, linking episodes of colonial violence and implicitly challenging the notion that such acts only occur in a distant elsewhere. Set in the mid-1980s, Lallaoui's *Les Beurs de Seine* (the third novel in French with October 17 content) features historically savvy *beur* protagonists whose encounters with French characters often become history lessons, as the outsiders school the insiders in the finer points of a recent past that has yet to appear in school textbooks.

In the numerous cases where *beur* novelists have taken up the subject of October 17, these books are, nearly without exception, *first* novels. The story of October 17 thus functions as originary material and as a foundational moment in the "coming to writing" of authors like Kettane, Lallaoui, Imache, and Mounsi, all of whom evoke October 17 in the works that served as their entrée into the world of letters.[38] (While it goes beyond our arbitrary boundary for the second wave, the same might be said for Faïza Guène: although her first novel, *Kiffe kiffe demain* (2004), does not deal explicitly with October 17, her very first creative work was a documentary short film titled *Mémoires du 17 octobre* (2002).)[39] The anarchival work of *beur* novels is thus multiple: It

he awoke to history." In *Writerly Identites in Beur Fiction and Beyond* (Lanham, MD: Lexington Books, 2011), 160.

37 Although I normally eschew qualifications that demand greater realism and verisimilitude of "minority" literature, Laura Reeck's engagement with Mary Louise Pratt's exploration of the notion of "peripheral" is compelling. Pratt views autoethnography as a writerly strategy that participates in determining and defining the metropolis. See Reeck, 81, and Pratt, *Imperial Eyes: Travel Writing and Transculturation* (New York: Routledge, 2007), especially the introduction "Criticism in the Contact Zone."

38 Significantly, Kettane would never write another novel after *Le Sourire de Brahim* but would become a major investor in *beur* culture, founding RadioBeur (BeurFM) and BeurTV. Lallaoui and Imache would take up October 17 again in subsequent works.

39 Guène's 17-minute documentary was produced in a film/video workshop

historicizes October 17 and narrativizes the subjective experience of the repression and its aftermath, while also positioning the *beur* as a central historical subject and agent.

The second wave of October 17 anarchival works also includes several little-known novels by mainstream French writers, a detail that suggests that October 17 was not simply a topic of predilection for activists (Daeninckx) or authors with a personal connection to the historical material (the *beurs*). Jean-François Vilar's pulp fiction *Bastille tango* does not explicitly mention the repression on October 17; it does, however, make reference to "Algerian bodies floating in the Saint Martin canal."[40] While the significance of this detail might be easy to miss (and certainly, it requires a historically informed reader in order to signify fully), the fact that it is caught up in a larger tale of Argentinian expatriates who fled that country's Dirty War and dictatorship in the late 1970s gives the novel the trappings of a comparative study in state crime. Meanwhile, *Algérie, bords de Seine* (1992), by Pierre-Jean Rémy (member of the French Academy), is a historical fresco in the realist style that traces the trajectory of a young *fonctionnaire* assigned to the Oran prefecture during the Algerian War. The politically naïve Gérard, who becomes sympathetic to the Algerian cause, returns in 1961 to Paris, where, narratively, the massacre on October 17 forms part of the historical ambiance of the "second front" of the Algerian War.

Like the first wave, the second wave also reflects a variety of genres and media, albeit on a grander scale. In addition to the abovementioned literary works, the second wave saw a rather intensive production of both documentary and fiction film. These include full-length feature and short fiction films, such as Denis Lévy's *Mémoire en blanc* (1981); Okacha Touita's *Les Sacrifiés* (1982); Heynemann's TV adaptation of *Meurtres pour mémoire* (1985); and Boualerm Guedj's film adaptation of the ironically titled novel-chronicle *Vivre au paradis* (1998). The last item is a unique case in the anarchive: Whereas the film contains a long sequence recreating the mass departure of Algerian protestors from the Nanterre *bidonville*, their arrival at the city limits, and the police

sponsored by *Les Engraineurs*, a neighborhood organization based in Pantin (eastern suburbs of Paris) devoted to citizenship, the environment, and grass-roots activism. For more on Guène's little-known and rarely studied cinema, see Dominic Thomas, "Documenting the Periphery: The Short Films of Faïza Guène," *French Forum* 35, no. 2–3 (Spring–Fall 2010): 191–208.

40   Jean-François Vilar, *Bastille tango* (Paris: Babelio, 1986), 113.

repression of the protest, the original novel, an autobiographical text published in 1992 by the Algerian writer Brahim Benaïcha, makes only passing reference to October 17. An international co-production with well-known actors, the film *Vivre au paradis* has become a significant October 17 cultural reference. Similarly, the Heynemann adaptation—which had a built-in national viewership on TF1 as part of the omnibus project *Série noire* and that capitalized on the popularity of the original novel—was one of the most visible representations of October 17 during the long second wave.[41]

Following in the unsung tradition of Panijel, the second wave also includes a relatively significant number of both feature-length and short documentary films. Several are only tangentially concerned with October 17: Jean-Pierre Krief's *Les années Kagan* (1989), for example, features a brief mention of October 17 in the context of a "day in the life" reportage on the photographer Élie Kagan, whose photographs constitute one of the few preserved visual records of October 17. Most of the documentaries, however, were made by committed October 17 activists such as journalist Virginie Delahautemaison, whose *Mémoire du fleuve* (1998) was produced by France 3, and novelist Mehdi Lallaoui, whose joint venture with Anne Tristan, *Le silence du fleuve* (1991), was accompanied by an activist art book, published the same year under the same title.

The most important documentary film of the second wave, however, came from outside the hexagon. *Drowning By Bullets*, by Philip Brooks and Alan Hayling, aired in 1992 on Channel 4 in the UK and in France on the Franco-German TV Station ARTE, under the title "Une journée portée disparue."[42] A work of investigative journalism, the 52-minute film features testimonial accounts from a variety of eyewitnesses, including protestors, policemen, and former officials, press clippings from the immediate aftermath of the massacre, and rarely seen film footage from state-owned television channels. *Drowning by Bullets* undoubtedly

41   Created in 1984, *Série noire* was an omnibus series of 37 90-minute episodes of international crime fiction that ran from 1984 to 1991 on TF1, France's first public television station.

42   First aired in the UK on Channel 4 as part of the series "Secret History." "Drowning" was season two, episode three. Season two also included features on the British bombing of villages in India during the Raj and on the Armenian genocide. Brooks was an Australian documentary filmmaker who had been based in Paris for years; Hayling, former head of BBC documentaries, co-founded Newsreel Collective.

constituted the first time the French public had been so directly confronted with such a complete vision of the crime and its cover-up.

The 25th anniversary year of the massacre, 1986, was pivotal in terms of activist production. For the first time since it was taken in 1961, the photo of the graffiti "Ici on noie les Algériens" appeared in the press. Prominently featured on the front page of the October 17, 1986, issue of *L'Humanité*, the photo was accompanied by an unequivocal caption referring to "the massacres of 1961" and a three-page reportage titled "25 Years Later."[43] Also in 1986, the review *Actualité de l'émigration* brought out a major special issue to commemorate the 25th anniversary of October 17— impressive both in scope and in the variety and quantity of contributions. Under the title "Hommage et témoignages" and the slogan "Pour ne pas oublier," the issue features essays by former FLN leader Ali Haroun and Pierre Vidal-Naquet (titled "La journée qui n'ébranla pas Paris" or The Day That Did Not Shake Paris); photos by Élie Kagan; commissioned artwork; and political cartoons by Larbi and Farid Boudjellel. Several pages of the special issue feature first editions of works that would later, in their more developed iterations, form part of the anarchive. Daeninckx's essay "Delphine pour mémoire," which details the genesis of *Meurtres pour memoire* and sets the stage for *Octobre noir*, appears in the pages preceding Kateb Yacine's "Dans la gueule du loup," which, in turn, shares a double-page spread with an essay by Leïla Sebbar titled "La Seine était rouge"—a precursor to her 1999 eponymous novella.[44]

The second wave of the anarchive corresponds with the publication of the first historical studies on October 17, notably Michel Lévine's *Les ratonnades d'octobre: Un meurtre collectif à Paris en 1961* (1985); Einaudi's *La Bataille de Paris* (1991); and Brunet's *Police contre FLN* (1999).[45] It was also during this time, in conjunction with the *beur* groundswell, that memory activists emerged in the public sphere through community outreach, publications, and eventually by dint of an online presence. The aforementioned *Silence du fleuve* works (documentary film and book) are the flagship productions of the association Au nom

43   *L'Humanité*, October 17, 1986, 1, 2–5. Reportage from 1985 by C. Leconte.
44   For all three texts, see *Actualité de l'émigration*: Daeninckx, 28–29; Kateb, 30; Sebbar, 31.
45   Einaudi's book was written in spite of having been denied access to most state-controlled archives. Brunet's later addition is a kind of rebuttal to Einaudi, commissioned by the state and for which Brunet was granted access to the police archives.

de la mémoire, founded in 1990 by Lallaoui, journalist and editor Samia Messaoudi, and historian Benjamin Stora.[46] Devoted to other instances of "oubli colonial" as well, Au nom de la mémoire was nonetheless the first official association to take up the cause of October 17 and to actively lobby for its recognition.

The Post-Papon Anarchive: The Third Wave, 1999 and Beyond

Distinguishing the end of the second wave from the beginning of the third is an exercise that highlights the arbitrary nature of periodization. Logical as it may be to bracket the entire second wave with the Papon affair by positing his conviction in 1998 as a natural limit to that period of anarchival activity, this assumes that culture can be indexed precisely to current events. Moreover, it stamps an expiration date on a saga that, in fact, seemed to live on with its protagonist. While the trial itself came to an end with the 1998 verdict, a series of appeals, reversals, and polemics kept the affair in the media spotlight until Papon's death in 2007.[47]

Positing 1999 as the start of the third wave also means drawing a somewhat random internal border in the cultural field. After all, the anarchive's continuities over time also make it difficult to pinpoint anything like an aesthetic or representational pivot. While the third wave is distinctive for its abundance of material, as well as for the emergence of several subgenres of representation not previously seen in the anarchive (namely young adult literature and theatre), post-1999 cultural texts continue to manifest many of the features previously highlighted in the first and second waves: the works still represent a wide variety of genres and media, and they remain collectively idiosyncratic in their aesthetic and political investments.

It is possible, nonetheless, to locate a perceptible shift in tone and discourse at the turn of the century. While Rousso has called the 1990s the beginning of *hypermnésie,* or the "obsessional" phase for memory

---

46   An association called Le 17 octobre, contre l'oubli was also founded during this period, but was eventually subsumed into Au nom de la mémoire. Their original website is still online, although not actively updated.

47   The polemics in question include, notably: Papon's attempt to evade prison by fleeing to Switzerland; continued requests for leniency due to his advanced age and ill health; and a scandal in which Papon was fined for wearing his *Légion d'honneur* medal after having been stripped of the decoration in 1999.

of the Algerian War, an "obsessive" cultural memory of October 17, specifically, only began in earnest in 1999—the year marked by the highly publicized Papon-Einaudi libel trial and the publication of Leïla Sebbar's novel *La Seine était rouge*.[48] Although the *Canard enchaîné* article of 1981 had drawn a connection between Papon's Vichy and colonial crimes, it was not until 1998, when historian Einaudi published an op-ed article in *Le Monde* titled "Octobre 1961: Pour la verité, enfin," that Papon's responsibility for the massacre on October 17 would return to public and political consciousness. On October 16, 1997, during the testimony phase of the Papon trial in Bordeaux, Einaudi was called to the stand by the prosecution to rebut Papon's allegations of the previous day. The former chief of police, when interrogated about the events of October 17, had recited the fiction he rehearsed in 1961 and had been performing ever since: Only two Algerians were killed, and the arrest of 11,700 Algerians was not a "rafle" (a raid) but rather a "mise à l'abri"—a measure taken to protect the Algerian community.[49] Brought forward with the precise goal of contradicting Papon, Einaudi offered detailed evidence of police violence and asserted "a minimum of 200 victims," ending with the solemn statement, "Je suis venu ici en mémoire de ces victimes algériennes, enterrées comme des chiens dans la fosse commune réservée aux musulmans inconnus du cimetière de Thiais" (I came here in memory of these Algerian victims, buried like dogs in a common grave reserved for unidentified Muslims in the Thiais Cemetery).[50]

It seems that Papon did not hide his immediate reaction to Einaudi's accusation—a journalist from *Le Monde* observed that the former prefect seemed to "lose his composure" and began nervously fumbling with his legal pad.[51] Yet it would take Papon eight months to react officially: In July of 1998 he brought charges of defamation against Einaudi, and the legal proceedings began in earnest in February of 1999. The libel case was the only moment of the larger Papon affair in which details of October 17 and the former prefect's responsibility for the massacre—indeed, the very term "massacre" was at the heart of

48   Rousso, "Rasins verts de la guerre d'Algérie," 139–40.
49   Fabrice Riceputi, *La Bataille d'Einaudi, ou comment la mémoire du 17 octobre 1961 revint à la république* (Paris: Le Passager clandestin, 2015), 21.
50   Riceputi, 21.
51   Jean-Michel Daumay, "Les heures noires de la France resurgissent à Bordeaux," *Le Monde*, October 17, 1997.

the suit—appeared to translate into political action.[52] Handily won by Einaudi, the trial propelled October 17 into public consciousness for a time, making visible both the crime and its official, systematic dissimulation. The case also reignited debates over the police archives and their classified status: Several City of Paris archivists had taken the stand on Einaudi's behalf, offering testimony that proved essential in his ultimate exoneration.[53] Although Papon lost the libel suit, he would never be judged for his actions on October 17.

The trial nonetheless provided rich material for the third wave of the anarchive. Just a few years after the Papon-Einaudi showdown, Mehdi Lallaoui drew on the trial transcripts for his second October 17 novel, a speculative fiction titled *Une nuit d'octobre* (2001) in which a cast of truth seekers—eyewitnesses to October 17, anti-war activists, and children of survivors—collaborate to assist Renucci (Einaudi's fictional avatar) in his defense. Lallaoui's novel is the only one to feature the libel trial, but numerous other third-wave texts stage Papon at the scene of the action on October 17, including: Alain Tasma's made-for-TV docudrama *Nuit noire* (2005), Rachid Bouchareb's feature film *Hors-la-loi* (2010), the experimental play *La Pomme et le couteau* by Aziz Chouaki (2010), Médine's rap "17 octobre" (2006), and several novels (Eric Michel's *Algérie! Algérie!* and Natacha Michel's *Plein présent*). Michael Haneke's film *Caché* (2005) also makes a passing reference to Papon in a scene that uses the name of the former chief of police as a would-be transparent signifier. Although *Meurtres pour mémoire* had already speculated on Papon's "double role" nearly 20 years prior, post-1999 works no longer cloak the prefect's identity in a protective pseudonym.[54] This, along with the spike in occurrences of Papon as a character, suggests a kind of *représentation décomplexée*—a newfound freedom to both name and

---

52 Including the creation of the Mandelkern Commission, tasked with evaluating the police archives. In an article in *Le Monde* dated May 10, 1998, Einaudi upped the ante, writing, "*Je persiste et signe. En octobre 1961, il y eut à Paris un massacre perpétré par des forces de l'ordre agissant sous les ordres de Maurice Papon*" (I stand by what I've said: In October 1961 there was a massacre in Paris perpetrated by the police force acting on the orders of Maurice Papon) (emphasis in original).

53 See Riceputi, "Archives et raison d'état" (117–58) and "On choisit un autre métier si on ne veut pas d'ennuis," interview with archivists Brigitte Lainé and Philippe Grand, *Vacarme* 13 (Fall 2000), http://www.vacarme.org/article45.html.

54 While the pseudonym used by Daeninckx in *Meurtres* (Veillut) is neutral, the same cannot be said for the one used by Lallaoui in *Une nuit d'octobre*, where the prefect is referred to as "Crapon."

represent the perpetrator, an unfettered finger-pointing filling the void of legal action.

If 1999 is critical because it heralded the end of the Papon affair, that year also saw the publication of Sebbar's *La Seine était rouge*, a novel that, in both its timing and its content, embodies a notable shift in anarchival production.[55] *La Seine était rouge*—by virtue of its title alone—is a frontal attack on the "invisibility" of October 17 and a bold staging of three protagonists on a mission to uncover the truth about the massacre and its erasure from official and personal memory. Unquestionably a fiction, *La Seine était rouge* nevertheless makes no attempt to hide its activist agenda. In addition to the title's accusatory statement, the book is dedicated to the victims as well as to a host of "October 17" actors (the Audin Committee, Daeninckx, Panijel, Lallaoui, Kagan, and others), a gesture that situates the text on a continuum with first- and second-wave works.

Published by Thierry Mangier, a publishing house specializing in young adult (YA) and children's literature, *La Seine était rouge* is accessible to younger readers but not otherwise marketed as YA literature. Nor does the book prescribe a reading age. The style, moreover, unornamented and syntactically straightforward, is characteristic of Sebbar's prose in general and makes it difficult to categorize the text, which, in terms of content and narrative structure, makes no concessions to "easy" reading. And unlike most first- and second-wave works whose references to October 17 are either elliptical or embedded in a story-world whose main preoccupations are elsewhere, *La Seine était rouge* is the first fiction in the anarchive to devote the *entirety* of its narrative project to October 17.[56]

55   Leïla Sebbar, *La Seine était rouge* (Paris: Thierry Magnier, 2003; first published 1999); *The Seine Was Red*, trans. Mildred Mortimer (Bloomington: Indiana University Press, 2008). Note that the novel is an extension of the piece Sebbar wrote for the 25th-anniversary special issue of *Actualité de l'émigration*. (See n. 8.) Born in Algeria in 1941, Sebbar was a student at the university in Aix-en-Provence during the events of October 1961.

56   A short list of the major articles on *La Seine était rouge* includes: Laïla Amine, "Double Exposure: The Family Album and Alternate Memories in Leïla Sebbar's *The Seine was Red*," *Culture, Theory and Critique* 53, no. 2 (2012): 181–98; Anne Donadey, "Retour sur mémoire: *La Seine était rouge* de Leïla Sebbar," in *Leïla Sebbar*, ed. Michel Laronde (Paris: L'Harmattan, 2003): 187–98; Dawn Fulton, "Elsewhere in Paris: Creolised Geographies in Leïla Sebbar's *La Seine était rouge*," *Culture, Theory and Critique* 48, no. 1 (2007): 25–38; Jonathan Lewis, "Filling in

The particularities of Sebbar's novel draw our attention to two other issues of interest in the third wave, and indeed throughout the anarchive: first, the significant presence of what might be called *paraliterary* genres, or genres often dismissed as "pulp" or non-literary (detective novels—known as *romans policiers*, or *polars*, in French; young adult literature; and graphic novels); and second, the question of narrative proportion. Given the importance of Daeninckx's *Meurtres pour mémoire* (a classic *polar*) as the first work of French-language fiction to represent October 17, the paraliterary appears to be something of a foundational mode in the anarchive. The third wave expands this trend with another *polar*, Gérard Streiff's *Les caves de la Goutte d'or* (2001), which features a young female protagonist (cub reporter and doctoral student in history, to boot) determined to unravel the truth behind a series of archival documents left on her doorstep.[57]

If the *polar* is a crossover genre, moving from wave to wave, it is important to note that, with the exception of Jeanne Puchol's illustration of *Meurtres pour mémoire* (first published in 1991), the graphic novel is new to the third wave. The year 2011 not only saw the reissue of the Daeninckx/Puchol volume, it also witnessed the publication of the previously mentioned *Octobre noir* (a graphic novel by Daeninckx), as well as the arrival of the first graphic novel penned by an Algerian and published in Algeria. A sober pen-and-ink rendering, Benyoucef Abbas-Kebir's *17 octobre 1961, 17 bulles: Tragédie-sur-Seine* is a 40-page recreation of the moments leading up to the demonstration, the repression itself, and its aftermath.[58] More recently, Au nom de la mémoire edited an omnibus volume of sketches and comix titled *17*

the Blanks: Memories of 17 October 1961 in Leïla Sebbar's *La Seine était rouge*," *Modern & Contemporary France* 20, no. 3 (2012): 307–22; Mildred Mortimer, "Probing the Past: Leïla Sebbar, *La Seine était rouge/The Seine was Red*," *French Review* 83, no. 6 (May 2010): 1246–56; and Karin Schwerdtner, "Enquête, transmission et désordre dans *La Seine était rouge* de Leïla Sebbar," *Temps zéro. Revue d'étude des écritures contemporaines* 5 (2012). Online.

57 Published in 2001, *Les caves* is a prize-winning *polar* from the series "Polarchive" at Éditions Baleine—a relatively new French publishing house devoted to *polars* and *littérature populaire*.

58 Benyoucef Abbas-Kebir, *17 octobre 1961, 17 bulles: Tragédie-sur-Seine* (Algiers: Éditions Dalimen, 2011). Scholarship on October 17 BD has been notably quick to emerge. For a unique study of *17 bulles* in the context of Algerian graphic novels, see Veronica Dean, "The Algerian War of Independence in Algerian *bande dessinée*" (PhD diss., UCLA, 2020). See also Claire Gorrara, "Black October:

octobre 1961, 17 illustrators, including prefatory texts by Benjamin Stora, Mehdi Lallaoui, and Anne Tristan.[59]

The advent of October 17 as a proper subject for young adult literature is also unique to the third wave. *La Seine était rouge*, the inaugural work of this period, also has a complex relationship with its subgenre: Initially commissioned by Thierry Mangier and billed as a YA novel, it is generally considered to have escaped these boundaries and is rarely taught as youth literature. Several third-wave works, however, fall squarely in the young adult category: *Les yeux de Moktar* (2005), by the prolific and award-winning YA author Michel Le Bourhis, and Yaël Hassan's *Le professeur de musique* (2006). Moreover, the graphic novels of the third wave might be understood as participating in a similar phenomenon, insofar as both tend to target a younger audience and both may be understood as presenting "simplified" versions of history.

In different ways, what the various paraliterary genres share is an interest in mobilizing the teachability of October 17: The *polar*'s quest-based structure mimics the work of research, reasoning, and synthesizing; YA literature (particularly that found in the anarchive) sets youthful protagonists in conversation with older, more experienced characters who deliver "history lessons" in modes that seem more accessible than textbooks; and the graphic novel, through its combination of text and image, is often both attractive and accessible to younger readers for whom gains in knowledge are an added benefit to a good story. Moreover, it is worth noting that *Les yeux de Moktar* and *Le professeur de musique* were published at about the same time that the measure mandating the teaching of the positive role of the French presence overseas was passed into law.[60] Although both novels end on a note of uplift, auguring interethnic harmony and celebrating the transmission of difficult histories from generation to generation, neither

Comics, Memory and Cultural Representations of October 17, 1961," *French Politics, Culture and Society* 36, no. 1 (Spring 2018): 128–47.

59 Among the 17 illustrators who stepped forward to participate in this particular form of memorialization, we recognize the names Cabu, Charb, Tignous, and Honoré—killed during the January 15, 2015 attack on the editorial offices of *Charlie Hebdo*.

60 Article 4 of the law no. 2005-158, dated February 23, 2005, mandated teaching "the positive role" of colonization. This article was deleted in a 2006 revision of the law. The text and subsequent modifications can be read online at LégiFrance: https://www.legifrance.gouv.fr/affichTexte.do?cidTexte=JORFTEXT0000004448 98&categorieLien=id. (See Introduction, n. 30.)

one paints a rosy tableau of French colonization. While the publication date might be a mere coincidence, we might also read these novels as reacting to what many perceived as a move toward government-mandated history. Viewed in this light, the novels oppose the potential domination of a totalizing pedagogical narrative about colonial history.

These speculations notwithstanding, it is undeniable that the third wave contains proportionally more works that are didactic in nature, and that target younger people and non-specialists. Certainly, this shift should contribute to the overall visibility of October 17 and the anarchive. But what is to be made of a corpus comprised increasingly of texts that traffic in historical trauma yet are not considered works of "high culture"? Some genres have been elevated by their deployment in service of the memory of the Shoah, for example; this is certainly the case for the graphic novel, which has gained greater recognition and gravitas thanks to Art Spiegelman's *Maus* series. Similarly, significant scholarly work has been done on the detective novel to demonstrate the ways in which its form can represent the fractured structures of memory and its reconstruction.[61] And yet within the anarchive, the sheer amount of popular forms suggests a desire to vulgarize, to reach a broad constituency, and perhaps even, however unconsciously, to slip the attention of the academic and intellectual elites.

La Seine était rouge also points to narrative proportion as an aesthetic strategy that shifts over time. Indeed, many third-wave works have followed Sebbar's lead, producing historical fictions that are given over entirely to October 17. These include works such as *Nuit noire*, Médine's narrative rap, graphic novels by Daeninckx and Benyoucef, and works of theatre by Rouabhi, Granouillet, and Chouaki. This expanded narrative investment suggests a newfound recognition of October 17 as a "proper" historical and literary subject. It perhaps also responds to a burgeoning desire on the part of the public for stories about October 17. We should bear in mind, however, that using October 17 as primary narrative grist is not an innovation of the third wave; most, if not all of the documentary films, beginning with Panijel's *Octobre à Paris*, have focused solely on the massacre and its context. Nonetheless, *La Seine était rouge* inaugurates an important shift in the way works of the imagination have dealt with the representation of October 17.

Yet even as the massacre—and the story of its erasure and recovery—become the main narrative event of novels, plays, and films, the third

---

61   See Atack, 274, and Gorrara, "Reflections," 134.

wave of the anarchive continues to catalog works in which October 17 plays a minor role or appears as only a detail. In contemporary historical fiction such as Eric Michel's *Algérie! Algérie!* (2007) or Natacha Michel's *Plein présent* (2013), the story of the massacre is just one narrative thread in a series of interlaced stories about the Algerian War and its aftermath. Annie Ernaux's *Les années* (2008), an experimental autobiographical text, covers a wide swathe of French history from the 1940s to the 1980s and includes a brief retrospective evocation of October 17: "Plus tard, on apprendrait ce qui s'était passé le 17 octobre 61, on serait dans l'incapacité de dire ce qu'on avait *su* à l'époque des faits" (Later, we would learn what happened on October 17, 1961; we would find it impossible to say what we *knew* about the events at the time).[62]

To speak in terms of narrative proportion may sound vaguely esoteric, a throwback to the heyday of structuralism, when literary criticism was often accompanied by tables, graphs, and equations. Yet the question of the textual detail is not only structural and aesthetic but also political. Thus, narratological questions might be seen not as "old school," but rather as fundamental to analyses of the anarchive: Can a text be legitimately included in this corpus if its sole mention of October 17 is highly allusive and couched in a larger autobiographical project that has little stake in the Algerian War, as is the case in Ernaux's reference? How do we understand the value of reading the *beur* novel *Le Sourire de Brahim* as an October 17 text when the massacre is never again mentioned after the first chapter? What do we do with a film like *Caché*, in which the representation of October 17 is reduced to a passing mention? I return to these questions in the chapters that follow, and while my analyses vary in function of the nature of the text and its detail, they share a common against-the-grain approach: What would it mean to *discount* these texts based on their feeble quantities of October 17 material?

The Anarchive's Visual and Theatrical Turns

In addition to questions of content, matters of form both link the third wave to, and distinguish it from, the previous two waves of anarchival production. While both earlier waves produced significant visual images, the third wave's engagement with image-based works is arguably far greater. Moreover, the third wave catalogs a larger

---

62   Annie Ernaux, *Les années* (Paris: Gallimard, 2008), 81.

number of highly visible works, and by this I mean not only works that are image-based, but that have obtained a notable degree of fame and recognition. The cinema of the anarchive's third wave, for example, has been at once more prolific and better disseminated.[63] Alain Tasma's made-for-TV movie *Nuit noire* was written in collaboration with the well-known historian Patrick Rotman and produced by Canal+, which guaranteed a budget that allowed for a high-quality production and insured a built-in market. Feature-length fiction films, such as *Caché* and Algerian-born director Rachid Bouchareb's *Hors-la-loi*, benefited from the star-power of internationally recognizable casts and worldwide distribution. Bouchareb's historical drama is a family saga set during the Algerian War and culminating on October 17 with a dramatic staging of the repression, based in part on photos taken in the Concorde metro station that evening. *Hors-la-loi* premiered at the 2011 Cannes Film Festival and was nominated for Best Foreign Language film at the 2011 Academy Awards. As for *Caché*, although critics do not converge in their assessment of the film, and even if *Caché* may not transparently signify as an "October 17 film," it nonetheless does important representational work and remains one of the most visible cultural productions to evoke the massacre. Finally, the coordinated 2011 release of Panijel's 1961 *Octobre à Paris* and Yasmina Adi's prize-winning documentary *Ici on noie les algériens* is also a nodal point of the third wave of the anarchive and further evidence of the increased visibility of October 17 as a historical event and as grist for cultural production.

The third wave of anarchival works is also notable for its diversification of visual modes of representation and its inclusion of performance; unlike in the earlier waves, after 1999 we find works of theatre, music video, street performance, and web-based productions. Experimentation with new genres may be the result of changes in the epistemological status of October 17, which had gained in visibility over the course of the early aughts as a result of heightened public and political discourse on France's colonial heritage in general and, more specifically, in the wake of the Papon affair and the attention it brought to the status of the archives.

This may explain the turn, after 1999, to the very public and fundamentally visual genre of theatre. The third wave has seen the writing, and in most cases the production, of no fewer than eight plays,

---

63   This may also be related to technological matters, such as increased internet access and the advent of more portable platforms.

two of which premiered at the Avignon Theatre Festival in 2019.[64] Of this corpus, the theatrical works of French playwright Mohamed Rouabhi, *El Menfi/L'Exilé* (2000) and *Requiem Opus 61: une prière pour les morts* (2001) are the most formally and linguistically experimental. Both plays are text-driven spectacles whose temporal and spatial discontinuities destabilize the spectator. The setting of *El Menfi* ranges from the USA to the Parisian *banlieue* to Palestine, covering a temporal swathe from 1961 to the present day with October 17 both re-created and represented as a haunting memory. *Requiem Opus 61* is devoted wholly to the memory of the massacre and incorporates archival radiophonic and television footage, including a devastating interview with Papon by journalist Jean-Pierre Elkabbach in 1994.

Other theatrical works from the same period, such as *Nuit d'automne à Paris* (Gilles Granouillet, 2002), *C'était un 17 octobre* (Marie-Christine Prati-Belmokhtar, 2009), *La pomme et le couteau* (Chouaki, 2001), and *Monique H., Nanterre 1961* (Lallaoui, 2014), also relive or represent the repression of October 17, thus confronting a live audience with difficult material in a public forum. In addition to the visible nature of public performance, it is also significant that many of these works were either commissioned by activist theatre troupes, or produced with regional and arts council funding.[65] Such patronage marks a shift in anarchival practice: The lone cultural agent (such as Daeninckx or any of the first *beur* novelists), motivated solely by a personal ethical commitment, is now seconded by a collective acknowledgment of (and investment in) the importance of memorializing or disseminating information about October 17 in art.

A role for the community, and the communal, is also embodied in ephemeral performance pieces that take October 17 and the anarchive to the street. The art group Komplex Kapharnaüm, for example, whose mission involves "creating and transcending a poetry of the everyday,"

64   The second installment of Alexandra Badea's *Points de non-retour* trilogy, "Quais de Seine," premiered on the opening night of the festival (July 5, 2019); Rachid Benzine and Monia Boudiaf's *Née un 17 octobre* premiered in the "Off" festival on July 6, 2019.

65   *La pomme et le couteau* was commissioned by the association Les Oranges; Rouabhi's *El Menfi* began in theatre workshops led by the dramaturge in Ramallah before being brought to the stage in Paris by Nadine Varoutsikos (who has directed numerous regional theatres in France); Lallaoui's play was funded by Au nom de la mémoire; Granouillet's play was commissioned by Guy Rétoré for Le TEP—Théâtre de l'Est parisien.

is particularly interested in the urban fabric of French cities and the histories they contain.[66] Their "17 octobre" performance is based on archival texts (read aloud) and on a stylized recreation of the violence of the police repression. Highly interactive and adaptable, the piece has been staged in various cities in France, each time tailored to a particular urban space. The activist theatre group Pierre noire also created a commemorative, artistic *parcours* that leads to the dedication of a memorial wreath in honor of the October 17 victims.[67] More populist, perhaps, than the formal works of theatre discussed above, street performance not only testifies to the desire and ability of artists to visualize October 17 in the public sphere, but also incarnates the resurgence of a repressed memory into the "street."

In light of the proliferation of theatrical works in the third wave, it is worth pausing to consider the particular nature of the spectacle, or the performance, within the context of something calling itself an anarchive. Scholars of performance have long been conscious of the vanishing or disappearing nature of their object of study, sometimes lamenting the fact that it leaves no original, or no material trace, and thus cannot be archived.[68] Their rejection of the written text, or, at the very least, their reluctance to consider the script as a valid support, leaves me uneasy: After all, I have experienced only a few October 17 performances live; rather, I have come to them primarily through their material, published avatars. In other words, I have come to them as texts.

But I wonder whether works that purportedly resist archiving might in fact make themselves uniquely amenable to *anarchiving*? Insofar as the problem with archiving performance has to do with the notion that it "disappears" and provides no "saveable" original, we might suggest that the anarchive—which has no substrate, no domicile—provides a kind of ideal conceptual space for "saving" performance, particularly when performance is reconceived (somewhat subversively) as having the potential "to remain."[69] As Rebecca Schneider has noted, if "we approach performance not as that which disappears (as the archive expects), but as both the act of remaining and a means of re-appearance [...], we are forced

66   See the group's website at http://www.komplex-kapharnaum.net/.
67   See website *Compagnie de la Pierre noire*: http://www.pierrenoire.org/.
68   Rebecca Schneider, "Performance Remains," in *Perform, Repeat, Record: Live in Art History*, ed. Amelia Jones and Adrian Heathfield (Bristol: Intellect, 2012), 137–50. See Richard Schechner and other epigraphs in Schneider, 137.
69   Schneider, 139.

to admit that remains do not have to be isolated to the document."[70] The anarchive might then lend itself naturally to "containing" performance remains as well as scripts and other traces (audio or visual recordings of table readings, playbills, marketing materials), thus producing a thick record composed of both the material and the immaterial.

An ability or willingness to "visualize" October 17 is undoubtedly linked to a particular, post-Papon zeitgeist in a France that was busily beginning, in the early twenty-first century, to take stock of various traumatic memories and uncomfortable historical truths. Yet the turn to the "visual" in October 17 representation cannot be disassociated from distinctly material concerns and realities— namely, the possibilities presented by the advent of new technologies and platforms. Online video culture and streaming options such as YouTube have made older October 17 productions more visible and more immediately available, and have brought them into the realm of youth culture. Indeed, new technological practices have allowed younger auteurs—digital natives—to birth their creations directly on the web.

Médine, a committed *beur* rapper who has long been invested in issues of social justice and racism, releases his singles, lyrics, and video clips online, for free. The video of the rap "17 octobre" (from the album *Table d'écoute*, 2006) sets a narrative about October 17 against appropriated images of contemporary violence against immigrants in Paris. With its unacknowledged representation of two distinct historical moments—easily taken by the viewer as unitary—the video raises questions about the ethics of appropriation.[71] Unlike works of theatre, these types of visual production live online and thus are readily reproduced, shared, "liked," and commented upon; the commentary threads that respond to the works create, in turn, new anarchival material, insofar as viewers often comment on how the video has changed their knowledge of October 17 or offer personal testimonies (which can, in turn, be shared, "liked," and commented upon).

The internet has also become an opportune platform for a new genre of documentary, the webdoc. Broadly defined as "documentary remediated

---

70   Schneider, 142.
71   See Katelyn Knox, "Rapping Postmemory, Sampling the Archive: Reimagining 17 October 1961," *Modern and Contemporary France* 22, no. 3 (2014): 381–97.

for the internet age,"[72] webdocs deploy certain hallmark techniques of documentary film (such as evidentiary editing or expert commentary) while leveraging a wider array of web-based elements such as clickable access to information, interactive design, forums, and the potential for multiple authors and real-time broadcast.[73] In Raspouteam's *17.10.61*, for example, an interactive (or "clickable") map of Paris allows the viewer to begin the October 17 story at any number of different physical locations.[74] Archival artifacts such as press clippings, photographs, and video footage give the webdoc an authentic, historiographical edge, while the flexibility of the "choose your own adventure" structure endows the viewer with the power to mediate her experience. *Le Monde* also produced a webdoc titled *La nuit oubliée*, which similarly allows the viewer to select a certain experience of October 17 and uses interactive technologies to combine maps, photography, and archival materials.[75]

The visual turn of the third wave also includes paintings, art posters, political cartoons, and satirical drawings. Algerian painter Affif Cherfaoui's tableau "Les enfants d'octobre" features an abstract bridge that seems to collapse into a bright blue river below, with stylized bodies caught in suspended animation. The "October" in question in the painting is, in fact, a reference to the police repression of a student protest that took place in Algiers in 1988; however, the use of the painting as cover art for Prati-Belmokhtar's play *C'était un 17 octobre* allows it to signify beyond its original context. (See Fig. 3.) Similarly, Mustapha Boutadjine's "Paris, 17 octobre 1961," whose bold imagery shows a hand reaching up out of a body of water toward a figure on the embankment represented only by a pair of army boots and the tip of a billy club, was used as the playbill for Hamma Mélani's October 17 play *Lamento pour Paris*, and currently decorates memorials in La

72   Kate Nash, "Modes of Interactivity, Analyzing the Webdoc," *Media, Culture and Society* 34, no. 2 (2012): 195–210.

73   Melahat Hosseini and Ron Wakkary, "Influences of Concepts and Structure of Documentary Cinema on Documentary Practices in the Internet," *Museums and the Web 2004*, http://www.museumsandtheweb.com/mw2004/papers/hosseini/hosseini.html.

74   *17.10.61*, http://www.raspouteam.org/1961/.

75   *La nuit oubliée*, http://www.lemonde.fr/societe/visuel_interactif/2011/10/17/la-nuit-oubliee_1587567_3224.html. *Le Monde* has been particularly invested in the production of webdocs; see Margaret Flinn, "Documentary and Realism," in *Directory of World Cinema: France*, ed. Tim Palmer and Charlie Michael (Chicago: University of Chicago Press, 2013), 36.

Fig 3. Cover of play by Marie-Christine Prati-Belmokhtar.
Inset: painting by Affif Cherfaoui, "Enfants d'octobre" (Children of October).

Fig. 4. "Paris, le 17 octobre 1961." Graphics © Mustapha Boutadjine.

Courneuve and Bagneux.[76] (See Fig. 4.) (It perhaps bears mentioning that the poster is also featured on the cover of this book.) Despite the fact that poster culture has been slow to incorporate October 17, numerous commemorative posters also depict the river, the police, and Algerians falling into the Seine.[77] (See Chapter 4.) Although many of these works may be more "traditional" in their conception, materials, and execution (particularly as compared to webdocs and interactive

76   Boutadjine is a painter, graphic artist, and photographer working in Paris. See http://artbribus.com/. Hamma Méliani, *Lamento pour Paris: chroniques parisiennes sur le massacre des Algériens les 17 et 18 octobre 1961* (Paris: La Marsa, 2011).

77   For a history of the poster in the context of the Algerian War and the absence of October 17, see Sofia Papastmakou, "Le 17 octobre 1961: le silence des affiches," *Matérieux pour l'histoire de notre temps* 106, no. 2 (2012): 60–62.

internet sites), the fact remains that many of them can be located and viewed only on the internet.[78]

Reading the Anarchive *avant la lettre*

Just as scholars struggle to decide whether the study of the events of October 17 has been fully institutionalized—and we might ask what "institutionalization" would look like and what forms it would take—it remains difficult to state with certainty whether the cultural productions of October 17 constitute known and well-studied objects of inquiry. Certainly, one of the novelties of *Absent the Archive* is its attempt to define and analyze a corpus, working across time periods and genres. But while there are no other existing studies of the "October 17 corpus" (irrespective of what it might be called), scholarly attention to the representation of the massacre in cultural texts emerged alongside the second wave of anarchival production, and scholarship focusing on either individual works or smaller subsets of the corpus has increased dramatically in the era of the third wave. *Absent the Archive*, then, necessarily builds on existing scholarly interventions, many of which have focused on *Caché*, *Meurtres pour mémoire*, and *La Seine était rouge*.

The emergence of memory studies has been especially propitious for the study of October 17 cultural productions. Michael Rothberg's *Multidirectional Memory: Remembering the Holocaust in the Age of Decolonization* charts a path through a wide variety of (primarily) French-language texts and films, exploring the interactions of memories of the Holocaust and colonialism and the representation of intergenerational memory.[79] The titular model of memory as "multidirectional" offers a heuristic tool for reading the coexistence of different traumatic memories in a way that allows their interaction to emerge as "productive" rather than "privative." The book's third section, which is devoted to representations of October 17, relies on analyses of *Meurtres pour*

78 For a study of the memorialization of October 17 on the internet, see Philippe Brand, "Des nœuds dans le Web: la commemoration du 17 octobre 1961 sur Internet," *Entrelacs* (December 2016), http://journals.openedition.org/entrelacs/1874.

79 Michael Rothberg, *Multidirectional Memory: Remembering the Holocaust in the Age of Decolonization* (Stanford, CA: Stanford University Press, 2009).

mémoire, La Seine était rouge, and *Caché,* three cultural productions in which memories of October 17 are negotiated by the children of the generation who experienced the trauma directly, and set in dialogue with memories of the Holocaust (or tropes of Holocaust representation). In a similar vein, Max Silverman's *Palimpsestic Memory: The Holocaust and Colonialism in French and Francophone Fiction and Film* also develops a memory model that offers a way out of the impasse of competitive victimhood. To illustrate his notion of palimpsestic memory, Silverman calls on specific examples from *Meurtres* (an Algerian worker in 1983 scraping away layers of posters to uncover a Nazi order pasted to a wall of the Parisian subway in the early 1940s) and from *La Seine était rouge* (graffiti inscriptions on World War II memorials in Paris that signal their importance in the context of the Algerian War of Independence). The literal layering present in both examples allows Silverman to illustrate a vision of memory work that escapes the compartmentalization and "blinkered" views that have characterized memory studies in recent decades.[80] The palimpsest, Silverman argues, "captures most completely the superimposition and productive interaction of different inscriptions and the spatialization of time central to the work of memory."[81] At stake in both Rothberg's and Silverman's models, be they articulated in terms of vectors (multidirectionality) or layers (palimpsests), is the recognition of culture's capacity to encode events in a particular way. And in both cases, placing memories of October 17 alongside memories of the Holocaust serves to draw attention to, and perhaps to validate, the lesser-known event.

Other scholars working at the seam of Francophone and memory studies have produced significant essays that constitute what we might call a proto-anarchival critical gesture. By this I mean that while these studies do not explicitly purport to delimit an October 17 corpus, their consideration of multiple October 17 cultural productions functions as a kind of implicit hunch about the potential synergies of comingling multiple texts. Michel Laronde's substantial essay on "foreclosed" colonial history and the functions of literary and filmic anamnesis, for example, has contributed greatly to the visibility of October 17 cultural productions.[82] In a similar vein, Alison Rice's work on the role of fiction in

---

80 Max Silverman, *Palimpsestic Memory: The Holocaust and Colonialism in French and Francophone Fiction and Film* (New York: Berghahn Books, 2013), 4.
81 Silverman, *Palimpsestic Memory,* 4.
82 Michel Laronde, "Effets d'Histoire. Représenter l'Histoire coloniale forclose,"

remembering October 17 corrals novels and films to think through the question of how the events have been "rehearsed" in culture. In addition to works like *Caché*, Rice turns to lesser-known "October 17" texts such as Algerian novelist Abedelkader Djemaï's *Gare du nord* and Faïza Guène's *Kiffe kiffe demain*—a book celebrated as a new *beur* fiction privileging a female voice, but whose October 17 content is often overlooked.[83] Chadia Chambers-Samadi's *Répression des manifestants Algériens: La nuit meurtrière du 17 octobre* is unique in its pluridisciplinary approach that brings together novels, films, and survivor testimony to explore how the memory of October 17 has been kept alive.[84] Finally, Charles Forsdick's masterful comparative study, "'Ceci n'est pas un conte, mais une histoire de chair et de sang': Representing the Colonial Massacre in Francophone Literature and Culture," not only makes a proto-anarchival gesture by virtue of bringing together fictions by Sebbar, Lallaoui, Kettane, and Daeninckx, it also constitutes one of the only studies to engage in a comparative, transcolonial analysis of violence, placing representations of the events in Paris alongside the massacre at the Camp de Thiaroye in Senegal in 1944.[85]

The scholarship that has emerged in tandem with the third wave of the anarchive has also been notably interested in visual materials—namely film and photography. Haneke's *Caché* has undoubtedly generated the most critical and scholarly attention of any object in the anarchive, a phenomenon certainly linked to Haneke's status as an *auteur* filmmaker with an international reputation. (To offer an imperfect point of comparison, a 2019 Google Scholar search of *Caché* yields more than 2000 articles, whereas a search of Bouchareb's *Hors-la-loi*—another October 17 fiction film—yields only 484 results.) Unsurprisingly given Haneke's stature and filmography (not to mention the nature of his film's representation of October 17), the scholarship on *Caché* focuses less on the references to 1961 and more on filmic aspects of the work (the gaze, the haptic, phenomenology, space, and surveillance), as well as the film's place within Haneke's corpus. The fact that *Screen*—the leading academic journal of film and TV studies—devoted a special dossier to *Caché* in

---

International Journal of Francophone Studies 10, no. 1–2 (March 2007): 139–55.

83 Alison Rice, "Rehearsing October 17, 1961: The Role of Fiction in Remembering the Battle of Paris," *L'Esprit Créateur* 54, no. 4 (2014): 90–102.

84 Chadia Chambers-Samadi, *Répression des manifestants Algériens: La nuit meurtrière du 17 octobre* (Paris: L'Harmattan, 2015).

85 Forsdick, "'Ceci n'est pas un conte.'" (See Introduction, n. 26.)

2007 is certainly a barometer of the film's cult-status within the world of cinema studies. And within the field of postcolonial francophone studies, numerous monographs on the visual representation of the Algerian War include chapters on *Caché* and its treatment of October 17.[86]

Scholarship on the third wave's cinema has, of course, not been limited to *Caché*. The anarchive's other fiction and documentary films have inspired a small corpus of critical essays, notably by Maria Flood, Guy Austin, Michel Laronde, Anne Donadey, Alison Rice, and Mani Sharpe. While many of these deal with contemporaneous works of cinema (such as *Hors-la-loi*), there has also been, particularly since its issue on DVD in 2010, a rediscovery of Panijel's documentary *Octobre à Paris*, for spectators and film scholars alike. (See, for example, Flood's analysis, which excavates Bouchareb's critique of the documentary in his little-known *Naissance du cinéma algérien* (1971), and Joy C. Shaefer's interesting comparison of *Octobre à Paris* and *Caché*.[87])

Photography has also emerged as a serious site of scholarly inquiry, in the form of art historian Hannah Feldman's incisive reading of the photographs taken on October 17 by Élie Kagan and other journalists in *From a Nation Torn: Decolonizing Art and Representation in France, 1945–1962*. A novel and brilliant study of the intersection of spatial and visual culture during the decades Feldman aptly renames the "during-war period" as opposed to "post-war" (in recognition of the ongoing conflicts in Africa and Asia), *From a Nation* thinks through the ways "the experience of war motivates the production and justification of culture."[88] Inspired by Rancière, Didi-Huberman, and the Situationists, the chapter titled "The Eye of History: Photojournalism, Protest, and the Manifestation of October 17, 1961," offers a multilayered, historicized, and sited reading of the photos taken during the Algerian protest. A similarly complex tracing of the history of a photograph and its afterlives can be found in the historical detective work carried out by Vincent Lemire and Yann Potin in their long article "'Ici on noie les Algériens':

---

86   See Maria Flood, *France, Algeria, and the Moving Image: Screening Histories of Violence (1962–2010)* (Oxford: Legenda, 2017); Feldman, *From A Nation Torn*; Rothberg, *Multidirectional Memory*; and Silverman, *Palimpsestic Memory*.

87   See Flood, "(Un)Familiar Fictions," and Joy C. Schaefer, "The Spatial-Affective Economy of (Post)Colonial Paris: Reading Haneke's *Caché* (2005) through *Octobre à Paris* (1962)," *Studies in European Cinema* 14, no. 1 (2017): 48–65.

88   Feldman, 1.

Fabriques documentaires, avatars politiques et mémoires partagées d'une icône militante (1961–2001)." A study of a single photograph of a work of graffiti, Lemire and Potin's essay provides critical insight into the improvised, rogue, and ultimately ephemeral forms of protest that emerged in the immediate aftermath of the protest and its repression. Their analyses, together with Feldman's, forcefully drive home the initial visibility of October 17, while also accounting for the forces that conspired to relegate it to the blind spot of national history.

Beyond Periodization

In terms of themes, aesthetics, genres, representation, ethics, and even facts, the internal categories of the anarchive—that is, the three "waves"—quickly become porous to the point of disintegration. Nonetheless, organizing October 17 cultural production in three relatively discrete temporal waves offers certain critical conveniences, particularly given that each category can be read against or alongside established national narratives related to memories of troubling history (be it Vichy or France's colonial past). Thus, the political, historical, and cultural conditions in which works were produced serves not only as context but also as paratext. Works from the first period are clearly the product of the heat of the moment, created at a time when the average citizen may or may not have been aware of the extent of the repression, and when a significant amount of knowledge about the event (in the form of eyewitnesses, first-hand accounts, and press reports) was smothered by a news blackout. During the longer second wave, cultural production arrives on the scene in a fashion that mimics the way memories bobbed to the surface of public consciousness: in small amounts and often in ways not readily recognized.

The third wave is contemporaneous with the 50th anniversary of October 17, the Sarkozy government's largely unnoticed decision to declassify the police archives (in 2011), and a general flurry of memorialist activity and lobbying. At the same time, the third wave also shares time and space with the memorial activities of 2012, which commemorated the 50th anniversary of the Évian Accords and the end of the Algerian War, and marked the first official recognition of the French state's responsibility for Algerian deaths on October 17.[89] Works from the third period

---

89   While Hollande did not use the term "massacre," he did state that the Republic "lucidly recognizes" the fact that Algerians were killed during a "bloody

must thus be considered alongside the era's "hypermnésie"—a moment when archival politics and questions of recognition and reparation come to the fore, when major anniversaries provoke more public discourse, and when discussions of state violence are beginning to be naturalized in political and historical debates.

What should be obvious by now about the distinctions made here between various "waves" is that they are temporal rather than aesthetic or programmatic. October 17 cultural production does not lend itself to aesthetic periodization—at no given point does the anarchive produce works that are stylistically or generically coherent with one another. Like many art movements, the October 17 corpus is made up of works that neither cohere along considerations of style nor emerge as a unified program. Rather, it is the retrospective recognition of their points of convergence that permits them to be labeled as a group. Moreover, when it comes to questions of knowledge, the anarchive does not chart a steady rise in quantities of information over time; the first wave already suggests a high degree of awareness about what happened on October 17 and what happened to the story of October 17. While some of the more contemporary works provide significant detail (often relying on previous cultural texts, or on archival material such as press clippings and non-classified institutional archives), there is no substantially new knowledge on display in the later works.

One final comment on verisimilitude and historicity: Not all works included in the anarchive are faithful to the facts. Levels of historical authenticity and accuracy, for that matter, are not perquisites for inclusion. In the feature film *Hors-la-loi* (2010), for example, the line notoriously uttered by Papon—"Pour un coup reçu nous en donnerons dix!" (For every blow received we will dole out ten)—is placed in the mouth of an FLN organizer as he is rallying Algerians for an operation that will lead them into an armed altercation with the Parisian police. Yaël Hassan's *Professeur de musique* wildly conflates pre-October 17 confrontations between Algerians and police, the actual repression on October 17, and the Charonne massacre. And while *Vivre me tue* contains the story of a

repression." Criticized on the right and the left, Hollande nonetheless stopped short of naming the state as responsible, although he did sign the *Appel pour la reconnaissance du 17 octobre* circulated by Médiapart. See "Hollande reconnaît la répression du 17 octobre 1961, critiques à droite," *Le Monde*, Octobre 17, 2012, http://www.lemonde.fr/societe/article/2012/10/17/francois-hollande-reconnait-la-sanglante-repression-du-17-octobre-1961_1776918_3224.html.

Moroccan man murdered on October 17—a "factual error" picked up
by Azouz Begag to mount a full-scale attack on the novel's author—it
turns out that it was not implausible for a Moroccan to have been taken
for Algerian and arrested or beaten that night. (See Chapter 5.)

These errors are exemplary insofar as they seem to add meaning to
the representation of October 17 even as they stray from the historical
record. Bouchareb's misappropriation of Papon's words cannot be an
accident; the quote is too famous, too symbolically laden. Begag's
misreading of a plot element as a historical error may speak to the degree
to which the history of October 17 has been flattened. An anti-Algerian
attack during a war against Algeria is one thing; racial profiling is
another; and the fact that Begag—himself a *beur* and a person of public
importance in France—would not know this, is revelatory. Finally,
Hassan's conflation of three episodes may speak to the generalized and
persistent difficulty in untangling this particular historical knot.

And so I tend to agree with the answer Susan Suleiman offers in
response to the question she poses in her essay, "Do Facts Matter in
Holocaust Memoirs?"[90] As with autobiographical writing on the Shoah,
when it comes to October 17 literature and film, facts certainly matter.
But as Suleiman suggests, they may matter *differently*. When it comes to
the representation of episodes of historical trauma, I would argue that
mistakes such as these—regardless of whether they indicate ignorance
or consciously perverted history—constitute sites of meaning whose
value resides in their speculative potential. Daeninckx's theory that the
detective novel is a *hypothesis* about reality, not a slavish copy of it, is
particularly apposite here. Requiring cultural productions to function
as transparent representations of reality is to misconstrue their purpose
and their function. As far as the October 17 anarchive is concerned,
errors in fact, even errors that are not often noticed or contested, can be
turned into productive moments for interpretation. We might even say
that they contain within them a certain "poetic appropriateness."[91]

90   Susan Rubin Suleiman, "Do Facts Matter in Holocaust Memoirs? Wilkomirski/
Wiesel," in *Obliged by Memory: Literature, Religion, Ethics*, ed. Steven T. Katz
and Alan Rosen (Syracuse, NY: Syracuse University Press, 2006), 21–42.
91   Suleiman, "Do Facts Matter...?" 42.

CHAPTER TWO

Archive Stories

From Politics to Romances

In a certain way, the novel
becomes a hypothesis about reality.[1]

—Didier Daeninckx

In October 17 fiction, archives are nothing but trouble. In Daeninckx's *Meurtres pour mémoire* (1983), a doctoral student is shot dead upon exiting the municipal archives in Toulouse; after consulting those very same archives, the detective charged with investigating the murder is targeted for assassination by an archivist-turned-hit man. In Lallaoui's *Une nuit d'octobre* (2001), an anonymous employee of the Parisian police archives surreptitiously gives a truth seeker a slew of damning documents; as he is leaving the reading room he is felled by a violent blow to the head, and regains consciousness only to discover that the proof has been stolen. In Gérard Streiff's *Les caves de la Goutte d'or* (2001), cub reporter Chloé is initially delighted when "scoops"—large envelopes stuffed with archival documents about October 17—begin arriving in her mailbox, but her enthusiasm is tempered when she realizes that the paper trail has led a notorious torturer-turned-assassin directly to her doorstep. And, in Eric Michel's *Algérie! Algérie!* (2007), the archives at the police headquarters in Paris are the scene of a bloody confrontation on October 17, 1961, between two Algerian brothers, one a *Harki* in cahoots with the French police, the other an FLN operative fighting for a free Algeria.

---

1 Daeninckx, "Je la connais, mon histoire des massacres, jeune homme," interview, Françoise Kerleroux, Éditions Verdier, June 16, 2014, http://editions-verdier.fr/2014/06/16/entretien-avec-francoise-kerleroux/.

Hit men, "smoking guns," and evidence gone missing are the stock in trade of detective novels, but while the archival violence in the aforementioned novels heightens dramatic tension, it also alludes to a deeper malaise. In the context of October 17 fictions, the representation of physical aggression in proximity to archives and archival material—a distinctive trope in the second and third waves of the anarchive—takes on a metaphorical function. Necessarily bound up with questions of interpretation and access to state-controlled archives, these moments register, subtly and subtextually, the epistemological violence of the repression of knowledge. They also signal the existence and the troubled visibility of official archives during a time when those archives remained classified.

The forbidden archives, those dangerous sites, appeared in October 17 literature long before they were made available to the public. Because the anarchive emerged in the void left by the absence of the official police archives, the two may seem to belong to separate parallel universes, realms that would have little to say to one another. Yet these examples of "archives in the anarchive" suggest that the latter has always been aware of the former as a kind of absent presence, as a haunting voice caught between its potential to signify and the conditions that prohibit its signification. Historians and "archive rats" of all disciplines should rest assured: The existence of the anarchive does not obviate the usefulness of the police archive, particularly given that the official documents in question—long imagined as the missing lynchpin of a reliable narrative about the extent of the massacre and state culpability—are now available for public consultation.

The recent declassification of the police archive means that they now exist in the same time and space as the anarchive; for the first time in history, then, it becomes possible to think through the two corpuses together, to explore their interface, and to read for the ways they inform one another. Politically and practically, the current climate is propitious for a consideration of the October 17 police archives: In 2011, President Sarkozy declassified the police archives pertaining to October 17; in 2012, President Hollande officially acknowledged the scale and the stakes of October 17, calling it "une sanglante repression" (a bloody repression) and a tragedy, and recognizing the Algerians as victims.[2] Some would point to these acts of recognition and memorialization—coupled with the various cultural manifestations that cropped up with the 50th anniversary of October 17 and of the end of the Algerian

2 See Chapter 1, n. 89.

War—as emblematic of a new "obsessive" phase of memory. Others view this attention as salutary: Activists and scholars renew their calls to shed light on the events, sensing an opportunity to "work through" October 17 once and for all. Moreover, the police archives themselves have recently benefited from a material upgrade: Formerly available for consultation in a cramped, airless reading room on the fourth floor of the police station in the 5th *arrondissement*, in 2014 the archives and the police museum were relocated to new, roomier quarters in the Pré-Saint-Gervais (just outside of Paris) and grouped under the common title "Department of Memory and Cultural Affairs."

Beyond these practical concerns specific to the October 17 police archives, the critical shifts of the last two decades have given us new concepts and vocabularies with which to imagine and theorize the archive. In the wake of the "archival turn"—that is, with the understanding that the archive is no longer strictly a source but potentially a subject unto itself—archives must be understood as complex sites where questions of knowledge, power, and politics intersect.[3] If the turn "registers a rethinking of the materiality and imaginary of collections and what kinds of truth-claims lie in documentation,"[4] it also reveals new actors engaged in this act of "rethinking." In the early 1990s, literary scholar Alice Kaplan noted (and lamented) that literary scholarship eschewed the peritextual stories of how scholars experienced the archive: "conventional academic discourse requires that when you write up the results of your archival work, you tell a story about what you found, not about how you found it." Yet, for Kaplan, the genesis stories about getting to the archives, about what one finds or fails to find, and about the way its contents reorient ideas and research questions, are rife with potential, "thick with literature and amenable to being analyzed like a text."[5] Literary scholars and historians alike—we might think of

3   See Ann Laura Stoler, "Colonial Archives and the Arts of Governance," *Archival Science* 2 (2002): 93; Stoler, *Along the Archival Grain: Epistemic Anxieties and Colonial Common Sense* (Princeton, NJ: Princeton University Press, 2010), 44. For broader reflections on the intersection of archives and power, see Michel Foucault, *The Archaeology of Knowledge*, trans. A.M. Sheridan Smith (New York: Pantheon Books, 1972); Derrida, *Archive Fever*; and the edited collection *Refiguring the Archive*, ed. Carolyn Hamilton, et al. (Dordrecht: Kluwer Academic Publishers, 2002).

4   Stoler, "Colonial archives," 94.

5   Alice Kaplan, "Working in the Archives," *Yale French Studies* 77 (1990): 106–7.

Helen Freshwater, Arlette Farge, or Antoinette Burton—have called for researchers to attend to the tales that are spun over the course of archival consultation, and to account for their subjective experiences of the material.[6]

Heeding this call, I approach the October 17 archives in ways that account for (but do not necessarily privilege) their function as an index of the real. In addition to their actual contents, and beyond the premise that the official dossiers have the potential to reveal "hard facts," the story of their sequestration and eventual liberation is an important narrative thread in the story of October 17. For Burton, the epiphenomenal aspects of archives—their "provenance, histories, and effects on their users"—are as crucial to our investigations as the contents of the archives themselves.[7] Freshwater, similarly, has argued that "the researcher must foreground his or her own role in the process of the production of the past."[8] Taking its cue from Kaplan and appropriating a turn of phrase from Burton, this chapter recounts a series of "archive stories."

Given the belatedness of the October 17 archives and the intensity of expectation surrounding their contents, accounting for the peripheral stories that condition the experience of reading freshly declassified materials is particularly illuminating. In the first section, I chart the path of the archives' slow road to declassification and the various obstacles, real and imagined, that have led to the persistent belief that machinations of the French state make it impossible to ever fully know their content. The second section operates in two modes: ethnographically, detailing my own experience of consultation in the freshly declassified police archives; and hermeneutically, that is, in the manner of the literary critic, offering typological assessments and interpretations (think "distant" and "close" readings) of the archival material itself.

The final sections of this chapter connect the dusty materials of the archive to the abstract space of the anarchive, and in so doing they exceed the limits of Burton's definition of archive stories. "The representation of

---

6   Helen Freshwater, "The Allure of the Archive," *Poetics Today* 24, no. 4 (2003): 729–58; Arlette Farge, *The Allure of the Archives*, trans. Thomas Scott-Railton (New Haven, CT: Yale University Press, 2015); Antoinette Burton, *Archive Stories: Facts, Fictions, and the Writing of History* (Durham, NC: Duke University Press, 2006).

7   Burton, 6.

8   Freshwater, 738.

archives in literary works" is *not* what Burton intended when she solicited scholars' "archive stories" for inclusion in the eponymous collection.[9] Yet my analyses show that, in the case of October 17, the anarchive stages its own archive stories—narratives about the provenance of the archive, its history, and its effect on its user—by foregrounding the subjective experience of characters (researchers, detective, scholars, reporters) who work in, against, or in the absence of archives. The anarchive, then, produces "archive stories": Caught up in a fictionalized world, the experiences in and of the archives function to both index the real and metaphorize the archive, and these narratives turn out to be as critical as the stories told by the contents of the archives themselves.

Persistent Archive Fever: 20 Years of Ambiguous Discourse

On October 17, 2011, France 2 devoted a portion of its nightly news coverage to a special reportage titled "Guerre d'Algérie: les archives parlent" (The Algerian War: The Archives Speak). Dramatically braving signs forbidding access, news cameras traversed steel doors to find themselves in the inviolable halls of the police archives. The October 17 files were finally open. The prefecture's Director of Cultural Services, Jean-Marc Gentil, opined: "Ces archives, ce sont des documents historiques, elles répondent à ce que l'on pourrait appeler un devoir d'histoire. Et donc si on veut les utiliser de manière sereine [...] je crois qu'il faut leur porter un regard qui est suffisamment objectif, et ça, je crois que c'est une chose que seul le temps permet" (These archives are historical documents, they respond to what we might call a historical duty. And so, if we want to use them in a serene way [...] I think we have to view them as objectively as possible, and I think only time allows for such objectivity).[10] The declassification of the police archives in October 2011 may augur a new era of historiographical activity, the 50-year ban on consultation having putatively ensured, in accordance with French Republican principles of knowledge dissemination, that time will have produced the critical objectivity essential for a "serene use" of the documents. French laws governing archival access date to

---

9   Burton notes that the volume is comprised of "self-conscious ethnographies of one of the chief investigative foundations of History as a discipline" (6).
10   Newscast,   http://www.ina.fr/video/4565665001/20-heures-emission-du-17-octobre-2011-video.html.

the founding of the Republic, and are notoriously complex.[11] Although my goal here is neither to rehearse this legislation nor to question its wisdom, I do wonder whether it is truly possible to create conditions for objectivity, and whether the very notion of objectivity is as solid as we might like to believe. In the context of Holocaust documentation and memoir, for example, questions of delay and immediacy have been hotly debated.[12] Nonetheless, as historians and even literary scholars begin to take advantage of the passage of time, starved for knowledge about October 17 after five decades of archival absence and eager to excavate the "true" story and perhaps even to find the "smoking gun,"[13] it seems worth speculating on the impact of this half-century of deferral and the confused political discourse that has surrounded this archive. Has being *en mal d'archive* (in need of archives) for so long led to a contagious and debilitating *mal d'archive* (archive sickness)?[14] What narratives can be established about the vagaries of archival access and how do such narratives layer into the larger saga of October 17?

If the power of the state, as Achille Mbembe has argued, resides in its ability to "abolish the archive and anesthetize the past"—that is, in the very same epistemological violence symbolized metonymically in the novels cited above—that power is nonetheless far from absolute. To the contrary, according to Mbembe, in abolishing the archive (destroying it or simply removing it from sight), the state inadvertently creates the conditions for it to become a fetish object: "destroying or prohibiting

---

11   See Jennifer Milligan, "'What is an Archive?' in the History of Modern France," in *Archive Stories*, 159–83. In France, not all public archives can be consulted at will. A set of six categories (established by the January 1979 law) of documents are subject to a gag order lasting from 60 to 150 years depending on the type of information they contain (state secrets, medical histories, public safety, etc.). The text of the 1979 law can be consulted here: https://www.legifrance.gouv.fr/affichTexte.do?cidTexte=LEGITEXT000006068663.

12   See, for example: Marilyn B. Meyers, "Historic and Psychic Timeline: Opening and Closing the Space for Witnessing," in *The Power of Witnessing: Reflections, Reverberations and Traces of the Holocaust*, ed. Nancy R. Goodman and Marilyn B. Meyers (New York: Routledge, 2012), 27–45; and Schlomo Breznitz, "The Advantages of Delay: A Psychological Perspective on Memories of Trauma," in Katz and Rosen (eds), 43–51.

13   House and MacMaster, 12. See also Jean-Marc Berlière, "Archives de police/historiens policés?" *Revue d'histoire moderne et contemporaine* 48, no. 4b (2001): 58–59.

14   Derrida, *Archive Fever*, 12, 90–91.

the archive has only provided it with additional content. In this case that content is all the more unreal because it has been removed from sight and interred once and for all in the sphere of that which shall remain unknown, therefore allowing space for all manner of imaginary thoughts."[15] Mbembe underscores, in particular, the specificity of the archive of a massacre, which is "removed from the sphere of 'remains' and 'debris' and transformed into a talisman."[16]

The talismanic value of the October 17 archives began to assert itself in the early 1990s, a moment that coincided with the 30th anniversary of the massacre. Historical, political, and activist discourses became particularly interested in foregrounding not only what was known about October 17, but also in what remained invisible—namely, the archival material held by the Parisian police. Einaudi's *La Bataille de Paris*, an account of October 17 and the subsequent cover-up, railed against the state for its draconian (and seemingly ad hoc) archive policies while at the same time incarnating the type of historical work that could be produced through other methods.[17] But *Bataille de Paris* is also a record of Einaudi's multiple failed attempts to consult archives related to October 17: Requests made to the coroner's office, the prefecture of police, the Interior Minister, and the French National Archives were systematically denied, often with the reminder that the documents in question were scheduled to remain classified for 60 years after the initial events (in other words, until 2021).[18]

The general public would only become aware of this institutional stonewalling (and of Einaudi's book) during the final courtroom acts of the Papon affair, when the former chief of police sued Einaudi for libel. The highly publicized trial, held in Paris in 1999, featured the testimony of Brigitte Lainé and Philippe Grand, two conservationists from the Paris archives, who recounted, at some professional risk to themselves, the "neo-revisionism" they saw at work in the treatment of sensitive

---

15   Achille Mbembe, "The Power of the Archive and its Limits," in *Refiguring the Archive*, 23.

16   Mbembe, 24.

17   Jean-Luc Einaudi, *La Bataille de Paris*, 342–44. House and MacMaster identify eight main sources for "evidence" related to October 17, all of which Einaudi and others have attempted to cross-reference. See House and MacMaster, 162–63.

18   The 60-year ban on consultation refers to the law of January 3, 1979, legislating the status of public archives. (See n. 11.)

dossiers.[19] Lainé's testimony was decisive in Einaudi's exoneration; moreover, it served to make public the often-invisible practices of favoritism and elitism at work in decisions about who could access certain archives.[20] At the same time, however, Lainé's decision to testify was roundly condemned by the French Association of Archivists in a press release that recalled the particular "deontology" of the profession and advised "absolute neutrality."[21] As of 2000, Lainé and Grand were "placardés": They could not legally be fired for having complied with a court summons to testify, yet their superiors viewed them as turncoats, and as a result they were frozen out of their functions. Allowed to come to work but stripped of all responsibility, they were essentially, in Lainé's words, paid to do nothing.[22]

The Papon trial had already spurred the Jospin government to look into the contents and handling of the October 17 police archives.[23] Yet

19   See "On choisit un autre métier si on ne veut pas d'ennuis," interview with archivists Lainé and Grand, *Vacarme* 13 (Fall 2000), http://www.vacarme.org/article45.html. Lainé: "On l'a (Einaudi) mené en bateau jusqu'en janvier 99, onze mois plus tard, à la veille de l'audience, il n'avait toujours pas de réponse à sa dérogation, ce qui est aberrant. J'étais folle furieuse, je l'ai prévenu, et il m'a demandé si j'accepterais de témoigner" (They strung Einaudi along until January of 1999; 11 months later, right before the hearing, he still had not received an answer regarding his request for archival access, which is highly unusual. I was absolutely furious, I let him know, and he asked me if I'd agree to testify).
20   Interview, Lainé and Grand. See also Claude Liauzu, "Notes sur les archives de la guerre d'Algérie," *Revue d'histoire moderne et contemporaine* 5, no. 48–4bis (2001): 56, and Einaudi, *Bataille*, 367–68.
21   While the archivists in question and certain other experts maintain that bearing witness did not represent a legal infraction or a contract violation, the mayor of Paris at the time (Jean Tibéri) publicly demanded legal action against them, and both archivists reported being "frozen out" of their jobs (or "mis au placard"—see Liauzu, 2001, 56) as a direct result of their participation in the trial. See also the appeal published on Lainé's behalf: "Appel: Soutenons Brigitte Lainé," *Libération*, March 6, 1999, http://www.liberation.fr/tribune/0101276145-appel-soutenons-brigitte-laine. While the Association of French Archivists officially denounced Lainé and Grand, it also called for a large-scale release of the documents in question, in the name of greater transparence. The association's communiqué can be viewed on H-Net:http://h-net.msu.edu/cgi-bin/logbrowse.pl?trx=vx&list=h-francais&month=9903&week=b&msg=ZvTD7jm8gPVVyvtT6pbsrA&user=&pw.
22   Interview, Lainé and Grand.
23   Already at the Bordeaux trial in the fall of 1997, Papon had admitted that the initial death toll issued by the prefecture had been low—although he maintained

the various measures taken and the official statements made seem to have produced only more confusion about the state of the archives. In October 1997, Minister of the Interior Jean-Pierre Chevènement created the Mandelkern Commission, a group of senators tasked with reading and evaluating the contents of the October 17 police archives; that same fall, Catherine Trautmann, Minister of Culture, announced that she would make those same archives available to the general public.[24] Notwithstanding their earnest rhetoric, the various political actors appear to have been motivated less by the pursuit of justice than by a spirit of competition. In an official communiqué from Trautmann's office, the language of rivalry is barely concealed: "A quelques jours du procès Papon, le Premier ministre a demandé à ses ministres d'ouvrir plus largement les archives de la période 1939–1945. Quinze jours plus tard, c'est Catherine Trautmann qui décidait de lever le voile sur les archives du 17 octobre 1961" (A few days before the start of the Papon trial, the Prime Minister asked his ministers to make more archives from the 1939–1945 period available. Fifteen days later, it is Catherine Trautmann who has decided to lift the veil on the October 17 archives). This statement is followed by a broader declaration of political intention: Trautmann would also take steps to make the 1979 laws restricting archival access more flexible.[25]

By the time the ministers began jockeying for position as champion of archival access (and, by extension, of transparency and democracy), the press was a step ahead of them all: On October 22, 1997 (after Trautmann's public announcement but just before the creation of the Mandelkern Commission), *Libération* published an article whose title—"The Archives Speak"—was accompanied by an incriminatory tagline: "*Libération* has acquired pages from the records of the public prosecutor. The documents published here prove the reality of the violence unleashed on the pro-FLN demonstrators at the time when

---

that the higher number of fatalities was due to internecine vendettas between the FLN and the MNA (le Mouvement national algérien).

24 The four-member Mandelkern Commission, named for its president, Dieudonné Mandelkern (section president of the Board of State), included two members of the administration's Audit Office and one archivist. Trautmann was not a member. The report was released to the press in May 1998.

25 The office of the Minister of Culture issued a long statement regarding these measures in its monthly newsletter, which can be consulted here: http://www.culturecommunication.gouv.fr/var/culture/storage/mag-culture/17.pdf.

Maurice Papon was Chief of Police."[26] In just a single day's work (which was all his special pass to the archives allowed him), *Libération*'s investigator David Assouline was able to reliably establish 70 deaths at the hands of police on October 17—far more than the four allowed by Papon in 1961, and the six or seven that would be detailed by the Mandelkern Commission after three months of deliberation.[27]

At the turn of the century, nobody could have been faulted for thinking that the October 17 archives were finally open: These grand gestures on the part of politicians, coupled with an increasing visibility of the archives in the press at the end of the 1990s, produced an *aura* of transparency, if not the actual conditions for it. This positive spin was also promulgated by academics. In 2001, historian Jean-Marc Berlière announced (albeit with more than a hint of irony) that the good news had arrived: The police archives no longer constituted "an unassailable fortress."[28] That same year, however, in his epilogue to a new edition of *La Bataille de Paris* titled "Ten Years Later," Einaudi notes that, despite certain "spectacular declarations" by high ranking members of the government,[29] official practices of stonewalling persisted at all archival sites, in particular at the prefecture, which continued to deny him access while ostentatiously giving carte blanche to Jean-Paul Brunet, the historian who openly critiqued Einaudi's findings and published, in 1999, a "counter history" titled *Police contre FLN*.[30]

26 Béatrice Vallaeys, "17 Octobre 1961: des archives parlent," *Libération*, October 22, 1997. Assouline's report reveals that instead of investigating the various complaints filed by Algerians whose loved ones had disappeared, the cases were simply labeled as "abandoned." See also "Les archives d'un massacre: rapport octobre 1961," a France 3 reportage that aired on May 4, 1998, http://www.ina.fr/video/CAC98017761.

27 See Dieudonné Mandelkern, André Wiehn, and Mireille Jean, *Rapport sur les archives de la Préfecture de police relatives à la manifestation organisée par le FLN le 17 octobre 1961* (1998), Section 2.3.5. David Assouline was associated with the October 17 activist group Au nom de la mémoire and he was elected to the French Senate in 2004, representing Paris.

28 Berlière, "Archives de police/historiens policés?" 57.

29 Einaudi, *Bataille*, 366.

30 Brunet's narrative, one of the few existing works of historical scholarship based exclusively on the police archives, is distinctly forgiving of the police. In a curious move, the government granted Brunet special authorization to consult the police archives, while continuing to deny Einaudi. Jean-Paul Brunet, *Police contre FLN: Le drame du octobre 1961* (Paris: Flammarion, 1999). Brunet is acerbic in his critique of Einaudi; see pages 13–14 in particular.

Statements and promises regarding archival access created a veneer of transparency that cracked when pressured at the logistical level. In an official question raised in the Senate and published in that institution's official journal in July 2002, Parisian Senator and French Communist Party (PCF) member Nicole Borvo made the following observation and request:

> Les archives concernant ce jour-là—ainsi que les jours qui suivent— ne sont, depuis lors, consultables que par dérogation accordée très parcimonieusement par le préfet de police, alors que par un décret du 5 mai 1999, le Premier ministre stipulait que—concernant les archives relatives à cette manifestation et plus généralement aux faits commis à l'encontre des Français musulmans d'Algérie—"rien ne doit faire obstacle à ce que les chercheurs aient accès à cette période de notre histoire contemporaine." Ne serait-il pas nécessaire qu'il mette tout en œuvre afin de permettre l'accès, sans exclusive aucune, à l'ensemble des archives concernant ces heures noires de notre histoire pour l'ensemble des chercheurs, historiens, écrivains pour que la vérité soit enfin dite sur le 17 octobre 1961?[31]

> (The archives concerning that day, and the days that followed, have only ever been accessible by special dispensation doled out very stingily by the police prefect, notwithstanding the fact that by virtue of a decree issued on May 5, 1999, the Prime Minister stipulated that—concerning archives pertaining to this demonstration and, more generally, to other acts committed against French-Algerian Muslims—"nothing should impede researchers from having access to this period of our contemporary history." Wouldn't it be necessary to do everything within his power to allow all researchers, historians, and writers to have unrestricted access to all of the archives pertaining to these dark hours of our history, so that the truth about October 17, 1961, can finally be established?)

The response to Senator Borvo, issued two months later in the same bulletin, only reiterates the official position, stating that "the Prime Minister's memo dated April 13, 2001, and published in the official journal of the Senate on April 26, 2001, eased the restrictions on access to all of the public archives pertaining to the Algerian War."[32] The

---

31   Published in the official Senate newsletter, *Le Journal officiel du Sénat*, on July 25, 2002, https://www.senat.fr/questions/base/2002/qSEQ020701136.html.

32   The response to Borvo's question was published on September 5, 2002, and refers to the 1979 legislation governing archival access. The response also reminds readers that a memorandum issued by the Prime Minister and dated May 4, 1999,

response does not address the question of actual access nor does it speak to how policy was implemented.

A few years later, various political actors and activist groups once again took up the issue of archival access. In October 2004, the Socialist Party issued a communiqué in support of "the initiatives related to the events of October 17, 1961," claiming that the "recognition of this historical fact participates in collective memory," only to conclude "it is normal that all researchers and historians have access to the archives so that the reality of the facts can be pieced together again."[33] The reference to archive accessibility is baffling in light of the memo issued in 2001 that supposedly eased restrictions, but it is not the lone suggestion that the police archives remained, in the early aughts, a kind of forbidden fruit. Claude Liauzu's essay in *Le Monde diplomatique* (1999) had already opined that it was time for Catherine Trautmann to make good on her 1997 promise to open the archives.[34] In a vaguely ironic twist on this confusing state of affairs, it was precisely at this time that British historians Jim House and Neal MacMaster were in the process of culling the archives and compiling the notes for what would become *Paris 1961: Algerians, State Terror, and Memory*—to date the most exhaustive account of the processes that led to the events of October and their cover-up. The book was made possible, in large part, by the researchers' *"special and unrestricted access to the entire archive* of the Prefecture of Police for the Algerian War period."[35]

Given the intensity of demands for archival access, and the long period during which the archives' status remained unclear, it is reasonable to imagine that their official declassification in 2011 would have been met with cries of victory or, at the very least, evidence of satisfaction from certain camps. Yet the news was greeted with relatively little media attention. While activist associations such as Lallaoui's Au nom de la mémoire and Le 17 octobre contre l'oubli should have been pleased with the developments, their websites and other documentation bear no trace of this critical shift.

loosened some of the constraints stipulated in the 1979 documents. https://www. senat.fr/questions/base/2002/qSEQ020701136.html.

33   See "Le 17 octobre 1961: Le PS pour l'ouverture des archives," *Le Nouvel observateur*, October 17, 2004, http://tempsreel.nouvelobs.com/culture/20041016. OBS9176/17-octobre-1961-le-ps-pour-l-ouverture-des-archives.html.

34   Liauzu, "Les archives bâillonées de la guerre d'Algérie," *Le Monde diplomatique* (February 1999), http://www.monde-diplomatique.fr/1999/02/ LIAUZU/11629.

35   House and MacMaster, 11; my emphasis.

In fact, in its mission statement for the 52nd anniversary of the massacre in 2013 (two years after the archives were, in fact, declassified), Au nom de la mémoire specifically highlights the continued need for archival access: "In order to carry out their mission, historians need to have free access to the archives. It is time for the archives to be open to everyone, historians and citizens."[36] Pierre Laurent, national secretary of the French Communist Party, proposed a resolution before the Senate on October 23, 2012, in reaction to Hollande's official recognition of October 17: "We believe, in particular, that the recognition of [the events of October 17] by the President of the Republic should lead to the declassification of the archives pertaining to October 17, 1961, and, beyond that, of all archives pertaining to the colonial wars and their succession of repressions and massacres."[37]

The array of conclusions one could draw from these statements is dizzying: The archives have been open since 1997, 2001, or 2011; the archives aren't really open, despite the fact that President Sarkozy declared them open in 2011; or, politicians and activists are unaware of the 2011 declaration and thus continue to lobby. Regardless, it seems clear that from 1997 to 2011, promises and perhaps even genuine desires to declassify the archives existed only at the level of political discourse. In terms of practice and action, no orders were given, and no material changes were made to inform archivists about new policies and how to implement them. Given that the archives now appear to be accessible to all, how are we to understand continued demands, such as those made by Au nom de la mémoire or Pierre Laurent, to declassify the archives? Is the discourse of archival desire and denial so deeply entrenched that reality cannot dislodge it? Or are activists, politicians, and scholars haunted by the persistent *belief* that the archives have been expurgated and thus represent only a portion of what is available, and that the state remains invested in continuing to hide the "smoking gun"?[38]

36   The website for Au nom de la mémoire has been revamped; the 2013 call is no longer available on the site, but reclamations using the same language can be found on the Mouvement contre le racisme (MRAP) website. See communiqué posted in 2016 and titled "17 octobre 1961—17 octobre 2016, 55ème anniversaire—Vérité et justice," https://mrap.fr/17-octobre-1961-17-octobre-2016-55eme-Anniversaire-Verite-et-Justice (accessed August 27, 2020).

37   See "Reconnaissance de la répression d'une manifestation à Paris le 17 octobre 1961," in the summary of Senate debates on October 23, 2012, https://www.senat.fr/seances/s201210/s20121023/s20121023001.html.

38   For more musings on the state of the October 17 police archives, see: René Galissot, "Secret des archives et raison d'état," in *Le 17 octobre, un crime d'état*

For the narrative of the October 17 police archives, Mbembe's notion of the archive-turned-talisman, that is, of a fetish object whose disappearance allowed for myriad "imaginary thoughts," seems uncannily apropos, particularly as the years since declassification have yet to produce a new historical account of October 17 (all major scholarly interventions were published prior to 2011), nor have any scholars written of their experiences consulting these documents (until now). Decades of archival deferral have created a set of paradoxical conditions whereby the archives have become invested with something like total authority, and yet that authority ultimately either cannot or does not exert itself. While work on the material contained within the archives is undoubtedly still to come, for the moment the October 17 archives remain a fetish—a fixation, but also a symbolic object upon which desires are projected—drawing their power from the narrative created about them rather than the tales they contain.

A Literary Scholar's Archive Story

My own experiences with the police archives in 2012 and 2013 confirm two things: 1) the archives are indeed open for consultation without special permission; and 2) this fact is not well understood by everyone. On my first visit in 2012, I was greeted by an affable archivist who painstakingly explained the system of classification and how to request cartons from the H series ("H" designates all documents relating to the Algerian War). The archivist was also fascinated, and visibly stymied, by the idea that a *literary* scholar wanted to consult these particular documents. He was quick to provide me with what he called an *outil de recherche*—a "research tool" that consisted of a Word document created by the archivist responsible for inventorying the October 17 documents, and intended to provide the historical context essential to understanding the documents in the archives. He also brought forth a rather large stack

---

à Paris, ed. Olivier Le Cour Grandmaison (Paris: La Dispute, 2001), 103–12, and Annette Lévy-Willaiard, interview with Jean-Marc Berlière, "On risque de ne trouver dans les dossiers que des coupures de presse," *Libération*, October 18, 1997. For general debates on archival polemics in France, see Sonia Combe, *Archives interdites. L'histoire confisquée* (Paris: La Découverte, 2001) and Rousso and Eric Conan's critique of Combe in *Vichy, An Ever-Present Past*, trans. Nathan Bracher (Hanover, NH: University Press of New England, 1998).

of secondary reading on October 17, including the Brunet and House/ MacMaster books, which represent opposite ends of the ideological spectrum. (More on the usefulness of the "outil" in a moment.)

When I returned to the archives the following year, however, there was a different archivist on duty, and she had very different ideas about the status of those same H boxes: "The H Series?" she queried, looking at me as though I were crazy or dangerous. "H is the Algerian boxes; you'd need a special permission to consult them." I persisted, and by showing her the photos of documents I had taken the previous year, I was able to convince her *not* that the archives were indeed officially declassified—I'm certain she believes that the Algerian boxes still require special permissions—but that I would simply be reexamining documents I had already seen. Therefore, if any state secrets were revealed, it would certainly be the fault of the archivist on duty in 2012. She quite literally threw up her hands and ordered the cartons for me. Such diametrically opposed attitudes would seem to signal both a misunderstanding of policies and their recent modifications and, more pointedly, a deeply held institutional malaise regarding the nature of historical documents, their consultation, and the power of knowledge. Moreover, the fact that the archivist in 2013 yielded relatively easily suggests that ideas about what is classified may be fairly malleable, and that protocol can often be bent to fit a given situation.

These "archive stories," epiphenomenal though they may be, are constitutive of the multilayered narrative of October 17, as are the stories of how the police archives interact with the corpus of cultural productions that represent the massacre or the quest for knowledge about the massacre. As someone viewing historical archives through a literary filter, then, I am less motivated by a search for evidence or even "truth" than I am by the lure of excavating the narratives they contain and setting them in conversation with other October 17 stories from the anarchive. I have wondered what narratives we can extrapolate from these archives, what deeper questions they prompt us to ask, and what kind of discursive work they do.

The documents specifically related to October 17 are contained in two cartons labeled HA 110/111, and can be divided into two macro-categories of origin: documents *produced* by the police, and documents *received or collected* by the police. In the first we find: press communiqués; internal memos; official responses to letters of inquiry; notations of phone calls received; dossiers concerning specific investigations (which include transcripts of interrogations and interviews, decisions made on the outcomes, and sometimes medical reports); reports from informants; affidavits taken from wounded Algerians at various hospitals in Paris; transcriptions of conversations recorded by wiretaps (Pierre Vidal-Naquet's telephone line, for example, was under surveillance); and teletexts reporting bodies discovered in the river, the canals, or in wooded areas on the outskirts of Paris.

In the second category are a variety of documents *collected* by the police: press clippings; tracts and manifestos circulated by the FLN and other pro-Algerian groups (students, Communists); letters from business owners inquiring as to the whereabouts of their Algerian employees; letters from elected officials inquiring on behalf of Algerian families; official questions from senators; letters of advice from the community on how to handle the "Algerian problem"; letters castigating Papon; and letters from businesses whose activities were impacted by the detention of Algerians in sites intended for commerce (the dairy industry trade show, for example, was scheduled to take place at the Porte de Versailles November 8–14; a polite but panicked letter from the president of the group informed Papon of the losses that would be incurred if the event had to be cancelled). Finally, there are a few photographs of uncertain provenance floating around in the boxes.

If all archives can be read through literary techniques of close reading, numerous documents in the October 17 files lend themselves particularly well to a method known as *critique génétique*, which examines versions of manuscripts in order to uncover the process of a text's creation and modification, and to speculate on the meaning of the changes.[39] It is clear that the staff at the prefecture had a practice of retaining multiple drafts of the documents they produced. Studying the iterations of a given document—each of which bears the editing marks and marginalia of the vetting process—reveals changes in strategy, accommodations to ideology, and concessions to various actors or institutions.

The announcement of the curfew prohibiting Algerians from circulating at night and in groups is illustrative: The memo was revised

39 *La critique génétique*, or "genetic criticism," emerged in France in the 1970s among researchers at the CNRS. The method involves studying the versions or drafts that lead to the production of a final text, analyzing the changes and permutations, or the traces left by the process of editing. It presumes that the final version of a work contains within it "the memory of its own genesis." See Pierre-Marc de Biasi, "Manuscrits—La critique génétique," *Encyclopædia Universalis*, http://www.universalis.fr/encyclopedie/manuscrits-la-critique-genetique/.

multiple times prior to its release on October 5, 1961. The modifications are primarily concerned with the exact hours of the curfew and the types of establishments subject to closure. The final version set the hours of the curfew from 8:30pm to 5:30am and dictated that restaurants and cafés frequented by Algerians would close at 7pm. Algerian-run cabarets and nightclubs, on the other hand, originally on the list of establishments to be shuttered at night, were ultimately permitted to remain open. These clubs were notoriously subject to police extortion and used as "hunting grounds" for informants; to close them, then, would have had a negative impact on the ability of the police to monitor the Algerian community. The series of changes suggests an ongoing conversation as to how punitive the measures were to be, and to what degree the curfew could impact other types of police activities without reaching a point of diminishing returns.

The archives—their existence and their content—are evidence of a will to establish and control a master narrative of October 17 and related events. Of course, this is not unique to the October 17 archives, and it may be something of a truism with respect to state archives in general. However, whereas the notorious meticulousness of the Nazi archives ultimately provided proof of nefarious, genocidal intentions, the police archives of October 17 are at pains to foreground innocence, or to provide alternative theories of culpability. One curious set of documents literally places the FLN and police narratives side by side: The template for this series is oriented in landscape format, allowing for two wide columns; the left-hand side is labeled "Version donnée par le FLN" (Version given by the FLN), while the right-hand column heading reads "Exposé des faits" (Presentation of the facts). The formatting graphically symbolizes balance, even-handedness, objectivity, with equal space allotted to both sides of the story; yet, with the FLN story coded as a "version"—with its implications, in French, of "interpretation" or "variation"—and the police story coded as factual, the goal of discrediting one side to the benefit of the other is transparent.

Moreover, at one point in this set of documents it becomes possible to diagnose a case of "narrative fatigue": Of the dozen or so pages that follow this format, most of them present the FLN's side of the story briefly while spending several paragraphs fleshing out the police "presentation of the facts." But, on the penultimate page, the police response to the "version" put forward by the FLN is summed up in a single line: "Cette information est inventée de toutes pièces" (this story is a complete fabrication).[40] Rather than offer a detailed counter-narrative, the police seem content to forcefully rebut, a gesture that reads as particularly hollow given the painstaking invalidations present in similar documents. Just as it can be tricky to attribute intention to an author, it is hard to say with certainty that documents like these would have been created or consigned with an eye to "spinning" the story in favor of the police. They do, however, have a constructed, over-determined feel, as if the would-be authors—notwithstanding various guaranteed protections afforded by French archival policies—were working in anticipation of a future reader's gaze and with an eye to the creation of a legacy. And at the same time, these particular narratives appear to be purely self-fulfilling: With no indication that they are destined for readers outside of the prefecture (no addressee, letterhead, dates, or signatures), the documents seem to exist solely for the record.

At the same time that one might read for and recognize totalizing gestures of narrative control in the archive, one can also read for the detail, for the micro-stories that escape the dominance of the master narrative and refigure the archive as a source of subversive material. One such detail is the presence, woven into the archive through collected documents (letters and manifestos), of a comparative discourse that alludes to (and sometimes directly references) World War II and Vichy, without ever explicitly mentioning Papon's role in the deportation of Jews from Gironde. This material is examined in Chapter 6 of the present book, but in the context of excavating the archive, it is worth mentioning here that these documents conserve the traces of a public outrage with a very particular tenor, which in turn produces a narrative that brings the Holocaust into close discursive quarters with the end of the colonial era.

The archives also harbor a micronarrative related to race. Among the various letters and tracts collected by the police, a few make direct accusations of racism and charge the police with racial profiling, and I analyze this at some length in Chapter 5. Perhaps more interesting, however, are the latent traces of racism embedded in the documents produced by the police themselves. One example, taken from the rich microhistory of Moïse Sebbah, whose dossier is one of the thickest in the October 17 archives, reveals the thorny imbrications of race, ethnicity, religion, and nationality. An Algerian Jew and therefore not legally subject to the same regime as the FMA (Français musulmans d'Algérie),

---

40   Police archives, HA 110/111.

Sebbah filed a complaint after he was arrested, beaten, and detained overnight on October 19. Although the investigative report determined that Sebbah should receive a small compensation for his suffering, it also exonerated the perpetrating officers on the grounds that Sebbah—notwithstanding his name or his claims—"looked a lot like a North African."[41]

In addition to reading for the master narrative and the micronarratives that subvert it, one can also read the archives as part of an intertextual web comprised of historiography, public discourse, and cultural productions (and of course, these various types of reading are in no way mutually exclusive). Researchers familiar with the novels and films featuring October 17 cannot help but relish the indexical or cross referential synergy produced by reading the archives in light of the anarchive, and there is a certain delight in the discovery that official documents confirm, and sometimes justify, details of the cultural objects. For example, references to racial profiling in novels such as *Vivre me tue* have been met with skepticism, yet the archives appear to confirm that arrests were carried out based on phenotype, that is, based on what a given person's skin color, hair type, and features might seem to suggest about his "racial" origins.[42] Stories of empathy and solidarity—such as those in Leïla Sebbar's novel *La Seine était rouge* or Alain Tasma's docudrama *Nuit noire*—also find historical ballast in these archives.

Numerous other details give rise to a eureka sensation as the archives reverberate against the anarchive. And yet, to read this way is also unsettling; pitting archival "evidence" against fictional representation feels vaguely sophomoric, akin to reading for authorial intention, or for plot. Nonetheless, I want to treat this uneasiness as a way station on a path to somewhere more productive: Caught up as they are in an inevitable intertextual web, the archives—given their history as hidden objects, given their fetish qualities, as Mbembe would put it—question ordinary notions of reading order and narrative temporality. The archives exude a double contemporaneity: They are *of* the time of the events they document, while also being *of* the present moment,

---

41   Documents and correspondence related to the Sebbah affair are collected in a folder labeled "4563: Violence contre les Algériens, affaire Moïse Sebbah." (The name is occasionally spelled "Sebah.")

42   Azouz Begag's critique of *Vivre me tue* is based in part on the novel's suggestion that a Moroccan man might have been killed on October 17. The novel, and Begag's assessment of it, are taken up in Chapter 5 of this book.

the moment of their availability. The temptations of indexical reading, although certainly in need of complication, may be less facile than they initially appear.

By accident or by design, archival conditions—the setting, regulations, and atmosphere of consultation—play an important function in archive stories. If I was lucky to have dealt with such a pleasant and forthcoming archivist on my first foray into the October 17 archives, the institution itself nonetheless attempts to exert itself over the researcher. This influence takes the form, ironically, of what the archivists present as a "research tool." At 20 pages long, the text provides "context" for October 17; yet this paratext, if we can invoke Genette, is no less subjective and unstable than any other text. By underscoring the various methods deployed to keep the Algerian population of Paris safe, by positioning Papon as a defender of rank-and-file Algerians made vulnerable to nationalist ideologies, and by recourse to terms like "terrorism" and "counter terrorism" to describe the French front of the Algerian War, the "research tool" has the potential to radically over-determine interpretation of the archives.

The police archives contain incontrovertible evidence of the Algerian dead and wounded, and of police use of munitions, yet the one way we *cannot* read them is as resolving questions of culpability or resolving the debate over the number of dead.[43] So if, as appears to be the case, the archives contain no long-awaited smoking gun, why bother with them at all? A more probative question might be: If there were a smoking gun, what would it look like? Would we recognize it for what it is? And can our work have meaning even if the notion of a smoking gun turns out to be a red herring? Like any set of texts, more or less organized, more or less imbued with intention, the archives are available for hermeneutic activity, and indeed, the meaning we attribute to them demands to be deepened through their deployment in a broader field. While the archive fails to solve many open questions about what happened on October 17,

---

43 Not a single document in the cartons consulted mentions an official death count. Even the famous "research tool" hedges its bets when it comes to the number of dead, noting only that, in the final assessment, there were an "undetermined number of deaths (between 30 and 50, perhaps 100)." A footnote cites Brunet's *Police contre FLN* and Linda Amiri's thesis (based on archival research and completed under the direction of Benjamin Stora)—both of which report lower numbers of deaths. The note ends with an offhanded mention of "other authors such as Jean-Luc Einaudi," whose numbers are much higher, only to conclude that the subject remains "a source of lively debate." "Introduction – Série H," 3.

it does offer evidence of one critical element: By virtue of the various first-person documents addressed to the prefecture and the scrupulous collection and conservation of contemporaneous press clippings, the idea that nobody knew what happened, or that October 17 was somehow innately invisible, can no longer be tolerated.

Romancing the Anarchive: October 17 Fictions and Their "Archive Stories"

Both the second and third waves of the anarchive feature novels that literary scholar Suzanne Keen would undoubtedly call "romances of the archive": fictions set in archives, libraries, or other sites of knowledge production, or whose plots are driven by a quest related to historical material.[44] Although Keen's corpus is different from my own—she focuses on the contemporary Anglophone novel—her study is germane to this discussion insofar as she argues for a valorizing of "pulp" or paraliterary genres, often discounted in favor of "postmodern" literature. Moreover, Keen proposes a typology of the "romance of the archive," which articulates the major features of the subgenre: the presence of researcher-characters; adventure stories in which "research" is essential to the plot; discomforts and inconveniences suffered in the service of knowledge; sex and physical pleasure gained as a result of the quest; settings and locations that contain archives of actual papers; material traces of the past revealing the truth; and evocations of history from a post-imperial perspective.[45]

Many of these themes and motifs are mobilized in the October 17 anarchive, especially, but not exclusively, in detective novels or *polars*.

44 In her discussion of the contemporary Anglophone novel, Keen identifies fictional representations of archival material belonging to the era of British imperial dominance as a strategy for probing post-imperial anxieties without necessarily "celebrating the national past uncritically or adopting a single philosophy of history." Suzanne Keen, *Romances of the Archive in Contemporary British Fiction* (Toronto: University of Toronto Press, 2001), 4–5.

45 Keen, 7. Keen's plea to recognize the contributions of "other channels of the mainstream" (that is, pop fiction subgenres like the detective novel, fantasy, gothics, and thrillers) resonates with the October 17 anarchive insofar as it features proportionally more "pulp" genres. Her work relies on Raymond Williams for its notion that all forms of writing (pop and literary alike) "express and embody in culture some of the most pressing contests among residual, emergent, and dominant political ideals" (34–35).

Some representations depict the physical setting of official archival sites, staging researchers, detectives, or other types of investigators as they explore documents or are thwarted in their attempts to access them. Others use archival spaces as backdrops for action unrelated to documentary research but nonetheless symbolically significant. Still others feature the archive not as a site but as a set of material traces, as real or invented "evidentiary" documentation that can be produced within a fictional story world to generate, among other things, a reality effect. Finally, a number of texts produce a figural understanding of the "archive" as a concept, constructing unorthodox repositories of information available for interpretation (by readers in and outside of the text) that work to mitigate an absence of evidence, to stand in for documentary records where none existed, or simply to suggest that readers scratch the surface of "master narratives" and ask better questions.

To the already long list of "firsts" that describe Daeninckx's *Meurtres pour mémoire*, we can add its status as the inaugural October 17 "romance of the archive." And indeed, with its murderous archivist, an unmistakable quest structure, adventures in and around actual archives, and a love story between the lead detective and the widow of a victim, *Meurtres* fulfills nearly all of the criteria established by Keen. Set in 1983, the *polar* anticipates what would become the Papon affair by staging an investigation into the murder of a father and son who had the misfortune of consulting municipal archives in Toulouse (avatar of Bordeaux) that could inculpate André Veuillut, a certain Vichy functionary turned Paris Police Chief (and avatar of Papon). The Toulouse archives are only epiphenomenally related to October 17, yet their contents and, more importantly, their consultation by three different characters, at two different points in time, encode questions of interpretation and state control of knowledge.

In 1983, narrator and protagonist Inspector Cadin is charged with investigating the murder of Bernard Thiraud, a doctoral candidate in history gunned down upon exiting the municipal archives of Toulouse. Believing that what Bernard saw in the archives might be related to his violent demise, Cadin returns to the original scene to pore over the same documents: municipal administrative files from the years 1942 to 1943 filed (alphabetically by topic) under the code "DE." A seasoned investigator but a newcomer to archival work, Cadin does not see a connection between the years in question and topics beginning with the letters "DE"; however, the investigator's observation that "les hasards du classement faisaient se reoncontrer le burlesque et le tragique" (71, "the vagaries of filing mixed comedy with tragedy," 55)—for instance, "deforestation" and "deportation" exist in the same file—comments implicitly on the absence of a hierarchical structure that would organize and assign meaning to the documents. Here, as in all archives, elements of wildly divergent significance are presented as equal in semiotic value.

At this point in his investigation, Cadin does not possess the tools that would allow him to recognize the potential significance of "DE," yet the text's description of the archives lingers far longer on "deportation" than "deforestation": "La DÉportation était traitée de la même manière que les autres taches de l'administration: les fonctionnaires semblaient avoir rempli ces formulaires avec un soin identique à celui apporté aux bons de charbon ou à la rentrée scolaire. On manipulait la mort, en lieu et place de l'espoir" (72, "DÉportation was treated in exactly the same way as other administrative tasks. The bureaucrats seemed to have filled in these forms with the same punctiliousness they brought to coal coupons or the new school year. Death was being allocated in the place of hope," 56). Through this density of detail, reported without commentary by Cadin, the text itself assigns importance to "deportation" and thus initiates the process of interpreting the content of the archive in the context of Bernard's murder.

With no apparent motive and no damning evidence readily available in the archive, Cadin begins the patient gumshoe work of following leads, interviewing witnesses, and retracing steps, all of which eventually reveal that Roger Thiraud (Bernard's father and also a teacher of history) had been working on a historical monograph about his hometown of Drancy when he was killed, inexplicably, during the Algerian demonstration on October 17, 1961. Roger's monograph functions as a supplement to the archive; excerpts scripted in the novel (gleaned, certainly, from actual archives) offer evidence of Drancy's role as a transit camp during World War II, including actual statistics on the deportation of Jewish children from Gironde. The Drancy monograph brings the contents of the DE classification into sharper focus, and Cadin returns to the municipal archives in Toulouse armed with an ability to confer meaning and weight upon the various disparate documents: "J'écartai les DÉbroussaillage, DÉdommagements, DÉfense passive, et autre DÉsinfections pour concentrer mon attention sur les dizaines de pièces référencées DÉportation. J'affrontai avec dégoût l'horreur insidieuse de ces notes de service qu'échangeaient les fonctionnaires afin de parfaire l'efficacité de la machine à broyer des corps" (194, "I put aside DEforestation, DEmarcation, DEfense and DElousing to concentrate

my attention on the dozen items referenced DEportation. I felt disgust
in the face of the horror underlying these memoranda swapped by
bureaucrats with the aim of perfecting the human disposal machine,"
161). Moreover, Cadin would uncover documents demonstrating that
a highly placed Vichy functionary, André Veillut (Papon), had signed
orders to deport a surprising number of Jewish families from the
Toulouse region to Drancy.

That Cadin's discovery has implications beyond the resolution of a
history teacher's murder is made clear when archivist-in-chief Lécussan
follows him out of the archives and attempts to kill him: "You shouldn't
have stuck your nose in," he admonishes, just before Cadin—quicker
on the draw—fires off a fatal round. Lécussan, Cadin will learn, was
indirectly responsible for the deaths of the Thirauds: Using his position
in the archives to monitor researchers' activities, Lécussan informed on
individuals whose interests gravitated toward sensitive documents. A
phone call from the archivist set into motion the murders of both Roger
and, 20 years later, his son Bernard.

The municipal archives in Toulouse, then, are a violent crime scene in
multiple senses of the terms: The documents consigned there (the "DE"
dossier) are proof of past state violence; they constitute an ongoing threat
of exposure for those state actors who remain public servants; and in the
case of Bernard and Cadin, the site itself is quite literally the scene of a
murder or attempted murder—this physical crime functioning symbolically for the figurative "violence" of the repression of information, but
also for the real violence of deportation and, symbolically, for other state
crimes covered up through official practices (October 17).

The second set of archives in *Meurtres* are the October 17 police
dossiers, represented in the novel as an inaccessible space and an absent
trace. Cadin's efforts to understand the context of Roger's murder
are thwarted by the fact that the dossiers remain classified. Parisian
archivist Gerbet is a minor character in the novel, yet his role as
proxy for government policy places him squarely at the center of the
text's representation of epistemological repression. Less treacherous and
violent than Lécussan, Gerbet nonetheless takes his duties seriously,
giving Cadin a lesson in archival policy:

C'est absolument impossible. Personne n'y a accès. Seul le ministre est
habilité à le faire sortir du coffre et à en divulguer le contenu. Tu connais
les décrets concernant la publicité des documents d'État. Cinquante ans
de secret absolu. Il n'est pas dans mon pouvoir d'y déroger. Et certains
de ces dossiers explosifs pourriront pendant des siècles entiers avant de

revoir la lumière. Vous savez tout autant que moi que les gouvernements
ont besoin d'une police forte et unie. Remettre l'affaire d'octobre 1961 sur
la place publique produirait l'effet inverse. (90–91)

(It's out of the question. Nobody can get at [the October 17 archive].
Only the Minister has the authority to have it taken out of the safe and
to make its contents known. You know the law about publishing state
papers. Fifty years of total secrecy. It's not in my power to rescind it. And
there are some files so explosive they'll rot for centuries before they see
the light. You know as well as me that governments need a strong united
police force. Exposing what happened in October 1961 would have the
opposite effect.) (73)

Although the two archivists in *Meurtres* are fictional characters, they
nonetheless embody real aspects of archival politics and practice in
France. As gatekeepers, Lécussan and Gerbet control access in accordance
with the bylaws of the institutions they represent. Paradigmatic of the
consummate professional archivist, Gerbet acts under the aegis of state
legislation, invoking decrees as old as the Republic to prohibit the consultation of sensitive documents.[46] Lécussan, encouraged by high-placed
cronies, goes rogue: Given that municipal archives are not subject to the
same level of censorship as police archives, he is compelled to produce
documents like the "DE" files upon request, but effectively suppresses
any knowledge they might produce by silencing renegade researchers.

By the end of *Meurtres* and despite Cadin's keen investigative tactics,
the work of the archons at both the highest and lowest levels is successful.
Although the detective identified the Thirauds' killer and uncovered a
conspiracy, he is compelled, for the good of the state, to keep his findings
to himself. In the final scene of the novel, Cadin admits—to the reader,
if not to Bernard's young widow, who has become his lover—that he
had already been ordered to "mettre la pédale douce" (216, "to soft
pedal it," 183). In other words, knowledge about the Thirauds' murders
and their link to Veillut and state corruption is consigned to the same
fate as stories of October 17, with officials preparing "un scénario plus
conforme à l'idée que les citoyens devaient se faire des garants de l'ordre
public" (217, "drawing up a version more in keeping with the idea that
the citizenry had of the guardians of public order," 183). If the novel's
ending is unsatisfying for Cadin and other characters who must live with
the knowledge that a revisionist fiction has been erected in place of an

---

46 See Milligan, "'What is an Archive?'"161–65; and Sonia Combe, *Les archives
interdites*, Chapter 2.

unpalatable historical reality, the book performs an essential anarchival function by activating traces of that particular reality and problematizing questions of archival access.

The novel's engagement with archives, however, is not limited to these representations of actual sites or documents; it also proposes alternative archives and gestures to the existence of other repositories of knowledge not subject to state archival policies. For example, at the end of the book's first three chapters—which narrativize the October 17 repression (and the death of Thiraud *père*) and are the only portions of the book set in the past—we find a headline from the journal *Paris Jour*: "Les Algériens maîtres de Paris pendant trois heures" (40, "Algerians Take Over Paris for Three Hours," 32). Adapted from an actual headline published in *Paris Jour* on October 18—"'C'est inouï !' pendant trois heures 20 000 musulmans algériens ont été les maîtres absolus des rues de Paris" (Unprecedented! For Three Hours 20,000 Algerian Muslims Completely Took Over the Streets of Paris)—Daeninckx's version does the important historical work of demonstrating to readers in the 1980s that the so-called "hidden event" of October 17 was in fact reported in the mainstream press.[47] Combined with the information that follows—"Vers midi, la prefecture communiqua son bilan et annonçait trois morts (dont un Européen) soixante-quatre blessés et onze mille cinq cent trente-huit arrestations" (40, "Around noon, the Prefecture released its figures, giving three dead [one of them a European], sixty-four injured and 11,538 arrests," 32)—this gesture suggests that there exists an archive of journalistic material that might be culled for its details about the night in question while hinting at the notion of a nascent cover-up that haunts the remainder of the text, even as the actual events of October 17 fade from the pages.

Hence, although Cadin is denied access to classified police files, as he pressures his interlocutors, the potential for other sources emerges. This permits the novel to speculate about actual "missing evidence" from October 17: Cadin gets a lead on a set of photographs taken on October 17 by a police photographer named Marc Rosner and an hour-long film made by a team of Belgian TV reporters. The first trail has long since grown cold: Rosner's photos had been seized by the police

---

47   For studies on October 17 in the press, see Mogniss Abdallah, "Le 17 octobre 1961 et les médias," *Hommes et Migrations* 1228 (Nov.–Dec. 2000): 125–33, and Agnès Maillot, "La presse française et le 17 octobre 1961," *Irish Journal of French Studies* 1 (2001): 25–35.

after he was indicted for professional misconduct—a story that appears to have been fabricated in order for the police to take possession of the incriminating documents. The second trail, however, takes Cadin to Brussels, where the Belgian producer allows him to view the hour-long film, which turns out to be nothing less than a scathing indictment, a smoking gun if there ever was one.

The Rosner character is likely based on Georges Azenstarck or Élie Kagan, photojournalists who took photos on October 17 only to have those images confiscated by state censors. While both photographers have, more recently, released photos or negatives they had managed to hide from the police, at the time of *Meurtres*' publication these images would not have been in circulation.[48] Similarly, there has long been speculation that a Belgian TV crew, in Paris to cover the Jacques Brel concert, had footage of the repression that has since been destroyed.[49] The fictionalization of this type of damning proof imagines the possibility that such evidence might indeed exist in reality. It also recognizes the potential limits of the official archives, even if they were to be made available. Finally, contrary to the existing narrative at the time, both types of fictional evidence (photos and the film) imply the presence of eyewitnesses on the scene who might have attempted to create a lasting trace of what they saw.

More so than any other work in the anarchive, *Meurtres pour mémoire* embeds references to hidden histories, to seemingly elliptical, superfluous, and nearly extradiegetical microepisodes that compel readers to make connections. Details about a Situationist attack on the police administration; Cadin's obsession with the graffitied slogan "Free Henri Martin" (referring to the French pilot imprisoned for refusing to bomb Hai Phong during the war in Indochina); one character's disquisition on the *demi-monde* of the Paris periphery at the turn of the century; an Algerian worker scraping away layers of posters to reveal a World War II-era order issued by the occupying forces: These episodes bear an indexical relationship to historical realities, yet have nothing to do with the novel's plot.[50] If the superfluous in the

---

48   See Introduction, n. 39.

49   See Stora, "Mort et résurrection du 17 octobre," *Le Monde diplomatique*, October 17, 2016.

50   For an astute analysis of the Situationst subplot and other superfluous elements, see Atack, "From *Meurtres pour mémoire* to *Missak*," 276–77; for a key reading of the poster, see Golsan, "Memory's *bombes à retardement*," 169.

text does not directly correlate to October 17, these details have in common subjects removed from history, stories of marginal protest, and a critique of the state, elements that may be read as obliquely related to October 17 and its repression. Thus, through a sidelong critique, Daeninckx's novel archives—alongside actual historical material—a pervasive historical pathos. At the same time, this profusion of detail simulates the researcher-archive relationship by confronting the reader with a mass of hierarchically undifferentiated elements and compelling her to select the ones to which meaning will be attributed.

Nearly 20 years separate *Meurtres* from Mehdi Lallaoui's *Une nuit d'octobre* (One October Night), and in that interval, the political, historiographical, and cultural landscape shifted significantly.[51] Notwithstanding changes over time, at stake in Lallaoui's 2001 novel are the same October 17 archives that Cadin is unable to access in *Meurtres*. Set in Paris in 1999, *Une nuit d'octobre* takes its inspiration from the actual "trial within the trial"—the libel case brought against Einaudi by Papon at the end of the latter's trial for crimes against humanity.[52] In Lallaoui's "ripped from the headlines" fiction, a group of friends—all of whom have a personal connection to October 17— work together to find evidence that will exonerate Renucci (avatar of Einaudi), a historian who has been charged with libel by former Police Chief "Maurice Crapon." Similar to *Meurtres*, *Une nuit d'octobre* stages physical violence in actual archival sites (again functioning metonymically for insidious violence against knowledge) and constructs alternative archives; in Lallaoui's novel, however, the archivists are heroes instead of assassins; the alternative archives imagined by the text are unearthed and allowed to signify; and the multiple narrative threads all have happy endings, one of which is a love story between the son of an Algerian survivor of October 17 and the daughter of a Parisian policeman.

51 Mehdi Lallaoui, *Une nuit d'octobre* (Paris: Éditions Alternatives, 2001). The novel is not available in English; all translations from the French are my own.

52 The "trial within the trial"—a term used by the French media—refers to the libel suit brought by Papon against Einaudi when the latter's testimony during the trial for crimes against humanity brought to light Papon's involvement in the massacre of Algerians in October 1961. Although Papon lost the libel suit in March 1999, he was never officially inculpated for his role in the October 17 massacre. See Josh Cole, "Entering History: The Memory of Police Violence in Paris, October 1961," in *Algeria & France 1800–2000: Identity, Memory, Nostalgia*, ed. Patricia M.E. Lorcin (Syracuse, NY: Syracuse University Press, 2006), 119–21.

As was the case in fact, in fiction, Renucci's defense rests on material presumed to be in the sealed archives: To defeat the libel charge brought by Crapon against the historian, the defense team must prove that a massacre indeed took place on October 17 and that the police were responsible. The novel's exposition introduces a group of Renucci supporters including Dadou, the son of an Algerian who survived the October 17 massacre and is haunted by it; Robert, a French priest who had actively supported Algerian independence and worked for the FLN; Pierre, Renucci's lawyer; Hélène, a French woman who aided the FLN; Monique Devaux, a friend and neighbor to Algerians living in the *bidonvilles*; and Agnès, a law student and daughter of a retired Parisian policeman. Many of these supporting characters recall real-life actors in the Algerian drama on October 17. Monique Devaux, for example, is a transparent calque of Monique Hervo, a social worker who lived in the Nanterre *bidonville* and who witnessed the violence on October 17.[53] Roger may be an amalgam of Georges Arnold (a priest who lived and worked alongside Algerians in Paris in 1961) and another priest whose testimony is captured in the BBC documentary *Drowning by Bullets*.[54]

Archival access is immediately problematized in the text when Pierre, the lawyer, tells the group to look elsewhere for proof: "On ne pourra pas compter sur l'ouverture des archives, ce qui aurait permis d'établir le déroulement de cette nuit-là; et il faut s'attendre à tout de la partie adverse: ils jouent gros dans cette histoire. Pas seulement l'honneur d'un Préfet, il s'agit d'une affaire d'État, voilà" (15, We can't count on being able to consult the archives, which would have allowed us to establish what happened the night in question. As far as the prosecution is concerned, they've got everything on the line here. Not just the honor of the former Chief of Police; this is nothing less than an affair of state). Written in 2001, at a moment when demands for access had become the stuff of public discourse yet promises of declassification had yet to be

53 Hervo lived in the Nanterre *bidonville* until its destruction in 1971, and is the author of *Chroniques du bidonville: Nanterre en guerre d'Algérie, 1959–1962* (Paris: Seuil, 2001). For more on Hervo, see: House and MacMaster; E. Blanchard, "Monique Hervo, une vie avec les Algériens et les mal-logés," *Plein droit* 4, no. 91 (2011): 36–40; and the play by Mehdi Lallaoui, *Monique H., Nanterre 1961* (Montigny-lès-Cormeilles: Au nom de la mémoire, 2014).
54 Philip Brooks and Alan Hayling, *Drowning by Bullets* (2003). For another interview with Georges Arnold, see Sébastien Pascot's short documentary *Témoignage d'Octobre* (2002).

fulfilled, *Une nuit d'octobre* features a credulous lawyer who clearly believes that the police archives, were they only to be declassified, would contain irrefutable proof of the events on October 17.

In the absence of the archives, this band of ragtag researchers and amateur investigators attempts to locate alternative evidence for Renucci's assertions regarding Crapon's authorization of police brutality and the number of victims. One promising lead points them to the archives of the river police, yet despite the goodwill of the lockkeeper, Dupond, who remembers the night in question as "une bien sale histoire" (48, a really nasty story), those documents are a dead end: The archives had been permanently removed from circulation just before Dadou's visit. Dupond notes: "J'ai trouvé ça étonnant, c'est une procédure vraiment inhabituelle.... Mais ce que je vais vous dire est la vérité. Ces archives ont été détruites il y a à peine trois semaines" (48, I found it astonishing; that's not in our procedures.... But I'm telling you the truth. Those archives were destroyed barely three weeks ago). Although this reversal of fortune reads like a set piece of crime-and-caper fiction, the detail is accurate: The Mandelkern Report observes that the department responsible for the archives of the *brigade fluviale* "proceeded, several years ago, with the destruction of its old archives."[55]

A break in the case comes once the trial is underway, when a mysterious caller leaves a message on Dadou's answering machine: "Je ne peux pas vous dire qui je suis [...] Sachez seulement que je possède des documents qui démontrent le nombre élévé de victimes le 17 octobre 1961 [...] Je vous les remettrai demain à la bibliothèque du Palais de justice" (138–39, I can't tell you who I am [...] All you need to know is that I have documents that attest to the high number of victims on October 17, 1961 [...] I'll give them to you tomorrow at the Hall of Justice library). The following day at the library, Dadou and Roger are dumbfounded when an unknown woman hands them an envelope and then disappears. The value of its contents is immediately apparent:

> Il s'agit d'une photocopie d'un registre du parquet... Ce sont les descriptifs des homicides concernant les Français musulmans d'Algérie se rattachant au 17 octobre. "Noyé mort par balle—mort—mort—mort—Repêchage en Seine... FMA pont de Bezons. Homicide volontaire—homicide volontaire—mort—repêché..." (140)

---

55 Rapport Mandelkern, section I.3.b.

(It's a photocopy of the court report... These are descriptions of homicides of French Algerian Muslims on October 17. "Drowned by bullets—dead— dead—dead—Fished out of the Seine... Dead Algerian near the Bezons bridge. Voluntary homicide—Voluntary homicide—dead—floater...")

The researchers' hopes are dashed, however, when Roger, on his way to photocopy the documents in question, is knocked unconscious and the irrefutable, incriminating evidence is stolen.

The Renucci case is saved from this tough break when the unknown woman, who turns out to be a curator at the City of Paris archives, takes it upon herself to testify at the trial. Lallaoui's representation of archivist Brigitte Glenot is nothing short of heroic: Not only does she attempt to transmit information from the archives to Dadou and Roger, but when this fails, she agrees to speak out in court. Modeled on Brigitte Lainé, one of two employees of the Paris archives who came forward during the Einaudi-Papon libel trial, and whose testimony was crucial to its outcome, the Glenot character reproduces in the text a nearly verbatim transcription of Lainé's testimony.[56] The novel's references to actual documentary material essentially perform the missing archive by alluding to proof of the number of victims and citing actual statistics that confirm Renucci's statements (198–99). In exonerating Renucci from the libel charge, Glénot's testimony also liberates the "truth" of October 17 while at the same time implicitly accusing the state of orchestrating the repression of knowledge and suggesting to readers that the archives indeed contain the "smoking gun." Unlike Lécussan or Gerbet, Glenot is nonplussed by the judge's insinuation that her participation runs counter to deontological ethics. She is convinced that human rights must be defended even in the face of state collusion in their destruction.

Like *Meurtres*, *Une nuit d'octobre* gestures to missing evidence and alternatives to the police archives. Agnès, a law student and the daughter of a retired Parisian policeman, attends the "Renucci-Crapon" trial first out of curiosity, only to discover a personal connection to October 17. The testimony of Georges Leblanc, a journalist who recounts filming the violence on October 17 and having his camera seized and his film confiscated, triggers Agnès's memory:

Elle classait les diapositives des vacances d'été lorsqu'elle était tombée sur cette boîte ronde et rouillée. [...] Elle se rappelait, comme si c'était la

---

56 For a discussion on the real-life archivists, see nn. 19–22.

veille, avoir levé le ruban de vinyle tout contre l'ampoule poussière. Sur ces minuscules photogrammes, elle avait encore dans les yeux mouillés, la vision de cette masse de gens, qui semblait glisser dans la nuit en levant les mains. (156)

(She was organizing her vacation slides when she stumbled on the round, rusty canister. […] She remembered, as if it were yesterday, that she had held the vinyl strip up to the dusty light bulb. Teary at the thought of it, she could still see, in her mind's eye, those tiny photograms and the mass of humanity that seemed to slide through the night, hands in the air.)

Having met Dadou and learned about October 17, Agnès realizes that her father's colleague Serge Grantier was instrumental in the October 17 repression, and had hidden proof among her family photos. Agnès proposes to unearth the canister and deliver it for the Renucci trial, but Grantier has already retrieved his smoking gun. When Angès and Dadou try to recover the film from Grantier's apartment they end up in a high-speed chase through Paris that lands Agnès in the hospital with a concussion and results in Grantier's theft and destruction of the film.

This lost archive of images is irrecoverable, yet in its place Lallaoui invents an alternative archive, filmed by the same journalist whose 1961 footage was destroyed. When Leblanc is called to testify on behalf of Renucci, the need to provide proof reactivates in him the memory of the footage confiscated years prior.[57] The retired photojournalist thus sets about filming testimonials of October 17 in an attempt to fill the void of the stolen evidence: "Depuis l'annonce du procès, une soudaine lubie s'était emparée de lui. Il s'était fixé pour tâche d'enregistrer avec sa caméra DV 1000 tous ceux qu'il découvrirait ayant eu un lien avec octobre 61" (31–2, Ever since the trial was announced, he had been overcome by a sudden impulse: He'd set himself the task of using his video camera to record everyone he could find with a link to October 1961). The novel is thus punctuated by eight intercalated, "filmed" testimonials, titled with the names of the witnesses in question and narrated with the immediacy of direct discourse.[58] By textually representing filmed, first-hand accounts of victims, eyewitnesses, collaborators, and *refusnik* police officers, *Une*

57 The Leblanc character is likely based on Georges Azenstarck. (See Introduction, n. 39.)

58 The intercalated filmic portraits in Lallaoui's novel are reminiscent of a technique used in Sebbar's *La Seine était rouge* in which a fictional character, a young filmmaker, makes a documentary about October 17.

nuit d'octobre invents permanent traces of the experiences of a variety of individuals whose lives were touched by the massacre and its repression.

Despite what can only be classified as a Hollywood-style happy ending—a triumph of good over evil; a celebration of previously hidden knowledge now brought to light; a flourishing romance between Agnès and Dadou; and a dramatic reconciliation between victim and perpetrator (none other than Agnès's and Dadou's fathers)—*Une nuit d'octobre* remains true to its vocation as a realist novel (or, more precisely, as a novel invested in representing the events of a certain reality). And yet, by staging Roger reading the documents and by ventriloquizing Lainé's testimony, the text speculates on and represents (however briefly) elements of the archive, figuring its actual contents as indisputable evidence of the scale of the massacre.

Archives and archival material are also at the heart of Gérard Streiff's *Les caves de la Goutte d'or* (The Cellars of the Goutte d'or), a quest narrative in which the protagonist, a young reporter and PhD candidate in history named Chloé, ends up investigating the October 17 repression.[59] Early in the novel, Chloé receives a tip that determines the course of her research and the narrative itself: In a brown paper envelope addressed to her, Chloé finds an old tract: "Deux feuillets, recto verso, imprimées sur un paper jauni, dont les bords commençaient à s'effriter. Le texte, dactylographié, était intitule: 'Un groupe de policiers républicains déclare'" (16, two pages, double-sided, printed on old, yellowed paper whose edges were beginning to fray. The typed text was titled "A group of Republican police officers declares"). Excerpts from this authentic tract—dated October 31, 1961, and written by a group of Parisian police outraged by the behavior of their colleagues on October 17— are reproduced (ostensibly verbatim) and interspersed with glosses, summaries, and Chloé's reaction to the material.

Like the other "romances of the archive," *Les caves* deploys archives in ways that are occasionally suggestive and symbolic rather than directly related to the classified October 17 archives. While the archival material inspires Chloé's research, her investigation advances primarily through interviews and conversations with her former lover, current best friend, and primary source of historical information: an archivist named Antoine Cavaignac. Once assigned to an important position

---

59 Gérard Streiff, *Les caves de la Goutte d'or* (Paris: Éditions Baleine, 2001). The novel has not been translated into English; all translations from the French are my own.

within the French National Archives, having authored an incendiary essay titled "Ces archives qu'on vous cache" (19, The Archives Hidden from You)—a tract denouncing the so-called rules restricting access to and consultation of sensitive dossiers—Cavaignac finds himself professionally disgraced and demoted to the rank of "gardien des enfers," or gatekeeper of hell, where the "hell" in question is the nickname given to the reading room devoted to formerly banned books at the National Library.[60]

Like the real-life archivists Lainé and Grand, Cavaignac places "sa conscience civique au-dessus de sa conscience professionnelle" (20, his civic duty above his professional conscience). In addition to his ethically motivated but insubordinate essay, he had revealed classified documents proving the Nazi past of a highly placed state actor (a thinly disguised reference to Papon). Depicted as a principled archivist, Cavaignac is nonetheless a character whose odd sexual proclivities make him something of an archive romance anti-hero; at one point Chloé feels compelled to defend him as eccentric but not a pervert, a troubling denial that makes Cavaignac a potentially unsavory character. Understood symbolically rather than literally, however, these details about the archivist's inclinations may refract the various fears, conspiracies, and rumors about archival management in France at the time of the novel's publication in 2001.

Les caves de la Goutte d'or also uses archival sites as touchstones throughout the text. Chloé lives, literally, in "Les Archives" (an area of the Marais neighborhood), and is a *habituée* (regular) of the nearby CARAN, or National Archives, where she spends hours "à attendre, febrile, des 'cartons' qu'allaient quérir des employés indolents; à découvrir avec une émotion recommencée les 'papiers' apportés; à contribuer à la mise au jour d'histoires oubliées" (31, waiting, feverishly, for the 'boxes' that lazy employees had gone to fetch; discovering with new zeal the 'documents' that they delivered; making forgotten histories known).[61] Her archival bliss is only interrupted by the occasional frustration when "la police de la mémoire lui faisait savoir que tel document ne pouvait être consulté" (32, the memory police decided that a certain document could not be consulted). While

60 The title of Cavaignac's fictional essay is undoubtedly inspired by Sonia Combe's *Archives interdites*, which made similar accusations.
61 The CARAN is the Centre d'accueil et de recherche des archives nationales, or the National Archive Research Center.

the vocabulary of the feverish wait and the possibility of frustration evoke Keen's notions of the archive as a site of libidinal investment, and the mention of classified documents underscores, albeit subtly, very real concerns about transparency and state secrets, what is even more interesting about the two paragraphs devoted to Chloé's "archive stories" is the brief paragraph that interrupts them. Although not completely nondiegetic, the paragraph sits awkwardly in its context, seemingly unmotivated by action or context:

> [...] elle était passé un jour sur une écluse, non loin de chez elle : on procédait à la réfection d'un canal. Avec la décrue des eaux, l'apparition progressive d'une étrange faune aquatique, carcasses de voitures ou de vélos, mobiliers disparates, restes de divers larcins, était un spectacle trivial dont elle ne se lassait pas. (32)

> ([...] one day she was walking over the locks not far from her house, the canal was being cleaned out. As the waters receded, the strangest aquatic fauna began to appear: carcasses of cars or bikes, odd bits of furniture, the ill-gotten goods from robberies gone awry. Chloé never tired of this trivial spectacle.)

Sandwiched between archive stories of pleasure and frustration, this brief episode can be read as a sidelong critique of archival practices and politics, with "access" to the canal's contents only occasional, regulated by state institutions and according to the vagaries of municipal decisions regarding the cleanup of the capital's waterways. More to the point, however, the canal also played a role in October 17, when its waters would have hidden not stolen cars but stolen lives.

If the passing mention of the canal's hidden contents seems to borrow a trope from Daeninckx by encouraging readers to identify quotidian elements as sources of information about history, knowledge, and state power, references in *Les caves* to actual archival materials hew closer to the representations found in *Une nuit d'octobre*. Published in the same year, Lallaoui's novel and *Les caves* both evince a greater awareness of details found in the classified police archives, perhaps due to the contemporary conjuncture: By 2001, even if the archives remained largely inaccessible, a certain amount of information had certainly trickled into the public domain. Yet the two works treat their source material differently: While Lallaoui does not cite the real documents to which it alludes, *Les caves*, in keeping with the ethos of the "Polarchives" series in which it was published, signals its archival basis through footnotes and appendices. Moreover, all material taken from archival sources is printed in small caps in the text, thus differentiating it from the fictional narrative thread. The appendix gives detailed information on the provenance of all cited materials, and reprints in its entirety the key document featured in the novel, the officers' tract that inspires Chloé's quest.

Unlike the previous novels, the narrative of Eric Michel's Algerian War saga *Algérie! Algérie!* (2007) is not based on investigation. It does, however, refer to and represent archives in a variety of ways that resonate with the notion of the "romance of the archive," most notably, perhaps, in its use of the physical setting of the *salle des archives*, or records room, at the Police Prefecture as the stage for its violent denouement. The novel is also structured as a quest—for truth, for a murderer, ultimately, for justice. *Algérie! Algérie!* is a tale of two brothers, Amar and Tahar: The former is an FLN fighter, devoted to the cause of a free Algeria; the latter, a *Harki*, has gone to work for the French, defending their presence in Algeria and, in Paris, actively tracking and torturing FLN operatives.[62] The brothers' trajectories are woven together with the story of Amar's daughter, Nedjma, exiled in Paris and believing that her father was killed in Algeria, and the tale of her boyfriend, Léo, a French Jew whose father died in Auschwitz and who has become an FLN sympathizer and *porteur de valise*. As the action moves, like the war, from Algeria to the center of Paris, the conflict between nations is allegorized in the struggle between brothers.

As a novel whose action is contemporaneous with the demonstration and repression on October 17—indeed, the plot comes to a head on the 17th and ends shortly thereafter—the representation of archives necessarily functions differently than it does in texts like *Meurtres*, *Une nuit d'octobre*, or *Les caves*, novels whose retrospective viewpoints allow for a certain amount of knowledge about the fate of the police archives. Set in 1961, *Algérie! Algérie!* cannot realistically contend with issues of archival access and deferred knowledge; it is, however, infused with historical hindsight by virtue of operations that mobilize

---

62   The term *harki*, derived from the Arabic *haraka*, meaning movement, refers to Algerians who served in the French Army during the war for independence (both in Algeria and later in metropolitan France). The story of the *Harkis*, now often considered synonymous with treason or collaboration with the enemy, is complex and often tragic. For an excellent history of this particular group and its post-war abandonment on both sides of the Mediterranean, see Vincent Crapanzo, *The Harkis: The Wound That Never Heals* (Chicago: Chicago University Press, 2011).

the archive as a symbolic space. Nedjma and Léo, who have identified Papon as the author of their personal tragedies, plot to assassinate him using the October 17 demonstration as cover. That night, as the couple clandestinely enters the Prefecture, the courtyard has already become a scene of terrible violence where police officers, hidden from public scrutiny, unleash rage upon their Algerian captives in a scene that has been established as authentic.[63] Narrative focus pans from Léo and Nedjma to the violence in the courtyard, to the point of view of a third character, an archivist observing the scene: "Guy Cochard assiste, depuis le soupirail, à leur arrêt dans la cour d'isolement [...] Il est seul ce soir aux archives. Il a fermé les portes à clé et observe les mouvements, prenant des notes maladroites avec sa main gantée, alors qu'on frappe à l'accès d'acier" (470, From a tiny window, Guy Cochard watches the arrest of Algerians in the interior courtyard [...] Tonight he is alone in the archives. He has locked all the doors and is observing the movements, taking clumsy notes with his gloved left hand, while in the courtyard steel blows fall).

In the context of a novel about an event that will be repressed in public memory and political discourse, and whose archival traces were still classified at the time the novel was published, the deployment of archivist characters (Guy is joined by a colleague, Armand, who is described as "tapi dans le noir de la salle des archives," or crouched in the darkness of the archives, 473) observing the massacre in the courtyard from their hidden position *in the records room* is an unmistakable invitation to interpretation. This scene is one of densely significant, historically informed foreshadowing: The archives—the space where documents are held and classified, and the future repository of October 17 "evidence"— are situated in close physical proximity to the violent repression. Here, the scene of the physical crime and the scene of the epistemological crime are one and the same, with the archivists witnessing from above the sadistic violence of police repression in the courtyard of the very seat of power, a site officially symbolic of the protection of citizens and democracy. Guy and Armand eventually leave the space of the actual archives to create alternative records of the massacre: When they go to the editorial offices of *France Observateur* to report what they have witnessed, they encounter there a small phalanx of outraged policemen

---

63 See "La manifestation du FLN à Paris le 17 octobre 1961: le témoignage du lieutenant-colonel Montaner," *Guerres mondiales et conflits contemporains* 206, no. 2 (2002): 87–93; and Haroun.

determined to go on the record about the abuses they, too, have seen in the courtyard and in the streets of Paris. The actions of Guy and Armand speak to the notion of the "ethical archivist," while also foreshadowing the difficulty that would arise in consulting the police archives and using them to create a narrative of the events of October 17.

Algérie! Algérie! is rife with actual historical documentation that lends authenticity and ballast to the historical fiction. Michel may have been able to obtain a special dispensation to consult the October 17 police archives, but it would not have been necessary: By 2007 all of the documentation reproduced in the text (some of which is not directly related to October 17) would have been in circulation via networks outside of the state's control, including the Wuillaume Report on torture in Algeria (which we observe then-President René Coty reading quite early in the novel), and the anonymous police tract, whose creation is witnessed by Guy and Armand when they leave the archives in order to report what they have seen at the editorial offices of *France Observateur*.[64] Michel also reproduces excerpts from various tracts distributed by the FLN and the OAS (Organisation armée secrète, or Secret Army Organization, a French terrorist organization active during the Algerian War).[65]

As in *Les caves*, the use of *realia* in *Algérie!* is signaled by a change in typeface and size, but this distinction is complicated by the fact that fictitious letters exchanged between characters also appear in the font reserved for archival material. Such a slippage in the presentation of "historical evidence" is further complicated by the inclusion, at the end of the novel, of a section titled "Selected Bibliography and Filmography." Here, alphabetical order removes distinctions of genre and method: Fiction, film, documentary, and historiography are all on equal footing, with none claiming more authenticity or authority than another. No distinction is made, for example, between *La Seine était rouge*, Ali Haroun's *La 7e wilaya*, and Saïd's *Culture and Imperialism*, and the lack of footnotes or other bibliographic apparatus makes it impossible to understand how the author has mobilized the selected sources. Moreover, the list does not mention any archival material, despite its obvious inclusion.

---

64 The Wuillaume Report, dated March 2, 1955, was considered damning. See Jean-Pierre Rioux, "Torture: l'état coupable mais amnestié," *Libération*, December 11, 2000. Portions of the report are reproduced in the novel; see 20–24.
65 See page 378, for example.

Pondering the bibliography at the end of *Algérie! Algérie!* reveals an interesting phenomenon: the frequency with which more recent October 17 works reference earlier works from the anarchive. Such a gesture suggests that first- and second-wave fictions (and earlier third-wave texts) may have taken on the aura of "archival" documents, or at the very least, of primary (read: historiographical) material.[66] Descriptions found in *Algérie! Algérie!*, for example, of anonymous letters from doctors working at the city morgue (341) were previously fictionalized in Jean-François Vilar's 1986 *Bastille tango* (although that novel is not mentioned in the bibliography). Conversely, the novels by Streiff, Sebbar, Daeninckx, and Lallaoui are all cited in the bibliography, and while the reader would be hard-pressed to identify them as source material, it is impossible not to wonder whether Michel's reference to the anonymous police tract leads not to the archives but to the novels that preceded his. Such notions may complicate the functioning of the anarchive in interesting ways, as it begins to feed upon itself and potentially signal types of operations and statuses to which it cannot necessarily lay claim.

The representation of history, be it evenemential or archival, is obviously a key facet of this project, and the questions it raises are neither unique to the "romances of the archive" found in the October 17 corpus, nor are they even limited to this particular chapter. Yet, as I have mentioned before, I am less interested in verifiable authenticity than in how recourse to the real and to indexical documents functions in the anarchive. And so it seems apt to conclude these "Archive Stories" with a discussion of the repeated representation of the police tract titled "Un group de policiers républicains declare..." (A Group of Republican Police Officers Declares...), which we have seen now, to varying degrees of transparency, in *Une nuit d'octobre*, *Les caves*, and *Algérie! Algérie!*

Comparative reading across the third wave of the anarchive reveals a curious trajectory in the representation of "A Group Declares..."— the archival document perhaps most often cited in October 17 cultural productions and, thus, the most common "archive story" told in the anarchive. We encounter it for the first time in *La Seine était rouge* (1999)—a novel coterminous with the Papon-Einaudi libel trial and the beginning of a particularly fraught period about the knowledge of the archive. Here the reference to the whistle-blowers' document is

---

66 *La Seine était rouge* is dedicated to several anarchival works that preceded Sebbar's, including *Meurtres pour mémoire* and *Octobre à Paris*.

allusive but unmistakable: In the testimony of a character called "le flic de Clichy" (121–22, "the cop at Clichy," 107–8), the police officer recounts that he had no connection to the Resistance during World War II; he even notes that he had only been on the police force for two years at the time of the events. He also mentions that he doesn't really like Arabs. His youth, his relatively recent start on the job, and his political positioning seem to make him an unlikely signatory of the actual document. But the "flic de Clichy" adds that he was "not the only one who witnessed it" (107), and this fictional version thus speculates on the potential for a more mixed, diverse group of policemen to have protested the actions of their comrades on the night in question. Indeed, the document itself mentions the *divergences* (or differences of opinion) within the group, but without offering detail as to their nature.[67]

As in the Sebbar novel, in Lallaoui's *Une nuit d'octobre* the document is referenced, although not cited directly: The character Émile Lopner—introduced as a witness in the Crapon-Rennucci libel trial—is a former police officer described as being "à l'origine du tract des policiers qu'on a appelés républicains" (189, the instigator of the tract written by the officers who came to be called the republicans). Unlike the "flic de Clichy," Lopner identifies himself as an "veteran of the resistance" whose ethical motivations have deep roots:

> Le 17 octobre, de nombreux camarades en service, dans les commissariats ou sur le voie publique, furent témoins des ratonnnades et des meurtres de cette nuit-là. Nous étions révoltés, car beaucoup d'entre nous avaient eu affaire à la Gestapo. C'était inadmissible de voir des Français agir de la même façon. (189–90)

> (On October 17, many of our colleagues on duty, in police stations and on the street, bore witness to racially motivated violence and murder. We were horrified because many of us had dealt with the Gestapo. It was unacceptable to see French officers acting the same way.)

---

67   The original document makes no specific mention of Resistance activities of the signatories, although the conclusion does connect the activities of 1961 to the Vichy years: "Nous avons trop souffert de la conduite de certains des nôtres pendant l'occupation allemande" (During the German occupation, the behavior of some of our colleagues caused us great suffering). Manceron, *Textes de l'époque*, 91.

Without citing the tract directly, Lopner's testimony summarizes its main ideological points.

Other novels reference the "Groupe de policiers" document more transparently. In *Les caves*, as mentioned earlier, the tract spurs Chloé's investigation, with excerpts reproduced verbatim in the novel, and the entire document reprinted in the appendix. Works such as *Algérie! Algérie!* and the film *Nuit noire*, however, produce a speculative origin story for the tract. In Michel's novel, Guy and Armand not only observe the group of police officers giving an account of the events so that "ces morts aient une voix" (477, the dead may have a voice), they are also responsible for sending the text to President de Gaulle. Reproduced in its entirety, the letter is read by a nonplussed de Gaulle, for whom "these abuses are regrettable" but will "soon be forgotten"—a reflection reminiscent of de Gaulle's reported comment on the events of October 17 as "secondary but unacceptable" (482–84).

The docudrama *Nuit noire*, which recreates the tense atmosphere of October 1961, as well as the demonstration, its repression, and reactions on the part of the police, the press, and the Algerian community, also stages the genesis of the letter.[68] Toward the end of the film, we bear witness to one officer struggling with his conscience, only to be called "worse than a collabo" by his colleagues. Several scenes later, in an episode bearing the time stamp "20 October 1961," an officer enters the editorial offices of an unnamed newspaper and announces his difficult mission "to denounce his colleagues."

The tract referenced in these five anarchival works is indeed the real letter authored by disheartened Parisian police officers. Written in the name of a Republican duty to "salvage the honor of the Paris police and of France" and to denounce the illegal violence to which they were witness, the four-page, single-spaced document is a litany of horrors perpetrated by rank-and-file police but also an indictment of the state.[69] Although it has always been described as an "anonymous tract," Émile Portzer,

---

68 Directed by Alain Tasma, *Nuit noire 17 octobre 1961* is a made-for-TV historical film produced by Canal+. It aired on France 3 in 2005 and enjoyed a limited release in movie theatres.

69 In this regard, the text states: "Nous ne pouvons pas croire que cela se produise sous la seule autorité de Monsieur le Préfet. Le ministre de l'intérieur, le chef d'état lui-même, ne peuvent pas les ignorer, au moins dans leur ampleur" (We cannot believe that this would happen as a result of the Prefect's authority alone. The Minister of the Interior, even the head of state himself, cannot possibly ignore these events, at least not their scale). Manceron, *Textes de l'époque*, 90–91.

a Communist militant who had been illegally expelled from the police force, is said to be the author.[70] The document is archived in the "H" series of the police archives; however, it is clear that this particular tract slipped the bonds of state censorship, becoming a work of *samizdat* even as it was consigned to police archives that remained classified for decades (sources mention hundreds and thousands of copies).[71] The text has since been republished in numerous venues, both in popular (magazines such as *Pour!* and *L'Humanité Dimanche*) and in specialized (the 2000 edition of Péju's *Ratonnades* and *Le 17 octobre 1961 par les textes de l'époque*). It is also available on various websites, including the sites of the MRAP, *Au nom de la mémoire*, and *Le Monde*, which provides a downloadable PDF file that is a facsimile of the archival document.

The ways these various fictionalized accounts do and do not reinforce each other, and their respective departures from the original document, are worthy of note. At the beginning of the third wave (in 1999), at a moment when the tract would have been available in various forms, including on the internet, the discrepancies regarding its creation and appearance are striking. *Algérie! Algérie!* situates the tract's origins in the heat of the action, on the very night of October 17; *Nuit noire* dates the police revelations to several days later. And yet we are able to verify that the tract was signed on October 31, 1961. In *Les caves*, set more than 30 years later, the tract takes on the allure of an ancient artifact: yellowed, its edges are beginning to wear, and its fragility is underscored by the fact that it is delivered in a plastic sleeve. This description gives the document the air of gravitas one might associate with an authentic artifact. That it appears to be old lends it a sense of immediate connection to the era in question, endowing it with the authority of a smoking gun, despite the fact the author might well have discovered it on the internet.[72]

Any of the works citing this document, then, could have located it without permission to consult the archival materials held by the police, and perhaps its very availability is the key factor in this "archive story." Simply stated, the most often recounted story of archives in the

70   House and MacMaster, 146, n. 45. In order to cover his tracks, Portzer apparently threw the typewriter he used to write the tract into the Seine.

71   For a history of the tract and the divisions within the police force, see Blanchard's epilogue in *Police parisienne*. See also Berlière, *Le monde des polices en France, XIX–XX siècles* (Paris: Éditions Complexe, 1996), 222.

72   In the novel's appendix, Streiff notes that he obtained the full text from the version printed in *L'Humanité Dimanche* 398, October 30, 1997.

anarchive pivots on a document that didn't need to wait until 2011 to be made available to the public. But it is also critical to consider the content of the text and its authorship, for indeed, even if this is one of the few texts that circulated outside the frontiers tightly patrolled by the archons, it is also perhaps the only document that looks anything like conclusive evidence of a state crime. In this tract, the eyewitnesses to the violence are not only bystanders, they are members of the brotherhood, colleagues of the very same individuals engaged in a brutal and bloody massacre. Whereas the inclusion of an FLN document might have held a whiff of conspiracy or over-determinism, the fact of policemen (particularly former members of the Resistance) reporting the crimes of their own, at some personal risk to themselves, carries more historical ballast, more gravitas, and more drama.

———

Pierre Nora's observation that "Modern memory is first of all archival," relying "exclusively on the specificity of the trace, the materiality of the vestige,"[73] is troubled by the October 17 anarchive: by its existence, which shows that memory may be first of all something other than archival; and by its contents, which refer to and deploy archives in ways that underscore their importance while at the same time revealing the ways in which their signification is thwarted. The October 17 anarchive constitutes a collection of traces that refer to real past events and participate in the production of knowledge about those events, particularly in the absence of the official archive. That knowledge, moreover, need not be exclusively historical; it may also concern subjective and aesthetic experiences related to October 17, its repression, and the transmission of knowledge about the massacre.

"Romances of the archive" activate the hidden archives not only by revealing their very existence, but also by speculating on their contents and staging the subjective, if thwarted, experience of their use. Beyond the fact and function of such representations, which draw the reader's attention to and circumscribe an egregious absence and its epistemological implications, these novels also point us elsewhere, gesturing to

73 Pierre Nora, "Between Memory and History," in *Realms of Memory: Construction of the French Past,* ed. Lawrence Kritzman (New York: Columbia University Press, 1996), 8.

the possibility that knowledge resides in other institutional repositories. Be it Roger Thiraud's unfinished Drancy monograph (in *Meurtres*) or Georges Leblanc's collection of filmed testimonies (in *Une nuit d'octobre*), both novels counter the absence of the "official story" by pointing to the existence of the numerous rogue archives available to the historian, the researcher, the investigator, the reader.

Indeed, *Meurtres pour mémoire, Une nuit d'octobre, Les caves de la Goutte d'or,* and *Algérie! Algérie!* suggest that archives are all around us, unguarded by archons who would limit our access or impose a single interpretation. At the same time that these texts underscore the existence of alternative archives, they also embody them; that is, the novels themselves operate as repositories where myriad elements are brought into contact with one another, caught up in a synchronic but non-hierarchical web that is available for hermeneutical activity.

Beyond their representation of the October 17 archives—official or otherwise—as nodal points in a broader history of institutionalized forgetting and its concomitant political discourse, and in addition to their archival function, the novels also offer up "archive stories": narratives that tell us, to varying degrees, "how archives are created, drawn upon, and experienced."[74] Even in instances where the experience is one of lack or absence, such stories are not incidental to knowledge, or even to knowledge about the archive; they are critical to a more complete understanding of how a particular set of archives has functioned during a period of time when its contents have not been allowed to signify. Whether or not we espouse Mbembe's problematic assertion that archives "have no meaning outside the subjective experience of those individuals who, at a given moment, come to use them," it is certainly true that literary representation of the subjective experience of archives has constituted one of the few ways in which the October 17 archives, prior to 2011, could be made visible to a broad public.[75] The novels, then, not only fill in missing pieces of the historical narrative, they also provide readers with precisely that "subjective experience" presumably reserved for, but in fact denied, the would-be archival researcher.

74 Burton, 6.
75 Mbembe, 24.

CHAPTER THREE

Non-lieux de mémoire

Maps and Graffiti in the Scriptable City

> The city…is in itself an archive of memory,
> from which the storyteller can pluck endless objects,
> symbols and traces to develop a narrative,
> utilizing the "teeming archive" of his inward eye.[1]
> —Ciaran Carson

During the weeks following the massacre on October 17, 1961, if you happened to be wandering the streets of Paris at night or in the early morning hours, you might have come upon a peculiar slogan spray-painted, in black or white letters, along the side of a bridge or on a balustrade overlooking the Seine. The graffiti declared "Ici on noie les Algériens" (Here we drown Algerians). By the next day, however, the inscription would have disappeared, revealing only a clean, blank surface. In a tense rondo of declaration and repression (of outcry and censorship), surfaces in the heart of the city were tagged, scrubbed clean by municipal authorities, and tagged again, as anonymous activists sought to make visible, and *legible*, an event whose history was quite literally being erased as quickly as it was being written. While the lifespan of each tag was limited, each one surviving only a few hours before being whitewashed, the gesture itself nonetheless constituted a tenacious bid to inscribe the massacre onto the planes of the city, to etch its trace on the very urban landscape that had witnessed the crime.[2]

---

1 Ciaran Carson, *The Star Factory* (London: Granta, 1997), 80.

2 See Lemire and Potin. For personal recollections of members of the group who may have been responsible for the graffiti, see Arthur Adamov, *Ici et maintenant* (Paris: Gallimard, 1964) and Jean-Michel Mension, *Le temps gage. Aventures politiques et artistiques d'un irrégulier à Paris* (Paris: Noésis, 2001).

That cities bear intentional, physical traces of their histories is a commonplace, one that is perhaps made most obvious in twenty-first-century European capitals, which both valorize existing historical sites (the catacombs in Paris, for example, or the Brandenburg Gate in Berlin) and produce material, visible recognitions of the past in the form of memorials, monuments, commemorative plaques, and named thoroughfares. There is also a long history of thinking about the city as text, as an "immense texturology" (de Certeau); as a palimpsest (Huyssen, Mongin); or as a "space of signs where no materiality remains un-semiotized" (Stierle).[3] In the case of October 17, however, reading Paris has been a fraught endeavor from the very beginning: the graffito mentioned above—the first October 17 text, after all—was radically edited by the state, setting the tone for the fate of future inscriptions. How, then, do we read a city when important passages of its narrative have been deleted, when key elements of its history have not found purchase in its urban landscape? How do we "semiotize" signs that have been erased, or account for missing layers of a palimpsest?

One city-thinker's textual musings provide a useful model. Roland Barthes has written amply on the city as text, calling it a discourse, "a writing," and suggesting that the user of the city is a reader.[4] But in all his metaphorical glossing of the city as text and language, Barthes was apparently never tempted to leverage his literary distinctions of *lisible* (readerly) and *scriptible* (writerly/scriptable) in service of a reading of urban space. Of course, the sorting of all literature along these two models was never, for Barthes, anything like a thoroughgoing program, and if his notion of the *texte lisible* is elucidated through example, the *scriptible* remains abstract and conceptually thorny. Barthes never so much defines *le scriptible* as he sketches it impressionistically, calling it "a

3   Walter Benjamin, *Arcades Project* (Cambridge, MA: Harvard University Press, 1999), 416; Michel de Certeau, *The Practice of Everyday Life*, trans. Stephen Rendall (Berkeley: University of California Press, 1984), 91–92; Andreas Huyssen, *Present Pasts: Urban Palimpsests and the Politics of Memory* (Stanford, CA: Stanford University Press, 2003), 7; Olivier Mognin, *La condition urbaine, la ville à l'heure de la mondialisation* (Paris: Seuil, 2005 [2007]), 50; Karlheinz Stierle, *La Capitale des signes. Paris et son discours*, trans. Marianne Rocher-Jacquin (Paris: Éditions de la Maison des sciences de l'homme, 2001), 3.

4   Roland Barthes, "Semiology and the Urban," in *Rethinking Architecture: A Reader in Cultural Theory*, ed. Neil Leach (New York: Routledge, 1997), 170. Citation in French from *L'aventure sémiologique* (Paris: Seuil, 1985).

perpetual present," or "ourselves writing."[5] As Thomas Pavel has noted, *le scriptible* for Barthes is an ideal, not a practice.[6] Such complexities notwithstanding, mobilizing these broad distinctions as a lens through which to think the city-as-text is a fruitful exercise—particularly so in the case of the Paris produced by October 17.

To consider the city-text as either *lisible* or *scriptible*, we might boil down Barthes's categories in this way: Readerly texts signify transparently and allow the reader to remain passive, whereas writerly/ scriptable texts destabilize and multiply meaning, creating a reader who is "no longer a consumer [...] but a producer."[7] For example, when it comes to the First and Second World Wars, to the Commune, or to the nation's monarchic past, the text that is Paris is plainly *lisible*. Here, I use the term denotatively—Paris is *readable*, able to be read and understood, but also in its Barthesian sense—Paris is *readerly*, a "classic text": Its codes are recognizable, their meaning is fixed, and the text communicates transparently with its "reader," who can passively take it in. To see the pertinence of Barthes's term in this context, we have only to conjure a mental image of the French capital's *axe historique*—that parade of monumental architecture running east to west from the *cour carrée* of the Louvre to La Grande Arche de la Défense—and overlay it with Barbara Johnson's gloss of the readerly as "irreversible, natural, decidable, continuous, totalisable, and unified into a coherent whole based on the signified."[8]

Yet with respect to October 17, Paris ceases to be *lisible*, instead becoming distinctly *illegible*: The city bears only the faintest traces of the event and its afterlives; few if any signs attest to the nature of the repression or the lives lost. Nonetheless, we might also understand this text as scriptable, insofar as it impels, even requires, the reader's participation in its creation. After all, the margins of the city-text have much to reveal if one is willing to look away from the memorialscape of the *axe historique*—if one is prepared to abandon the comfort of

---

5   Barthes also writes that *le scriptible* is "not a thing; we would have a hard time finding it in a bookstore." Barthes, *S/Z*, trans. Richard Miller (New York: Farrar, Straus and Giroux, 1974), 5.

6   Thomas Pavel, "S/Z: utopie et ascèse," *Communications*, 63 (1996): 159–74.

7   Barthes, *S/Z*, 4.

8   Barbara Johnson, "The Critical Difference: BartheS/BalZac," in *The Critical Difference: Essays in the Contemporary Rhetoric of Reading* (Baltimore: Johns Hopkins University Press, 1978), 5–6.

standard codes, conventions, and completeness. As I have been arguing about October 17's traces more generally, those left on the city by the massacre have also been displaced into the realm of representation, that is, into the realm of the anarchive. Already in 1961, for example, a photo sequence in Panijel's *Octobre à Paris*—a five-minute, non-verbal succession of black-and-white images that show the demonstrators in recognizable locales throughout Paris—provides a distinctly *sited* representation of Algerians within the space of the capital. Later, in the early texts of the second wave, Daeninckx and Kettane both open their novels with descriptions of October 17 rich in Parisian toponyms, choreographing characters moving through the city on the night of the massacre. And in Lallaoui's *Les Beurs de Seine*, a novel set two decades after the massacre, one character remembers and remarks upon the event's particular disposition within the city: "The assassinations of October 1961 *in the very center of Paris* have completely disappeared from collective memory, as if none of the dead had ever been killed."[9]

This chapter is interested in exploring the intersection of spatial practices, the representation of urban space, and the way both of these interact with the visibility of October 17 and its inscriptions (or lack thereof) on the city. I suggest that the anarchive produces a *scriptable* Paris—one that is opaque rather than transparent, and that demands an energetic engagement on the part of its reader. I begin in the contemporary moment with a discussion of current policies concerning the representation of October 17 in the Parisian memorialscape. Then, traveling back in time to October 1961, the chapter explores the spatial politics of the demonstration and its representation, teasing out a cartographic impulse that connects up with both earlier colonial technologies of mapping and representation, and that emerges, later, as a trope in the anarchive (notably in documentary film). Then, jumping firmly into the post-facto representations of October 17, I explore the ways the anarchive has represented October 17 and the particular space of Paris through revisionist cartography, pop- or counter-cultural subversive tactics such as graffiti, and rogue spatial practices. Like the original graffiti, "Ici on noie les Algériens," the works of the anarchive have revised Paris by writing on it (literally and figuratively), participating in the creation of an open narrative.

9   Mehdi Lallaoui, *Les Beurs de Seine* (Paris: Arcantère, 1986), 159; emphasis mine.

Sign-Posting the City and the Politics of Memory in Paris

Pierre Nora once remarked that he was struck by "the absence of visible traces" of the colonial experience in the French collective consciousness, particularly given its weight and importance.[10] There has been no shortage of criticism surrounding the lack of attention to imperialism and its aftermath in Nora's vast multivolume project to catalog French national memory, and the omissions of *Les lieux de mémoire* with regard to colonialism are now something of a minor legend in certain academic and intellectual circles. Writing in 1993, Nora may have been incorrect about the absence of visible traces of colonialism broadly construed, but it was certainly true that the Parisian memorialscape at that time contained no monuments, streets, or metro stations dedicated to the memory of the Algerian victims of the October 17 repression.[11] Today, though, a handful of gestures—commemorative plaques, a "17 octobre" square in Aubervilliers, a "Fatima Bédar Park" in Saint-Denis, and ephemeral interventions into the memorialscape—do attempt to inscribe the event on the city. Yet the visibility of these notations is complicated by a variety of factors (political and topographical), and the text they produce, insofar as it requires deciphering, is decidedly a scriptable one.

Inserting October 17 into the network of Parisian "lieux de mémoire" is a political gesture often met with significant political opposition. In 2007, for example, activists proposed to name the new Asnières-Gennevilliers metro station "17 octobre 1961."[12] During a week devoted to anti-colonial action and happenings, a collective led by Mourad Slimani unofficially baptized the station, hanging a sign with the new name conforming to the RATP iconography.[13] A public statement was

---

10 Nora, "Les Lieux de mémoire," interview, Pierre Kerleroux and Hubert Tison, *Historiens et géographes* 340 (May–June 1993): 358.
11 I borrow the term "memorialscape" from Gillian Carr, "Examining the Memorialscape of Occupation and Liberation, a study from the Channel Islands," *International Journal of Heritage Studies* 18, no. 2 (March 2012): 174–93.
12 The station is on line 13, which travels north and south through the western half of Paris, and currently runs from Châtillon-Montrouge to Asnières/Gennevilliers/Les Courtilles and to Saint-Denis-Université.
13 Mourad Slimani is journalist and activist with various associations devoted to educating the public about the history of colonialism. A bid to name the new station had been in the works long before the event in 2007. RATP stands for *Régie Autonome des Transports Parisiens* (Autonomous Parisian Transportation Administration).

read: "Inscrire la mémoire des événements du 17 Octobre 1961 dans l'espace public à travers une station de métro, ce serait reconnaître cette mémoire comme partie intégrante de la mémoire nationale" (To inscribe the memory of the events of October 17, 1961, on the public space by naming a subway station would be to recognize this memory as an integral part of national memory). In a petition to have the name officially changed, Slimani pointed out the irony of the absence of visible traces: "Dans la ville où se sont en partie déroulés les massacres du 17 Octobre 1961, se construisent deux stations de métro dans le cadre de l'extension de la ligne 13. Aujourd'hui, aucun monument, aucun signe distinctif ne fait référence à ces évènements tragiques qui s'y sont déroulés" (In the city where part of the October 17, 1961 massacres took place, two subway stations are being constructed as part of the extension of Line 13. Today, no monument, no distinctive sign testifies to the tragic events that took place there).[14]

Although the station itself did not exist in 1961, the chosen site was symbolic on several levels: Maghrebi immigrants or descendants of immigrants make up a large portion of the population of Asnières-Gennevilliers; while this metro was not a site of violence on October 17, police violence in subway stations that night is a documented fact, and this adds important symbolic weight to the memorial capacity of a named station; and, finally, the RATP has a long history of naming stations for important historical moments, such as battles (Austerlitz, Stalingrad, Bir Hakeim) or commemorative dates (La Courneuve—8 mai 1945). The RATP's official response to the request was a resounding no, arguing that a long and complicated name such as "17 octobre 1961" did not conform to the agency's charter, which purportedly prefers station names that are "simple et le plus court possible" (simple and as short as possible), a logic that begs disbelief, as one immediately considers that existing station names, such as "La Courneuve—8 mai 1945," are no simpler than "17 Octobre 1961," and that the new station's ultimate name, "Asnières-Gennevilliers-Les Courtilles," is not particularly short.[15]

14   Slimani's long letter to the RATP can be found here: http://anticolonial.free.fr/IMG/pdf/CourrierRATP-2.pdf. While undated, the letter clearly preceded the unofficial renaming ceremony in October 2007.
15   The RATP's response, dated October 2, 2006, can be found here: http://anticolonial.free.fr/IMG/pdf/Reponse_RATP.pdf. For a discussion of the attempts to inscribe October 17 on the Parisian memorialscape, see Clotilde Lebas, "Au fil

Other attempts at writing October 17 into the urban text of Paris have been more successful. In 2001, the mayors of Paris and the northern suburb of Aubervilliers (Bertrand Delanoë and Jack Ralite, respectively) became the first municipal leaders to brave the political turbulence associated with official recognition of the event.[16] In solemn ceremonies on the 40th anniversary of the massacre, both mayors inaugurated plaques bearing identical inscriptions: "À la mémoire des nombreux Algériens tués lors de la répression sanglante de la manifestation pacifique du 17 octobre 1961" (In memory of the numerous Algerians killed during the bloody repression of the peaceful demonstration on October 17, 1961). Ten years later, similar gestures of commemoration were made by mayors of Bezons, Clichy-la-Garenne, and Colombes, all cities in the *banlieue* with large populations of North African origin (and often with Communist mayors).[17] While the establishment of such memorials attests to a desire to inscribe October 17 on Paris, and by extension in French history, and while the "unveiling" ceremonies have often involved a convergence of politicians, scholars, and activist groups (both French and Algerian), it is also true that such acts have been limited to the municipal level and the private sector.[18] The lack of political and economic investment at the national level is emblematic of

de nos souvenirs: le 17 octobre 1961, emblème des violences policières," *Revue des mondes musulmans et de la Méditerranée* 119–20 (November 2007): 233–48.

16   Delanoë's gesture had been a subject of heated debate, with the right-leaning Parisian politicians accusing the mayor of "provocation." See Philippe Bernard and Christine Garin, "Le massacre du 17 octobre 1961 obtient un début de reconnaissance officielle," *Le Monde*, October 17, 2001, http://www.lemonde.fr/societe/article/2011/10/17/archives-du-monde-17-octobre-2001-le-massacre-du-17-octobre-1961-obtient-un-debut-de-reconnaissance-officielle_1588198_3224.html.

17   Many of the commemorative plaques in towns adjacent to Paris were inaugurated in 2011, on the occasion of the 50th anniversary of the massacre. It is worth noting that the French Communist Party's (PCF's) reaction to October 17 in the heat of the moment was considered a failure. On October 17 and the PCF, see: Henri Malberg and Sébastien Crepel, "Henri Malberg: On a sous-estimé la portée du 17 octobre 1961," interview, House and MacMaster, *L'Humanité*, October 16, 2011.

18   In Paris, in 2001, Mehdi Lallaoui was present at the ceremony, along with right-wing politicians Bruno Mégret and Jean-Yves Le Gallou. The ceremony in Aubervilliers that same year brought together Didier Daeninckx and Fadila Belkebla, an actress of Algerian origin who appeared in *Vivre au paradis*. Belkebla claims that she only learned about October 17 when she was doing research for the role. See "À la mémoire des Algériens...", *Libération*, October 18, 2001, http://www.liberation.fr/societe/2001/10/18/a-la-memoire-des-algeriens_380833.

a broader denial of October 17, thus contributing to its failure to gain traction in the national narrative.

Moreover, with the exception of the plaque in Paris, which is centrally located near the Pont Saint-Michel, these small memorials stand in the margins of the city, accessible, theoretically, to many of the communities that suffered losses on October 17, but physically removed from the sites of the violence they commemorate. In this way, they symbolically displace the narrative into the margins of the capital's history. Nearly all of the plaques are situated in sites that make them difficult to read—even the plaque in Paris sits below eye level along the balustrade next to the Pont Saint-Michel, and the plaque in Aubervilliers is under a footbridge in a desolate area—ensuring that they command little attention. And any contribution the plaques might make to the national narrative is further undermined by frequent vandalizing or theft, leaving a void of meaning in their place.[19]

The codes of the October 17 Parisian memorialscape (to the degree that it exists) are anything but those of the conventional monumental narrative; they do not reveal themselves to the reader of the city, but rather require an active engagement in meaning-making. In short, they impel the reader to participate in the production of a text. And if the ensemble of commemorative plaques can be understood as scriptable, it is also the case that many of the micro-narratives—that is, the memorial inscriptions themselves—are also scriptable in the Barthesian sense. This is particularly true of the earliest plaques (in Paris and Aubervilliers), but also of the Bezons memorial (2011), which uses the same phrase as the 2001 plaques.[20] In these cases, it is incumbent upon the reader to fill in various gaps, as the statement does not identify the perpetrator nor does it contextualize the violence. Only the plaque in Saint-Denis (a northern suburb) produces a "classic" memorial, and thus *lisible*, or readerly, text:

> Le 17 octobre 1961, pendant la guerre d'Algérie, trente mille Algériennes et Algériens de la région Parisienne manifestèrent pacifiquement contre

19   The plaque inaugurated in Clichy, for example, was stolen one year later.

20   There is a very similar statement on the plaque at Fontenay: "The city of Fontenay-sous-Bois pays homage to the hundreds of Algerians who were victims of the bloody repression that took place during the peaceful demonstration against the curfew imposed on them." See: http://eluscommunistescitoyensfontenay.elunet.fr/index.php/post/20/10/2011/50eme-anniversaire-de-la-commemoration-du-17-octobre-61et-pose-dune-plaque-en-hommage-aux-victimes-discours-de-Jean-Francois-Voguet.

le couvre-feu qui leur était imposé. Cette mobilisation fut brutalement réprimée sur ordre du préfet de police de Paris. Des manifestants furent tués par balles, des centaines d'hommes et de femmes furent jetés dans la Seine et des milliers furent battus et emprisonnés. On retrouva des cadavres dans le canal de Saint-Denis. Contre le racisme et l'oubli, pour la démocratie et les droits humains, cette plaque a été dévoilée par Didier Paillard, maire de Saint-Denis, le 21 mars 2007.

(On October 17 1961, during the Algerian War, 30,000 Algerian men and women of Paris and its environs protested against the curfew that had been imposed on them. This demonstration was brutally repressed at the order of the Prefect of Police. Protesters were shot, hundreds of men and women were thrown in the Seine, and thousands were beaten and imprisoned. Cadavers were found in the Saint-Denis Canal. Against racism and forgetting and in the name of democracy and human rights, this plaque was unveiled by Didier Paillard, Mayor of Saint-Denis, on March 21, 2007.)[21]

Cultural Capital: Mapping the Demonstration

The need to make a mark on Paris does not belong exclusively to the afterlives of October 17. If the post-facto activities seek to memorialize the event in the urban fabric of the capital, the demonstration itself—a spatial practice in its own right—sought to establish the Algerians' existence in the fabric of the nation. The practical and semiotic potential of Paris was well understood and strategically leveraged by both the FF-FLN and the French state, and the capital was of course the logical site for the demonstration: Most of the Algerians living in France at the time were settled in and around Paris, and the curfew itself (the ostensible reason for the protest) only applied to Algerians living in the capital. But the FLN organizers were very aware of what today might be called "the optics"—or the "public relations" value—of such an event: The City of Light was, at the time, both the capital of the French empire and the emblematic seat of the nation that invented the notion of human rights and codified tolerance. As Paulette Péju wrote shortly after the events, "With stupor and a bit of anxiety, Parisians very quickly

21   For the full text, see: http://www.micheldandelot1.com/saint-denis-le-16-de-cembre-2015-en-memoire-de-fatima-bedar-assassinee--a118994312. There is now a *Jardin Fatima Bédar* in Saint-Denis and a *Place 17 octobre* in Aubervilliers.

discovered the existence of these men who had been hidden out of sight, like a wound."[22]

The political gesture enacted by the Algerians on October 17 was also eminently spatial and visual. The FLN laid the groundwork for a "spectacular" event, with carefully selected routes that would ensure a presence in and a pacific disruption of spaces of leisure and entertainment (the cinemas, theatres, concert halls, and cafés of the *grands boulevards*), but that would also parade thousands of Algerian families in front of the offices of major news outlets (such as *Paris Match* and *L'Humanité*).[23] In becoming visible within the space of a Paris at work and at play, the Algerian demonstration turned the city into a canvas upon which to paint an alternative vision of sovereignty.[24]

Politics, space, and the visual come together in a particular emblem of the October 17 demonstration and its repression, one that, paradoxically, erases Algerian political subjectivity and reasserts colonial technologies of control while simultaneously testifying to the visibility of the event. On October 19, 1961, the daily newspaper *France-Soir* published a graphic titled "Trois 'bases' de depart en banlieue" (Three starting points in the suburbs).[25] (See Fig. 5.) The map of the city—represented schematically in its classic ovoid form traversed by the arc of the Seine—features little detail, noting only a few key locations in and outside of the city. The captions, placed around the periphery of Paris like numbers on a clock, contain time stamps and descriptions of police actions but no real assessment of the violence. Most visually dominant, however,

22   Paulette Péju, *Ratonnades à Paris* (Paris: La Découverte, 2000), 137.

23   Feldman, 172–73.

24   Dawn Fulton has observed, "The Algerian demonstrators' call to make their existence manifest in Paris's most public spaces thus reveals the extent to which the war to reclaim Algeria for Algerians is also a war to reject the politically and culturally peripheral status of Algerians in French national identity when they had crossed the real borders of the hexagon" (35).

25   *France-Soir*, October 19, 1961, 3. The amount of press coverage—much of which has been collected in the police archives—is remarkable in light of the censure. On this topic, see Charlotte Nordmann and Jérome Vidal, "La politique de la mémoire," in Le Cour Grandmaison, 171–81. See also Julien Buzenet, "Manifestation du 17 octobre 1961 à Paris: l'oubli pour mémoire collective d'une violente répression policière," *Conserveries mémorielles* 10 (2011), https://cm.revues.org/899. For a review of the French press coverage in the first weeks after October 17, see House and MacMaster, 222–26; and Abdallah, "Le 17 octobre 1961 et les médias."

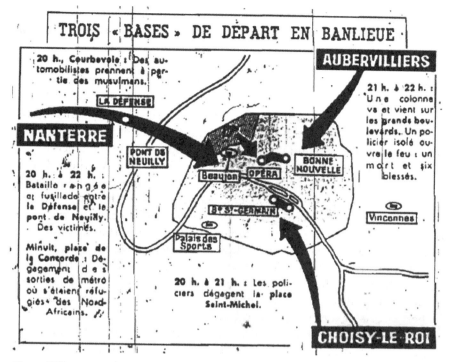

Fig. 5. "Three starting points in the suburbs." Graphic by *France-Soir*. October 19, 1961.

are three thick black arrows that originate in sites in the *banlieue* whose names are situated at the edges of the graphic. With white lettering on black backgrounds that appear to emit the arrows that grow in size as they traverse the Paris periphery, the toponyms Nanterre, Aubervilliers, and Choisy-le-Roi (all peripheral sites associated, at the time, with large Algerian populations) are easily the largest elements on the map.

At first glance, the map seems to produce a neutral, even "journalistic," readerly narrative of October 17. Yet the representation of a multi-pronged attack emanating from outside of Paris and resulting in a successful breaching of the frontier separating the capital from its surrounding zones looks like something we might, today, call "fake news." Unwittingly or ironically, it encodes the failure of the state (embodied on the ground by Papon's police forces) to "defend" the territory. Interior Minister Roger Frey had given orders to "hold the capital," and Papon understood that he had carte blanche to do so. Keeping the protest—that is, the Algerians—invisible was not a direct command, but it was implicit in the operational tactics, which, as early as the afternoon of October 17, involved stopping the columns of protesters before they entered the city.

This strategy would have had the dual effect of "holding Paris" (keeping both violence and evidence of the colonial problem out), while allowing the police to deal with the Algerians in the peri-urban blind spots of Paris, rather than in full view of the state and its citizenry. The map hints at this attempt with the caption: "20h à 22h: Bataille rangée et fusillade entre la Défense et le pont de Neuilly. Des victimes" (8pm to 10pm: Pitched battle and gunfire between la Défense and the Neuilly bridge. Victims). It is a matter of historical record that nearly 10,000 Algerians from points west of the city converged on the bridge as they made a bid for the Champs-Élysées, and that they were greeted with gunfire and an extremely violent police charge. This was no "pitched" battle, but rather a one-sided aggression.[26] While the caption allows that there were victims, it does not mention from which side, nor does it suggest that the barrage was successful; indeed, the *France-Soir* map, with the point of its "Nanterre" arrow firmly embedded in Paris proper, suggests that the capital, despite the best efforts of the state, was indeed "taken."

Yet this cartographic representation of October 17 also speaks to the particular spatial configuration of Algerians in the French imaginary. In what we might call the "demographic unconscious" of the *France-Soir* map, Algerians come from somewhere other than Paris, from a zone nearly emptied of signifiers; they are literally outsiders. While it is true that many (perhaps even half) of the protesters that night would have traveled from the outskirts or *banlieues*, what the map erases is the existence of significant numbers of Algerians residing *in* Paris, who would also have joined the demonstration.[27] The map, of course,

26   House and MacMaster, 118. Algerians were converging from Nanterre, Courbevoie, and other points west and north. The archival audio recording of police communication featured in Adi's documentary film *Ici on noie les Algériens* reveals orders being given on the night in question: "Rappel! Il faut appréhender le maximum de manifestants à leur arrivée aux points désignés, soit par le métro, soit par les autobus. Il faut les intercepter aux portes et ponts de Paris" (Attention! We need to apprehend a maximum of protesters as soon as they converge on designated spots, either by subway or by bus. They need to be stopped at the gates and bridges of Paris).

27   In 1960, the 13th, 15th, and 18th to 20th *arrondissements* of the capital were home to more Algerians than Nanterre, Choisy-Le-Roi, or Courbevoie. See statistics in House and MacMaster, 64, and E. Blanchard, "'Montrer à de Gaulle

reinforces a spatial configuration reflected in the Algerians' politically marginal status, and visually (albeit erroneously) codes them as an external menace. In fact, not only did many Algerians live in the city, administratively they were considered "French," or *français musulmans d'Algérie* (French Muslims of Algeria).[28]

Moreover, *France-Soir*'s spatial representation of the demonstration unwittingly enacts a Fanonian prophecy: In depicting the arrival of the colonized in the "colonial city," the map is a visual enactment of Fanon's harbinger of the end of the colonial order, the "dislocation of the colonial world," or that moment when "décidant d'être l'histoire en actes, la masse colonisée s'engouferera dans les villes interdites" (71, "taking history into their own hands, the colonized swarm into the forbidden cities," 6).[29] The graphics testify to the appropriation of the "European zone" by "les indigènes"; long an object of desire, Paris (here, its image) is possessed by tentacles reaching in from dark elsewheres; and possession, in all its polysemy, is what Fanon's colonizer fears—"[Les colonisés] veulent prendre notre place" (70, "[They colonized] want to take our place," 5), and what his "indigène" dreams of—"s'asseoir à la table du colon, coucher dans le lit du colon, avec sa femme, si possible" (70, "sitting at the colonist's table and sleeping in his bed, with his wife, if possible," 5).

Both Fanon's colonizer and the *France-Soir* map are painfully aware of the spatial dimensions of this tenuous privilege. But the map also lays bare the domestication of colonial spatial order: After October 17, the

que nous voulons notre indépendance, s'il faut crever,' Algériens et Algériennes dans les manifestations d'octobre 1961," *La ville en ébullition. Sociétés urbaines à l'épreuve*, ed. Pierre Bergel and Vincent Milliot (Rennes: Presses universitaires de Rennes, 2014), 205–36.

28 The administrative status of Algerians during the colonial period is complex. While certain categories of the population had been given French citizenship at different moments during the colonial period (such as the Jews of Algeria, who were made French by virtue of the Crémieux Decree in 1870), citizenship was, theoretically, conferred upon all Algerians by de Gaulle after his speech in Constantine in 1943. In practice, most Algerians did not benefit from the full rights that would normally accompany citizenship. See Weil, "Le Statut des musulmans en Algérie coloniale"; Stora, *Les mots de la guerre d'Algérie* (Toulouse: Presses universitaires du Mirail, 2005), 57; Hervé Bleuchot, *Droit musulman: Tome 1, Histoire* (Aix-en-Provence: Presses universitaires d'Aix, 2000), 192.

29 Frantz Fanon, *Wretched of the Earth*, trans. Richard Philcox (New York: Grove Press, 2005).

"ville coloniale" described by Fanon, "coupée en deux" (cut in two) and governed by principles of "exclusion réciproque" (reciprocal exclusion) could no longer be understood as a faraway place in the hinterlands of the French empire. That world where a clean, protected, impenetrable European zone abutted the "native quarters"—that "disreputable place inhabited by disreputable people"— was now, too, Paris.[30]

The *France-Soir* map suggests a kind of grand narrative of Algerian spatial mastery over Paris; yet the micro-narrative, the on-the-ground realities of spatial knowledge were quite different. In a caustic article published in *L'Express* at the end of October, Jean Cau noted that thousands of Algerians had been living, largely unnoticed, "only 5 minutes from la Place de l'Étoile"; as Emmanuel Blanchard has remarked, Cau's "5 minutes" belie an important social and geographical distance.[31] Actual proximity notwithstanding, many Algerians residing in the *banlieue* had never set foot in the capital, and this lack of cartographic knowledge put them at a distinct disadvantage on October 17: Unfamiliar with the sites to which they were dispatched for the various marches, some protestors found themselves disoriented and thus more easily targeted by the police. Despite attempts by the FLN organizers to guide and orient their charges, many—without a map with which to apprehend and control the space of the capital—found themselves not only topographically but also, to borrow a term from Blanchard, lexically, lost: Certain protesters reported finding themselves near the "Château de Versailles" (rather than at la Porte de Versailles, on the southwest edge of the city).[32]

The graphic tropes used in the *France-Soir* map to spatialize the October 17 demonstration connect up with other cartographic processes and representations of the relationship between putative centers of power and colonized spaces. The 1938 colonial propaganda documentary *France is an Empire* situates the French empire in the world while schooling viewers in the good works of her civilizing mission. After a five-minute preface (filmed on location in various French colonies), designed to convince viewers of the desperate need for French technology, education,

30 Fanon, *Wretched*, 4. Feldman has also observed that the demonstration incarnates Fanon's description of colonial space, and conforms to "the mandate inherent in Fanon's urging colonial subjects to overturn and so decolonize these lamentable conditions" (175).

31 Jean Cau, "Jean Cau chez les Ratons," *L'Express*, October 27, 1961. Cited in E. Blanchard, "Montrer à de Gaulle," 17.

32 E. Blanchard, "Montrer à de Gaulle," 17–18.

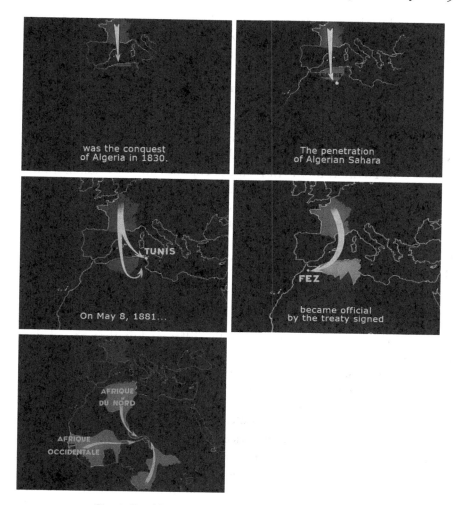

Fig. 6. Graphic representations of colonial incursions in
La France est un empire (France is an Empire).
Documentary. Dir. Jean D'Agraives. France, 1939.

and authority, the film cuts to a three-minute graphic sequence that narrates, through voice-over, the genesis of the French empire. On a black background, thick, animated white arrows originate in France and stretch out across the Mediterranean and through the Suez Canal, offering a teleological, graphic representation of imperial expansion. As the arrows visually invade Algeria, Tunisia, Morocco, and the interior of Africa, the voice-over describes the process in terms that will later be reprised and inverted by Fanon: "The first act was destined to be the *taking* of Algiers [...] the *penetration* of the Algerian Sahara was more difficult [...] May 8, 1881, our troupes *penetrated* Tunis [...] Our *penetration* efforts would be pursued without fail until we succeeded in joining together our three large colonies."[33] (See Fig. 6.)

In pointing out the common lexicon and visual thematics of a map produced by *France-Soir* in 1961 and a colonial documentary filmed in 1938, I am not suggesting conscious imitation. Rather, I want to call attention to a trope and its inversion. In the 1938 film—a project underwritten by the Bureau des colonies and the Colonial Film Commission with the goal of "making the colonies known to France"— the graphic arrows start in France and point outward, "penetrating" the territories in question and becoming vectors of a violence that is metaphorically sexual in nature.[34] The arrows likewise double the figurative rays of "light" that radiate from the *métropole*, illuminating the dark corners of the world it has blessed with its presence, as seen in a later sequence of the documentary.[35] Rehearsed here visually and verbally, the metaphor of penetration is nothing less than the clarion call of the civilizing mission; some decades later, the *France-Soir* map—a representation whose context is wholly different but that nonetheless captures a certain colonial reality—would reverse the trajectory of those outbound arrows. The violence that produced colonialism is now, on the cusp of decolonization, refracted back upon its creators; *les indigènes*, as Fanon predicted, have internalized the lessons of empire.

By the time *France-Soir* published its map of the October 17 demonstration, cartographic practices had come under some scrutiny, notably from the Situationist International (SI), whose rogue urban spatial practices sought to reveal and disrupt the previously undisputed dominance of the conventional map. In 1955, SI founder Guy Debord published the *Guide psychogéographique de Paris*, and later, in 1958, a tract titled "The Naked City: Illustration de l'hypothèse des plaques

33   Jean d'Agraives and Emmanuel Bourcier, *La France est un empire* (1939).

34   See Peter Bloom, *French Colonial Documentary: Mythologies of Humanitarianism* (Minneapolis: University of Minnesota Press, 2008), 127. See also Alison Levine, "Film, Propaganda, and Politics: *La France est un empire* 1939–1943," *Contemporary French Civilization* 40, no. 1 (2015): 71–90.

35   Alison Levine has remarked that "the trope of rayonnement was often depicted as rays of light emanating from France across the world." See Levine, *Framing the Nation: Documentary Film in Interwar France* (London: Bloomsbury, 2010), xiii.

tournantes en psychogéographie."[36] The images depicted therein—
psychogeographic maps—are material representations of SI's co-opting
of Paris (and city space in general) through urban practices such as the
dérive. Contesting the authority of cartography, Debord's guides are the
opposite of navigational tools: Chunks of official maps are removed from
their context, resituated in an empty field, and linked together via thick
red arrows, not unlike the black ones indicating the Algerian incursion
into Paris (and equally reminiscent of the white arrows of imperial
expansion/penetration in *France is an Empire*). Feldman has remarked
that the demonstration's production of space on October 17 bears a
striking resemblance to the abstract concepts espoused by Debord in
The Naked City.[37] *France-Soir*'s perhaps unwitting reprise of the graphic
motif of arrows—used to such different effect in the SI "guides"—
allows us to link spatial practice and its representation more concretely.
Although the newspaper's deployment of arrows is clearly intended to
serve a totalizing and authoritative narrative (in other words, to produce
the very effects that psychogeography sought to upend), its echo of those
"useless," non-authoritative arrows—Debord's arrows often point to
everything and nothing at all—subtly undermines its own project, giving
it the effect of making one final, stalwart effort at spatial control, in
representation if not in reality.

The map of the 1961 demonstration has also surfaced in the anarchive,
albeit in slightly different forms that attest to the staying power of
the colonial technology of cartography, while unsettling it in subtle
ways. In 2002, before she was known as a breakout *beur* novelist,
Faïza Guène wrote, directed, and produced a documentary short titled
"Mémoires du 17 octobre 1961."[38] The 20-minute film is made in the
classic "talking-head" style, with eyewitnesses and experts providing
commentary on the demonstration, the massacre, and its repression in
memory. Two minutes into the film, the image cuts from an interview
with eyewitness Monique Hervo to a close-up of a map of Paris drawn

36   For images, see: http://imaginarymuseum.org/LPG/Mapsitu1.htm, and
http://laboratoireurbanismeinsurrectionnel.blogspot.com/2011/05/psychogeog-
raphie.html.
37   Feldman, 178–79.
38   Bernard Richard, Guène's industry mentor, shares credit for this film,
which was made under the auspices of a *banlieue* video workshop called *Les
Engraineurs*, based in Les Courtillières. For information on the association, see:
http://les-engraineurs.org/content/lassociation. Film available at: http://juralib-
ertaire.over-blog.com/article-6818241.html.

on white paper with Magic Marker.[39] As Hervo, now hardly visible in the frame, narrates the demonstration's progression from the *banlieue* into Paris, she recreates, almost "verbatim," a map that in many ways resembles the *France-Soir* graphic. (See Fig. 7.) Here, however, as we observe the creation of a visual aid and hear Hervo telling her story (narrating with the first-person plural "we"), cartography is figured as an embodied practice and the map becomes voiced, infused both with Hervo's belief in the Algerians' right to demonstrate and with her own affinity for their cause. Although the schematics of Paris are the same as in the *France-Soir* map, Hervo's version multiplies the arrows, thus multiplying the Algerians' origins, trajectories, and existence. Moreover, these arrows are shorter—they originate in sites, both named and unnamed, that are quite close to Paris's periphery. Hence, in Guène's film, the cartographic impulse contests the totalizing rationalistic aims of the official maps discussed earlier, suggesting, instead, a greater intimacy between "outside" and "inside," giving the impression that the "European" and "indigenous" zones were closer—physically but also affectively—than many might have imagined. The hand-drawn aspect of this image, finally, is a subversive gesture: It points to the *affective* and *embodied* status of Hervo/Guène's map, in opposition to the "official" (and technologically produced) maps mentioned earlier and to those we will discuss below. The embodied condition of this map, which is being drawn before our eyes, is precisely what marks its resistance to the *totalizing* nature of almost all official maps.

Institutional maps of Paris make yet another anarchival appearance in Yasmina Adi's film *Ici on noie les Algériens* (2011). Like Guène's (and like most other October 17 documentaries), Adi's film is structured by the testimony of eyewitnesses and expert commentators. What distinguishes her film from the others in the anarchive, however, is the amount and variety of archival footage (both visual and audio) incorporated into the film's narrative. One particular episode has special relevance to our discussion of maps and space: The sequence that runs from 00:08:08 to 00:08:45 consists of still images representing the central office of *les renseignements généraux* (the RG, or intelligence service of the

39 Monique Hervo was more than just an eyewitness to the violence on October 17; she had dedicated herself to public service and social work. In 1959 she moved into the Nanterre *bidonville* in order to live alongside, and in the same conditions as, the population she served. Hervo remained there until the *bidonville* was destroyed in 1971. See Chapter 2, n. 53.

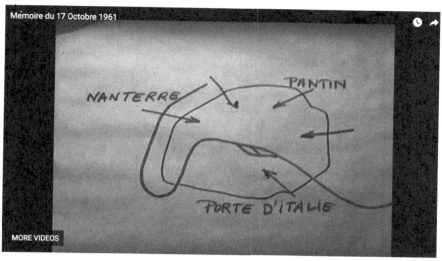

Fig. 7. Hand-drawn map of the demonstration on October 17, 1961, in
Mémoires du 17 octobre. Documentary short. Dir. Faïza Guène. France, 2002.

French police). The images themselves, which depict agents manning
the phones and consulting large maps of the city, are "animated" (using
a "pan and zoom" technique known as the Ken Burns effect), and the
sequence is overlaid with actual audio recordings of information and
orders disseminated by authorities to officers in the field as operations
unfolded on October 17.[40] As the camera moves over the images, we
hear the agents informing the units in Paris: "Ici les RG, nous venons
d'avoir plus de précisions. Les Algériens ont reçu comme consigne de
se rendre sur les voies de rassemblement suivantes: Place de l'Étoile,
Place de la Concorde, les grands boulevards d'Opéra à Bonne nouvelle,
et Saint-Michel" ("We have received more intelligence. The Algerians
have been ordered to gather in these places: Place de l'Étoile, Place de
la Concorde, the boulevards around the Opéra and the Saint-Michel
area"). While it is highly unlikely that the audio and video tracks are
taken from the same moment (that is, that the photographs were taken
on the night of October 17), the juxtaposition of these particular images

40 The recordings come from live transmissions over "TNZ 1," the radio
frequency reserved for the police authorities. See Brunet, *Police contre FLN*,
184–85; he notes that a transcription of the recordings is preserved in the archives
of the prefecture, FA/413, dossier 2.

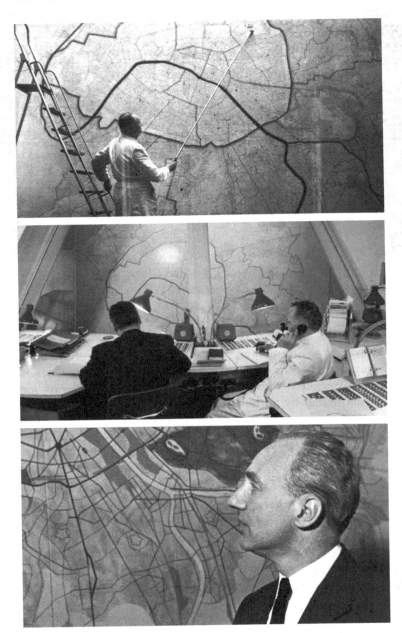

Fig. 8. Inside "les RG," the intelligence service of the French Police.
Ici on noie les Algériens (Here we drown Algerians). Documentary. Dir. Yasmina Adi.
France, 2011.

with the selected voice recordings from officers describing their location in Paris and the conditions on the ground produces a plausibly authentic scenario.

However realistic its elements may be, and however much the film may indeed "document" history, the scene itself is oddly eerie and reminiscent, in certain ways, of Chris Marker's science-fiction film *La Jetée* (1962), which is nearly contemporaneous with the moment depicted in Adi's film.[41] The white lab coats worn by the agents of the RG, the mostly white, highly sterile-looking environment of the offices, and the numerous high camera angles that gaze down on men at work behind glass walls produce an overall effect of mad scientists in a futuristic lab, plotting something top secret and potentially toxic.

With its evidentiary editing, this sequence produces a useful narrative: In the context of a documentary about the repression on October 17, it demonstrates that agents at headquarters and police in the field knew the routes and sites of the Algerian protestors, and were able to place those actors in the broader spatial field that is Paris; in other words, it suggests that the police dominated, controlled, and disseminated knowledge about the demonstration. And of course, the mere existence of a centralized bureau responsible for collecting and disseminating information testifies to the ability of the state to control knowledge. Removed from the physical space of the city, the agents nonetheless benefit from the type of information that a "bird's-eye view" affords of the Parisian text; this in turn allows them to imagine the "whole" in a way not available to those on the ground, whether the police or the demonstrators. The combined effect of surveillance, technology, and superiority is further heightened by the images of maps of Paris present in nearly every shot of the 40-second sequence. (See Fig. 8.) The agents appear to be dominated by the large maps that loom over them, yet are able to use them for purposes of control. In this archival montage, agents of the state become mediators between a colonial technology of totalizing control and the ability of the state to limit the risk to its physical space.

In the context of a discussion about city space, maps, and colonial critique of imperial means of knowing, and in the context of a film that is very much about the Algerian victims of October 17, it is tempting

---

41 A short film with a decidedly cult status, Marker's *La Jetée* is said to have inspired Terry Gilliam's *Twelve Monkeys* (1995). *La Jetée* is notable both for its apocalyptic scenario and its unique aesthetic: It is entirely constructed out of black-and-white photographs.

to seek out and read the small cracks in this coherent narrative of state control. First, we might notice that the very notion of a bird's-eye perspective is inversed in these shots: The maps, which often consume entire walls, dominate the men who appear in the frame and who are either engulfed by Paris or compelled to look up to view the city in its entirety. Here, the agents may be mediators, but it is the "vast texturology" that gazes down upon them and thus, spatially at any rate, man is dominated by a technology he has created and that has expanded to fill his entire frame of reference. (Here, again, we might circle back to Fanon's presaging of the end of the colonial project as a moment of radical change in the spatial order of things.)

Second, and this observation is in tension with the first, Adi's editing techniques create a situation in which no single map of Paris is ever shown in its entirety. Each segment begins from a fragment of a map, and even longer shots that allow for deep space depict the ovoid of Paris as cut off, partial, incomplete. The choices made at the level of montage, then, speak of the ways in which spatial representation exceeds its mere utilitarian function to become a hegemonic, overbearing presence, while at the same time suggesting the possibility of artfully undermining those very colonial technologies depicted within these archival images. Moreover, the fact that the audio and video do not necessarily come from the same source impels the viewer to engage the film-text critically, to wonder if it really represents totalizing control (as it would have us believe), to be skeptical of montage as a visual technique and as a rewriting of history.

Revising Paris: Urban Space in the Anarchive

Beginning with the first texts of the second wave, the anarchive establishes a thick record of Parisian toponyms associated with the sites of the demonstration and its repression, tracing routes upon the city or delving deeply into a particular neighborhood or site. Certainly, any cultural production representing October 17 or its memory is more likely than not to be set in Paris; certain anarchival works, however, insist on urban spaces in such a way as to revise the city map or to stage spatial practices that propose counternarratives, both of which tend to reveal how violence in the urban landscape has become naturalized.

The first chapter of Brahim Kettane's novel *Le Sourire de Brahim*, titled "Octobre à Paris" (a sidelong glance at Panijel's documentary, still missing in action in 1985, when the novel was published), recounts the trajectory of Brahim's family from the *banlieue* to the city center. The directions are clear enough to allow the reader to ascertain that the family lives in a southeastern zone: "La voiture roulait vers Paris. [...] Une fois franchi le pont d'Ivry [...] dans un crissement de pneus, la voiture s'arrêta net. Ils étaient devant Notre-Dame de Paris. [...] Ils entreprirent de rejoindre à pied la place Saint-Michel" (10–11, The car headed toward Paris. [...] Once they crossed the Ivry Bridge [...] the car screeched to a halt. They were in front of Notre-Dame de Paris. [...] They decided to make their way to place Saint-Michel on foot). From Notre-Dame to Saint-Michel is just a short walk over the river, yet the narrative dilates time, with flashbacks to the hardship of life in Algeria and the complications of life as an Algerian immigrant in Paris, slowing the spatial progression of Brahim's family toward what will become their tragedy. Several pages and multiple anecdotes after the family arrives at Notre-Dame, the narration recounts: "La place Saint-Michel était maintenant en vue" (16, Place Saint-Michel was now in view), but it is only three pages and several more flashbacks later that we read, "Ils étaient maintenant Place Saint-Michel, avec la fontaine en face d'eux" (19, They were now at Place Saint-Michel, with the fountain in front of them). The first chapter's insistence on the setting of Paris, and specifically, on Place Saint-Michel, takes on particular relief in light of the novel's overall reticence to name places, with the exception of several longer, nearly poetic passages on the *banlieue* and Brahim's trip to Algeria. Paris only returns in a significant way in the last episode of the novel, set at the Place de la République in 1985; here, the occasion is a concert, and the "Republic" is described as being taken over by "la France des cités" (178, the France of the housing projects), while descriptions of a heavy police presence connect this visible emergence of a minority in the space of the capital with October 17.[42]

If *Sourire* is narratively straightforward and, in many ways, a readerly text, its treatment of October 17 and the memory of the massacre is not wholly transparent. Certainly, the novel's first pages provide a description of the subjective experience of police violence; yet October 17

---

42   The concert at the end of *Sourire* may allude to the concert organized in June 1985 by the newly launched anti-racism organization SOS Racisme, which emerged onto the French scene with a large-scale, multi-artist musical event held at the symbolic Place de la Concorde. Sometimes called the first *concert des potes* (buddy concert), this was also the first time the SOS Racisme slogan *touche pas à mon pote* (don't touch my buddy) was introduced to the French public.

is never mentioned again after the first chapter, not even in passing. This is astonishing in the context of the story world, as Brahim's little brother is killed that night, a tragedy that should serve as a narrative touchstone in this *beur bildungsroman*. Yet the denarration of October 17 is also surprising in the real world, as Kettane's novel was one of the first to treat the massacre. In this sense, the event's textual disappearing act seems to reify the original disappearance of October 17 from the political landscape.

While this may indeed be the case, it is also plausible that October 17 has only disappeared from the text in the most "readerly" of fashions. As Brahim and his family drive away from the massacre, the body of his felled younger brother cradled in his mother's arms, the text tells us that "Ce jour-là, le sourire de Brahim s'envola" (Brahim's smile vanished that day). From that moment on, while October 17 is never again mentioned, each instance of Brahim's smile—rare and often mysteriously haunted— serves as a metonymic reminder of the massacre and its impact. With Brahim's smile (the book's title, after all) standing in for the massacre, its mentions become nodal points on a network, or map, that "emplots" October 17 throughout the novel.

Also published in the early 1980s, at a moment when the *beurs* had begun to mobilize, Mehdi Lallaoui's *Les Beurs de Seine* (1986) is something of a city-symphony novel, with a cast of mostly *beur* characters ranging far and wide in La Seine—the name given in 1790 to the region today known as L'Île de France—which included Paris but also peripheral communes with important Algerian communities, such as Argenteuil and Nanterre. Like *Sourire*, *Beurs* presents itself as a realist novel. The book features a trio of protagonists, Kaci, Belka, and Mourad, who are as literate in the space of the zones and the *banlieue* as they are in the various sites within Paris. The action is set firmly in the early 1980s, and although it does not represent the October 17 demonstration, it does recall the massacre in an episode inspired by other Parisian memorial practices and one character's capacity to analyze the city as a text. Kaci—described as the historian of the group and the guide to the dodgiest areas of Paris—notes that the Algerian Consulate in Nanterre is located on a street named "8 mai 1945." For the French, the street name is readerly (readily legible, transparent): It marks the end of World War II. Kaci's historical knowledge, however, allows him to decipher the hidden double meaning of this date: May 8, 1945 was the end of one war but the symbolic beginning of another: It marks the Sétif Massacre in Algeria, a date often considered the beginning of the Algerian War of Independence (which would begin in earnest nine years later).[43] Kaci downplays his own virtuosic reading performance, telling his interlocutors that his method is a simple one: "ça vaut le coup de gratter un peu la couche de vernis qui recouvre, en France, l'histoire de la guerre d'Algérie" (158, it's worth scratching at the layer of varnish that covers the history of the Algerian War in France). The story of October 17, 1961, which he heard from elderly workers, becomes visible in Paris once one knows what to look for; armed with knowledge, sites all over the center of Paris—the Île de la Cité, la Préfecture de Paris, even simply the Seine—become *scriptible* (writerly) texts, capable of revealing the traces of histories otherwise unwritten.

Daeninckx's *Meurtres pour mémoire* similarly "scratches at the layers" that hide the story of the Algerian War by mobilizing a connection between history and place, and by prompting the reader to engage Paris as a text. Although the story is primarily set in 1980s Toulouse, like *Le Sourire de Brahim*, *Meurtres* begins on the night of October 17, 1961, and features Algerian characters making their way from points in the suburbs into the center of Paris. Saïd, Lounès, and Käira fulfill the key narrative function of tracing routes across Paris and marking the sites within the capital where state violence occurred in plain sight. In these preliminary chapters, the cartographic record is dense with detail. Saïd's perambulations in Paris call out Algerian-run cafés and bars (Chez Rosa, Chez Marius, Café de la Justice), signaling the embeddedness of Algerians in Parisian culture. Discussions between Saïd, Lounès, and Kaïra situate them at points within the urban networks of Paris: Gare de l'Est, Strasbourg Saint-Denis, Bonne Nouvelle. The opening chapters, in certain ways, hark back to Élie Kagan's photos of the demonstration and Panijel's photomontage sequence in *Octobre à Paris*: Just as the photos offer visual information to establish the action in place and time (we see, for instance, that Jean Gabin's film is playing at the Berlitz), Daeninckx's novel offers textual vignettes of Paris on October 17, 1961:

> Saïd et Lounès garèrent la quatre chevaux à la Villette, boulevard MacDonald, juste après l'arrêt du PC [...] La caserne des Gardes mobiles semblait calme bien que le parc de stationnement fût entièrement occupé par les Berliet bleus de la Compagnies républicaines de sécurité [...] Au Grand Rex on jouait les *Canons de Navarone*. (16–17)

---

43 See Chapter 1, n. 7.

> Saïd and Lounès parked the 4CV in La Villette on boulevard MacDonald, just past the ring road bus stop [...] The *Gardes Mobiles* barracks seemed quiet, although the parking area was packed full, with the blue Berliet vans of the *Compagnies Républicaines de Sécurité*, the CRS. [...] At the Rex they were showing *The Guns of Navarone*. (10–11)

The time and place of the massacre come together at the end of the first chapter: "A la devanture de la bijouterie qui faisait l'angle de la rue Notre-Dame-de-bonne-nouvelle, une imposante horloge munie d'un baladier de cuivre marquait dix-neuf heures vingt-cinq. Le 17 octobre 1961" (28, "On the façade of the jeweller's shop at the corner of rue Notre-Dame de Bonne-Nouvelle, the imposing clock with the copper pendulum showed it was 7:25pm. It was 17 October 1961," 21).

As they travel by metro from La Villette to Bonne Nouvelle—from the northeastern edge of Paris to the center, Saïd shows Lounès a poster he had taken from the print shop where he works. It is a movie poster for Jacques Rivette's first film, *Paris nous appartient* (Paris Belongs to Us). Saïd adopts the title as a slogan: "Tu te rends compte, Lounès, Paris nous appartient" (17, "Do you realize, Lounès, Paris belongs to us," 11). Here, the poster, appropriated by an Algerian, serves as a metonym for Paris; the possession of the former, by Saïd, augurs the possession of the latter by all Algerians. Ironically, on that night, Algerians were significantly dispossessed of any claims to the capital; Paris only belonged to Lounès and Saïd for a short time, if at all.

While the early chapters of *Meurtres* depict characters involved in the disruptive spatial practices that would allow them to become visible in the symbolic space of the capital, thus participating in the creation of textual "maps" of October 17, the fact that the novel shifts temporally (to the 1980s) and spatially (to Toulouse) would tend to suggest that its contributions to "siting" October 17 remain limited. Yet various idiosyncratic narrative elements allow other times and settings to participate, symbolically, in a spatial critique of October 17. As a "hard-boiled" detective novel with a number of strands of intrigue, all intricately braided together, *Meurtres* nonetheless features, proportionally, a remarkable amount of what I will call "superfluous" narrative elements. These moments of superfluity are woven into the story, adding local color, specificity, and sometimes humor; however, given that the superfluous in this tale interrupts the main narrative and diverts, albeit momentarily, the reader's attention, it is tempting to pay attention to this excess rather than skirt it, to view it not as flabby storytelling, but rather as a site of potential meaning with particular hermeneutical value. While

I would argue that *most* of the moments of superfluity in *Meurtres* can be read in light of the text's imperative to stimulate knowledge about October 17, two episodes in particular stand out for their engagement with the Parisian city-text, bringing to the surfaces of urban geography the repressed memories of the massacre.

In the first of these two episodes, we encounter a minor character in the text, Claudine Chenet. The girlfriend of the murdered historian Bernard Thiraud, Claudine comes to be, in keeping with a classic trope of noir fiction, the love interest of Cadin, the detective charged with investigating her fiancé's murder. Like Bernard and his father, Claudine is a historian; her specialization is early twentieth-century Parisian urbanization, and she is writing a thesis titled "La Zone de Paris en 1930" about the marginal population that took up residence on the edges of the capital, erecting shanties on the site formerly occupied by the city's fortifications. Beyond her role as a bereaved young widow and Cadin's love interest, Claudine is, like Kaci in *Les Beurs de Seine*, an unofficial guide to the dodgy parts of Paris. This minor actor is thus a key vector of the novel's spatial and historical critique. In the episode in question, as she guides Cadin through the primary ground for her doctoral research (the edge of the 13th *arrondissement* between the Porte d'Italie and the Porte de Gentilly), Claudine delivers a lesson in marginal Parisian urban history that charts the vagaries of this "zone" and its poor inhabitants.[44]

Narratively negligible, this episode does nothing to advance the investigation, nor is it significant in terms of Cadin's romantic aspirations. Yet if its facts are superfluous to the story, its symbolic potential is essential to the anarchive: It is here that Claudine emerges as the authoritative voice of lost memories of the city, and as the keeper and defender of the memories of a marginalized population of laborers who were often viewed with suspicion. As a portrait of a particular zone of Paris takes on life, it becomes possible to infer a metonymical operation from Claudine's discourse. A mention of the term *bidonville* (139) in the context of a novel whose opening chapter is set partially in the Nanterre *bidonville* in 1961, reactivates a memory of the place from which many Algerians departed on the night of October 17. In addition, it subtly

---

44 As Margaret Atack has noted, "the fortifications" (the zone Claudine studies and glosses for Cadin) "are an historical and social archive in their own right." Atack, "From *Meurtres pour mémoire* to *Missak*," 277.

reinscribes the scene from the first chapter into the heart of the text, while also articulating comparisons with the narrative present:

> Prenez un journal, ouvrez-le à la page des faits divers, vous vous apercevrez que rien n'a vraiment changé. Les brebis galeuses sont maintenant ceux qui logent dans les grands ensembles, en lointaine banlieue. Les Minguettes, les Quatre Mille. Les immigrés ont remplacé les romanichels, les jeunes chômeurs ont pris la place des biffins. [...] Certains avait intérêt à donner une image négative du people de la zone. Ils ont utilisé le phénomène de rejet pour les chasser de la périphérie immédiate de la ville. Ça continue avec l'utilisation actuelle du thème de l'insécurité. On tente d'assimiler les couches sociales les plus durement frappés par la crise à des groupes présentant des dangers pour la société. [...] Et ça marche! La grand-mère la mieux intentionnée serre son sac à main sur son ventre dès qu'elle croise un garçon aux cheveux un peu trop bouclés. (140)

> (Take a newspaper, open it at the *faits divers*, and you'll find that nothing much has changed. The black sheep are now the ones living in the big housing projects in the outer suburbs. The Minguette flats, the 4000. The immigrants have replaced the vagrants, the young unemployed have succeeded the rag pickers. [...] There were those with an interest in giving a negative image to the poorer sections of the working class. They made use of this outcast status to push them beyond the city limits. This continues today in the way everyday insecurities are played on. There's an attempt to identify the social groups most hard hit by the crises as groups endangering the rest of society. [...] And it works. The kindliest old lady will hug her bag to her chest the minute she encounters a boy whose complexion is on the dark side.) (116)

Claudine's references here to 1980s spatial and social politics (the relation of the poor immigrant classes to *les grands ensembles*) remind us that the young people in question, the "black sheep" with "complexions on the dark side"—on the verge of becoming *les beurs*—are the children of the demonstrators on October 17.[45] If her representation of the downtrodden who lived in the zone in question is humanizing and democratizing—she continually prompts Cadin to rethink his received ideas about criminality in the area by citing statistics, as the conversation shifts to how the zone was controlled, she blatantly accuses the press of sensationalizing and, more importantly, accuses the police of covering

---

45   This of course predates the most well-known representation of the *banlieue*, racism, and the effects of unemployment and exclusion, Mathieu Kassovitz's feature film *La Haine* (1995).

up "upper class" crimes in order to foreground the poor as inherently criminal: "On peut acheter certains journaux, on ferait la même constatation: assassins, sadiques, violeurs, tous les sales rôles sont tenus par des ouvriers, des miséreux. Jamais de notables [...] Vous courez uniquement après les plus petits et vous laissez les gros se repaître tranquillement [...] Le système se protégé efficacement. La police constitue l'un des éléments majeurs du dispositif" (141, "Popular newspapers today have not changed: murderers, sadists, rapists, all the filthy roles are played by workers, have-nots. Never any big shots [...] You only chase the little ones and you let the big ones prosper undisturbed [...] The system has a good line of self-protection. The police play a crucial role," 116–17).

While Claudine's history lesson makes no direct reference to October 17, it nonetheless performs the very historical and spatial critique that *Meurtres* itself advocates and embodies by excavating marginal stories. Like Kaci in *Les Beurs de Seine*, Claudine, through her attention to the non-monumental, "scratches the varnish" that covers uncomfortable histories. By doing her fieldwork in, and writing about, the zone, Claudine re-draws the mental maps of Paris, pulling the focus away from the center and reorienting our gaze to the edges and, by extension, to those who inhabit them. Unlike a promenade along the Champs-Élysées, this stroll through "forgotten" Paris has the effect of recuperating a part of the city that had fallen off the mental map.

The second episode of *Meurtres* to stage urban geography's ability to make repressed memories visible is not situated in Paris, but rather in Toulouse. Much like Claudine's lesson in urban history, the passage in question—Cadin's description of graffiti on a wall outside his office—is firmly diegetic but utterly incidental to the plot. The scene occurs halfway through the novel, at a moment when Cadin has amassed numerous puzzle pieces regarding the murder of Roger Thiraud in Paris on the night of October 17, 1961, and that of his son Bernard some 20 years later in Toulouse, yet still cannot see the relationship between them. He sits back in his office chair to contemplate the graffiti-covered wall outside his window, and the page-long description of the ever-morphing "writing on the wall" produces a subtle comment on the legibility of cities and the writing of history, as well as a sidelong glance at October 17. Although the wall in question is not set in Paris, the fact that Cadin contemplates its writings while investigating the murders related to October 17 creates a symbolic contiguity. Notwithstanding the shift in locales, then, we can understand the scene in question as foregrounding the scriptable planes of the city and quite specifically reactivating a

memory of the disappeared Parisian graffiti "Ici on noie les Algériens"—
the original "text" of October 17. In the case of Cadin's wall, the parade
of historically conscious graffiti has turned it into a kind of barometer
of the planet: "Le mur face au commissariat résonnait depuis toujours
des événements qui secouaient le monde" (161, "The wall opposite the
station had always carried echoes of events that shook the world," 135),
and Cadin's initial musings raise issues inherent to reading graffiti.
Necessarily anonymous, mutable, and subject to incessant editing, the
genre is naturally resistant to ascriptions of intention. In the graffito "I
AU REFERENDUM" Cadin notes, the "I" could indicate "yes" (the *ou*
of "oui" having been drawn over) or "no," with the I being in fact the
final leg of the N in "non." This graffito, then, has been rewritten to such
a degree that its meaning has been rendered ambivalent; there is no way
to know its position on the referendum (nor to what referendum it refers).
Similarly, Cadin observes how changes to other tags chart the vagaries
of time and ideology: In the slogan "Solidarité avec l'Iran," a first rewrite
suppresses Iran in favor of Palestine; a second edit substitutes Israel for
Palestine; and a final modification deletes all modifiers to light on the
simple declaration of "Solidarité."

   The tag "Libérez Henri Martin" poses a different reading challenge,
as "Henri Martin" is to French as "John Smith" is to English. Cadin
works through a list of possible Henri Martins, some of whom present
interesting interpretative possibilities: The first was an eminent French
historian, pertinent within the context of the novel's engagement with
history; Henri Martin was also a French architect responsible for the
Paris *périphérique* project, thus for having demolished the environment
that is the subject of Claudine's doctoral research. One of Cadin's
colleagues claims that the Henri Martin immortalized on the wall
in white letters was in fact a *refusnik* pilot during the French war
in Indochina, imprisoned for having disobeyed the order to release
his payload of bombs on the Vietnamese port of Hai Phong.[46] Like
Claudine's thesis, this actual act of military subversion has no direct link
to October 17; however, the story of a soldier disobeying state orders
so as to do what he deemed to be "right" is both aspirational and has
resonances with the French police officers on October 17 who published
the tract denouncing the behavior of their colleagues. The homage to a
refusnik pilot may cast gazes both backward and forward: back to the

---

46   See *L'Affaire Henri Martin et la lutte contre la guerre d'Indochine*, ed. Alain
Ruscio (Paris: Le Temps des cerises, 2005).

"groupe de policiers républicains" who refused to go along with the cover-up of the scale and nature of the crimes on October 17, but also forward to the representation of those *refusnik* police officers in fictions of the third wave.

Reading the Walls: Graffiti, Maps, Graffiti as Map

Walls, both written upon and read, are an important feature of the anarchive. They serve a key function in Leïla Sebbar's short novel *La Seine était rouge* (1999). Perhaps the most notable "city-text" in the anarchive, *La Seine* (unlike *Meurtres*) represents the act of writing on the wall as well as the contemplation of these texts. Moreover, whereas in *Meurtres* each graffito morphs with subsequent edits while the site remains the same, *La Seine* embeds graffiti in multiple sites throughout Paris, creating a network, and even a map. More specifically, the graffiti produced in *La Seine* directly engage the original graffito "Ici on noie les Algériens," and participate in the novel's project of rogue cartography.

As the first text of the third wave, *Seine* builds on several anarchival works that predate it, yet it is the first novel to devote the entirety of its narrative content to October 17 and one of the few cultural texts whose entire aesthetic project is given over to staging the afterlives of the massacre. *Seine* has a clear instructive (we might even say didactic) aspect: It offers up historical detail and, through its production of testimonial accounts, also represents subjective experiences of both survivors and perpetrators. Formally, however, the text's insistence on gaps and the unspoken, not to mention its enigmatic conclusion, tend to signal a literary and historiographical operation that is less interested in what happened on October 17 than in what happened—and what continues to happen—to the memories of October 17. Moreover, the particular spatial practices of its characters—who set out to map October 17 onto the contemporary cityscape—imply a desire to displace personal memories into the public space of the city, that is, to mobilize the scriptable attributes of October 17.

That traditional vectors of knowledge transmission have been broken is made evident in the first line of the novel: "Sa mère ne lui a rien dit ni la mère de sa mère" (15, "Her mother said nothing to her, nor did her mother's mother," 1). With possessive pronouns referring to Amel, the female protagonist, the short phrase's multiplication of negation (ne, rien, ni) encodes the foreclosure of intergenerational knowledge:

Nobody, neither her mother nor her mother's mother, has bothered to tell Amel anything. Notwithstanding these ruptures in transmission, the notion that knowledge can be restored is one of the main thrusts of *La Seine était rouge*. The novel not only enacts and embodies this restoration, it figures the complexities and inadequacies of retrieval and representation. Indeed, Sebbar's work does not so much repair broken vectors as establish new paths.

Sebbar sets in motion a trio of protagonists who practice the space of the city. Amel, daughter and granddaughter of October 17 survivors, is a student of classical languages who knows nothing of her own family history. Omer is an Algerian journalist who has left his country to escape the violence of the Dark Decade (that is, the Algerian Civil War); he accompanies Amel through Paris, leaving an occasional graffito in his wake. Louis, a Frenchman and son of *porteurs de valise*, has just made a documentary film about October 17.[47] In fact, Amel learns about October 17 only through watching Louis's film, which is composed of testimonials (including Amel's mother's own account), and so her coming to historical consciousness is not achieved through family or formal education but rather is mediated through cinematic technology and a young Frenchman's desire to reconstruct a lost portion of the recent past.[48] Vignettes of Louis's documentary are interwoven with the story of Amel and Omer's excursions in the capital, and these moving images provide the impetus for their wanderings, as the two visit the sites described in the film. Louis, in turn, appears to follow Amel and Omer through the city unbeknownst to them, filming the traces they leave behind. Louis's trailing presence, visible only to the reader, is thus

47   *Les porteurs de valise*, or suitcase carriers, was the name given to left-leaning French activists and members of the Jeanson network who assisted the Algerian cause (most often by carrying money or documents in suitcases). The notion dates to the French Resistance during World War II. See Hervé Hamon and Patrick Rotman, *Les porteurs de valises* (Paris: Albin Michel, 1979). On Francis Jeanson and his activism see Marie-Pierre Ulloa, trans. Jane Marie Todd, *Francis Jeanson: A Dissident Intellectual from the French Resistance to the Algerian War* (Stanford, CA: Stanford University Press, 2009).

48   The relationship between a young female of Algerian origin and a young French male who knows a great deal about Algeria is something of a trope in Sebbar's fiction. The *Shérazade* trilogy, which began in 1982, features a character named Julien who, like Louis in *La Seine était rouge*, is something of a *nouveau* Orientalist.

signaled solely through the novel's representation of his filmed images of Omer's graffiti.

Sebbar's text is keenly aware of Paris as a mute protagonist in the events of October 17, and the characters engage the city both directly and obliquely. They produce alternative cartographies of Paris and challenge the existing "memorialscape" by revising and editing the text of the city, creating signs where currently only blanks exist. The repeated references to Parisian toponyms in the chapter titles (Paris, Nanterre, La Défense, République, rue de la Santé, Concorde, Saint-Michel) foreground the importance of place, and the characters' practice of urban space adds another dimension to the already complex referential web created by the text. The first chapter, titled "Nanterre," does not reveal much about the western Parisian suburb, although the historical significance is clear: Nanterre was the site of the largest slum in Europe in the middle of the century and home to a large population of the Algerian immigrants working in the region. The "Nanterre" chapter is the only one to end with a kind of time stamp, a "signature" that reads: "Nanterre—Université—Le RER—Paris. Octobre 1996" (17/3). The brief litany of this final line of the chapter also serves as an itinerary, a map. That the following chapter is titled "Paris" seems to confirm this notation as signaling a one-way trip into the city, a journey from the margins to the center—echoing both the movement from the outskirts of the city into the center by Algerian protesters on the night of the massacre and, perhaps more abstractly, the emerging centrality of Algerian history in French discourse.[49]

The chapter is also a first indication of Amel's interest in cartography. Indeed, my interpretation of the chapter's so-called signature as a map is partly conditioned by the mention of an actual map pinned to the wall of the dining room in Amel's house, above the TV. Evoked in reference to Amel's grandparents' trip to Mecca (17/3), this map appears to have a vaguely talismanic value for Amel, who realizes that once she leaves home, "elle n'entendra plus parler de ce fameux pèlerinage et répéter les noms de villes et des pays à traverser. La carte est épinglée sur le mur de la salle à manger, au-dessus de la télévision" (17, "She'll no longer hear

---

49 Fulton similarly argues that *La Seine était rouge* "decenters the métropole" (25), while staging a "process of excavation and creation undertaken." The actions of the characters in the novel, "like the demonstration of October 1961, claims a central presence and visibility of the colonial nation's elsewhere in the main streets of Paris" (36).

them talking about this famous pilgrimage, repeating the names of the cities and countries they'll cross. The map is tacked on to the dining room wall, above the TV," 3). The reality of this trip is less interesting for Amel than its visual representation, which traces key sites of the *hadj*. Its appearance just before the chapter's signature ("Nanterre—Université—Le RER—Paris") brings two very different toponymic litanies into close textual proximity, amalgamating a holy pilgrimage (stations of the *hadj*) and a journey into Paris on public transportation (stations of the metro), endowing Amel's own trajectory with a sacred component.

The significance of these first cartographic moments in *La Seine* is amplified by a second explicit reference to a map. Observing Omer reading the newspaper, Amel asks, "C'est la page des massacres? [...] Lis à haute voix, que je sache, comme si j'avais une carte sous les yeux: Tlemcen, Aïn Defla, Médéa, Tiaret, Aflou, Blida, Alger...Tizi-Ouzou..." (39, "Is this the page about the massacres? [...] Read aloud so I can follow, as if I had a map in front of my eyes: Tlemcen, Aïn Delfa, Médéa, Tiaret, Aflou, Blida, Algiers...Tizi-Ouzou...," 25).[50] Amel has never been to Algeria, but she tells Omer: "Dans ma chambre j'ai une carte de l'Algérie. Je mets une épingle rouge pour marquer les massacres" (39, "I stick in red pins to mark the massacres," 25), a mapping that allows her to "savoir la géographie terroriste" (39, [to know] "terrorist geography," 25). While the two maps in Amel's house chart very different territories—a millenary pilgrimage to a holy land and the brutal civil war of a postcolonial republic—both suggest that her understanding of the world demands geographic referents. To encode realities, she must be able to grid the unknown onto a knowable index.

The established penchant for maps, this worldview that requires a geographic index, is at the root of Amel's reaction to the knowledge she acquires about October 17 in viewing Louis's film. The need to comprehend the massacre by charting its spatial movements and identifying its key sites spurs Amel to enact (with the exile Omer in tow) an idiosyncratic cartography of Paris, one that is vaguely reminiscent of the Situationist International's psychogeography insofar as it contests the sovereignty of the institutional map by chopping it up and connecting its "unités d'ambiance."[51] Amel's mental remapping will combine with

50   Amel's reference to the "massacre page" refers to the violent Algerian Civil War of the 1990s, when death tolls were routinely front-page news in the French press.
51   The *unité d'ambiance* corresponds to the smallest unit of urban analysis (a

Omer's practice of graffiti to reveal the links between monumental
Parisian sites and the October 17 massacre, ultimately producing Paris as
a *scriptable* text, that is, as a text that requires the mediation of a reader
willing and able to move beyond an initial opacity, able to "scratch the
surface of the varnish" (to once again invoke Kaci in *Beurs*).

Amel's mapping practice is twofold, revealing the difficulty of writing
a new history in sites where a dominant narrative has already made
its mark. First, she continually draws Omer's attention to the physical
layout of Paris, and specifically to the capital's historical axis, in an
attempt to teach the Parisian cityscape and to make established urban
landscapes reveal their hidden stories by mentally calquing episodes
from Louis's film onto the physical city before them: "Si tu as vraiment
regardé le film de Louis, tu sais qu'à la Défense, au rond point de la
Défense, au pont de Neuilly, à la Concorde, la police française et les
harkis de Papon ont raflé, frappé, tué des algériens, le 17 octobre 1961"
(51, "If you had really watched Louis's film, you would know that at
Défense, the Défense traffic circle, Neuilly bridge, Place de la Concorde,
French police and Papon's harkis rounded up, beat, and killed Algerians
on October 17, 1961," 37–38).

In addition to charting new territory by narratively "emplotting"
October 17 sites within the Parisian urban landscape, Amel also *edits*
existing historical traces that have no relationship to the 1961 massacre.
This editing looks accidental: She reads aloud the text of monumental
inscriptions and memorial plaques she encounters, but the versions
produced are always partial, with portions of the established history
elided or de-narrated. At the Marianne statue at La Défense, for
example, the reproduction of the plaque's text contains several ellipses:

> La statue
> LA DÉFENSE DE PARIS
> inaugurée…
> afin de rappeler le courage des Parisiens
> pendant le terrible siège de 1870–1871.
> A été réinstallée à son emplacement initial…
> Elle a été inaugurée le 21 septembre 1983. (53)

neighborhood, an urban *îlot*). See Debord, "La Théorie de la derive," in *Les Lèvres
nues* 9 (December 1956). It has been glossed as "an area of particularly intense
urban atmosphere." See Simon Sadler, *The Situationist City* (Cambridge, MA:
MIT Press, 1998), 69.

(The statue
THE DEFENSE OF PARIS
inaugurated…
to recall the courage of the Parisians
during the terrible siege of 1870–1871.
Reinstalled at its original site…
It was inaugurated September 21, 1983.) (39)

These gaps are explained away as the result of Amel reading fast, skipping words.

Later, near the Saint-Michel fountain, a similar revision occurs; here, however, the missing text is represented as *visually* inaccessible, blocked out by Omer's shoulder (101).[52] In both cases, we might read such acts as denying the plenitude of the official marks of French history, as writing them out of the Parisian memorialscape. (We might also remember the framing techniques in Adi's documentary that served to depict the map of Paris as always partial, amputated, or incomplete.) However, insofar as the missing words seem to hold no particular symbolic value, the significance of the act may derive less from what is left out than from the very fact of the erasure itself, which calls attention to other, unnamed and unrecognized historical erasures. We might even say that her edits participate in making the text *scriptable*, compelling the reader to fill in gaps.

Amel thus functions as a revisionist cartographer, anxiously repeating the story of October 17 through its sites and trajectories so as to reconfigure the map of Paris in a way that charts an invisible spatial and historical reality. But if Amel is busy redrawing the maps through language, Omer, despite his feigned indifference to Amel's geography lessons, is also busy "writing" wrongs. In exile in Paris, the Algerian journalist practices a different form of "reportage": In a bid to make readable a story that has no textual presence in the city, he gives himself over to the renegade act of tagging, inscribing Algerian history onto the existing monuments of Paris.[53] Written with red spray paint

---

52   As Rothberg has observed, here "Sebbar literalizes the partiality of official memory at the site of another memorial" (*Multidirectional Memory*, 299).

53   David Fieni's concept of "nomad grammatology" is apropos here; Fieni points out the relationship between "letters of graffiti and the letter of the law," noting "the imbrication of structures of authority and graffiti's critique of them: the graffitist positions him or herself outside the law, while also writing on the very material surfaces of the law (property, the walls built by the state); graffiti does

and "incrusté dans la pierre" (28, "etched in the stone," 14), Omer's graffiti represent a form of alternative history, as he sprays the invisible stories of Algerians in Paris alongside official, institutionally sanctioned monuments and commemorative plaques. Indeed, the French verb that designates writing with a spray can, *bomber*, adds a violent dimension to Omer's revisions: Omer does not write, "il bombe."

Omer's tags stand out as one of the most salient features of Sebbar's memorial and historical interventions. Not surprisingly, then, the graffiti are perhaps one of the most commented features of *La Seine était rouge*, having been held up as exemplifying "multidirectional" and "palimpsestic" memory, and as proof of the text's engagement with "creolization."[54] Here, however, I would like to engage a number of details that have been left unattended, details crucial to a deeper understanding of how *La Seine était rouge* produces knowledge about October 17, and providing an example of how the anarchive can be made to interact, productively, with archival material.

First, it is worth noting that Omer does not indiscriminately tag all of the statues and monuments he visits with Amel. In fact, although the pair spends a significant amount of time contemplating "Mariannes" (at La Défense and again at République), these monuments to French glory are left unedited by Omer. Second, the places where he does leave his mark— the Prison de la Santé, the Hôtel de Crillon on the Place de la Concorde, and near the Saint-Michel fountain—are not only sites of Algerian memory but places with a particular significance for World War II.[55] This graffiti narrative thus makes the existing memorialscape of Paris less *lisible* (readerly, in Barthes's sense)—that is, less directly communicative, less transparent—and renders it more scriptable/writerly, dependent upon the reader's mediation and operating outside of, or against, the established "codes" of memorialization and historical knowledge.

Each of Omer's tags has its own particularity. At the Hôpital Sainte-Anne/la Prison de la Santé (in the 14th), he inscribes the site's

---

not simply stand outside or against the state, but always links up with the state, disfigures the representatives of the state, and becomes barred by state science." See "What a Wall Wants, or How Graffiti Thinks: Nomad Grammatology in the French *Banlieue*," *Diacritics* 40, no. 2 (Summer 2012): 3.

54 Rothberg, Silverman, Fulton (in that order).

55 Whereas the Hôtel de Crillon was used as the headquarters of the German military authorities, the Prison de la Santé and the Saint-Michel fountain are sites where Parisian resistance to the occupying forces is glorified.

significance for Algerian history alongside the official memorial of French suffering during World War II. The original plaque reads:

EN CETTE PRISON
LE 11 NOVEMBRE 1940
FURENT INCARCÉRÉS DES LYCÉENS ET DES ÉTUDIANTS
QUI À L'APPEL DU GÉNÉRAL DE GAULLE
SE DRESSÈRENT LES PREMIERS CONTRE L'OCCUPANT. (28)

(ON NOVEMBER 11 1940
IN THIS PRISON WERE HELD
HIGH SCHOOL AND UNIVERSITY STUDENTS
WHO, AT THE CALL OF GENERAL DE GAULLE,
WERE THE FIRST TO RISE UP
AGAINST THE OCCUPATION.) (14)

Omer's revision replaces Algerians in this memorial:

1954–1962
DANS CETTE PRISON
FURENT GUILLOTINÉS
DES RÉSISTANTS ALGÉRIENS
QUI SE DRESSÈRENT
CONTRE L'OCCUPANT FRANÇAIS. (29)

(1954–1962
IN THIS PRISON
WERE GUILLOTINED
ALGERIAN RESISTERS
WHO ROSE UP
AGAINST THE FRENCH OCCUPATION.) (15)

Parallel to the plaque in both its physical position and its grammatical structure (note the use of the *passé simple*, the slightly rarefied expression "se dresser"), the tag creates an implicit adequation between the German occupation of France and the French colonial forces occupying Algeria. Moreover, Omer reminds readers that the preferred killing technology of the Revolution, the guillotine, was still in use in twentieth-century Paris.

Omer also tags the Hôtel de Crillon, the pre-revolutionary *palace* that stands on the Place de la Concorde. Here, the new tag does not share space with an existing inscription; the hotel's connection to World War II is known—it was used to billet German military officers—but it is certainly not the stuff of commemorative plaques. With its initial deictic marker, Omer's tag—"*Ici* des Algériens ont été matraqués sauvagement par la police du préfet Papon le 17 octobre 1961"—activates a memory of the 1961 graffito with which we began this chapter ("Ici on noie les Algériens"). Yet Omer's version goes beyond the 1961 tag in its direct accusations; its reference to the date and its addition of the qualifier "sauvagement" bring to the surface—of the building, literally, and of collective consciousness, symbolically—a repressed French history of occupation and collaboration.

The final tag of *La Seine était rouge* appears along the riverbank near the Pont Saint-Michel, toward the end of the novel, immediately after we see Amel and Omer contemplating the plaques at the Saint-Michel fountain. Whereas the first two graffiti are physically placed in a direct relationship to the material objects whose signifying valences they seek to reorient, the third tag represents a break: It is no longer tethered to, nor in competition with, existing histories. Omer's last tag evinces its own narrative, historical, and spatial authority: "Ici des Algériens sont tombés pour l'indépendance de l'Algérie le 17 octobre 1961" (107, "On this spot Algerians fell for the independence of Algeria October 17, 1961," 93). The expression "tombés pour l'indépendance" parrots standard "memorial speak" ("ici est tombé pour la France," and so forth), and this battlefield lexicon suggests that, on October 17, Algerians participated in a worthy, even glorious national project. Of Omer's three tags, this is the only one to make a direct connection between October 17 and Algerian independence, characterizing the events of that day as part and parcel of the struggle for national liberation. In this context, of course, the turn of phrase "sont tombés pour l'indépendance" is also heavy with irony, as many Algerians quite literally "sont tombés" in the Seine, while the text itself is situated just above the river.

Even more so than the graffito at the Crillon, this tag clearly reactivates the semantics of the 1961 "Ici on noie les Algériens," again echoing the deictic marker "ici," which, now, points to the Seine itself and thus implicates the river in the massacre (as does Sebbar's title *La Seine était rouge*). Despite the striking similarities between the two tags, Omer's version nonetheless contains a substantive revision: Whereas in 1961 "on" a noyé les Algériens—with *on* signifying at once "us" (in a gesture of collective self-accusation) and "one" (a nameless guilty party)—in Omer's present-day formulation, "les Algérians sont tombés." If this edit causes the tag to lose its accusatory tone, we cannot fail to notice that Omer's tag effectively changes the subject, giving the Algerians grammatical agency and linking the Parisian massacre to the Algerian

liberation struggle and thus holding up the fallen of October 17 as
martyrs.

With his final tag situated along the Quai Saint-Michel, on the edge of
the Latin Quarter and just across from the Île de la Cité, Omer's graffiti
historiography has brought Sebbar's text centripetally closer to the heart
of the city. Here, it enters the physical and discursive vicinity of both
the original graffiti with which this story began and Bertrand Delanoë's
memorial plaque, positioned along the Saint-Michel Bridge. But it
also enters a zone crackling with invisible semiotic traffic. Indeed, as I
have mentioned, the original graffiti from 1961 painted along the Quai
de Conti, facing the Institut de France, has today become a veritable
"militant icon" of October 17.[56] Given the status of October 17 in public
discourse as an "événement occulté" (an occluded or unseen event) it is
perhaps fitting that its first Parisian inscription was made in the form of
graffiti. Presumably anonymous, necessarily political, and ephemeral by
nature of its form and its means of production, the genre of graffiti seems
to encapsulate an essential truth about representations of the massacre.[57]
Like the graffiti, cultural productions of October 17 appeared in the heat
of the moment, only to have their "readability" compromised by erasure
and other constraints.

Thanks to the detective work of a couple of French historians, we
know that capturing this particular graffito was a matter of chance:
Jean Texier, a woodworker and volunteer journalist at *Avant Garde*
(the weekly newsletter of the *Mouvement des jeunes communistes
de France*), was at the paper's offices in early November 1961 when a
colleague reported seeing the graffiti. Texier hustled back to the site
in his colleague's car, jumping out just fast enough to make a quick
snapshot before the two gendarmes guarding the tag could react. By
accident or by design, the forces of order were edited out of the snapshot

56   Lemire and Potin. The image was featured on the cover of *L'Humanité* in 1986
(25 years later after it was taken); it was used as the emblem for the association Le
17 octobre contre l'oubli (founded in 1988); reproduced on tracts, posters, stickers,
even hung as a banderole on the Pont Saint-Michel, in a kind of restaging of the
original graffiti; a photoshopped version serves as the cover image for La Cour
Grandmaison's *17 Octobre 1961* and of Adi's documentary (2011); finally, publicity
material for nearly every conference or event devoted to the events of October 17
features this image.
57   See Keely B. Harris, "Graffiti as Public Pedagogy: The Educative Potential of
Street Art," in *Metropedagogy*, ed. Joe Kincheloe and Kecia Hayes (Rotterdam:
Sense Publishers, 2006), 97–112.

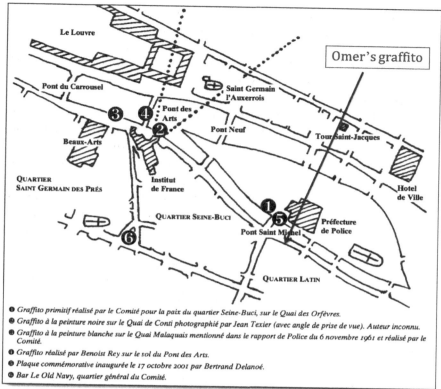

Omer's graffito

Le Louvre

Pont du Carrousel

Saint Germain l'Auxerrois

Pont des Arts

Pont Neuf

Beaux-Arts

Tour Saint-Jacques

QUARTIER SAINT GERMAIN DES PRÉS

Institut de France

Hotel de Ville

QUARTIER SEINE-BUCI

Préfecture de Police

Pont Saint Michel

QUARTIER LATIN

❶ *Graffito primitif réalisé par le Comité pour la paix du quartier Seine-Buci, sur le Quai des Orfèvres.*
❷ *Graffito à la peinture noire sur le Quai de Conti photographié par Jean Texier (avec angle de prise de vue). Auteur inconnu.*
❸ *Graffito à la peinture blanche sur le Quai Malaquais mentionné dans le rapport de Police du 6 novembre 1961 et réalisé par le Comité.*
❹ *Graffito réalisé par Benoist Rey sur le sol du Pont des Arts.*
❺ *Plaque commémorative inaugurée le 17 octobre 2001 par Bertrand Delanoé.*
❻ *Bar Le Old Navy, quartier général du Comité.*

Document 10. Plan du quartier Seine-Buci et localisation des graffitis. © Dessin Yann Potin, Vincent Lemire.

Fig. 9. Mapping the October 17 graffiti.
Map created by Yann Potin and Vincent Lemire. © 2002.
(The location of Omer's graffiti is my own addition to the map.)

at the moment it was taken (not in post-production). This capture is all the more significant in light of the fact that numerous denunciatory tags were made in this area in the wake of the October 17 massacre—all within a few blocks running between the Pont Saint-Michel and the Pont des Arts—although no others were captured on film.

Through interviews and archival research, the same historians who tracked down Texier (the photographer) have reconstituted traces of these erased tags and recreated a bygone, ephemeral memorialscape by "emplotting" the sites of the 1961 graffiti on the map of central Paris. (See Fig. 9.) Omer's tag, then, participates in and extends this network of variously visible traces, thickening the cartographic record. And while his graffiti stands along the same *quai* as the graffito captured in the Texier photo, it also casts a sidelong glance across the river to the space that now marks the absence of the very first known October 17 graffiti. In gazing across the river to its forerunner, Omer's declaration also looks askance at the Préfecture de police, the physical and symbolic site of state power, the site from which emanated, on October 17, state terror.

Ultimately, in its treatment of graffiti, *La Seine était rouge* reproduces and extends the logic of representation: Just as Texier's photographic image has been reproduced, giving legs to the original 1961 graffito, so Omer's tags achieve a kind of permanence through the novel's representation of Louis's filmed images: The reader only "sees" Omer's graffiti through the lens of Louis's camera, as it records the palimpsest created by the superimposition of rogue historiography on the classic memorialscape. Literature itself thus functions as a form of reproducible technology, endowing ephemeral traces with real staying power. Omer's additions, together with Amel's subtractions/edits and remappings, produce a network of nodal points and connective tissue that can be laid over the existing map of Paris, much like a calque. This calque, or text, has the effect of reclaiming—and perhaps even decolonizing—that imperial practice of mapping, that gesture of totalizing knowledge and control.

It is fitting, in this regard, that, at the end of Sebbar's novella, the action goes literally off the map. The brief, and somewhat unexpected, final chapter finds all three protagonists together at a café in Alexandria, Egypt. Louis is scouting locations for a film on Bonaparte's "Orientalists"; Omer claims to be writing a play that, from its description, is a reprise of *Antigone*. Amel appears in this chapter as an ancillary character, an object, never a subject. A dozen years later, in 2011, Sebbar wrote a brief epilogue to *La Seine était rouge*, titled "L'île Seguin, le retour," published in a volume of memorial essays/short stories titled *17 écrivains se souviennent*.[58] Situated downstream from Paris, the île Seguin is an island in the Seine where the Renault factory employed an almost exclusively Algerian workforce during the boom known as the "Glorious Thirty."[59]

The short story begins in medias res, clearly evoking (at a significant temporal distance) the end of *La Seine était rouge*:

58 Sebbar, "L'île Seguin, le retour," in Harzoune and Messaoudi, 185–92.
59 See Chapter 1, p. 41.

Ils ne voulaient plus quitter l'Égypte. Louis et Omer, chaque jour sur la place de la colère au Caire [...] criaient avec les Égyptiens, en arabe et en français, «Dégage MOUBARAK.» [...] Amel, de retour à Paris, avait suivi à l'image jour après jour les Révoltes arabes [...] Elle avait défilé dans les rues de Paris, hurlant des slogans en arabe, on la prenait pour une Égyptienne. (187)[60]

(They didn't want to leave Egypt anymore. Every day at Anger Square in Cairo, Louis and Omer [...] chanted with the Egyptians, in Arabic and in French, "Get out MOUBARAK." [...] Amel, when she got back to Paris, had followed the Arab revolutions closely [...]. She'd protested in the streets of Paris, yelling slogans in Arabic. People took her for an Egyptian.)

Amel remembers that she had "parcouru les stations du martyr algérien, ce terrible 17 octobre 1961, pensant donner, par ce pèlerinage avec Omer, une tombe [...] aux Algériens qui n'avaient pas été sauvés des eaux" (188, traveled the stations of the Algerian ordeal, the terrible October 17, 1961, thinking that her pilgrimage with Omer might offer a tomb [...] to those Algerians who hadn't been saved from drowning), calling explicit attention to the spatial practice of her activities with Omer, reconnecting with the very beginning of *La Seine était rouge* and the map of her grandparents' devotional voyage to Mecca. Sebbar's narrative chronology is implausible: Are we to believe the three protagonists had been simply killing time in Egypt since their arrival at the end of *La Seine était rouge*, that is, more than ten years prior? Nonetheless, the "sequel" closes the physical distance between the Arab Spring and October 17, between Cairo and Paris, folding the world map upon itself to bring the story of today's revolutions against tyranny into the textual territory of those of yesterday.

Site Specific?

I have argued, in the introduction to this book and throughout this particular chapter, that the sited nature of October 17 is perhaps its most poignant feature, that the meaning of the event is amplified by its having taken place in Paris. The site of October 17 is what distinguishes it from other acts of colonial violence and what contributes to the sense

---

60 "Place de la colère," which I have translated as "Anger Square" in order to remain faithful to Sebbar's idiosyncratic language, is clearly a reference to Tahrir Square, the focal point of the 2011 Egyptian Revolution.

that October 17 is not yet resolved (either in history or in memory). My argument about place is of course grounded in the fact that the anarchive so frequently points up the importance of the *lieu*, the site, and engages it in various ways, making visible what I have called "non-lieux de mémoire"—understood multiply as alternatives (or even challenges) to Nora's "classic" *lieux* of franco-French national memory; as a riff on Marc Augé's *non-lieux*, spaces of supermodernity and anonymity—but also spaces that "cannot be defined as relational, or historical" and that are not "concerned with identity"; and, finally, as emblems of incomplete processes of justice (borrowing here from the juridical term *non-lieu* in French).[61] But I wonder if this insistence on the site—the need to return to the scene—is, or will always be, necessary? After all, even as they negotiate "non-lieux" of October 17, the characters *of Meurtres pour mémoire, Le Sourire de Brahim, Les Beurs de Seine,* and *La Seine était rouge* reify the importance of place, of the site. Are *non-lieux*, once mobilized, simply destined to become *lieux*? Do *lieux* exercise a hegemony over our thinking and, if so, how would this play out in a theory-world where we have come to emphasize concepts like deterritorialization, nomadism, and un-homing, and where place-bound identities are increasingly unstable or impossible? As Miwon Kwon has observed, nostalgia for a place upon which to anchor identity is "out of synch with our prevalent description of contemporary life as a network of unanchored flows."[62] At what point, then, might recuperating the site become undesirable, or even unnecessary? Is the return to the scene of a crime destined to become an empty gesture?

My perhaps paradoxical interest in the potential for detachment from the primacy of the site, however, is inspired not by theory trends, but rather by the way one particular late work from the anarchive seems to have called into question the primacy of the site in representations of October 17. The performance piece "Memento" was created in 2009 by Komplex Kapharnaüm (KXKM), a self-labeled "art team" based in a suburb of Lyon, whose mission statement is unmistakably redolent of Debord's Situationists: "Nous traversons des histoires, nous composons à partir de lieux, nous croyons en la poésie du quotidien, nous

---

61   Nora, *Les lieux de mémoire*, 7 vols (Paris: Gallimard, 1984–92); Marc Augé, *Non-lieux: Introduction à une anthropologie de la surmodernité* (Paris: Seuil, 1991). The juridical term "non-lieu" is translated as "dismissal" in English.
62   Miwon Kwon, *One Place After Another: Site-Specific Art and Locational Identity* (Cambridge, MA: MIT Press, 2002), 164.

cherchons à la transcender. La ville est notre terrain de jeu, notre source d'inspiration et notre espace de représentation" (We cross histories, we create site-specific work, we believe in the poetry of the everyday, we try to transcend it. The city is our playground, our source of inspiration and our place of performance).[63] "Memento" has been performed at least 15 times since its creation in 2009, yet, like the handful of site-specific or street performance pieces that have arrived in the anarchive in the last decade (at a moment when the anarchive may be on the verge of exhaustion), the spectacle is ephemeral, existing only through the traces made by those who have witnessed it.[64]

"Memento" has a genesis story that makes no mention of October 17. Billed, on the company's website, as "speaking out in the city," the description of the performance is both specific and vague:

> Avis de recherche, collages, traces... autant de signes qui interpellent passants et riverains, et ce faisant, tracent un fil d'Ariane dans le quartier. Bientôt, sur ce parcours, des prises d'espace ont lieu. Des agents neutralisent des bouts de murs, des morceaux de façade. Un soir, des commandos circulent dans le quartier, faisant halte çà et là, pour y perpétrer des plasticages : fabrication en images, sons, collages et graffs d'une fresque pérenne. A l'issue des deux soirées d'intervention, une série de "plaques commémoratives" perdure sur les murs. Une sorte de 'fresque-manifeste' qui continue d'interroger passants et riverains sur les résistances d'hier et d'aujourd'hui.[65]

> (Wanted posters, collages, traces... so many signs that call out to passersby and locals, and in so doing, leave a trail of breadcrumbs in the neighborhood. Soon, along the path, spaces are taken over. Agents neutralize large swathes of wall, bits of façades. Then, one night, commandos invade the area and bomb it all: layering images, sound, collages, and graffiti, they create long-lasting frescos. At the end of an evening of interventions, a series of commemorative plaques is revealed on the wall. These "fresco-manifestos" interrogate passersby and locals about the resistances of today and yesterday.)

63   See the group's website: http://www.kxkm.net/la-compagnie.
64   Other street performances include "Remouvances" (by the Compagnie de la Pierre noire), which uses the city space in Bobigny and ends with the memorial gesture of throwing a wreath in the Seine. Street performance "takes back" the street, but without relying on a specific street.
65   Komplex Kapharnaüm, *Mémento*, dossier de presse, https://www.calameo.com/books/00014993632bacc96e0c2.

"Memento" in fact seems to be a placeholder for any number of site-specific interventions in urban locations that prompt an ambulatory audience to question received ideas on topics generally related to history, inequalities, social justice, and human rights. A report on the spectacle's first show in 2009 in Villeurbane (Lyon) mentions that the "commando-spectacle," which begins with a series of generalities, then unfolds to include October 17 through video projections accompanied by a voice-over description of the *bidonvilles* outside of Paris, the political climate, and Papon, culminating with filmed testimonials by survivors.[66] Based on published reviews in the press, it seems that "Memento" has often included a variety of other materials unrelated to October 17, and indeed, despite the information available on the KXKM website, it is difficult to ascertain the level of October 17 content for any given performance.[67]

In October 2014, I attended a performance of "Memento" in Marseille. Komplex Kapharnaüm's intervention was one of a variety of memorial events that had been programmed over the course of a week-long commemoration of October 17. The version of "Memento" I witnessed appeared to have been streamlined to feature only elements related to October 17, and rather than move through Marseille, the action took place solely at Leon Blum Square, in the center of the city. The performance seemed deliberately ad hoc, beginning in medias res, with actors who had been milling among the crowd stepping forward to play "Algerians." First, they postered documents to a wall that had been erected in the park—closer examination after the spectacle revealed these to be facsimiles of the police's declaration of the curfew. Actors playing agents of the state entered the scene to "arrest" the Algerians and arrange them in frisk positions against the wall; all layers of this tableau—a makeshift wall, a series of historical documents, bodies representing Algerians in a position of submission to the state—were then bombarded with a paint gun while violent music and strobe lighting heightened the tension of the scene. After a few moments, when the sensory display came to an end, each figure was removed one by one, the outline of the body remaining an empty space against the wall. The resulting "plaque"—as KXKM calls these visual palimpsests created during the spectacles—was a condensation of historical material and a fictional emblem of the fate of Algerians. (See Fig. 10.)

66 Anonymous, https://rebellyon.info/Spectacle-du-Komplex-Kapharnaum.
67 Frédérique Roussel, "Chalon en large," *Libération*, July 25–26, 2009.

Fig. 10. "Résister à l'oublis" [*sic*]. (Resist forgetting.) "Fresco" created during street performance by Komplex Kapharnaüm. Marseille, October 17, 2014. Photo: Lia Brozgal.

Although the narrative of the performance was difficult to follow, its specific relationship to October 17 was unmistakable, and the venue—such as it was—had even been outfitted with some historical context (posters, leaflets, a timeline of events). But in reflecting on the experience of watching what amounted to, at least in part, a reenactment of the police violence on October 17, I was struck by how little this street art had to do with the very streets where the violence occurred. We were in the center of Marseille; we could have been anywhere. "Memento" required a street—its ethos and aesthetics emerge in the "hijacking" of urban spaces—but it did not require a specific street in Paris to represent October 17, nor, for that matter, was there any attempt to reconstruct Paris as a set. The distinctly sited nature of the violence seemed less important in this production than the human toll, the subjective experience of submission to forces of the state. In the late works of the anarchive, particularly those invested with the potential to mobilize space in a very direct way, the representation of October 17 seems to have moved beyond the limits of Paris.

CHAPTER FOUR

The Seine's Exceptional Bodies

Ma grande, ma seule, mon absorbente passion,
pendant dix ans, ce fut la Seine.[1]

—Guy de Maupassant

Je me souviens de ceux qui voulaient nous jeter à la
mer, la mer étant trop lointaine, on en a retrouvé
certains jetés à la Seine.[2]

—Mounsi

On May 1, 1995, Brahim Bouarram, a 29-year-old Moroccan father of two, was pushed into the Seine in central Paris, where he drowned nearly instantly. The murder took place in broad daylight, and the assailants were four young men who had come to the capital from the provincial city of Reims to participate in the "Joan of Arc" parade organized annually by the Front national, or National Front, France's far-right political party. The parade that year was more politically charged than others: May 1, 1995, marked the halfway point between the two rounds of the French presidential elections; although the FN candidate, Jean-Marie Le Pen, did not advance to the second round, he had achieved a record number of votes, arriving in fourth position with a score of 15 percent.[3]

---

1   Guy de Maupassant, "Mouche, Souvenir d'un canotier," in *L'inutile beauté* (Paris: Victor-Harvard, 1890), 105. (Translation: My great, my only, my all-consuming passion was, for ten years, the Seine.)
2   Mohand Mounsi, "Bâtard," *Seconde génération* (1984). (Translation: I remember those who wanted to throw us in the ocean/The ocean was too far away so they threw us in the Seine.)
3   Le Pen came in fourth behind Jacques Chirac, Lionel Jospin, and Edouard

As the rowdy cortege passed over the Pont du Carrousel on its way to the statue of Joan of Arc, the four men decided to drop down to the embankment below. It was along this stretch of the riverbank that they encountered Bouarram: According to the assailants' accounts, the lone Moroccan insulted them, calling them "sons of bitches" and "skinheads"; according to eyewitnesses, the assailants could be heard yelling racial slurs at Bouarram before one of them shoved him into the river, where he drowned.[4] A week later, Jacques Chirac was elected president, and a political commentator from a major network observed that, all said and done, it had been a civilized campaign, with no bloodshed and no deaths.[5]

The crime was abundantly reported in the French press. A few days afterwards, François Mitterrand, in one of his last official gestures as president and before a crowd of some 12,000 onlookers, threw a bouquet of lilies of the valley into the Seine at the precise spot where Bouarram had drowned. Gazing at the current and seeming to address the river directly, Mitterrand announced that the bouquet served as a sign that the disappeared man was not forgotten.[6] In many ways, Brahim Bouarram's murder received the public and political attention it merited, both as a tragic human loss and as a symbol of a rising tide of racist violence.[7] Yet the

---

Balladur, but his score placed him higher than long-standing Communist candidate Robert Hue, *Lutte ouvrière* (ultra-left Trotskyist) leader Arlette Laguiller, and Philippe de Villiers, an ultra-right-wing conservative.

4   Karen Saranga, "Le jeune homme qui suivait le FN," *L'Express*, April 10, 1998.

5   As the activist and philosopher Pierre Tevanian has pointed out, the commentator's remark is largely figurative, but it ignores the fact that the campaign began with the death of a young man from the Comoro Islands, and ended with Brahim's murder. In other words, the 1995 presidential campaign was a site of violence by FN extremists against French citizens of immigrant origins. See Tevanian, "Hommage à Brahim Bouarram: retour sur un crime raciste et son effacement," http://lmsi.net/Hommage-a-Brahim-Bouarram.

6   Mitterrand's speech can be seen online: "Mitterrand/Carrousel," *F2 Le Journal 20h*, May 3, 1995, http://www.ina.fr/video/CAB95028427.

7   The death of Brahim Bouarram belongs to a series of racially motivated murders that took place in the mid-1990s in France, a number of which were significantly more mediatized, including the death of Makomé M'Bowolé—a young man from Zaire killed while in police custody—which inspired Mathieu Kassovitz's *La Haine*. See Brigitte Vital-Durand, "1995. L'Année noire de la violence raciste. Sept meurtres à caractère xénophobe ont été recensés en France l'année dernière," *Libération*, March 21, 1996.

death of an innocent Arab in the Seine (and at the hands of angry racists), in all its symbolic horror, did not seem to trigger a return to consciousness of the murder, in the not so distant past, of so many innocent Algerians in the very same river. Not a single news outlet mentioned the uncanny echo, and as Mitterrand gazed into the very waters that had swallowed protesters on October 17 but failed to connect history's dots, his promises of perennial memory already rang hollow.

Bouarram's story is of course only epiphenomenally related to October 17, yet it trains our focus on several important continuities between these two violent episodes. Certainly, it testifies to the persistent symbolic and discursive invisibility of October 17, some 35 years after the facts. Indeed, given what we know about the structures of traumatic memory, the details of Bouarram's murder should have prompted a "return of the repressed." That it failed to disperse the national fog surrounding those events only attests to the density of the cover. But it also underscores the common site and embodied nature of both episodes, which (again, notwithstanding differences of scale and "ideology") saw unwanted bodies beaten and disposed of in the Seine. A second important continuity, then, between the murder of a young Moroccan grocer by four civilians in 1995 and the massacre of Algerians by forces of the state in 1961, is the implicit construction of the North African as *un corps d'exception*, or an exceptional body, where "exceptional" is understood not as superlatively positive, but rather as "unusual," or as "presenting a special problem."[8] The victims in 1961 were *indigènes*, indigenous peoples of a colonized state, and thus necessarily subjected to *un régime d'exception* (an exceptional regime) of discipline and control.[9]

---

8   The concept of the exceptional body has been articulated by Sidi Mohammed Barakat in *Corps d'exception: Les artifices du pouvoir colonial et la destruction de la vie* (Paris: Éditions Amsterdam, 2005); and in his essay "Corps et état," in special issue "Corps en guerre: Imaginaires, idéologies, destructions," *Quasimodo* 9 (Spring 2006): 153–62. Pierre Tevanian has also done important work to mobilize this concept. See "Le 'corps d'exception' et ses métamorphoses. Réflexions sur la construction et la destruction de 'l'immigré' et du 'jeune' issu de l'immigration coloniale et post-coloniale," *Quasimodo* 9 (Spring 2006): 163–80.

9   The exceptional regime in question was a rule of law: The *code de l'indigénat*, which established the difference between Europeans and Algerians, was codified in 1881 and officially repealed in 1944. Emmanuel Blanchard's work on the notion of "citoyens diminués," or diminished citizens, is useful here. See *Encadrer des "citoyens diminués". La police des Algériens en région parisienne (1944–1962)* (doctoral thesis, Université de Bourgogne, 2008). See also Weil, "Le Statut des

Years after the fact, Bouarram could no longer technically be considered an "indigène," yet the fact that he was subjected to a form of "discipline and control" (however rogue), points up the enduring structures of colonial mentality.

The notion of the iconic Parisian river as a mass burial site—the very thought of bodies in the Seine—remains one of the most gruesome aspects of the massacre. And while not all of the dead on October 17 fell victim to the river, it is nonetheless true that the Seine has come to occupy significant symbolic territory in the realm of representation, to a degree that perhaps surpasses the representation of analogous "killing fields" or "technologies" of destruction in other episodes of state violence. The anarchive is replete with images of the Seine and of the experience of exceptional bodies, all of which participate in an implicit project of resignifying the river. Certain anarchival productions—the graphic posters produced for the 50th anniversary of the massacre, for example—are uncompromising and unambiguous in their representation of the Seine as a dumping ground for "exceptional" bodies. Others depict the river in a documentary style whose ostensible straightforwardness often belies a subtle critique. And many anarchival works treat the river in ways that are complex and equivocal, thus unsettling the reader above and beyond the decidedly unsettling facts of the matter. In exploring these representations of the Seine, I seek to make visible a poetic and political discourse about the nature of the violence on October 17 and to explore the way culture has dealt with the weighty implications of a state hiding the evidence of its crimes in a site so geographically, affectively, and symbolically central.

"For Some Time Now, the Seine Has Been Full of Cadavers"

The police archives contain a series of teletexts produced in October 1961. Written in sparse, bureaucratic shorthand, these fragments tell a grisly story:

> Le corps d'un musulman algérien, qui portait des traces de coups à la tête a été retiré hier de la Seine près du Pont Neuf (Paris, 25 octobre, 13h46)

musulmans en Algérie coloniale"; Weil, *Qu'est-ce qu'un français? Histoire de la nationalité française depuis la Révolution* (Paris: Grasset, 2002).

(Body of an Algerian Muslim showing signs of blows to the head pulled out of the Seine yesterday near Pont Neuf. [October 25, 1:46pm])

Le corps d'un FMA a été retiré du canal de l'Ourcq 19e, ce matin à 8h20, par les pompiers. (October 30)

(Body of an FMA pulled out of the Ourcq Canal in the 19th, this morning at 8:20am, by the fire brigade. [October 30])

A 16h20. A été repeché dans le canal Saint-Denis à Aubervilliers à hauteur de la 2e écluse le cadavre d'un homme inconnu de type nord africain paraissant agé de 35 ans environ. (13 oct 1961)

(Today at 4:20pm. Male cadaver, identity unknown, ethnicity North African, aged about 35, pulled out of the Saint-Denis Canal in Aubervilliers, at the level of the 2nd lock. [October 13, 1961])

Unavailable to the public at the time of their creation, today, as part of the declassified police archives, the teletexts would seem to give evidentiary ballast to the accusation made in 1961 by the iconic graffiti "Ici on noie les Algériens." By gesturing directly to the river, the tag placed the Seine at the scene of the crime, implicating it in state terror and compelling readers to reconceive the "soul of Paris" as a watery grave for Algerians. Certainly, the power of the slogan and its image resides in the bald brutality of the statement, but it also lies in the elastic nature of the deictic marker "here." In this case, "here" could be as capacious as the national territory of France—an implicit indictment of the state's role in the massacre. In a geographically reduced but no less symbolically charged context, "here" might also refer to Paris—the administrative, cultural, and symbolic capital of the nation. But the graffiti's placement along the embankments of the Seine is also a clear indication that "here" quite explicitly means "in this river."

Unlike the graffiti, the teletexts are removed from the site they describe; yet they nonetheless function in a similar manner, re-signifying the river and "emplotting" the violence onto the city center though references to toponyms familiar to all Parisians who might cross these same bridges on their way to work, and even to casual tourists who might pass beneath them as they experience the city via *bateau-mouche*. But where the graffiti is symbolic, the teletexts—administrative work product, after all—are literal. They not only concentrate our attention on the fact that October 17 occurred in the heart of Paris, but also remind us of the actual dispersal of the violence by both humans and nature. On one hand, a body might have ended up in the Saint-Denis

Canal because the killing took place in Aubervilliers; on the other, a cadaver dumped in one site could easily have been borne along the currents of the waterways, traveling through the canals to the Seine and the center of Paris, or from the center of Paris to locations downstream (Colombes, Bezons). The teletexts speak to the fate of these anonymous, exceptional bodies, while reminding us that although the river is at the very heart of Paris, it also exceeds the city.

In many ways, the Seine has always been symbolically and geographically synonymous with Paris, its elegant arc through the capital a topographical happenstance and an organizing spatial principle, creating, over time, neighborhoods with strong historical, cultural, and affective identities. Paris originated in the Seine: Its two central islands (today's *Île de la Cité* and *Île St Louis*) are the oldest part of the city, first discovered by Gallo-Romans who named them Lutèce, or Lutecia.[10] Their particular shape, reminiscent of early modern galleons with their "bows" pointed downstream (the Seine flows from east to west), inspired Paris's Latin motto *fluctuat nec mergitur* (generally translated as "rocked [by waves] but not sunk"), which has long appeared on the city's official coat of arms and was re-popularized after the terror attacks of November 13, 2015, in a gesture of defiance.[11]

Certainly, it is important to account for the Seine's powerful poetic function as metonym, or even as a synecdoche, for Paris, and to recognize that the river's capacity to produce meaning is undoubtedly a function of its relationship to the urban space through which it runs. (It is also worth noting that from 1795 until 1968, the administrative region known as the Île de France—of which Paris is the seat—was known as the "La Seine.") To the degree that Paris and the Seine share literal and symbolic space in the cultural imaginary, and that anarchival references to the river participate in a cartographic project of spatializing October 17 and inscribing it on the city, this chapter extends and develops the logic of the previous one. It is, however, critical to consider the specificity of the Seine, and the way in which its very flow both concentrates meaning in, and takes meaning beyond the capital to the space of the nation.

Like any major river—the Nile, the Ganges, the Volga, the Thames, or the Mississippi—the Seine generates powerful narratives that

---

10   Lutèce became "Paris" in about 310 CE.

11   In use since at least 1358, the motto supposedly originated with the Guild of the Water Merchants. It has been on Paris's coat of arms since 1853 (when it was made official by Baron Haussmann).

are at once linked to and distinct from its natural setting and its alluvial attributes. Rivers have long served national interests in myriad pragmatic ways, a waterway being a natural conveyance for goods and services; a system of transportation for people; a fortification or boundary; and a natural resource. Since the nineteenth century and the coming of the industrial age, the modern European nation-state, and the formation of nationalist movements, the importance of rivers has also been recognizably metaphorical. As Teresa Cusak has noted, their very nature was mobilized in the service of national myth-making: "because rivers signify life and renewal, they have been appropriated as symbols of national vitality, and in representing the passage of time, they offer an excellent metaphor for the uninterrupted 'flow' or 'course' of national history."[12] Riverscapes—the textual or visual stories mobilizing such tropes as fertility, regeneration, and purification—thus became the natural vectors for disseminating ideas and concepts of nationalism.[13]

Paris's river was a particularly powerful symbol in national myth-making projects in late nineteenth-century France. Following the devastating loss of the Franco-Prussian War (1870) and the disruption of the Paris Commune (1871), the nation's way forward was galvanized by a narrative of selective memory, perhaps best codified by Ernst Renan's call for a kind of "collective forgetting" (even if it led to "historical error") as an essential component of national unity.[14] The Seine provided an ideal canvas upon which to blend a cautiously optimistic vision of the future with selective uses of France's glorious past. Reconceived in the nineteenth century as a "grand imperial passageway," the river was depicted by Impressionist painters whose representations captured the essence of a timeless, idealized present. According to Cusack, "Edenic scenes located on the Seine employed the classic connotations for water and river to symbolize purification and regeneration, metaphorically cleansing the city and its environs, lending to the depiction of the suburban riverscape and bourgeois leisure an aura of freshness, salubrity

---

12   Tricia Cusack, *Riverscapes and National Identities* (Syracuse, NY: Syracuse University Press, 2010), 2. Cusack's work on the Seine focuses on the Third Republic (1870–1940), triangulating the relationship between the river, Impressionist art, and a particular nationalist agenda.

13   Cusack, *Riverscapes*, 2–3.

14   Ernst Renan, "What is a Nation?" trans. Ethan Rundell, ucparis.fr/ files/9313/6549/9943/What_is_a_Nation.pdf. (Punctuation of translation modified slightly.) Original title: "Qu'est-ce qu'une nation?" Lecture delivered at the Sorbonne on March 11, 1882.

and timelessness."[15] The representations themselves testified to "the progressive values of a new French society based on science, secularism and modernity," while the presence of the river and its flow "provided a metaphor for continuity with the country's past."[16]

But the notion of a glittering, eternal summer staged along the banks of the Seine by Third-Republic Impressionist painters is of course only one chapter in the story of how the river has been represented over time. Indeed, that chapter's particularly idealized vision of the Seine was in tension with the realities of the river's functions, both at the moment when Monet, Seurat, and Caillebotte were painting the river *en plein air*, and in centuries prior.[17] The Seine, after all, has a long history of being pressed into service as an improvised burial ground, with cadavers thrown into its waters following the St. Bartholomew's Day massacre of Huguenots by marauding mobs of Catholics, the bloodshed of the Revolutions of 1789 and 1848, the Franco-Prussian War (1870), and the Commune (1871), to name only a few of the historical episodes that saw the Seine transformed into a watery grave.

If Impressionist painting offered a luminous counter-narrative to these historical realities, other cultural productions nonetheless intervened with a starker picture.[18] Victor Hugo's *L'Année terrible* (1872), a collection of poems recounting daily life in Paris during the Franco-Prussian War, features a short poem titled "En voyant flotter sur la Seine des cadavres prussiens" ("On seeing Prussian cadavers floating in the Seine"). However straightforward the title, Hugo's poem is tinged with irony as he describes the river as a "supple pillow

15   Cusack, "Bourgeois Leisure on the Seine: Impressionism, Forgetting and National Identity in the French Third Republic," *National Identities* 9, no. 2 (2007): 170.

16   Cusack, "Bourgeois Leisure," 174–79.

17   Cusack, "Bourgeois Leisure," 179.

18   Worthy of mention is Peter Greenaway's film *Death in the Seine* (1988), based on mortuary reports of some 300–400 bodies brought to the morgue from 1795 to 1801, and on scholarly work by historian Richard Cobb. Greenaway writes of the mortuary log: "It was a list of death, a catalogue of corpses—incomplete, unfinished—like all catalogues—providing findings and statistics which, as always, asked more questions than they provided answers. What I wanted to do was to attempt some sort of resurrection of these people dredged dripping from the Seine—the people of the Paris crowd just after the Revolution." See http://petergreenaway.org.uk/seine.htm.

of soft water" supporting the heads of the nation's dead enemies.[19]
The fifteenth-century legend of the Tour de Nesle—reprised to great
acclaim in 1823 by Alexandre Dumas—also features the Seine as a
crime scene.[20] In this case, however, the river is no soft pillow but
rather an unwitting accomplice in homicide: The legend holds that
queen Marguerite de Bourgogne used the riverside Nesle Tower in
Paris for romantic trysts, after which her unfortunate lover would
be placed in a burlap sack and thrown into the Seine to drown.
So voracious was the queen's appetite that a character in Dumas's
version remarked wryly that "depuis quelque temps la Seine charrie
bien des cadavres" (27, "for some time, the Seine has carried many
corpses," 18).[21]

In addition, then, to the ways in which exceptional bodies are
recuperated and represented in the anarchive, this chapter is particularly
interested in how anarchival images of the river participate in a long
history of ambivalent cultural representations of the Seine, mobilizing
and unsettling putatively positive tropes of nostalgia, nature, erstwhile
bourgeois leisure activities, and human improvement through technology,
while also drawing on a history of darker narratives of the Seine's role in
crime, war, and political reckonings.

19 Victor Hugo, "En voyant flotter sur la Seine des cadavres prussiens," in
L'Année terrible, 8th ed. (Paris: Michel Lévy frères; Librairie nouvelle, 1872),
75–76.
20 Known in English as *The Tower of Death*, the five-act play would become the
most frequently staged play of nineteenth-century France.
21 The story has become grist for cinematic and literary adaptations, the most
famous of which, Alexandre Dumas's *La tour de Nesle* (1832), provided the line
cited here (Brussels: Meline, Cans et Compagnie, 1838); *The Tower of Nesle*,
trans. Adam L. Gowans (London: Gowans and Gray, 1906). Also of note: In the
early twentieth century, Louis Aragon's novel *Aurélien* drew on the *fait divers*
known as "l'inconnue de la Seine." Reported in the news and the "talk of the
town," a mortician had been so taken by the beauty of a young woman who had
apparently drowned herself in the river that he made a plaster cast of her face.
The cast, reproduced and photographed, became a fetish object, such that it
became fashionable, in certain circles, to display a reproduction of the mask in
one's home.

Poetic Justice/History Lessons

The representation of the Seine as "carrying many corpses" emerges as a key aesthetic and political strategy in the first wave of anarchival productions, suggesting a contemporaneous awareness not only of the crime, but of its scale and its cover-up. Written less than a year after the events it describes, the poem "Dans la gueule du loup" (In the jaws of the wolf), published in 1962 by the Algerian poet, playwright, and novelist Kateb Yacine, posits the details of the massacre as information, not interpretation, and identifies the river as a key element in Algerian deaths.[22] The poem is composed of 18 brief lines that directly address "the French people," establish a historical connection between October 17 and the Commune, and culminate in a demand for action.

The force and intensity of Kateb's poem reside in its unornamented style and declarative tone: The details of the massacre are presented as a *précis*, a simplification of what was in fact a complicated, multi-sited repression. In compressing the factual elements into a few gestures—"Tu as vu la police / Assommer les manifestants / Et les jeter dans la Seine. / La Seine rougissante..." (You saw the police / beat the protesters / and throw them in the Seine. / The reddening Seine...)—Kateb's poem becomes a schematic emblem of the massacre, with the "reddening Seine" at its center. The equivalence between the Seine and the titular "jaws of the wolf" is implied on several levels. Both are dangerous places into which one can be thrown, and as the river morphs into a vomiting maw it becomes a nearly pure animal signifier. At the same time, the river's "reddening" is ambiguous, obviously referring to the staining of the river with the blood of dead Algerians—a stain that perhaps renders the Seine complicit—but also personifying the river, its "reddening" understood as "blushing," implying embarrassment or shame. And if the poem anthropomorphizes the Seine by endowing it with the capacity to feel shame, the same operation serves to further underscore the river's animal qualities: *rougissante* (reddening) is just a vowel away from *rugissante* (roaring), which describes the threating cries of wild beasts, not unlike those emitted from the jaws of the wolf.

In apostrophizing the French, the implied narrator does not wonder whether or not the events of October 17 were visible. Instead, the poem's point of departure is a statement of incontrovertible fact: "Peuple

22   Kateb Yacine, "Dans la gueule du loup," *Jeune Afrique* 90 (June 25, 1962): 22–23.

français, tu as tout vu / tout vu de tes propres yeux" (People of France, you saw it all / saw it all with your own eyes). The unusual choice to refer to the "people of France" with the singular pronoun of "tu" both reduces the French to a singular entity and creates an awkward sense of intimacy, as "tu" is also used to address close friends and family. The singular, familiar form of address inverts, or at the very least, *levels* the hierarchy between Kateb, a colonized Algerian, and the colonizing nation of France. In particular, the final lines of the poem, with their questions ("Et maintenant vas-tu parler? Et maintenant vas-tu te taire?" (And now will you speak? And now will you be silent?)) situate Kateb as a kind of father figure, cajoling a child to do the right thing. These lines also imply an awareness that the "people of France" bore witness to a crime, thus making visible the imminently *visible* nature of the repression.

This presumption of intimacy, however, is critical to Kateb's history lesson. In making October 17 visible, in emblematizing it, the poem moves seamlessly between colonial violence and the Commune (1871), allowing an Algerian story to take its place alongside distinctly more Franco-French ones: "La Seine rougissante / N'a pas cessé les jours suivants / De vomir à la face / Du peuple de la Commune / Ces corps martyrisés / Qui rappelaient aux Parisiens / Leurs propres révolutions / Leur propre résistance" (The reddening Seine / in the following days didn't stop / vomiting in the face / of the people of the Commune / these martyred bodies / that reminded the Parisians / of their own revolutions / of their own resistance). The Seine's visceral reaction— it regurgitates what it has been compelled to swallow and cannot digest—should, according to the poem's parallelism, remind Parisians of the violent struggles in which *they* were the victims. Martyred bodies of Algerians (note that the word "martyr" turns these victims into heroes of the Algerian War) thus signify the Parisians of the Commune and the Revolution, two capital yet bloody moments in the formation and establishment of the Republic and, not incidentally, two moments when the Seine was a site of violence and undoubtedly "reddened." The Seine here becomes the common ground for the poem's bid for cross-cultural empathy, one made possible through the poet's intimate knowledge of French history: Evoking other revolutions and resistances, ones in which the French themselves might have participated and been "martyred," Kateb elicits the substitution of one history for another, one people for another, in an attempt to generate fellow feeling and political action.

Kateb's poem has been reprinted in multiple venues and sites—very often by October 17 activists and almost always in publications whose readership is unlikely to be "Franco-French." The author himself has been directly involved in several of the poem's afterlives, taking an active role in positioning it within new contexts that shift both the meaning of the poem and its particular representation of the Seine. In the 25th anniversary issue of *Actualité de l'émigration*, a brief essay by Kateb, also titled "Dans la gueule du loup," shares a double-page spread with an essay by Leïla Sebbar and two evocative, hand-drawn works of original art depicting bodies falling into the Seine.[23] The two essays' titles, placed on the same horizontal line and separated only by one of the images, seem to form nearly a complete phrase and thought: "Dans la gueule du loup...la Seine était rouge" (In the jaws of the wolf...the Seine was red). Sebbar's title and the visual material reinforce a reading of Kateb's poem as one in which the "gueule du loup" is indeed the Seine, and the river stands in, metonymically, for France and the French.

In his short essay, however, Kateb subtly recontextualizes both October 17 and his poem by placing the two in counterpoint with another anti-colonial demonstration that took place in December 1960, in Algiers.[24] For Kateb, the success of the spontaneous protest in Algiers less than a year prior to the repression on October 17 was unexpected and unprecedented, and he questions the FLN's wisdom in risking Algerian lives with a similar protest in October 1961: "Réussir à Alger, une telle demonstration de force face à l'armée française, [...] c'était déjà énorme. Mais refaire, moins d'un an après, à Paris, la capital d'un empire [...] c'était se jeter dans la gueule du loup! Et c'est bien ce qui s'est passé" (30, Such a successful show of force, in Algiers, before the French army, [...] that was already incredible. But to re-attempt the same thing, one month later in Paris, the capital of an empire, [...] it was like throwing yourself into the jaws of the wolf! And that's exactly what happened). Here, Kateb explains that, in the days after October 17, the newspapers were full of "ces images insoutenables"—unbearable images that inspired the poem "Dans la geule du loup" (reprinted in its entirety in the essay). This recontextualization shifts the signification of the title: No longer just the

<hr />

23   Kateb Yacine, *Actualité de l'émigration*, 30–31.
24   The demonstration in 1960 in Algiers inspired Kateb's poem "La Femme sauvage" (which is also reprinted in *Actualité*). According to Kateb, the poem was published in the clandestine journal *El Moudjahid*, no. 81, on June 4, 1960.

river, or even the Parisian police who threw Algerians into it, the title now implies that it was the FLN who threw its rank and file into the yawning maw of imperial power and all its potential force of repression. If this presentation of the poem suggests that the results of October 17 were predictable, it also figures the river less as complicit and more as another victim of Parisian police brutality and the FLN's political hubris.

Like Kateb's controlled tirade, Ludovic Janvier's "Du nouveau sous le pont" (Something New Under the Bridge) (1987), uses poetry to make a point about Algerian bodies, the Seine, and October 17.[25] From its opening lines, the poem's project of binding historical horror and quotidian routine is explicit: "Paris, 1961 dix-sept octobre on est à l'heure grise / où le pays se met à table en disant c'est l'automne" (40, Paris, 1961, October seventeen it's the witching hour / when the country sits down to dinner saying fall is here). The poem is divided into three parts: a prologue that ironically and contrapuntally situates dinnertime rituals alongside the moment Algerians were preparing to join the march, setting up the major leitmotif of the poem; a second section that moves from the general to the specific, narrating, in a few lines each, the death of three Algerians who perished that night (and who are identified by their proper names), before relating the story of four workers who were drowned and 30 men from Nanterre whose bodies were dumped in the Seine; the third and final section is saturated with irony as the Seine is described as "filled with cadavers" and a series of landmarks chart the final, fluvial trajectory of what is "new" under the bridges: the bodies of Arabs that float by as France sleeps.

"Du nouveau sous le pont" does not narrativize the events of October 17 so much as schematize the violence by creating a litany of ordinary victims, Algerians whose names have no particular significance other than the fact that their deaths on October 17 have been edited out of history. Repetition is a key tactic in this three-stanza prose poem. The anaphora of the second stanza is established through a grammatical bridge that begins at the end of the first stanza: "il pleut sur les marcheurs et sur les casques; il va pleuvoir bientôt sur les cris sur le sang" (41, it's raining on the marchers and on the helmets; soon it will rain on cries and blood). The notion that it rains upon everyone is picked up in the second stanza, whose structure is articulated in several mini-series, each one beginning "Sur" or "Et sur" (continuing the reference to rain falling

25 Ludovic Janvier, "Du nouveau sous le pont," *La Mer à boire* (Paris: Gallimard, 1987), 40–44.

on people and things), and ending with progressive references to the banal stages of dinnertime. All of the actors "upon which it rained" are described as "jeté[s] à l'eau; lancés dans l'eau froide aller simple; [tombé] depuis le mont; culbuté dans l'éau noir" (42, thrown in the water; tossed into the cold water a one-way ticket; fallen from on high; kicked into the black water).

The third section represents the aftermath of the killing, and deploys yet another series of anaphora that are in keeping with the tension produced by the chafing of gruesome facts against a (falsely) lighthearted tone:

> C'est mains dans le dos qu'on en retrouve
> ils flottent enchaînés pour quelques jours à la poussée du fleuve
> c'est la pêche miraculeuse ah pour mordre ça mord
> on en repêche au pont d'Austerlitz
> on en repêche au quai d'Argenteuil
> on en repêche au pont de Bezons
> La France dort. (44)

> (It's with their hands behind their backs that we find them
> floating in chains for a few days carried along on the current of the river
> it's the miraculous catch ah the fish are biting today
> some are fished out by the Austerlitz Bridge
> some are fished out by the Argenteuil riverbanks
> some are fished out by the Bezons Bridge
> France sleeps.)

Janvier traces the trajectory of bodies moving east to west, along the current of the river, from Paris intra muros to the *banlieue*, thus producing a fluvial cartography of the horror.

Like "Dans la gueule du loup," in which Kateb binds Algerian and French realities together by virtue of the Seine and its role in the nation's violent convulsions, in "Du nouveau sous le pont," Janvier creates an inextricable parallel between October 17 and French reality through recourse not to major historical events but rather the banal structures of daily life. As the fate of each Algerian is described, the poem signals the passage of time through references to the various courses of a traditional French dinner, a second strand of anaphora braided into the first:

> La France, elle en est à la soupe;
> [...]
> La France elle en est au fromage;
> [...]

la France elle en est au dessert;
[...]
La France elle en est à roter;
[...]
la France elle est bonne à dormir. (42–43)

(France is having the soup course;
[...]
France is having the cheese course;
[...]
France is having dessert;
[...]
France is ready for a good belch;
[...]
France is ready for bed.)

By using the dinner ritual to chart the passage of time and the suffering of the Algerians on October 17, the poem depicts brutality alongside the quotidian, implicitly accusing "France" (a singular personified noun here) of continuing about its business while a crime was being committed outside its collective dining-room windows. At the same time, the poem suggests—albeit ironically—that the violence of state terror was already, at the time, disturbingly naturalized. Subtly, Janvier's poem also complicates the metaphor of indigestion established in "Dans la gueule du loup": Whereas Kateb's Seine "vomited martyred bodies," Janvier's river is troublingly bountiful, full of "good fishing" ("c'est la pêche miraculeuse!"); meanwhile, France ends its dinner with a solid belch ("La France elle en est à roter"), a sure sign of a good meal and a strong stomach.

The history lessons of "Du nouveau sous le pont" are rooted in the moment of October 17, with the second section offering an elliptical yet detailed narration of the varieties of violence experienced by Algerians at different sites throughout Paris and its suburbs. Less explicitly than Kateb, Janvier nonetheless reaches back in time to connect the particular use of the river in October 1961 to darker histories: The mention of "les noyés habituels" (the usual drowned)—"les rats crevés les poissons ventre en l'air les godasses / ne filent plus tout à fait seuls avec les vieux cartons / et les noyés habituels venus donner contre les piles" (44, dead rats belly-up fish old shoes / no longer float alone with old cardboard boxes / and the usual drowned that get hung up on the piers)—underscores the Seine's function as a dumping ground for ordinary crime, while at the same time reminding readers that these drowning victims are exceptional.

It is the final lines of the poem, however, that are the most explicit in their historical reference: "on peut dire qu'il y a du nouveau sous les ponts / la Seine s'est mise à charrier des Arabes" (44, it seems there's something new under the bridges / the Seine's begun churning up Arabs). With these two lines, Janvier embeds the material of his poem in a network of cultural representation that emblematizes the Seine's history of ambivalent signification. The mention of "sous les ponts" will remind many readers of one of the most famous works of French poetry, Symbolist poet Guillaume Apollinaire's "Le pont Mirabeau" (1912). A story of the end of love, the poem's elegiac tone and haunting final lines—"Sous le pont Mirabeau / Coule la Seine / [...] / Vienne la nuit sonne l'heure / les jours s'en vont je demeure" ("Under the Mirabeau flows the Seine / [...] / Comes the night sounds the hour / The days go by I endure")—evoke tropes of the passing of time, but also of permanence—despite the river's flow, underscored by the successive enjambments, both the bridge and the narrator "remain." Notwithstanding the starkly different subject matter in the two poems, the renown of "Le pont Mirabeau" is such that Janvier's "sous le pont" almost reflexively conjures Apollinaire's iconic lines. Yet, if the reference to Symbolist poetry produces a vision of the Seine that is melancholy but not sinister, the penultimate phrase of Janiver's poem—"La Seine s'est mise à charrier des Arabes"—appropriates a line from the Tour de Nesle legend whereby the Seine was said to "charrier" (churn up) the cadavers of a heartless queen. Janvier's pointed reference thus links the dead on October 17 to a centuries-old ironic quip about the river's uses as a convenient, anonymous burial ground.[26]

Unsettling Tropes of Nostalgia

However figurative, representations of the Seine such as those found in the poems of Kateb and Janvier reinforce a very real dimension of

26   Unlike Kateb, who refers specifically to "Algerians," Janvier refers to "Arabs." Kateb, as an Algerian writing in 1962, would have been more attentive to the question of national specificity; in 1987, Janvier's extrapolation may signal an awareness of the Arab world simmering in the collective subconscious: In 1983 the *beur* movement had just begun in France, and 1987 saw both the inauguration of the Insititut du monde arabe in Paris and, in December, the start of the First Intifada.

the October 17 repression—the unwitting participation of the river in the violence and its aftermath. Indeed, in the anarchive more generally, the river is often presented in a documentary fashion, as a necessary element of mise-en-scène in a story whose historical accuracy would otherwise be lacking. Yet throughout the anarchive we also find cultural productions that tap into the ways the Seine has been mobilized, over time, in service of various narratives—not all of which are negatively inflected. In particular, several works have recourse to the tropes and set pieces of nostalgia associated with the river (particularly in the late nineteenth century and early twentieth), only to trouble that wistful imagery with intrusions of the real.

As in Janvier's poem, in Nacer Kettane's novel *Le Sourire de Brahim*, the partial reprise of Apollinaire's "Le pont Mirabeau" introduces a curious intertextual juxtaposition. In the first chapter (the only chapter that directly refers to the massacre), Brahim participates in the demonstration and witnesses its degeneration. That night, his father goes missing and his younger brother is killed. Although Brahim does not mention the Seine during his description of the violence, the river becomes a central figure in the final portion of the chapter, a three-paragraph long "epilogue" whose tone and register set it apart from the rest of the book. In the middle of this epilogue, a reference to the "use" of the Seine on October 17 becomes the occasion not only for an appropriation of Apollinaire's famous poem, but also for a brief narrative digression centered on the river:

> Les berges de la Seine étaient jalonnées de cadavres et sous le pont Mirabeau avait coulé le sang. Hommes noyés, fusillés, torturés, à jamais témoins de la barbarie, **vous êtes** comme un souffle de vie suspendue qui rafraîchira la mémoire des générations en pèlerinage d'identité. En se promenant, les amoureux des bords de Seine pourraient voir **votre** sourire, au fond de l'eau, bénir leurs baisers. Les ronds provoqués dans l'eau du fleuve par les jets de pierre des enfants seront autant de portées musicales dont les notes chanteront la révolte. (23) (My emphasis.)

> (The banks of the Seine were littered with cadavers and under the Mirabeau bridge blood had flowed. Men drowned, shot, tortured, forever witnesses to barbarism, **you are** like a breath of suspended life that will refresh the memory of generations in search of their identity. As they stroll along the riverbanks, lovers will be able to see **your** smile in the depths of the water, and their kisses will be blessed. Children will throw stones in the river and the ripples they produce will be a musical notation whose notes will sing the melody of revolt.)

The obvious hijacking of Apollinaire's iconic line—here, beneath the Mirabeau bridge it was blood, not the Seine, that flowed—capitalizes on the symbolic potential and familiar rhythm of the original only to denaturalize the river. No longer is the Seine's course under a bridge a nostalgic measure of the passage of time; it is evidence of a crime. Yet the very gesture of recuperation seems to detract from the gravitas of the scene described in the novel. Neither "Le pont Mirabeau" nor *Le Sourire de Brahim* are light in tone, yet Kettane's transformation of Apollinaire's decasyllabic, or ten-foot line into an alexandrine (12 feet), gives the macabre phrase a light, almost tripping tone.

The oddity of the tonal shift is made stranger still by a change in narration (from third- to second-person address or apostrophe) and by a reference to lovers who would observe, as they meander along the banks of the Seine, the smiles of the dead from the depths of the water.[27] Although the meaning of the paragraph is clearly one that seeks to glorify the dead, the notion that they remain at the bottom of the river, smiling up at lovers, seems ill fitting for the seriousness of the topic and the chapter in general, whose storytelling imperatives include setting the stage for Brahim's loss—a trauma that conditions the remainder of his experiences in this *bildungsroman*. Moreover, in imagining lovers embracing along the banks of the Seine, the paragraph simultaneously activates another historical narrative about the Seine—the river as a site of bucolic leisure. Kettane's appropriation of Apollinaire's lyrics disrupts their meaning, as well as the poetic valences of the Seine as representing continuity. The clash here of tone and topic, of traditional iconography of the Seine and its refiguration in a less flattering light, provoke a discontinuity in both the text and in the telling of October 17—an aspect of the novel that, however troubling, mirrors the ways in which the story of October 17 itself has been discontinuous.

The Seine's association with leisure and entertainment is mobilized to great ironic effect in the musical adaptation of Kateb's "Dans la gueule du loup" by the French indie-rock group Têtes Raides. While the poem has had numerous afterlives since its original publication in 1962, the version produced by Têtes Raides has given Kateb's words a much

---

27   This type of sudden shift in the pronoun of the speaker is a feature of Arabic rhetoric (called *iltifāt*, or "turning") found, notably, in the Coran. It is certainly possible that Kettane's French is (consciously or otherwise) mobilizing Arabic rhetorical tropes. I am grateful to Kareem James Abu-Zeid for calling this to my attention.

broader platform, and is perhaps the only iteration with the potential to reach the very group whose empathy Kateb sought to stir. The song itself, which reprises the poem exactly as it was written, first appeared on the album *Chamboultou* (1998) and has had an internet presence since 2007, when the group posted a music video to YouTube.[28] Initially, the text's grave representation of the Seine (as a burial site, as stained by the blood of the victims, as the jaws of a beast) is foiled by an instrumental track that recalls the bygone culture of the *guinguettes*. Popular in the late nineteenth century and early twentieth, *guinguettes*—working-class cabaret-restaurants often situated along the riverbanks—today conjure nostalgic notions of leisure and times when Sunday afternoons could be whiled away with cheap wine and the strains of a small orchestra dominated by an accordion.[29] Têtes Raides' version of "Dans la gueule du loup" is set, somewhat improbably, to the music of a lone accordion, accompanied only by a triangle and a harmonica. Rather than sing the lyrics, the singer speaks Kateb's words over a musical air whose accordion liltingly lays down a 3/4 tempo reminiscent of the waltzes of *bal musettes*, evoking images of riverside reveries and the French working class at play in their shirtsleeves.

Above and beyond the lyrics, then, the instrumentation produces strong, if discordant, mental images of the Seine, despite the fact that the accompanying video images never reveal any actual shots of the river. The visual aspects of the music video, however, further trouble the relationship between representation and meaning. Shot in

---

28 Têtes Raides, "Dans la gueule du loup," *Chamboultou* (1998), https://www.youtube.com/watch?v=lNWLEAXdSqw. The album features a second track that is also a reprise of a poem that refers to a traumatic history: "Le Coeur a sa mémoire," originally written by Mauricette Leibowitch, is dedicated to the memory of the victims of concentration camps.

29 Established in the eighteenth century but reaching a kind of cultural iconicity in the nineteenth (thanks, in part, to their ample representation in Impressionist painting—see Renoir's "Luncheon of the Boating Party," for example), *guinguettes* began in Paris and then moved to the riverbanks in the *banlieue* due to tax issues. Their popularity peaked in the nineteenth century. They were shuttered in the 1960s due to increased traffic on the rivers and degraded water quality (when it became illegal to swim in the river). See Robert Beck, *Histoire du dimanche, de 1700 à nos jours* (Paris: Éditions Ouvrières, 1997), 83. *Guinguette* music evokes the *canotiers* and their bars, and the leisure activities of the banks of the Seine and Marne rivers of the nineteenth century and early twentieth. In other words, the belle époque, nostalgic, middle class. See Jean Gabin in *La belle équipe* (1936).

black and white with a pared down mise-en-scène featuring the lead singer in a décor that appears to be a stage, the video is filmed in an intense chiaroscuro and appears to be lit diegetically, that is, by a single light swinging on its cord over the head of the lead singer. This bare lighting feature recalls the classic film tropes of jail or torture scenes in which a cell is lit only by a bulb suspended on a fraying cord, or where a light is shone into a person's eyes to compel him to speak. Without explicitly referencing the Algerian War, the implied reference to torture in the video activates a painful and unresolved aspect of that conflict. But the lighting and mise-en-scène also produce a highly stylized image of the Seine on October 17: As the singer's face is alternately lit by the cone of light and hidden by the shadows, and as solid forms toggle between planes of opacity and transparency, the screen is transformed into a surface that hides and reveals, not unlike the surface of a dark body of water punctuated by a bobbing face, alternately hidden and revealed.

The recruitment of the Seine in the original poem is destabilized and ultimately resignified by Têtes Raides' video clip. Pulled in by the familiar, comforting music of the *guinguettes*—which can only signal good times, abundant wine, relaxation in nature—the listener/viewer experiences a reversal as she moves beyond the siren call of the accordion to apprehend images and words that coalesce to unsettle the very nostalgic imagery they produce. Notwithstanding the strength of the metaphors of the Seine, its history is multiple, nefarious, and ultimately more complicated than the air of an accordion.

The ambiguous aesthetics produced by Têtes Raides' particular film-grammar has a precedent in the anarchive's very first images of the Seine. In Jacques Panijel's documentary *Octobre à Paris* (1962), the river is endowed with the same semiotic complexity the Seine has produced historically; it is at once a site of leisure and technology, and a dumping ground for the dead. The documentary begins with a black screen and a 50-second prologue spoken by an off-screen (presumably Algerian) voice before cutting to its very first image: a static shot of the Seine with the sun glimmering on the light current and the wooden Pont des Arts at the top edge of the frame. After five seconds, the camera pans left ever so slightly as a *bateau-mouche* enters the frame; as the camera reverses course again, now following the boat's slow progression to the right, a different off-screen voice, in lightly accented French, announces: "J'étais venu en France, on m'avait dit au bled, en France, c'est le pays de la liberté…vas-y là-bas, on te fera pas de mal...les Français sont gentils" (I had come to France, they told me, back at home, France, it's the country of liberty...go over there, nobody will hurt you...the French are nice).[30] This narration provides a sound bridge to connect the image of leisure on the Seine to a shot of two Algerian factory workers (one of whom is the speaker). The camera then cuts to an interior setting where another Algerian relates the discourse of freedom, fun, and bounty that conditioned his vision of France prior to arrival: "Il y avait beaucoup d'amis qui sont arrivés de France [...] ils m'ont raconté qu'ils ont passé une belle vie, au cinéma, en voiture...Puis, avec des filles, des promenades..." (There were lots of friends coming back from France [...] they told me that they'd had a good time, at the movies, in cars...And with girls, long walks...). Again, the speaker's story is used as a sound bridge to stitch together the shots that follow: a mobile framing of young women strolling along Parisian sidewalk; an image of the Saint-Michel cinema; another medium shot of the man speaking; and a static shot of the Seine with the very same *bateau mouche* now passing under the Pont des Arts.

It is at this moment that the film's genteel images of the river, its light melodic soundtrack, and a narration that confirms the positive valences of a sun-dappled Seine plied by pleasure boats, are replaced by a bleaker vision and a discordant clamor. *Octobre à Paris* cuts abruptly from the city center to a desolate riverbank *extra muros* where the Seine flows through a semi-industrial wasteland, devoid of traces of civilization or humanity. In a destabilizing four-second scene, the camera point of view (POV) reproduces the back-and-forth of a body being swung to gain momentum before it is heaved into the river. Disturbing for its embodied representation of the killing of Algerians and its contrast with the preceding imagery, this scene is all the more shocking for its unvarnished reenactment, just months post facto, of the very acts perpetrated by Parisian police. We then cut to an Algerian survivor of October 17 who announces: "La police m'a jeté à la Seine" (The police threw me in the Seine)—a line that begins a litany of economical, one-line testimonials by Algerians filmed in close-up.[31]

---

30 My translation attempts to capture the sometimes halting, sometimes incorrect nature of the French spoken by many of the Algerians filmed by Panijel. Unless presented in square brackets, ellipses indicate pauses in speech.
31 The other four men recount different forms of torture, sometimes with quite a bit of detail, at the hands of the police or of the *Harki* forces.

In moving from pleasant images to disturbing ones, and from narratives of hope and liberty to stories of torture, Panijel initially seems to be staging the conditions for a chronological, even teleological, shift, as if to say that the Seine has changed over time: Once signifying leisure, now it is synonymous with torture. However, if we look carefully at the very first image of the Seine in the film—the still shot of the glistening surface of the river that then moves to follow the boat—we can see that not all is smooth in this representation. Near the center of the screen, directly in the path of the ray of sunlight, a difficult-to-identify object hovers just beneath the surface of the water. (See Fig. 11.) Enough elements emerge from the river to suggest that this may be a wheelbarrow, or a wheeled cart of some sort. Certainly, the notion of an unidentified body barely perceptible at the surface of the water darkens this sunny tableau: As a visual metonym of Algerians drowned in the Seine and rendered anonymous, it becomes a harbinger, in these early moments of the film, of the violence that would shortly be both reenacted and narrated. But the fact that this is not just any object, but very likely a wheeled cart or *un char*, is also significant: The image of a cart or wheeled conveyance circles back (again) to the line popularized in Dumas's version of *La tour de Nesle*—"la Seine charrie bien des cadavres"—meaning the river transports the dead along on its current.[32] The noun (un char) and the verb (charrier) share a common etymology, and thus an image of *un char* triggers the grammatical unconscious of the viewer, reminding her of the Seine's notorious history and becoming a metonym for drowned Algerians.[33]

Later in the film, the very few other depictions of the river hew more closely to documentary principles, presenting the Seine as a straightforward and necessary element of mise-en-scène. In a sequence dubbed in the press "L'Algérien sauvé des eaux" (The Algerian Saved from Drowning)—an oddly humorous riff on the title of the 1932 Renoir film *Boudu sauvé des eaux* (*Boudu Saved from Drowning*)—an Algerian recounts how the police threatened him ("Il faut aller à la Seine maintenant"/Now you have to go to the Seine); he then goes on to reenact being driven in a paddy wagon to the outskirts of Paris, and even to mime the experience of being heaved to and fro just before being thrown into the river near Alfortville. The man was able to swim underwater to

---

32   The polysemia of the verb *charrier* is lost in the English translation, which has Dumas's Gaultier noting only that the river "carries" cadavers.

33   Indeed, "chariot" (or char) and "charrier" have the same etymological root.

Fig. 11. A foreign body in the Seine? *Octobre à Paris.*
Documentary. Dir. Jacques Panijel. France, 1962.

a hiding place along the embankment before hoisting himself out once the coast was clear. This later depiction of the river makes the opening sequence all the more complex and significant: Before a full two minutes of film have rolled, Panijel has subtly both demonstrated and undercut the significance of the Seine as a site of pleasure associated with bygone nostalgia. In those same two minutes, the film also mobilizes negative tropes of the Seine as a dumping ground, as a surface with the potential to hide horrors.

Ironically, by the end of the 1950s, just a few years before Panijel made his documentary, the *guinguettes* had all but ceased activity as boat traffic had increased considerably and the quality of the Seine's water was deemed insalubrious. Like the river itself, Panijel's seemingly innocuous image of a sun-dappled Seine also hides, just below its surface, a searing reality: Those same waters considered unfit for Parisian leisure activities had become a burial site for Algerians.

Visualizing Embodied Experience

More so than any of the cultural productions discussed thus far, *Octobre à Paris* represents the river in a fashion that is distinctly interested in Algerians' embodied experiences. What little press the film received upon its semi-clandestine release in May 1962 tended to focus on the film's capture of Algerian political subjectivity, yet the very gesture of turning the camera into a drowning victim already suggests, early on in the documentary, a filmic investment in the body.[34] This is confirmed in the last third of the film, in a sequence immediately following the representation of the massacre: a silent, one-minute series of medium and close-up shots features Algerians wordlessly revealing their wounds and scars to the camera, creating a mobile tableau of the suffering inflicted on these exceptional bodies, the first representation of the visible evidence of state-sponsored violence on October 17.

Panijel's depiction of wounded bodies reminds us (already in 1962) that not all Algerians fell victim to the river, and not all of the violence perpetrated was linked to the Seine. In later cultural productions, however, death in the Seine emerges as the enduring image of October 17, with numerous works taking up the question of violence and embodiment by narrativizing—however improbably—the experience of being thrown in the river to drown. In Médine's rap "17 octobre" (from the 2007 album *Table d'écoute*), a protagonist named Ahmed narrates his journey from Algiers to Paris in 1961; he recounts his experiences of racism in France, of the preparation for the demonstration on October 17, and his own death at the hands of police on October 17.[35] The rap contains numerous irony-laden references to the river as a place of death, particularly as the demonstrators are subjected to the violence of the police: "une fois sur la berge j'aperçois le comité d'acceuil / Qui souhaite faire de ce pont notre cerceuil [...] Nous allons voir si les rats savent nager / Au fond de la Seine vous ne pourrez

---

34   Robert Benayoun, "Où commence le témoignage?" *Positif* 49 (November 1962): 23–28. At least 20 reviews of the film were published in 1962, in venues both specialized (*Positif, Cinéma*) and more mainstream (*Libération, Témoignage chrétien, Lettres françaises, France-Observateur, Avanti*).

35   I've chosen to focus exclusively on the lyrics of this rap; Katelyn Knox has written expertly about both the lyrics and their mise-en-scène in the video produced by Larab. See "Rapping Postmemory, Sampling the Archive: Reimagining 17 October 1961," *Modern and Contemporary France* 22, no. 3 (2014): 381–97.

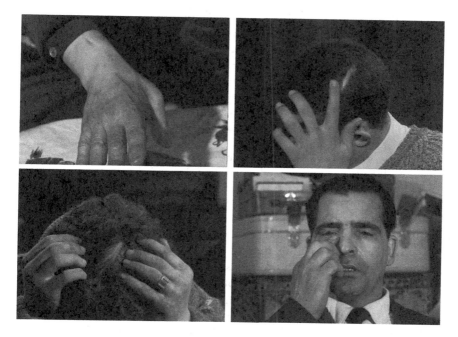

Fig. 12. The scars of October 17. *Octobre à Paris.*
Documentary. Dir. Jacques Panijel. France, 1962.

plus vous venger" (when I get to the riverbank I see the welcome wagon
/ Who want to turn this bridge into our coffin. [...] Let's see if rats know
how to swim / From the bottom of the Seine you won't be able to get
even). In a curious and implausible narrative gesture, the narrator goes
on to recount his own death in the river:

> Les brigadiers en chef par tous les membres me saisissant
> Amorce ma descente là où passent les péniches
> S'assurent de ma mort frappant ma tête sur la corniche
> Je tombe comme un déchet au vide-ordure
> Dans la chute violemment ma nuque a touché la bordure
> Liquide poignardant tous mes orifices, le fleuve glacial un bûcher
> chaud pour mon sacrifice
> Monsieur Papon a jugé bon de nous noyer
> Aucun pompier pour étouffer le foyer
> [...]
> Mon cadavre emporté par le courant
> Sera repêché dans les environs de Rouen.

(The officers in charge grab me by all four limbs
Thus begins my fall toward where the barges float
They guarantee my death, striking my head on the edge
I fall like trash through a chute
My neck hits the edge as I plummet violently
Water stabs my orifices, the glacial river a hot braise for my sacrifice
Monsieur Papon thought it was a good idea to drown us
There's no firefighter to snuff this out
[...]
My cadaver borne by the current
Will be fished out somewhere around Rouen.)

Médine's rap narrativizes the gruesome reality of cadavers transiting along the river, borne by its current from central Paris to its outskirts. And, similarly to Têtes Raides' sceneography of "Dans la gueule du loup" and Panijel's opening images of the Seine, Ahmed's story also refers to the river's other, more pleasurable uses: His fall happens right where the barges travel, referring both to the leisure activity associated with *péniches*, houseboats, and *guinguettes,* as well as to the utilitarian aspect of the Seine as a thoroughfare for goods traveling by boat. "17 octobre" thus subtly activates the river's ambivalent symbolism.

Whereas Kateb reached back to the Commune and "other revolutions," inscribing violence and the Seine along a Franco-French trajectory, Médine's rap situates Ahmed's experiences within a story of colonial violence and representation. The references to the "tirailleurs et combattants zouaves" invoke the contingents of indigenous soldiers deployed in France's European wars, when significant manpower was supplied by French's African colonies. The phrase "Dégât des eaux pour les gens des humans-zoo / Déshumanisés les basanés ne font pas de vieux os" (Water damage for the folks from the human-zoos / Dehumanized, the darkies aren't long for this world), with its biting wordplay riffing on an expression for water damage and rhyming it with "gens des humans-zoo," also refers to French imperial practices of staging indigenous subjects in human zoos at colonial exhibitions.[36] This web of references works to historicize October 17 not just within the context of the Algerian War, but also within broader colonial practices that sought to control, discipline, and even display the colonialized subject.

36   There is a great deal of excellent scholarship on "human zoos" at colonial fairs; see, for example, *Zoos humains: au temps des exhibitions humaines*, ed. Nicholas Bancel, et al. (Paris: La Découverte, 2004).

As invested as the rap may be in the French imperial context, an odd image in the final stanza initially appears to depoliticize Médine's message by transforming the drowned bodies—of Ahmed and others—into naturally occurring fluvial flora. After his body is "fished out of the water near Rouen," Ahmed offers this meta-reflection on the scene:

> D'étranges nénuphars flottent sur la Seine
> Séquence long métrage les yeux plongés dans la Seine
>
> (Strange water lilies float on the Seine
> A feature-length sequence eyes fixed on the Seine)

These lines are the only ones to mention the Seine by name, a rarity that is reinforced through repetition. This particular reference to the river, however, is unsettling not for its violence, but rather for its unexpected loveliness: the "étranges nénuphars," or strange water lilies floating on the river are an odd metaphor for dead Algerians, one that conjures Monet's large-scale tableaux more readily than it evokes colonial violence.[37] But the image in fact resonates with another, earlier, musical representation of victims of institutionalized racial violence, namely, the "strange fruit" swinging from poplar trees in Billie Holiday's eponymous song first recorded in 1939:

> Southern trees bear strange fruit,
> Blood on the leaves and blood at the root,
> Black bodies swinging in the southern breeze,
> Strange fruit hanging from the poplar trees.[38]

Different bodies, similarly made "strange": Holiday's "fruit" are, of course, the corpses of black men who had been lynched and hung from trees. Médine's transnational comparison works associatively: In both cases, bodies—exceptional bodies—are imagined as organic extensions of the same natural elements used in their assassination. As an engaged rap artist whose repertoire includes numerous references to racism

---

37 This gentle image is also somewhat reminiscent of Kettane's reference to the dead at the bottom of the river, who would bless the kisses of lovers on the riverbank.

38 Billy Holiday was the first to sing and record "Strange Fruit" (recorded April 20, 1939 and released that year on Commodore Records). The song has been covered by artists such as Nina Simone. The lyrics were written in 1937 by Abel Meeropol, a Jewish songwriter from the Bronx. It was originally a poem published under the title "Bitter Fruit."

in the American South and notorious incidents of racially motivated violence in the US, it seems impossible that Médine's "strange water lilies" are not a deliberate appropriation of Holiday's "strange fruit," connecting racial violence transnationally and creating a powerful analogy between black American struggles and those of the Algerian people.[39]

Like the "17 octobre" rap, the play *La pomme et le couteau* (The Apple and the Knife) represents the subjective, embodied experience of drowning, all the more improbably because as a work of theatre, the stagecraft required to depict characters drowning becomes as much a function of the audience's imagination as of the mise-en-scène. Written by Algerian dramaturge and novelist Aziz Chouaki, *La Pomme et le couteau* suggests the Seine primarily through sound, but also through dialogue.[40] The first scene opens with the stage indication "La scène se déroule dans le noir, on entend des bruits d'eau et des sirens de police" (The scene unfolds in darkness, we hear sounds of water and police sirens), followed by a conversation between Ramdane and Ali, two Algerians who have been, as the audience or the reader is given to understand, thrown into the water:

> Ramdane: Au secours. [...] Je sais pas nager, j'en peux plus, ça y est c'est fini. [...] J'ai un bastos dans le ventre, je peux pas flotter, non, foutu. [...]
> Ali: J'en ai deux dans la cuisse, alors tais-toi. [...]
> Ramdane: Eh là-bas, t'as entendu? [...] Plouf. Oui, ils en ont jeté d'autres, plouf, t'as pas entendu. (3–4)

> (Ramdane: Help. [...] I can't swim, I can't go any further, that's it, it's over. [...] I've got a bullet in my belly, I can't float, no, I'm a goner. [...]
> Ali: I've got two bullets in my leg, so shut up. [...]

39 Other works by Médine that reference or engage the US context include his third album, titled *Arabian Panther* (2008), in reference to the Black Panthers.
40 Aziz Chouaki, *La Pomme et le couteau* (Paris: Éditions Les Cygnes, 2011). The play was originally commissioned by Le Théatre des Quartiers d'Ivry (a national center for the dramatic arts in Val-de-Marne, outside of Paris). An initial public reading took place in May 2011 in Nanterre, animated by Gerard Noirel and Gilles Manceron. A staged reading was performed at the Festival de la Mousson d'été (August 25, 2011), directed by Adel Hakim, produced by Les Petits Ruisseaux, le Théâtre des Quartiers d'Ivry, and the City of Nanterre, in partnership with the organizations Daja and Les Oranges. The commission asked Chouaki to use texts by Abdelmalek Sayad and Jean-Luc Einaudi. *France Culture* recorded a live public reading that was broadcast on October 16, 2011. See also http://www.daja.fr/index. php/fr/spectacles/spectacles-passes/la-pomme-et-le-couteau.

Ramdane: Hey, over there, did you hear? [...] Plop. Yeah, they threw in others, plop, you didn't hear.)

The onomatopoeia "plouf"—the French sound for an object splashing into water—recurs throughout the play, as episodes toggle back and forth in time and in location. In the seventh scene, set just before the demonstration, Ali and Ramdane stand by a balustrade overlooking the Seine. Stage directions indicate that Ali "ramasse un caillou et le jette dans la Seine, on entend un plouf" (37, picks up a stone and throws it in the Seine, we hear a plop). A clear form of foreshadowing, the sound made by the sinking rock also temporally links the various disparate moments of the play, and will appear one last time in the final stage direction given: "le plateau est vide, noir progressif, on entend plusieurs 'plouf'" (68, the stage is empty, growing progressively darker, we hear several plops). From the darkness, Ramdane once again says, "Je ne sais pas nager. Au secours" (I can't swim. Help). Framed with the words of a drowning man pleading for help, *La Pomme et le couteau* begins and ends in the Seine, and while the river is never visually represented on stage, the audience is drawn into the characters' immersion through sound.

Set in 1961, both Médine's rap and Chouaki's play stage plausible events, even if such intimate, subjective depictions of the experience of being drowned are highly stylized, and can only belong to the realm of representation. Both performances, moreover, seem less concerned with provoking catharsis in the classical sense than with exploring, via the improbable representation of a character narrating his own death, a certain form of alienation. By contrast, the representation of drowning—or of a near-drowning experience—in Mehdi Lallaoui's novel *Une nuit d'octobre* (2001) is pitched in such a way as to provide the character in question with a cathartic experience (in the psychoanalytic sense) but also to symbolize a more generalizable form of catharsis for Algeria and France. Lallaoui's second "October 17" book is something of a fan-fiction version of the Papon-Einaudi libel trial. The main character, Dadou—the son of an Algerian man who survived October 17 but whose brothers did not—along with a band of truth seekers, attempts to find proof of the scale of the violence on October 17 in order to exonerate Renucci (the fictional avatar of the historian Jean-Luc Einaudi).

Lallaoui's first novel, *Les Beurs de Seine* (1985), was one of the earliest *beur* fictions published and, against type, it was less overtly autobiographical than most, even if Lallaoui has familial connections to October 17 and has long been active in associations devoted to educating the public about the massacre.[41] *Les Beurs de Seine* in fact features only a short mention of October 17, despite the fact that the title itself inscribes the river as an origin for the *beurs*, and plays on the equivalence between the river itself and the administrative department for which it was named (until 1968).[42] But the representation of the river in the novel is otherwise significant; the main character Kaci tells the story of an Algerian friend who, whenever he passes by the police headquarters on the Seine, buys a bouquet of carnations and throws them into the water. Delivered as a kind of mini-historical lecture to two minor characters in the novel, one French, one Franco-Algerian, what is significant is that neither has ever heard this story (158–60).

More than ten years later, in *Une nuit d'Octobre*, the Seine comes back to haunt the scene, and in this case the haunting in question, and the return of the repressed, are figured in nearly explicit psycho-analytical terms. When the reader first encounters Dadou, he is happily riding his scooter along the banks of the Seine. For reasons that will only be elucidated later in the novel, Dadou is run off the road, summarily beaten, and thrown into the Seine (7–8). Narrative time dilates, and the few seconds it would have taken Dadou to fall from the bridge to the water last for two pages. During this extended time, Dadou reflects with surprising lucidity on the symbolism of what is happening to him:

Il n'essaie pas de battre des ailes pour se soustraire à la fatalité, tant l'évidence de cette chute était inscrite dans sa mémoire [...] Dans un cauchemar d'enfance, il avait déjà vu en noir et blanc des corps dégringoler dans la Seine. Cette descente qui n'en finissait pas confirmait les dires de ceux qui avaient fait l'aller-retour mystérieux. (8)

(He doesn't even try to break his fall, to resist destiny; this fall is engraved in his memory [...] In a childhood nightmare he had already seen, in black and white, bodies tumbling into the Seine. This unending dive only confirmed the accounts given by those who had survived this mysterious round trip.)

41   Writer and filmmaker Mehdi Lallaoui co-founded the organization Au nom de la mémoire (1990). His first film was the October 17 documentary *Le silence du fleuve* (1991).
42   Although, of course, at the time "Seine" was also the name given to the administrative *département* that now corresponds to Paris and the limitrophe areas of Seine-Saint-Denis, Hauts-de-Seine, and Val-de-Marne. Initially named "département de Paris" in 1790, the agglomeration was renamed "Seine" in 1790. Officially broken apart in 1968, the department was slightly smaller than today's regional designation "Île de France," so named in 1976.

The classic tropes of the near-death experience are in evidence here. Dadou revisits the important moments and symbols of his life: his first kiss, his father's hands, his favorite teacher. And yet the finality of the fall is narratively deferred. As he imagines the small obituary that would appear in a third-rate newspaper and wonders who will remember him, the story cuts to the next chapter, one whose temporal relationship to Dadou's fall has to be inferred from the subtlest of clues in the opening line of Chapter Two: "À Argenteuil, la nuit n'était pas encore tombée" (In Argenteuil, night had not yet fallen). Like the night, Dadou's fall is not yet complete, and as the reader waits for him to land, the narrative takes us back in time, retracing, over the next 100 pages or so, the steps that led him to the moment when he finds himself repeating the fatal trajectory of his uncles in October 1961.

As the third-person narration unspools, we follow Dadou and his friends as they try to collect evidence to exonerate Renucci, a task made difficult by the fact that the police archives are still closed. It also becomes clear that Dadou has an intimate relationship with the Seine, whose trace he follows back and forth from Argenteuil to central Paris on his beloved scooter. The text takes a certain toponymic pleasure in rehearsing the names of towns along the loops of the Seine: Dadou follows "les bords de Seine par Conflans-Saint-Honorine jusqu'à Herblay et la Frette, puis coupa par Sartrouville" (43, the riverbanks from Conflans-Saint-Honorine to Herblay and la Frette, then cut over to Sartrouville). It's not the most direct route, but Dadou prefers itineraries that keep him as close to the river as possible, cutting away from its banks only when absolutely necessary. If Dadou's experience of the Seine is synesthetic and deeply nostalgic, it is a complex nostalgia, tinged with a sadness that returns him to primal experiences:

Il avait l'habitude de rouler sur ces berges tranquilles [...] Il aimait sentir l'humidité du fleuve, goûter à la sensation primitive de l'intérieur du ventre d'une mère, se donner l'illusion d'une complicité, d'une parenté, ou simplement adresser un message illusoire à la Seine, serpent paisible qui avait englouti ces hommes qu'il fallait faire resurgir du néant. (43)

(He was used to driving along these calm riverbanks [...] He liked to smell the dampness of the river, to feel the primordial sensation of being back in the womb, to imagine a deep connection to the river, or just to fantasize about sending a message to the Seine, that peaceful serpent who had swallowed up the men who he now had to bring back from the void.)

The Seine's role in the October 17 massacre is signified as a passive one: The river is a "calm serpent" that may have "swallowed up" victims but had not actively hunted them.

The vision of the Seine presented by Dadou is in tension with a description of the river he offers in another passage. One of the Renucci defenders is filming testimonials of individuals whose lives were touched by October 17, in order to save the story for posterity. In Dadou's monologue, he admits that the river also conjures for him a traumatic memory, one that can only be properly called "postmemory,"[43] for as he recounts a recurring nightmare about the river, it is clear that the trauma in question is not his own, but rather the one experienced by his father and uncles on October 17:

> Cette nuit me possède et me dépossède aussi. Chaque jour pour me rendre à Paris je dois traverser deux fois les boucles de la Seine, et sur les ponts, l'angoisse m'étreint toujours [...] Enfant il m'est arrivé une chose étrange et véridique. C'était la fin de l'été, de retour d'une colonie de vacances. Le car avait roulé toute la nuit et les enfants étaient tous endormis. Nous étions bercés par les mouvements du véhicule. Soudain, je me suis réveillé en nage. Je me souviens d'un mauvais rêve où je voyais des hommes voler dans les airs. Nous étions en train de traverser le pont de Neuilly. Plus tard, des années plus tard, au même endroit, les images de ce cauchemar me sont revenues. Les hommes que je voyais voler avaient le visage déformé par la peur. Ils ne volaient pas, ils tombaient tout habillés dans la Seine. (52)

> (I am possessed and dispossessed by this night. To get to Paris, I have to cross the Seine twice every day, and each time I cross a bridge I'm gripped with anxiety [...] As a child, I had a strange experience. It was the end of the summer, we were coming back from summer camp. The bus has been driving all night and all of the children were asleep. We were rocked by the lullaby of the road. Suddenly, I woke up in a cold sweat. I remember a bad dream where I saw men flying through the air. We were crossing the Neuilly Bridge. Later, years later, at the same spot, images of this nightmare came back to me. The faces of the men I'd seen flying were deformed by fear. They weren't flying, they were falling, fully dressed, into the Seine.)

43 Theorized by Marianne Hirsch, "postmemory" refers to the relationship a person may have to a set of traumatic memories and experiences that are not her own. It "describes the relationship that the 'generation after' bears to the personal, the collective, and the cultural trauma of those who came before." *The Generation of Postmemory: Writing and Visual Culture after the Holocaust* (New York: Columbia University Press, 2012), 5.

The river that causes Dadou so much anguish will become a source of salvation, for him and for others. Dadou's confession about his nightmare occurs only after he has a revelatory meeting with a lockkeeper who works on the Paris canals and who, in 1961, was an officer in the river brigade. Following up on a tip that the lockkeeper might know something about the river brigade's missing archives, Dadou is confronted with another dead end. "Les collègues de l'époque ont eu l'interdiction, je dis bien l'interdiction, de révéler combien ils avaient repêché de corps de Nord africains dans le fleuve," the lockkeeper tells him. "Ces archives ont été détruites il y a à peine trois semaines" (48, at the time, my colleagues were forbidden—and yes, I mean forbidden—from revealing how many North African bodies they'd fished out of the river. The archives were destroyed barely three weeks ago). Despite the disappointment, it is this revelation and the moment of complicity with the lockkeeper—a man whose life is devoted to the waterways of Paris—that brings to the surface Dadou's dream and the trauma it reveals.

Dadou resurfaces—literally and narratively—more than three quarters of the way through the novel. His fall from the bridge in Argenteuil is finally broken when he lands squarely on a barge that just happens to be passing beneath the bridge, piloted by the aptly named sailor, Sauveur. Although he has been compelled to reenact the fatal trajectory of his uncles and so many others on October 17, Dadou encounters a different ending; however passively, he has essentially repeated and worked through a trauma, exorcising it not only for himself, but, symbolically, for an entire generation. And this positivity is born not only of the fact that he has been saved, but of the nature of his savior, a man who understands the river deeply, and knows the story the Seine would tell, if she could speak: "Ah, la Seine…si elle pouvait parler, elle en révèlerait des choses, et des pas catholiques" (162, Ah, la Seine…if she could speak, she would have some stories to tell, and I don't mean fairy tales). Moreover, Sauveur's worldview is deeply connected to the Seine, such that the murder of men in the river is a personal affront to him and to the sanctity of the river itself and what it represents for the nation:

> Ce métier […] c'est notre héritage. Le fleuve est une seule et même veine, nourrie par une multitude de sources. C'est une seule et même toile d'araignée qui irrigue le pays. Aujourd'hui, il se meurt à petit feu. D'année en année, j'ai vu disparaître la transparence de l'eau. La Seine est devenue une poubelle. On y jette des frigidaires, des voitures et toutes sortes de choses dont les gens ne veulent plus. Tout compte fait, vaut mieux balancer ça que des hommes. Je ne crois pas aux silences du fleuve.

Au contraire, ceux qui y vivent diront que les nouvelles s'y transmettent très vite [...] Il n'y a pas un marinier qui ignorait les Algériens jetés à la Seine. Nous étions les premiers à signaler qu'un corps remontait à la surface. (164–65)

(This job [...], it's our heritage. The river is one long vein, fed by many sources. It's a single spider web that irrigates the country. Today, the river is slowly dying. From year to year, I've seen the water grow cloudy. The Seine has become a garbage can. People throw refrigerators, cars, and all kinds of things they don't want any more. That being said, better to throw things than to throw men. I don't believe in the silences of the river. On the contrary, people who live on the river will tell you that news travels fast [...] There's not a sailor out there who didn't know about the Algerians thrown in the Seine. We were the first ones to report the bodies floating in our river.)

Sauveur paints the river as entwined in a deeply symbiotic relationship with France: The river is fed by numerous sources from far and wide, but it also spreads out its water web to feed the country in turn. Yet if this monologue recalls late nineteenth-century discourse on the river as a metonymy for the nation, it also contains a distinctly ecological critique that implies a need for stewardship of the land, as well as a comment about modernity and the state of the environment. Indeed, images of refrigerators and cars are reminiscent of France's mid-century obsession with the trappings of modern convenience, and with the emerging discourse of a modernity that provided a welcome alternative to the colonial narrative.[44] Now, however, both stories find themselves submerged in a river whose transparency—understood both literally and metaphorically—has become cloudy.

Une nuit d'octobre ends on the same bridge from which Dadou had been thrown. In the final dramatic scene of this pulp fiction, a retired police officer named Gérard, wracked with guilt over his complicity in the murders of October 1961, teeters on the balustrade of the bridge, contemplating suicide. Alerted to his plan, Gérard's daughter and Dadou arrive at the bridge "au moment où le brouillard se dissipait" (204, at the moment the fog was lifting). There, they find not only Gérard, the

---

44   See Ross, *Fast Cars, Clean Bodies*, 7. Ross argues that, during the 1960s, the French felt compelled to choose between two guiding narratives—"the story of French modernization and Americanization" and "the story of decolonization." For Ross, "holding the two in tension" is crucial to understanding the contradictions of the period in question.

perpetrator, but also Dadou's father, a survivor of October 17. Acts of empathy, forgiveness, a desire to move on: Dadou's father takes Gérard by the arm, the fog lifts, and the Seine breaks its silence as Sauveur and the other barge drivers sound their horns in a river concerto.

Notwithstanding its varying levels of plausibility and verisimilitude, fiction possesses a particular ability to account for uncommon embodied experiences such as falling into the Seine. Yet, as seen earlier in our discussion of Panijel, this quality is not the exclusive purview of works of the imagination; although typically less subjective, documentary and memorial productions have also mobilized the river and the trope of the falling body as a means of both situating the violence of October 17 and engaging with a history of representation of the Seine. Yasmina Adi's 2011 documentary *Ici on noie les Algériens* has emerged as a kind of companion film to Panijel's *Octobre à Paris,* and in her updated story of October 17, the very first image to appear on screen is also a still shot of the Seine. Framed in what might be considered an extreme close-up, the shot of the surface of water eliminates all landmarks, allowing the river to fill the screen and its rippling surface to become a background against which the opening credits roll.

In the first sequence of the film, Mme Khalfi, an Algerian woman widowed on October 17, is filmed as a passenger in a moving car as she gazes out the window and recounts, in Arabic, the loss of her husband.[45] If the spectator is able to infer that she is riding along the banks of the Seine, it is in part because of the sound bridge of eerie, quavering music linking the credits and this first sequence; a few moments into the film, Khalfi implicitly confirms this by gesturing to the river, accusing it of hiding her husband: "October 1961. He left me, I was 25. With four children. I know he's there, in the water." Images alternate between Khalfi, narrating from the backseat of the car, and the roiling waters of the Seine. After offering a few more details about her own suffering and that of her children, Khalfi turns more fully toward the river to address

---

45   Khalfi speaks Arabic, as do all the other Algerians interviewed in the film. In a review of both Adi's film (which had just been released in theatres) and Panijel's *Octobre à Paris* (which had just been released on DVD), Jacques Mandelbaum notes that "tous les personnages d'*Octobre à Paris* parlent français, tous ceux d'*Ici on noie les Algériens* parlent arabe. A croire que le demi-siècle d'intégration qui les sépare charrie bien des cadavres" (all the characters in *Octobre à Paris* speak French; all those in *Ici on noie les Algériens* speak Arabic. It would seem that the half-century of integration that separates them carries many cadavers). *Le Monde,* October 14, 2011.

her husband directly: "I know you are there in the water. The enemy put you there. They put you there and left you there. I know you're there. You'll be there forever." If Khalfi's direct address to the river speaks to a certain pathos present throughout the documentary, her testimonial also assumes its importance in comparison with others: A handful of individuals are also filmed in proximity to the Seine, yet none of them engage the river directly, and none of them make such obvious reference to bodies disappeared in the Seine.

The end of Adi's documentary returns to the river, redeploying the same extreme close-up of the turbulent surface of the Seine as a leitmotif. The final three minutes form a video palimpsest that begins with a static, full-frame shot of the photo of the graffito "Ici on noie les Algériens." (See Fig. 13.) The solidity of the photograph is unsettled as water appears at the lower edges of the frame and seems to lap at the borders of the picture, with technical manipulation producing the effect of the river having left its bed to flood the embankments. Slowly, in a variation on the lap dissolve (a film editing technique in which one image gradually fades into the next), the photo is replaced by a full-screen shot of water, identical to the one that opened the film. Over the sound of a gentle rippling, we hear an ostensibly archival recording from a newscast announcing the investigation of "the deaths of some 60 North Africans." The image of the water's surface now ebbs and flows, alternating between total opacity and just enough transparency to reveal, first, images of newspaper headlines from October 1961, nearly all of which mention bodies in the Seine; then a photograph of Algerian men protesting on October 17; and, lastly, a set of titles that function as an epilogue to the film, relating that the 60 cases brought on behalf of missing Algerians were never brought to trial, and that there has been no restitution or official recognition.[46] This final image of the documentary freezes on a triple-layer of sedimentation: An archival photo of well-dressed Algerian men on the *grands boulevards* lies beneath the accusatory text, while the layer constituted by the river functions ambiguously. Depending on how we read this image, the river is either at the bottom, that is, *au fond*—in the sense of being both the background and the heart of the matter—or the top layer, suggesting that the Algerians we see lie beneath

---

46 The headlines read: "Les cadavres de deux Algériens retirés de la Seine" (Cadavers of two Algerians pulled out of the Seine) and "Encore trois cadavres d'Algériens retirés de la Seine" (Three more Algerian cadavers pulled out of the Seine).

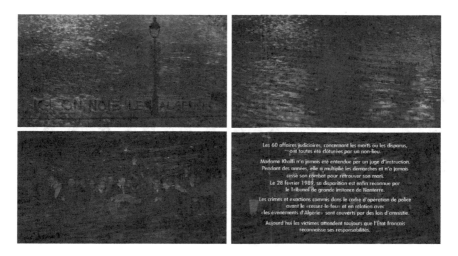

Fig. 13. Beneath the surface; last images of *Ici on noie les Algériens*.
Documentary. Dir. Yasmina Adi. France, 2011.

the Seine's surface both literally (in terms of the order of the calques) and symbolically.

If the palimpsest that concludes Adi's film offers an emblem of Algerians (here, their photo) falling into the Seine, activist posters commemorating various anniversaries of the massacre feature images that are uncompromising in their visualization of bodies and the river. Two graphic posters, signed by artist, photographer, and activist Miloud Kerzazi and issued in 2011 to mark the 40th anniversary of October 17, depict slightly different variations on a main theme: Dark figures reminiscent of crime-scene chalk outlines fall or are thrown from a parapet. (See Fig. 14.) The poster on the right features strong horizontal motifs that suggest a bridge: Just above a band featuring the reproduction of the graffito "Ici on noie les Algériens," a horizontal frieze portrays policemen clashing with demonstrators, beating them until they fall into the river below. The date "17.10.61" is the largest element on the poster, and a bust of Marianne is bisected by the number "10," suggesting that "October" remains a divisive element for the Republic. In Kerzazi's second version of the poster (on the left), used by the movement Indigènes de la République to advertise commemorative activities for the 50th anniversary of the massacre, the colors of the French flag form the background of the poster, while the bridge

Fig. 14. Two commemorative posters: "17 octobre 1961. Bleu, blanc, rouge" and
"17 octobre 1961. Noir et blanc." Graphics © Miloud Kerzazi.

in question is clearly the Pont Neuf. What both versions share are the
names of 12 actual victims of October 17, depicted falling into the river
alongside the schematic bodies that represent them.

Insofar as they advertise commemorative events, these posters are
clearly designed to transmit a certain amount of logistical information.
Their message, however, is also coded in their imagery, which quite
efficiently tells a certain story of October 17. Its historical accuracy
notwithstanding, it is certainly true that foregrounding bodies falling
into the Seine allows these posters to achieve maximum dramatic
impact, even at the risk of telescoping the narrative and reducing
October 17 to one particular element. But the motif of bodies in the
Seine can also be found in posters whose absence of verbiage places
them more squarely in the category of graphic art. An unsigned blue
and white image featuring only a large stylized hand reaching up out of
waves toward a bridge was used by the city of Bezons on its October 17
memorial web page. The motif of the extended hand can also be seen in
Mustapha Boutadjine's poster "Paris, 17 octobre, 1961." (See Chapter 1,
Fig. 4 and n. 76.) Vaguely reminiscent of the May '68 *atelier populaire*

posters, the wordless bold image depicts a large hand reaching up from the water toward a pair of military boots.

Ultimately, any representation of the Seine in the anarchive is implicitly about the disappearance of Algerian bodies, even when the river is depicted without a human presence (such as the very first images of Panijel's and Adi's documentaries). The attention to embodied experience depicted in Kateb's poem and Panijel's film make it impossible to say that concern with the exceptional body is new in the anarchive. Yet, the third wave does contain proportionally more images of bodies falling in the Seine, particularly visual images. Despite the fact that not all Algerian victims on October 17 died by drowning, and notwithstanding the ample evidence of other forms of violence in parts of the city removed from the river, the Seine and the stylized falling body have clearly become the emblem par excellence of October 17.

While I do not wish to enter into comparisons of scale, ideology, repercussions, or any other analogy-based argument about October 17 and other instances of historical trauma or genocide, I must nonetheless confess my curiosity about how such blatant imagery fits within a history of representation of horrors perpetrated by humans on humans. It strikes me, first of all, that recourse to a form of iconic shorthand is hardly uncommon as a representational strategy for commemorative imagery: Posters or memes honoring the memory of the 9/11 terrorist attacks very often feature New York's Twin Towers, even though the attacks were multi-sited and not all victims that day perished in lower Manhattan. And yet, such 9/11 memorial material stops short of using actual or stylized images of falling bodies, even though we know that photographs taken on September 11 show individuals falling from the skyscrapers.[47] Similarly, memorial representations of the Shoah often use the Star of David, barbed wire, or a single flame as symbolic images, generally steering away from imagery that would recall too precisely the experience of death in a gas chamber.[48]

---

47 I am thinking, of course, of "The Falling Man," a photo by Richard Drew of the Associated Press that depicts a man falling, seemingly headfirst, from one of the towers of the World Trade Center on September 11, 2001.
48 Memorial posters of the Rwandan genocide also tend to feature a single flame. Of course, museums, exhibits, and performance pieces devoted to remembering the Holocaust, the Rwandan genocide, and other episodes of historical trauma often use more explicit imagery and objects, and certainly photographs exist that testify to the various horrors committed (images of skeletons or machetes, for example).

It is certainly the case that difficult, even intolerable images of cruelty and human suffering exist, and are occasionally displayed to pedagogical and/or political ends. What strikes me as unique in the quiver of October 17 representations is the relative speed—and apparent ease—with which something like being thrown off a bridge by the local police has become *iconic* to the point of quite nearly being a logo. Ironically, even as such works make visible the exceptional body of the disappeared Algerian, that very body is converted into a banalized figure, one without particularities or origins, the very horror of the act perhaps drowned in its blatant representation and reproduction.

Hidden Rivers/Reading for the Detail

Made nearly five decades after the events of October 17, Michael Haneke's 2005 feature film *Caché* (Hidden) stages neither the massacre, nor even the memory of it; in fact, the film makes only one reference to October 17.[49] Instead, *Caché* attempts to represent the complex processes of repression at work in subjects whose lives were touched, even only glancingly, by the events, while at the same time serving as an allegorical exploration of collective guilt.[50] In the context of this particular discussion, *Caché* is doubly superlative. It is undoubtedly the best-known work in the anarchive: Of all the cultural productions featuring some aspect of October 17, the film's renown among a general,

49 With seven films to his credit, Haneke had already established himself as an award-winning director when *Caché* was released in 2005. The film went on to win three awards at Cannes that year, in addition to a raft of French and international prizes, and is featured on multiple "100 best film" lists. (*Caché* was listed first in *New York Times'* "Best 100 Films of the Decade" feature; 44th in *Daily Telegraph*'s equivalent list; and 36th in *Guardian*'s.)

50 I write "attempts to represent" because, as scholars have noted, the film is, among other things, keenly interested in the foibles and failures of representation. With regard to the film's allegorical potential, Haneke has said, "You could find a similar story in any country [...] There's always a collective guilt which can be connected to a personal story..." He also notes that he learned about October 17 from a documentary on the Franco-German public TV station Arte. (This would most likely be the BBC film *Drowning by Bullets*, which aired on Arte under the French title *Une journée portée disparue*.) Haneke, interview with Karin Schiefer, Austrian Film Commission (May 2005), http://www.austrianfilms.com/news/en/bodymichael_haneke_talks_about_cachbody.

international public and the quantity of scholarship it has inspired are unequaled. At the same time, *Caché* is also, to the naked eye, one of the anarchival works least likely to be discussed in the context of representations of the Seine: The river, like the massacre itself, is mentioned exactly once in a film that, for all intents and purposes, seems to have little to do with October 17. But rivers, as it turns out, are just one of the many things hidden in *Hidden*.

Caché parachutes the viewer into the lives of Anne and Georges Laurent, a couple of upper-middle-class Parisian intellectuals with a teenaged son named Pierrot. The smooth veneer of their existence is troubled when they begin receiving anonymous videocassettes in the mail. At first these seem to suggest nothing extraordinary, other than the fact that the house is under surveillance. With time, the videos and the drawings that accompany them reveal disturbing images, ones that Georges recognizes as belonging to his past: A scene of the country home where he grew up suggests that the sender knows who he is and where he is from. Georges begins to have nightmares that hark back to traumatic scenes of his childhood; a rooster's throat being cut, a young boy coughing up blood. With these buried memories now triggered, Georges begins to imagine who might want to disturb him: When he was a child, his family employed an Algerian couple who lived at the family farm along with their son, Majid, who was the same age as Georges. The couple went to Paris to join the protest on October 17 and never returned. Majid stayed on with the family until Georges, jealous at sharing his parents' attention, schemed to have Majid removed to foster care. Now, Georges suspects Majid of harboring resentment and seeking revenge by psychologically torturing Georges and his family.

Georges confronts Majid twice, and on the second of these occasions, the Algerian man slits his own throat with a razor blade, offering, as his only explanation to Georges: "Je voulais que tu sois présent" ("I wanted you to be present").[51] Georges flees the scene, retreats to the plush, darkened interior of his own home, and proceeds to swallow a

---

51 The suicide scene is undoubtedly the most analyzed moment of *Caché*; see Max Silverman, "The Violence of the Cut: Michael Haneke's *Caché* and Cultural Memory," *French Cultural Studies* 21, no. 1 (2010): 57–65; Flood, "Brutal Visibility: Framing Majid's Suicide in Michael Haneke's *Caché* (2005)," *Nottingham French Studies* 56, no. 1 (2017): 82–97; Ipek A. Celik, "'I Wanted You to Be Present': Guilt and the History of Violence in Michael Haneke's *Caché*," *Cinema Journal* 50, no. 1 (Fall 2010): 59–80.

few "cachets"—sleeping pills (and yet another meaning we could impute to the film's title)—that allow him to further escape a reality that he has witnessed, but to which he has failed to react. After Majid's death, suspicions concerning the origins of the videocassettes and drawings, that is, the origin of the unidentified menace, come to land on his son. Yet, although Majid's son makes two more appearances in the film— he confronts Georges somewhat aggressively at his office and, in the mysterious final shot of the film, we see him mount the steps outside Pierrot's school and consult with the boy briefly—there is never any clear resolution to the question posed, in various contexts, throughout the film: Who is responsible?

The question of responsibility permeates *Caché* and, in a metafashion that Haneke could not have intended or anticipated, it also surfaces in some of the most pointed criticism leveled at the film. Paul Gilroy, perhaps *Caché*'s most fervent detractor, calls the film's minimalist reference to October 17 "overly casual" and a cinematic expression of "bad faith":

> That unmourned and unremembered real event does a lot of narrative work for Haneke. Many people involved in building a habitable multicultural Europe will feel that there are pressing issues of morality and responsibility involved in raising that history only to reduce it to nothing more than a piece of tragic machinery in the fatal antagonism that undoes *Caché*'s protagonists. The dead deserve better than that passing acknowledgement.[52]

Gilroy goes on to castigate the film for centering our attention on the tortured conscience of the privileged white male (Georges), a *topos* he calls "well-trodden ground," and to rebuke Haneke for his apparent "collusion with the comforting idea that the colonial native can be made to disappear in an instant through the auto-combustive agency of their own violence."[53] Gilroy's critique raises important questions about the types of demands we make on art and artists, as well as about what constitutes responsible representation; it also, however inadvertently, pushes us to think about responsible *interpretation*: Isn't it possible that Gilroy's condemnation of the film as "antipolitical" (233) lies in his apparent refusal to read its details carefully? In *Caché*, as in other works where the representation of the massacre and its repression are "limited"

---

52   Gilroy, "Shooting Crabs in a Barrel," *Screen* 48, no. 3 (Summer 2007): 233.
53   Gilroy, "Shooting Crabs," 233–34.

to a wink, the containment, minimizing, or "reduction" of October 17 creates emblematic signs charged with meaning. These sidelong glances are not furtive but indicative; they prompt the reader to follow the gaze. It may be worth wondering if calling October 17 "unremembered" in this film is not, in itself, a form of bad faith.[54]

Even before we turn our attention to the hidden rivers in *Caché*, it is possible to begin tugging at the loose threads of Gilroy's assertions. It is certainly true that, diegetically, the history of October 17 is figured as a detail in a plot that otherwise does not explicitly deal with colonial history, Algerians, or racial politics. In terms of temporal proportionality, colonial history is inarguably minimized. At a pivotal point in the film, Georges recounts the story of Majid's parents to Anne:

> Ces parents travaillaient pour nous. Papa les aimait bien. Ça devait être de bons ouvriers. En octobre 61 le FLN appelait les Algériens à manifester. Ils sont allés à Paris. Le 17 octobre 16, je te fais pas un dessin. Papon. Le massacre policier. Ils ont noyé à peu près 200 Arabes dans la Seine. Il semble que les parents de Majid étaient de ceux-là, en tout cas ils sont jamais revenus. Papa est allé à Paris pour se renseigner, ils lui ont dit qu'il devrait être bien content d'être débarrassé de ces bougnouls.

> ([Majid's] parents worked for us. Dad liked them. I guess they were good workers. In October '61 the FLN called all Algerians to a demonstration in Paris. October 17, 1961. Enough said. Papon. The police massacre. They drowned about 200 Arabs in the Seine. Including Majid's parents, most likely. They never came back. Dad went to Paris to look for them. [The police] said he should be glad to be rid of a couple of jigaboos.)

On the surface of things, Georges appears to think that announcing the date alone is sufficient to recount an entire history: "Enough said," he tells Anne (in the English version), but then goes on to add significant detail, including names of historical actors and the number of dead. The supplement of information suggests in fact that "the 17th October 1961" does not say *enough*, that it is not a transparent signifier. Here, through its representation of October 17 as both a complete sign and one that needs more information to signify, as both transparent and opaque, the film captures and crystalizes the date's essential ambiguity.

---

54   Patrick Crowley also takes issue with Gilroy's critique of the film. See "When Forgetting is Remembering: Haneke's *Caché* and the Events of October 17, 1961," in *On Michael Haneke*, ed. Brian Price and John David Rhodes (Detroit, MI: Wayne State University Press, 2010), 274.

206 Absent the Archive

This is the moment Gilroy refers to when he calls the film's mention of October 17 an "overly casual citation." But there is nothing casual about the construction of this scene or the textual account of October 17 that it offers: Just as its opacity reproduces the historical handling of the massacre, the syntactical fragments alone—each a kind of semiotic isolate—replicate the morcellated memory of colonial violence. Moreover, the condensed content of this moment is centrifuged throughout the film, flung out into other scenes representing other violence while metonymically reflecting back on the ur-trauma at the center of *Caché*. As Max Silverman has pointed out, for example, the nearly omnipresent TV news broadcasts in the background are meant to be *read*: Scenes from the Iraq War, the Abu Ghraib torture trials, and Israeli violence are Haneke's way of suggesting that "what is hidden beneath the normalized surface of everyday metropolitan life is a cultural imaginary of overlapping layers of violence and trauma."[55] Through various filmic and textual tactics, October 17 is multiplied—however implicitly—throughout the film. Ultimately, then, to ignore the amplitude of October 17 in *Caché* is to ignore the power of the detail.

Beyond the lone explicit mention of the Seine in Georges's patchy history lesson, there are two ways in which the river wends its way into *Caché*'s representational subconscious. Recognizing the first appearance of the Seine depends on attention to small details of Laurent family's home in Paris and knowledge of the capital's underground cartography. Numerous scholars have commented upon the architecture of the house—an actual modernist structure that, viewed from both within and without, constitutes a fortress-like space.[56] Few, though, have lingered on the particular place the house occupies in Paris's 13th *arrondissement*. Despite the fact that the home is "protected" from the outside world by multiple barriers to access (a gate, a front door, numerous internal doors), and despite the fact that the interior thwarts the exterior (interior shots of windows turn these surfaces into mirrors that reflect the inside back rather than permit a view out), the scenes of video-surveillance footage reveal an actual address that can be located on the map of Paris: 49 rue Brillat-Savarin.[57]

55   Silverman, "Violence of the Cut," 134.
56   For a particularly in-depth study of private and public space in *Caché*, see Brianne Gallagher, "Policing Paris: Private Publics and Architectural Media in Michael Haneke's *Caché*," *Journal for Cultural Research* 12, no. 1 (2008): 19–38.
57   Gallagher's observations on windows and mirrors are particularly perceptive:

A home address is a detail that creates vulnerability—for the Laurents, after all, one of the most disturbing aspects of the videocassettes is their revelation that a potentially nefarious individual *knows where they live*. In a film that depicts very few, if any, recognizable Parisian addresses or landmarks, the visibility of the street name and house number is a surprising moment of transparency; likewise, it offers the viewer access to information that can be used to expose the vulnerabilities of the film's representation. Rue Brillat-Savarin, as it has been known since 1894, is one of a number of streets that owe their existence and configuration to the path of the Bièvre, Paris's little-known "second river." Indeed, rue Brillat-Savarin is a surface trace of a hidden river: Once a source of potable water, the 33-kilometer-long Bièvre (running from the Yvelines region south of Paris to the Seine) came to be known in the nineteenth century as an open-air sewer, and was condemned by Baron Haussmann in 1858. Plans to canalize and cover over the river began in 1860, and by 1902 nearly all of the Bièvre had been backfilled; the portion that still ran underground was diverted from the Seine to the capital's sewer system.[58]

Arguably a main character in *Caché*, the Laurents' home—notwithstanding all about it that is hidden from view—is visibly situated on a Parisian street with a particular history related to rivers. Rue Brillat-Savarin shows no signs of its hidden past, of its historical underbelly; to mobilize any kind of interpretation thus requires a degree of historical and topographic knowledge. But once we know that the Laurents' house is built upon a site deemed offensive and therefore hidden away from view, and that this very site is a river, it becomes nearly impossible not

"The window in Georges's bedroom, moreover, functions as a reflection image of his past, reflecting the image of him as a young boy. The bedroom window in this sense functions more as a media space—as well as a temporal frame that oscillates between the past and present—than as a functional frame to capture an exterior view from the home" (35). It is also worth noting that, given the configuration of exterior shots of the home, these most likely were taken from a position on the Rue des Iris. In the context of a film about gazes, the hidden, and the seen, the symbolism of this street name cannot be missed.

58   On the history of the Bièvre, see Thomas Le Roux, "Une rivière industrielle avant l'industrialisation: la Bièvre et le fardeau de la prédestination, 1670–1830," *Géocarrefour* 85, no. 3 (2010): 193–207, and Jean Anckaert, "La Bièvre parisienne: son asservissement, sa capture, sa disparition (1902–1912)" (doctoral thesis, École pratique des hautes études, Paris, 1999).

to see references to October 17 everywhere, flowing under and through the film.

If the implied Bièvre River stands in for the Seine—itself a metonym for October 17—and if this in turn suggests that the Laurents' home, symbolically, rests upon a palimpsest of historical and cultural signs, it is worth noting that the Seine is also implicated in the home's interior. To understand how, we need to return to the scene of Georges's comment on October 17, and the notion that the film takes this compact reference to the massacre and centrifuges it, in this case quite literally forcing it onto the walls. First, it is worth noting that, while in the English translation Georges tells Anne: "October 17, 1961. Enough said," the original language of the exchange complicates matters substantially. In French, Georges uses the idiomatic expression "je te fais pas un dessin"; literally, "I'm not going to draw you a picture." The reference to a picture, a work of visual representation, activates the mise en abyme at work in the film; in other words, we are now forced to contemplate the actual "dessins" (or drawings), the still pictures represented in this "moving picture."

The camera placement throughout Georges's explanation is, like the text itself, anything but casual. During the monologue about October 17, the camera is trained statically on Georges, who is seated on a white couch before a mostly white background (with the exception of a bookcase visible on the left side of the screen). It is only when Georges is done talking that the camera point of view switches to fix its gaze on Anne, who is sitting on a similar white couch. Here, in the deep space of the shot—which retains Georges in perfect focus in the foreground— we see not only Anne, but, also in perfect focus, a busier backdrop featuring two long, narrow, minimalist, horizontal tableaux comprised of a sinusoidal dark blue line that meanders back and forth across a lichen-green splotched canvas. (See Fig. 15, top.) The paintings are placed on perpendicular walls so as to appear continuous; the strong blue line turns the corner nearly seamlessly.

In the scenes of this cosseted interior where nearly all the walls are insulated with books but no other ornamental art appears to be visible, this set of paintings has appeared just twice before: once when, in a conversation similar to this one, Georges admits to Anne that he suspects he knows who is sending the tapes, and once earlier in the film, when Anne receives an anonymous phone call.[59] (See Fig. 15, bottom

59 Scholars have noted the importance of the interior decoration in the Laurent home, many remarking on the bookshelves, the DVDs, and the TV screen. Few,

right and bottom left, respectively.) (Innocuous in and of itself, the call—like the barest glimpse of the painting we see in the frame—takes on a more troubling signification in light of the context.) The painting may be a work of abstract art, but this meandering line looks very much like a schematic, aerial map of a river, and of course the Seine is very much characterized by its *méandres*—or meanders, the pronounced bends and curves that make it visually distinctive when viewed from above. The color and sinuous quality of the meandering blue line of the tableaux thus recall the Parisian river-turned-gravesite by the state's attempts to erase the visible traces of October 17. Georges does not need to "draw Anne a picture" because their domestic space is haunted by (and built upon) signs of the Seine, a metonymic figure of the fate of Majid's parents and French Muslims of Algeria.

The Fine Line of Hypervisiblity

The subtlety of *Caché*'s handling of river motifs, be they historically implied or artistically rendered, contrasts sharply with nearly all of the anarchival representations of the Seine discussed thus far. Indeed, in the poems by Kateb and Janvier, as well as in Lallaoui's novel, Panijel's and Adi's documentaries, and activist posters, the river is an obvious, if unwitting, participant in the tragedy of October 17. As such, its representation—even when abstract or figurative—cannot be divorced from the bodily experience of death. Particularly when read alongside Haneke's almost subliminal messaging, depictions of the dead speaking (such as in Médine's rap), or of death in process (in Chouaki's play and, to an extent, in Lallaoui's novel), can seem contrived. Above and beyond the discomfiture produced by the content itself, the treatment of such scenes risks coming across as lachrymose and even, in certain instances, pathetic.

As a reader and a critic, I feel no special obligation to steer away from cultural productions whose level of craft might be considered less than "high art." This is particularly true of my work on the anarchive, which contains a certain amount of "pulp" fiction, paraliterature, or

---

if any, have noted the paintings, which constitute the only ornamentation in the interior. See Crowley, "When Forgetting is Remembering," 273; and Asborn Gronstad, *Screening the Unwatchable: Spaces of Negation in Post-Millennial Art Cinema* (New York: Palgrave Macmillan, 2012), 158—both of which discuss various features hung on the walls, but not the paintings.

Fig. 15. Juliette Binoche and Daniel Auteuil in *Caché*.
Feature film. Dir. Michael Haneke, 2005.

commissioned works whose ultimate status is indeterminate (this is the
case of Chouaki's play, for example, which was published in book form
but has never been given a public production). Moreover, gimmicky
representations strike me as no less valuable than, say, the sophisti-
cation of Haneke's filmmaking and, conversely, I would not suggest that
Haneke's aesthetic sensibilities are the opposite of contrivances. The
accounts produced by Médine's drowning Ahmed or Chouaki's sinking
Algerians may traffic in pathos; the ambition nonetheless deserves
recognition. Death, no matter the circumstances, may be understood as
an "interruption in the production of meaning," something abundantly
clear in the case of October 17, when the dead have been prohibited
from signifying, whether forensically, politically, or historically.[60] In

60   Colin Davis, *Haunted Subjects: Deconstruction, Psychoanalysis and the
Return of the Dead* (New York: Palgrave Macmillan 2007), 111.

their recourse to prosopopoeia, the rhetorical device whereby the dead are made to speak, the works in question defy the blockage in meaning produced by the murder of their characters.

Regardless of the way that death in the Seine is depicted in the anarchive, and notwithstanding any subjective assessments of their aesthetic and/or political value, all of the works discussed in this chapter (with the notable exception of *Caché*) participate in what we might consider an iconotextual hypervisibility of the Seine. This perhaps disproportionate attention to the river in October 17 fictions finds its echo in ultra-contemporary activist material (the posters, for example) in which the Seine becomes an ur-signifier, telegraphing meaning above and beyond its factual role in Algerian deaths. The reproducibility—the "shareability" and even "meme-ification" of visual imagery in particular—makes it possible to see bodies falling into the Seine (more precisely: representations thereof) with the click of a button.

Scholars who work on hypervisiblity, particularly in the context of race and gender, have argued that more exposure does not necessarily lead to more awareness, better politics, or even smarter behavior or better outcomes for individuals and groups previously sentenced to cultural and political invisibility. Paradoxically, more visibility seems to departicularize and ultimately desensitize, leading to another, perhaps more insidious form of invisibility. Of course, it is impossible to argue that the Seine's hypervisiblity in the anarchive is what has contributed to the metaphorical invisibility of October 17; the notional invisibility of the massacre of Algerians preexisted the proliferation of verbal and visual representations of bodies falling into the rivers and canals of the capital. However, it is certainly the case that anarchival images of the Seine are complicated by the river's ambivalent, albeit mythical, status in the French imaginary and the gravitational force it exerts within culture.

Perhaps, ultimately, it is the Seine itself that suffers from a form of hypervisibility: The early twenty-first century has brought with it a return to the river perhaps equaled only by the heyday of the *guinguettes*. Since the first "Paris plages" in 2002, which trucked tons of sand into the capital, transforming the cobblestone embankments into temporary beaches, the City of Paris has engaged in dogged efforts to give the river and its banks back to the people. Redolent with late nineteenth-century images of *guinguettes* and bourgeois leisure activities, a reinvestment in the Seine has allowed for the creation of beaches, *buvettes*, and myriad activities for young and old alike. Moreover, the refurbishing of the

Seine's banks has also become a showcase for progress and technology: Stands tout cutting-edge water filtration and recapture techniques, and new testing systems that allow for the detection of bacteria or pollutants upstream have made it possible to cordon off a section of Canal de l'Ourcq for supervised swimming. In 2015, Mayor of Paris Anne Hidalgo announced a plan to make the Seine itself available for swimming by 2024.

For the moment, however, swimming in the Seine and its tributary canals remains officially forbidden and punishable by fine. And yet, in recent summers the waterways have been full of all kinds of bodies at play: Teenage boys speaking a patois of French and Arabic leap from the *passerelles* over the basin de la Villette; *bobos* put down their apérol-spritz to dip into the Canal de l'Ourcq right in front of their regular bar; an Orthodox Jewish grandma dangles her feet in the water, a brief respite from the *canicule*; late one night, a man paddles right down the middle of the canal as his dog gallops alongside him on the tow path. To say that the Seine and its tributaries are hypervisible is to state the obvious; the river has always been an iconic emblem of Paris, captured in some of its most enduring photos and film scenes. Today, the ability to experience the water bodily means that Parisians can now see—and by extension, know—the waterways of their city from a wholly different perspective. But what does this increased hypervisiblity add to our knowledge? As I watch the frolicking of bearded thirty-something hipsters and teenaged boys of Maghrebi descent alike, I can't help but wonder if they know that, in 1961—less than a year after the degradation of the Seine's water quality led the last of the *guinguettes* to close and so many to abandon the riverbanks—"here" was where they drowned Algerians. I wonder what it would change if they did?

CHAPTER FIVE

"How Lucky Were the Blond Kabyles"
Reading Race in the Anarchive

Le racisme, finalement, c'est une affaire personnelle...
entre nous et nous...une affaire de l'inconscient.[1]
—Igor Barrère and Étienne Lalou

In 1997, working under the pseudonym Paul Smaïl, French author Jack-Alain Léger published *Vivre me tue*, a novel marketed as a lightly fictionalized autobiography of its protagonist.[2] Narrator Paul Smaïl is a twenty-something Parisian of Moroccan descent with a degree in comparative literature, a penchant for citing Melville and Rimbaud, and a dead-end job delivering pizza. The story of his tribulations in 1990s France—cultural alienation, political disenfranchisement, chronic underemployment, and discrimination—rang true for a generation of French young adults of Maghrebi origin. Léger (writing as Smaïl) appeared to bank on a novel combination of established themes of 1980s

---

1 "Racism, in the end, is a personal matter...between us and us...it is a matter of the unconscious." Igor Barrère and Étienne Lalou, "Le Racisme," September 11, 1961, narrated by Étienne Lalou, on *Faire face*, RTL. The documentary series *Faire face* ran on RTF from June 10, 1961 to February 9, 1962. The series included episodes on topics such as birth control, earthquakes, divorce, prostitution, TV, and the *pieds noirs*.

2 Literally translated, the novel's title means "life is killing me," but it has been translated into English under the title *Smile*, which plays on the pronunciation of the author's last name. The novel was adapted for the screen in 2002 by Jean-Pierre Sinapi, and the English-language version of the film was marketed under the title *Life Kills Me*.

beur literature dressed up in a decidedly hipper vernacular. Indeed, *Vivre me tue* read like something of a "new wave" in *beur* letters, comparatively less interested in tropes of coming of age and pathos than some of its predecessors, more attuned to popular culture and full of acts of microresistance.[3]

As a work of the anarchive, *Vivre me tue* belongs to a subset of cultural productions whose investment in October 17 is situated in details rather than in key plot points. Although October 17 neither drives the novel's plot nor motivates its characters' actions, the first two explicit mentions of that violent night raise important questions about the transmission, representation, and even the facts of history. In this episode, which finds Paul in conversation with his former French teacher Monsieur Hamel, our narrator critiques the high-school history curriculum for its partial vision of contemporary French history:

> Le peu que je connais d'histoire contemporaine je ne le tiens pas de mes profs d'histoire mais de M. Hamel...les mensonges de l'histoire officielle, les falsifications, le silence sur les crimes de la police parisienne pendant la guerre d'Algérie...ce qui s'est passé la terrible nuit du 17 octobre 1961, la nuit du pogrom des Arabes à Paris, la nuit où a été tué avec plus de cent autres ratonnés mon oncle Mehdi. [...] On a retrouvé son cadavre dans la Seine, à Conflans, le 21 je crois, ou le 22. [...] Il ne manifestait pas quand ils l'ont tué, [...] Il allait à son boulot: il était machiniste à l'Olympia. Il avait un permis pour circuler après le couvre-feu. *D'ailleurs, il n'était pas algérien.* (103–4)

> (The little I've learned about contemporary history doesn't come from my history teachers but from Mr. Hamel. The lies of official history, all the falsification, the silence about crimes committed by the Paris police during the Algerian War...What happened on that terrible night of October 17, 1961, the night of the Arab pogrom in Paris, the night when my Uncle Mehdi was killed along with more than a hundred other A-rabs, all victims of Arab-bashing. [...] They found his body in the Seine, at Conflans, the twenty-first, I think, or the twenty-second. [...] He wasn't demonstrating when they killed him. [...] He was on his way

3   The novel was a critical and popular success, selling 600 copies per day in October 1997. See also Brozgal, "Hostages of Authenticity: Paul Smaïl, Azouz Begag and the Invention of the *Beur* Author," *French Forum* 34, no. 2 (Spring 2009): 113–30. The Léger/Smaïl story is also taken up by Christopher Miller in *Imposters: Literary Hoaxes and Cultural Authenticity* (Chicago: University of Chicago Press, 2018).

to work. He was a stagehand at the Olympia. He had special permission
to be out during the curfew. *Besides, he wasn't Algerian.*)[4]

In a few lines of prose, repressed national and personal histories
collide: The hidden narrative Paul discovers through rogue channels
of knowledge transmission—that is, in conversation over coffee with a
former teacher and not through formal schooling—allows him to situate
the mysterious death of his Uncle Mehdi in the context of October 17.
What little detail Paul does offer seems to suggest that the circumstances of Uncle Mehdi's death were both tragic and ironic: Here was a
law-abiding individual who had taken pains to acquire a special permit
allowing him to breach the curfew; more to the point, he was not at the
protest because *he was not Algerian.*

Uncle Mehdi's narrative weight in the novel is light, at best. One
might even argue that the uncle could be removed without significantly altering the fabric of *Vivre me tue.* Yet the fact that he has
no backstory other than the one Paul recounts here allows Mehdi to
function as a pure political signifier. Phrased as an offhand remark,
"besides, he wasn't Algerian" intimates that Mehdi's death was a case
of mistaken identity—collateral damage wrought by racial profiling.
How else would one explain the murder of a Moroccan at a time when
police dragnets ostensibly targeted Algerians? Uncle Mehdi may be the
most minor of characters in *Vivre me tue,* but his death at the hands of
the Parisian police on October 17 *racializes* the violence in a particular
way—a political gesture that, in 1997, few cultural productions or works
of historiography had sought to make.

If this small detail from *Vivre me tue* serves as a literary punctum,
it is in part because it recasts apparently anodyne passages in the novel
as not only explicitly political, but as bound up with a longer history of
racism in France. In light of Uncle Mehdi's murder in 1961, the desperate
attempts of Paul's brother's in the 1990s to pass as "white," for example,

---

4 Paul Smaïl, *Smile,* trans. Simon Pleasance and Fronza Woods, with Janine
Dupont (London: Serpent's Tail, 2000), 79–80; my emphasis. Originally published
in French as *Vivre me tue* (Paris: Éditions Balland, 1997), 103–4. I've corrected
here an error in the translation, which understood the French expression "Il avait
un permis pour circuler après le couvre-feu" as "He had a license to drive after
the curfew." The "permis" in question is actually a pass, or a special dispensation
granted by the administration to Algerians working the night shift in factories.
In theory, this permission slip was intended to protect these workers from being
stopped by police; in practice, it offered no protections whatsoever.

might be cast as a form of traumatic postmemory. And beyond the role it plays within its own textual economy, the Uncle Mehdi detail emerges as a nodal point in a broader network, for when it comes to the politics of race, *Vivre me tue* is not a lone voice in the anarchive. A number of works (primarily published after 2001) mobilize tropes or stage scenarios of racism, racial profiling, and passing. However, if this detail has been largely unnoticed, it may be because some of the best-known and most widely circulating anarchival productions—Daeninckx's *Meurtres pour mémoire* (1985), Sebbar's *La Seine était rouge* (1999), and Haneke's *Caché* (2005)—do not engage the racial dimensions of October 17, or do so only in the most elliptical of fashions.

When read for its representations of race and racism, the anarchive produces a transhistorical discourse that is as instructive in its moments of ambivalence as it is in its most pointed critiques. The work of this chapter, then, involves excavating discourses of race as they have been produced, implicitly or explicitly, in more than 50 years' worth of cultural productions, ranging from documentary and feature film to historical and graphic novels. In each of the following sections, I am concerned with both the representational strategies and the synergies produced by reading a text against its particular microhistorical context, its conditions of publication or production, and other epiphenomena. At stake in reading race in the anarchive is a process of "race-ing" October 17, that is, of understanding the repression as not simply an inevitable skirmish in a war for independence, but as the fallout of a colonial ideology invested, tacitly but profoundly, in a racialized worldview.[5]

5   "Race-ing" is often used but rarely theorized or even defined (as tends to be the case in so many instances of "gerunding," in critical theory). "To race" a cultural production, situation, or paradigm implies an interpretation that accounts for race and racism as critical components. Its first use may have been in the title of the volume of essays on race and the Anita Hill-Clarence Thomas hearing, *Race-ing Justice, En-Gendering Power: Essays on Anita Hill, Clarence Thomas, and the Social Construction of Reality,* ed. Toni Morrison (New York: Random House, 1992).

"Race Talk" in France: Everywhere and Nowhere

Before delving into the anarchive's representations of race, it is useful to think through the complexities of talking about race, particularly in the French context. Indeed, when it comes to October 17, the anarchive, the police archives, and the cultural moment itself are abuzz with "race talk." This term itself, which seems to be something of a contemporary media buzzword in the United States, Canada, and Australia, is admittedly problematic. Race talk (sometimes written "racetalk") has often been used as a synonym for racist speech: In the early 1990s, Toni Morrison defined it as "the explicit insertion into everyday life of racial signs and symbols that have no meaning other than pressing African Americans to the lowest level of the racial hierarchy," and Morrison is not alone in understanding race talk as a way of creating and policing boundaries between people.[6] More recently, however, both in popular culture and in the academy, the term has taken on a more neutral meaning, referring to "talk" (discussions, commentary, or any kind of speech or discourse) that has to do with "race," and to the complex, difficult attempts to engage openly and honestly with topics that are emotionally charged and often explosive.[7] Race talk, as I understand its manifestations in the October 17 archives and anarchive, draws on both valences of the term: It can manifest as an expression of racism (on the part of a social actor or a fictional character) or as a critique of racist ideology; it may recount the subjective experience of racism or, conversely, of racial privilege; and it may be about emotions, politics, or ostensibly "scientific" discourse. Notwithstanding the variation and even contradictory valences of race talk in October 17 discourse, the phenomenon alone suggests that race was a critical component in both the violence itself and the way it has been represented in culture.[8]

---

6 Toni Morrison, "On the Backs of Blacks," *Time*, December 2, 1993, 57. Numerous scholars share this point of view. See, for example, Kristen A. Meyers, *Racetalk: Racism Hiding in Plain Sight* (Lanham, MD: Rowan and Littlefield, 2005), who posits that racetalk allows people to "imbue different racial and ethnic groups with meaning and oppositional status" (3).

7 This is particularly well argued in Derald Wing Sue's *Race Talk and the Conspiracy of Silence: Understanding and Facilitating Difficult Dialogues about Race* (Hoboken, NJ: John Wiley and Sons, 2015). Sue suggests that, "honest race talk is one of the most powerful means to display stereotypes and biases [...] to enhance a greater sense of belonging and connectedness" (x).

8 One of the most obvious racist features of the violence against Algerians is the particular name it carries in the French lexicon. Since the early nineteenth century,

Hovering in the background of this chapter are, of course, all of the anxieties that come with talking about race: the thorniness and fragility of the concept itself; its iterations as a bygone pseudoscientific category, a construct, a narrative; its function as an analytical tool or as a political cudgel. It is also tempting to sidestep the conversation altogether. After all, science, critical theory, and the law have all pointed us in the direction of a postracial world: Geneticists have proclaimed that "any attempt to classify races of people is both arbitrary and impossible";[9] the US-based legal scholars who developed Critical Race Theory converge in their assessment that "race and races are...categories that society invents, manipulates or retires when convenient"; and in 2018 the French government voted to remove the word "race" from the preamble to its constitution.[10] Yet, just as the scientific community has recognized that, notwithstanding the findings of the Human Genome Project, the concept of race is "likely to persist in both popular and scientific usage," many members of the French political community have also admitted that the wholesale editing of legislation remains symbolic at best, and is unlikely to do away with racism.[11]

Algerians have been referred to as *ratons* (little rats); the term *ratonnade* emerged during the Algerian War to describe violent acts committed against Algerians (and North Africans, more generally).

9   Luigi Cavalli-Sforza, *Qui sommes-nous? Une histoire de la diversité humaine*, trans. Françoise Brun (Paris: Albin Michel, 1994). See also Patricia McCann-Mortimer, Martha Augoustinos, and Amanda Lecouteur, "Race and the Human Genome Project: Constructions of Scientific Legitimacy," *Discourse and Society* 15, no. 4 (2004): 409–32.

10   The 1946 preamble stated that the Republic "assure l'égalité devant la loi de tous les citoyens sans distinction d'origine, de race ou de religion" (ensures the equality before the law, without distinction of origin, race, or religion); the modified version reads, "sans distinction de sexe, d'origine ou de religion" (without distinction of sex, origin, or religion). Proposed by the Front de gauche (or the Left Front), the removal of the word "race" from the Constitution was based on the following justification: "En supprimant la catégorie juridique de races, nous cesserions de donner une légitimité juridique aux idéologies racistes et nous affirmerions, enfin, qu'elles s'appuient sur un concept qui n'a aucun fondement scientifique" (By removing the juridical category of race, we would cease to give juridical legitimacy to racist ideology and we would assert, finally, that such ideology has no basis in science).

11   For the view from the scientific community, see McCann-Mortimer, et al.: "Despite the promissory representation of the HGP as having produced scientific evidence to discredit the biological legitimacy of race, the concept is likely to persist in both popular and scientific usage" (409).

Indeed, as the above anecdote about French legislative practices might already imply, a particular frame is needed in order to begin corralling and unpacking anxieties about race in France. In her essay on "colonial aphasia," historian Ann Laura Stoler observes that in France, "race talk" is everywhere. Writing in 2011, Stoler was responding specifically to what seemed to be a new visibility for race in French political and critical theory, and perhaps an increased legibility for what she calls "the racial coordinates of empire and the racial epistemics [*sic*] of governance."[12] And yet, Stoler is understandably wary about ascribing a *telos* to French "race talk": the sense that it is now "everywhere" certainly in no way precludes it having existed at other moments in time, even though race has often been described (particularly by American scholars) either as a nonexistent analytical category in France, or as a term that "makes [the French] shudder."[13]

To tease out some of these complexities, and to understand the essential ambiguities of a grand narrative of race in France, we might look to an example of race talk from the October 17 police archives. In the weeks following the October repression, Parisian university professors read the following statement to their students: "Un couvre-feu a été établi à 20h pour les Algériens. Quelles que soient les raisons invoquées, c'est une mesure à caractère raciste, inadmissible par principe. *Elle n'a de précédent en France, depuis 1789, que les mesures prises par les Nazis sous l'occupation*" (An 8pm curfew was established for Algerians. Whatever reasons may be invoked to justify this measure, it is *racist* in nature and inadmissible in principle. *The only precedent for such action*

---

12 Stoler, "Colonial Aphasia: Race and Disabled Histories in France," *Public Culture* 23, no. 1 (2011): 122. Of course, it is also important to underscore the fact that antiracist discourse (and organized activism) certainly exist in France. See Catherine Lloyd, *Discourses of Antiracism in France* (Brookfield, UK: Ashgate, 1998); and House, "Anti-Racism in France, 1898–1962: Modernity and Beyond," in *Rethinking Anti-Racisms: From Theory to Practice*, ed. Floya Anthias and Cathie Lloyd (New York: Routledge, 2005), 111–27.

13 See *Race in France: Interdisciplinary Perspectives on the Politics of Difference*, ed. Herrick Chapman and Laura L. Frader (New York: Berghahn Books, 2004), 1; and Eric Bleich, "Anti-Racism Without Races: Politics and Policy in a 'Color-Blind' State," in Chapman and Frader, 163. See also Nancy Green: "Race long was disparaged as an imported American category, but for many years, the majority of French researchers simply ignored the subject of racism in France." "Le Melting-Pot: Made in America, Produced in France," *Journal of American History* 86, no. 3 (December 1999): 1205.

in France, since 1789, are the measures taken by the Nazis during the Occupation).[14] The professors were not alone in voicing their solidarity with the Algerians and their dismay at their government's policies, nor were they the only ones to recognize the racist nature of the curfew. What is particular about their declaration, however, and what makes it, ultimately, emblematic of the complications involved in "race-ing" October 17 (and of race talk in France more generally), is that the grand narrative it implies is already mined with its own contradictions.

The reference to 1789 is shorthand for the complex and contradictory discourse that is French Republican universalism, and the statement's recourse to the Revolution as a signifier of the demise of the monarchy and the birth of the modern French state testifies to the existence, potency, and staying power of a foundational myth.[15] The myth itself is grounded in the "unitary, universalist and inclusive nature of the Republic of France," a unique vision of citizenship and national belonging based on an abstract egalitarianism, whereby the relationship between the individual and the state is sacrosanct, so long as the individual subordinates her communal allegiances to her national identity.[16] The encoding of these principles in the Declaration of the Rights of Man and Citizen (also from 1789) marked, in the words of one historian, "the legal triumph of a repudiation of any form of segregation based on race, religion or ethnic origin," the foundation of what would

14   Péju, *Le 17 octobre des Algériens*, 99; my emphasis. Excerpt from a brochure produced by the Ministère de l'information du GPRA (Gouvernement provisoire de la république Algérienne), apparently read aloud in classes at Parisian universities by certain professors at some point between October 23 and 30.

15   Naomi Schor, "The Crisis of French Universalism," *Yale French Studies* 100 (2001): 43–64. "To speak of French universalism is and is not an oxymoron" (43). It is worth noting that certain scholars have argued that Enlightenment philosophy (as manifested in universalism) is not anathema to racist policy; see Natalya Vince, "Transgressing Boundaries: Gender, Race, Religion and 'Françaises Muslmanes' during the Algerian War of Independence," *French Historical Studies* 33, no. 3 (2010): "In the nineteenth century and particularly under the Third Republic, categorizing according to race was not only the norm but in fact the product of French Republican values. Indeed, universalism and categorizing according to race have never been diametrically opposed but were symbiotic elements in the thought of a number of Enlightenment *philosophes*" (448).

16   Chapman and Frader, 1. Stanislas de Clermont-Tonnerre's discourse before the National Assembly in 1789 is the most oft-cited source for this principle. See "Speech on Religious Minorities and Questionable Professions" (December 23, 1789), https://chnm.gmu.edu/revolution/d/284/.

come to be known as "neutral" or "color-blind" race politics—a politics that would ostensibly obviate the need for any "race talk" at all.[17]

But the invocation of this myth in 1961 reveals its hubris; after all, such an interpretation of the so-called national novel is only made possible by skipping over its darkest chapters. To understand October 17 and the Nazi occupation as the sole inconsistencies in an otherwise smooth story requires the elimination of major swathes of French history, from slavery to colonization, and of important moments such as the rise of racial theory in the nineteenth century (embodied in the figure and theories of Joseph Arthur de Gobineau) and the Dreyfus affair, all of which have sorely tested narratives of universalism and its guarantees of tolerance and *laïcité*.[18] The professors' declaration is thus remarkable for the way it pitches the mid-twentieth century as an *exceptional* crisis for republican values, despite historical facts that would suggest otherwise. Yet it also hides French collaboration and the anti-Semitic policies of Vichy by gesturing ostentatiously to the foreign occupier (in a quintessential performance of what Henry Rousso, in his assessment of the "Vichy syndrome," called *le refoulement* or repression).[19]

Given the context of the Algerian War, it is worth pausing to consider the professors' restrictive comment that "other than the Nazi occupation, these measures had no precedent in France." On the one hand, the formulation implicitly discounts the racist nature of the colonial project and seems to ignore the abundance of race talk (in the form of critique) that would have been in circulation by 1961. After all, by the early 1960s, the essential synergy of racism and colonialism had been duly recognized.

17 Gerard Noirel, "French and Foreigners," in *Realms of Memory: The Construction of the French Past*, vol. 1: Conflicts and Divisions, ed. Pierre Nora (New York: Columbia University Press, 1996), 148. See also Giorgio Agamben's very interesting read on the ambiguity of "man and citizen" in the *Déclaration*: For Agamben, the expression can be understood as naming two separate realities, or as constituting a hendiadys, whereby the second term is a repetition of the first. Agamben, "We Refugees," trans. Michael Rocke, *Symposium* 49, no. 2 (1995): 114–19.
18 See Bleich, "Anti-Racism without Races."
19 Rousso, *The Vichy Syndrome: History and Memory in France Since 1944*, trans. Arthur Goldhammer (Cambridge, MA: Harvard University Press, 1994). The concept of the "Vichy syndrome" models the changing attitudes in French debates and discourse about the Second World War, the Occupation, and France's role in the Resistance.

We might think, in this regard, of Hannah Arendt's comment in 1944 that racism was "the powerful ideology of imperialistic policies since the turn of our century."[20] Closer to France, works by Albert Memmi, Frantz Fanon, and Aimé Césaire also laid bare the structural racism of the colonial system.[21] Of course, even prior to these analytical observations, there was never any shortage of race talk in French imperial discourse; to offer only the most obvious example, Jules Ferry's declaration of the Republic's "mission civilisatrice" (or civilizing mission) leaned heavily on vocabularies of nineteenth-century racial theory to argue that "les races supérieures ont un droit [...] de civiliser les races inférieures" ("superior races have a duty [...] to civilize the inferior races").[22]

The professors' stipulation that the measure had no precedent *in France* could, in the most literal understanding of "France," keep the question of the colonies at bay: France might have enacted racist measures throughout its empire, but these were faraway places peopled by "inferior races," whereas to imagine such practices in the hexagon would run counter to the principles of universalism.[23] Even if this wobbly logic could be maintained for a short distance, the specificity of Algeria topples it completely: Since 1870, Algeria had been not just occupied by the French but incorporated administratively as a part of France. When compared with other areas of French imperial administration, the deployment of racial categories in Algeria was far more energetic (and in some ways, more confused)—a situation made all the more ironic by the veneer of republican color-blind politics applied to French Algeria.[24] Lip-service to universalism in the Algerian context is perhaps

20   Hannah Arendt, "Race-thinking Before Racism," *The Review of Politics* 6, no. 1 (January 1944): 36.

21   Memmi, *The Colonizer and the Colonized* (1957); Fanon, *The Wretched of the Earth* (1961); Césaire, *Discourse on Colonialism* (1950).

22   Jules Ferry, "Speech Before the French Chamber of Deputies, March 28, 1884," *Discours et Opinions de Jules Ferry,* ed. Paul Robiquet (Paris: Armand Colin, 1897), 199–201, http://sourcebooks.fordham.edu/halsall/mod/1884ferry. asp. Original text available in the online archives of the Assemblée nationale: http://www2.assemblee-nationale.fr/decouvrir-l-assemblee/histoire/ grands-discours-parlementaires/jules-ferry-28-juillet-1885.

23   On the evolution of French national consciousness regarding colonialism and the French empire, see Raoul Giradet, *L'Idée coloniale en France de 1871 à 1962* (Paris: Hachette, 1972).

24   Todd Shepard, *The Invention of Decolonization: The Algerian War and the Remaking of France* (Ithaca, NY: Cornell University Press, 2008). "Local officials

best exemplified by the long and tortuous saga of personal status and nationality, which, in the case of Algerian Muslims in particular, has been summed up as a tale of "denatured French nationality." Specifically, indigenous Algerian Muslims could lay claim to being "French," yet benefited from none of the rights of citizenship.[25]

Ultimately, in their statement of solidarity with the Algerians, the professors *recognized the racism of the curfew but failed to identify the racism of the system*. As an illustration of France's ambivalent national narrative on race, it is hard to imagine a more evocative case in point. And yet, evidence of the racism of the system was on display in France in 1961, both politically and culturally. When the FLN opened a second front in mainland France, the Algerians' export of the conflict was met with the same regimes of surveillance and control already perfected in colonial experiments in North Africa. Seen as an extension of the "indigenous" colonial subject in Algeria, Algerians in France, and in Paris in particular, were treated to the same forms of muscular, militarized policing that had been developed in Algeria to pacify local populations.[26] These measures, however, implied that the police be able to identify their targets.[27] Already in the 1930s, the metropolitan Brigade de surveillance des Nord-Africains (North African Surveillance Team) had begun using racist criteria, and by 1961 the use of *la chasse au faciès*, or racial profiling, was widespread. (As we will see in the next section, a number of vocal journalists and politicians publicly decried this practice, often making a connection, as the professors did, with measures taken during World War II against French Jews.)

While the state's racist policies would have been visible in the streets in 1961, that same year, race talk was likewise making an appearance on the silver screen and on television. Filmed in the summer of 1960 and released in theatres on October 20, 1961, Jean Rouch and Edgar Morin's *Chronique d'un été* (Chronicle of a Summer) projects Holocaust

in Algeria encountered few sanctions when they ignored 'race-blind' French laws and regulations" (34).

25 Weil, "Le statut des musulmans en Algérie coloniale," 95–109.

26 See E. Blanchard, *La police parisienne et les Algériens*; Jean-Paul Brunet, "Le Racisme dans la répression policière des manifestations algériennes à Paris en 1961," *Cahiers de la Méditerranée* 61, no. 1 (2000): 69–89; and Rémy Valat, *Les calots bleus et la bataille de Paris: une force de police auxiliaire pendant la guerre d'Algérie* (Paris: Michalon, 2007).

27 See Mathiuex Rigouste, *L'ennemi intérieur: la généalogie coloniale et militaire de l'ordre sécuritaire dans la France contemporaine* (Paris: La Découverte, 2009).

memories (in the figure of camp survivor Marceline Loridan) against the backdrop of a dying colonialism, embodied not only by the shadow of the Algerian War but also by the two Congolese university students who participate in the film.[28] The race talk depicted by Rouch and Morin is complex and, in certain ways, oddly depoliticized. Michael Rothberg has argued that in *Chronicle of a Summer*, "Europe's contemporary experience of the limits of its colonial project [...] served to catalyze Holocaust memory."[29] While this may be true, it also suggests—at least at the level of representation—that references to the colonial project function primarily to orient and motivate the film's interest in Marceline and her experience. Rothberg, however, has also underscored how the scene in which the Congolese men are "relegated to the status of those who do not know" about the Holocaust is as awkward as it is "dubious," ultimately producing a perhaps unintentional critique of *Chronicle*'s own racial blind spot.[30] As for the Algerian War, it comes up just once, halfway through the film, in a halting dinnertime conversation where only one character has a chance to offer his viewpoint. However puzzling, this handling of the Algerian War may ultimately reflect a certain reality about its unwelcome presence around the putative national dinner table.

Just prior to the premiere of *Chronicle of a Summer* came a remarkably self-aware and self-critical episode of the televised biweekly newsmagazine *Faire face*.[31] The two-part series, titled "Le Racisme,"

28   Jean Rouch and Edgar Morin, directors, *Chronique d'un été* (released October 1961).

29   Rothberg, *Multidirectional Memory*, 179.

30   Rothberg, 185.

31   "Le Racisme" can be viewed online at: http://www.ina.fr/video/CPF86614340/le-racisme-1ere-partie-video.html. While the *Faire face* series is unknown abroad, it has been the object of significant media studies scholarship in French, notably in the context of political censorship of the media under de Gaulle. See Aude Vassallo, "Typologie de l'information contrôlée," in *La télévision sous de Gaulle: le contrôle gouvernemental de l'information (1958/1969)* (Brussels: De Boeck, 2005): 181–260; and Edouard Mills-Affif, "Le racisme: La malédiction des immigrés," in *Filmer les immigrés: Les représentations audiovisuelles de l'immigration à la télévision française, 1960–1986* (Brussels: De Boeck, 2004): 73–94. Note that Mills-Affif's assertion that the *Faire face* episodes focused on racism were never aired due to political censorship appears to be incorrect. While there does appear to have been some concern about the sensitive nature of the episode given the context of the Algerian War and the tenuous peace talks, several sources, including Vassallo, aver that the two episodes indeed aired (albeit several months later than planned). See Vassallo, 141.

was hosted by Etienne Lalou and aired on September 11, 1961, on France's national station RTF (it would have thus been available to all French homes with a TV).[32] The episode begins with a claim that slyly parrots the republican "foundational myth": With respect to racism, the offscreen voice narrates, "nous sommes le peuple à cet égard ayant la conscience la moins trouble" ([the French] are the people with the least troubled conscience). Archival footage of the rise of Nazism in Germany and of extermination camps fills the screen, followed by other, easily recognizable forms of racism (images of KKK rallies in the United States and footage of violent segregation in South Africa) before coming back to France to pose the question, "to you, all of this seems inconceivable in France; but are you sure?" Next, "man-in-the-street" interviews demonstrate a simultaneous rejection of racism as a principle and the practice of racism as a deeply held, if utterly unexamined, worldview. Nearly all those interviewed state that they are not racist, but they invariably reveal an embarrassed hypocrisy as they respond to a series of follow-up questions that move the discussion from the abstract to the concrete: Would you rent a room to someone of a different race? Would you let your daughter marry someone of a different race? Having declared themselves categorically not racist, the interviewees' answers to these specific questions nonetheless range from "no," and "people should know their place," to "mixing is not good." Perhaps the most shocking sequence features schoolchildren telling the interviewer that they prefer the color "white" to "black" because white is "pretty" and "clean," and black kids don't fit in. Lalou concludes with a searing observation: "La vérité, c'est que nous sommes tous plus ou moins, d'une façon ou d'une autre, racistes. Et que c'est seulement si nous en sommes conscients que nous éviterons de nous faire les complices de crimes contre l'humanité, tel qu'il y en étaient commis chez nous, il y a moins de 20 ans" (The truth is that we are all more or less, in one way or another, racist. And we need to be aware of this in order to avoid becoming accomplices in crimes against humanity, crimes like the ones committed here, less than 20 years ago). Papon issued his curfew for Algerians less than a month after France watched itself on *Faire face*.

Perhaps, given the complexities of race talk in France, the absence of a stable narrative about race and the Algerian War should come as

---

32   It may be worth noting, however, that in 1962, only 23 percent of French households had televisions. "L'équipement des français en biens durables en 1968," *Economie et statistique* 3 (July–August 1969): 65–68.

no surprise. Even historical studies devoted to the war of independence vary widely in their attention to and emphasis on race, racism, and racial discourse.[33] Yet, just as the widely held "invisibility" of October 17 itself flies in the face of evidence, so the deeply racist character of a massacre that might well have been called a large-scale *ratonnade* appears to be at once obvious and obscured. At stake in exploring the race talk of the anarchive is not to determine whether Algerians (or even North Africans) constitute a race unto themselves or whether races exist, but rather to understand the ways in which culture accounts for the complex traces of institutionalized prejudice and intolerance, while also complicating such representations in ways both compelling and troubling.

Contemporaneous Objects, Divergent Discourses

There is no doubt that Jacques Panijel's documentary film *Octobre à Paris* (October in Paris) (1962) is keenly interested in situating the events of October 17 within a broader context of state violence, a stance that quite naturally reads as sympathetic to the Algerians and their national liberation struggle. Through narrative and visual techniques, the film codes the Algerian as a social actor with an ethical, political, and collective consciousness, and as a victim of a fascist regime. Eschewing both explanatory voice-over narration and expert commentary, *Octobre à Paris* stages its Algerian subjects as the voice of authority by editing the experiences they recount into a coherent narrative. Throughout

---

33 In certain cases, the question of race is simply nonexistent: James LeSueur's *Uncivil War* and Alistair Horne's *A Savage War of Peace* devote little or no discussion to the racist valences of colonial policy in Algeria or to the racialized nature of the conflict. Connolly's *A Diplomatic Revolution*, however, presents a fascinating sub-narrative about race and the conflict, speculating on the way Algerian nationalists pitched the war as a "global struggle against western rule, sometimes defined in racial or religious terms" (46). Todd Shepard has suggested that, in most instances, local colonial authorities upheld—officially, at least—the republican race-neutral philosophy that animated policy in the *métropole*, and this in the face of attacks by prominent individuals (Gobineau, Renan, Saussure) exhorting French police to consider applying racial theory to its colonial policies. At the same time, however, he also notes that "racism had an enormous and direct effect on the daily experience of Algerians [...] as well as on popular, intellectual, and official thinking about 'Muslim' Algerians." See Shepard, 34.

most of the film, the presence of an off-screen interviewer is implied but never made manifest, reinforcing the perception that the story belongs to the Algerians. Panijel's decision to film in a variety of interior social spaces (the workplace, boarding houses, the Nanterre *bidonville*, kitchens, common areas), but also to recreate FLN cell meetings and the preparation for the demonstration, further underscores the idea of a political community.

Octobre à Paris engages issues of racism in a subtle manner, producing a tension in the film itself and within a larger discussion about race and October 17. In the film's first act, which sets the stage for the massacre by describing the mounting tension between police and the FLN in the weeks preceding the massacre, the viewer is introduced to the horrors of police violence as a number of Algerian men recount experiences that can only be understood as torture.[34] Of the several individuals interviewed, only Abdallah uses the word "racism" to describe police behavior and attitudes:

> Le système qu'ils ont amené, c'est la police d'Algérie qui l'ont montré... c'est la flicaille d'Algérie qui l'ont fait. C'est-à-dire des types qui sont... *racisme* ou quelque chose comme ça, je peux pas vous dire comment... C'est des *racismes*, ou par haine, ou par vengeance, ce qu'ils font. Mais les harkis, ils sont commandés par un français...mais c'est lui qui fait toute la pagaille. Ils ne sont pas venus pour mettre de l'ordre mais pour mettre le désordre. Ces types-là, ils ne cherchent qu'à tuer...[35]

> (The system they used, it was the police in Algeria who showed them... it's the low-level cops in Algeria who do it. What I mean is guys who are...*racism* or something like that. I can't tell you how...It's *racism*, hate, or vengeance, what they do. But the *Harkis*, they take orders from the French...but they're the ones who muck everything up. They didn't come to bring order but to bring disorder. Those guys, all they want to do is kill...)

34 There is an ample bibliography of scholarship on the use of torture during the Algerian War. For a more pointed study of the use of torture in mainland France during the war, see Pierre Vidal-Naquet's *La Torture dans la République: Essai d'histoire et de politique contemporaine (1954–1962)* (Paris: Éditions de Minuit, 1972).

35 My transcription of the original preserves the grammatical errors of some of the speakers in the film. The translation attempts to reproduce the sometimes halting language of this particular Algerian witness. Unless bracketed, ellipses indicate pauses in his speech rather than omitted material.

This is the sole moment in *Octobre à Paris* where police actions are labeled racist—indeed it is the only time in the documentary the word "racism" is used. If the victim's word choice is notable in part for its uniqueness, it is also worth observing that this particular Algerian appears reluctant to let the word stand, mitigating its impact through imprecision and hypothetical language ("racism or something like that"; or the suggestion that hate or vengeance might be something other than racism). These hesitations might be imputed to his somewhat approximate use of French; however, his observation that the violent tactics are imported, and that they are often carried out by *Harkis*, could have the effect of displacing the origin of the violence and diminishing the assessment of racism.[36] (After all, an uninformed viewer might not understand that the "police d'Algérie" refers, nonetheless, to French police.) The only explicit reference to racism in the film thus produces an ambiguous record of how Algerians might have perceived their treatment.

But *Octobre à Paris* makes other, implicit, moves when it comes to its invocation of racial difference and racism, and these contradict—or at the very least, complicate—the episode of racial profiling described in Smaïl's novel *Vivre me tue*. On two occasions, the film draws our attention to the police practice of racial profiling. In a sequence from the first part of the documentary, an Algerian worker with a "European" phenotype (paler skin, lighter hair) describes the improbable perspicacity of the police, who seem to be able to identify his origins just by looking at him.[37] He describes being stopped, frisked, and subjected to an identity verification by the police as he was leaving work. His tone is almost begrudgingly admiring: "Je n'ai pas la physionomie typique du Nord-Africain, mais il m'est arrivé quand-même d'avoir à faire des spécialistes qui savent même reconnaître l'Algérien à son allure, même à son regard" (I don't have the typical physiognomy of a North African, but it happens nonetheless that I sometimes have to deal with specialists who know how to recognize an Algerian simply by his bearing, or by his gaze).

36   On the *Harkis* see Chapter 2, n. 62.
37   Although some readers may bristle at this term "phenotype," it is useful when discussing triage practices such as racial profiling, which are rooted in a belief (however misguided) that a person's physical characteristics carry reliable information about his or her origins.

As if to confirm the police's ability to distinguish among "ethnic types," to pick an Algerian out of a crowd while avoiding the indiscriminate targeting of all men of a certain phenotype, a short while later the film takes the measure of a group of men in the Nanterre *bidonville*. A voice from off-screen (Panijel, in the only instance where an interview question is actually voiced) asks the group: "Who's been beaten up by the cops? Raise your hand." Many of the men raise their hands. The voice continues: "And who hasn't been beaten up? Anyone? How many?" When two men tentatively raise their hands, another voice from off-screen, an Algerian named Kader who is introduced at the very beginning of the film, interprets the scene for viewers: "Il n'y a que deux. Ils sont pas Algériens. C'est des marocains. Et la police ne les cherche pas" (There are only two. They aren't Algerians. They are Moroccans. And the police aren't looking for them). In an evidentiary gesture, the camera immediately cuts to still images of doors in the *bidonville* that bear handwritten signs indicating "Ici Marocain," presumably a shield against police raids.[38]

Without ever explicitly mentioning race or naming the practice of racial profiling, the logic of both sequences is nonetheless unmistakable: Police violence is figured as a surgical strike on known, identifiable targets, namely Algerians. The witnesses in Panijel's film tell a story of focused discrimination, and of a police force that is immune to the potential pitfalls of racial profiling. To hear Panijel's Algerians tell it, Parisian cops possessed preternatural powers of distinction, allowing them to root out even phenotypically white Algerians while also distinguishing between Algerians, Moroccans, and, presumably, other nationals of similar phenotype.[39]

My point is not to shed doubt on the authenticity of this testimonial evidence, nor to suggest that the experiences described in the

38 Evidentiary editing "uses cuts within a scene to present the impression of a single convincing argument supported by a logic." Bill Nichols, *Introduction to Documentary* (Bloomington: Indiana University Press, 2001), 30.
39 A contemporaneous and contradictory point of view can be found in Eve Dassarre's reportage in *France Observateur*. Walking through the Nanterre *bidonville* days after the massacre, she observes the following: "Sur une porte rudimentaire, je lisais, tracé au charbon: X—Maroc. La précaution ne sert pas à grand-chose. Personne n'est à l'abri, les Marocains pas plus que les Algériens" (On a makeshift door I noticed, written in coal: X—Morocco. The precaution is useless. No one is safe, and the Moroccans are no safer than the Algerians). "La marche du désespoir," *France Observateur*, October 26, 1961, 15.

documentary are implausible. What interests me is how these particular sequences cast episodes of racial profiling as pointedly and unerringly *anti-Algerian*, that is, as targeting a national group rather than an ethnic or religious one. Logically, of course, police cross-hairs would have been trained on Algerians—France and Algeria were at war and the FLN network had opened a second front in metropolitan France, taking the urban guerilla techniques rehearsed in Algiers to the streets of Paris and provoking generalized anxiety at all levels of the Parisian police force. Nonetheless, while *Octobre à Paris* is invested in showing the viewer that the police had no reason to suspect Moroccans, Tunisians, or even Algerian Jews, what it fails to show is the inevitable blurring of national and ethnic designations by on-the-ground forces. One of the perhaps unintended and ironic consequences of coding the enemy of the state as a "national" actor is the deracialization of the violence on October 17.

As the ur-text in the anarchive, *Octobre à Paris* is certainly informed and complicated by its proximity to the events it depicts, more so, perhaps, than any other October 17 cultural production. Given a certain evolution in political and scholarly thought about October 17, and given significant changes in archival access, it should come as no surprise that the film's racial politics are in tension with numerous subsequent works from the anarchive, notably with *Vivre me tue*, in which the "Uncle Mehdi" episode explicitly subverts the idea that Algerian nationals were the only victims on October 17. Questions of temporal proximity notwithstanding, however, it is essential to note that the discourse produced by the film also runs counter to a narrative that emerges from other contemporaneous documents—tracts, manifestos, letters, articles in the press, op-ed pieces, eyewitness accounts, and proceedings from the debates in the National Assembly—all collected and consigned to posterity by the archivists of the Parisian police.

It is not simply a matter of archival record that police tactics were hardly the surgical strikes on Algerian nationals portrayed in *Octobre à Paris*; the archive is verily abuzz with race talk emanating from a variety of different camps, including politicians, intellectuals, the mainstream press, and special interest groups. Perhaps unsurprisingly, one of the most conspicuously vocal groups was the FLN. Whereas FLN propaganda in Algeria may have hedged its bets when it came to race, on the metropolitan front the race issue was leveraged consistently and ruthlessly, with open letters addressed to the "people of France" that used historical precedent to highlight the government's assault on republican values.[40] A tract issued the day after the massacre not only called the curfew "racist" (indeed, FLN documents from this period rarely mention the curfew without the qualifier "racist"), but specifically raised the issue of national versus ethnic "types": "Pour ne pas les confondre avec les Italiens, les Espagnols et autres méditerranéens ou touristes sud-américains, à quand l'étoile jaune pour les Algériens?" (To avoid confusing them with Italians, Spaniards, other Mediterraneans, or South American tourists, why not force Algerians to wear a yellow star?)[41]

Yet accusations of racism were not the strict purview of FLN communications experts. Journalist Henri Kréa's interview with both rank-and-file Algerians (most often factory workers) and their French co-workers reveals a sophisticated awareness of racism. One of the Algerians tells Kréa, "quant au racisme, vous n'aurez guère de mal à le découvrir; il est partout, même chez ceux qui pleurent en regardant le film *Exodus*" (as for racism, you'll have no trouble finding it; everyone is racist, even the ones who cry when they watch the film *Exodus*).[42] Even prior to the repression on October 17, Algerians expressed a sentiment of racial exclusion: "On nous considère comme des Français, nous avons une carte d'identité nationale. Ce n'est pas parce que notre peau et notre religion sont différentes que nous n'avons pas le droit de sortir la nuit" (We are considered French; we have a national identity card. Having different skin and a different religion shouldn't mean that we can't go out at night).[43] The man's French co-workers, interviewed separately, are

40 On differences between race-based politics in Algeria and in France, see Shepard.

41 Police archives, HA 110/111. This two-page manifesto is titled "Un Appel au Peuple Français." Issued by the FLN on October 18, 1961, it was distributed to all major news outlets, trade unions, student groups, and certain political figures. The version in the police archives contains a cover note explaining the manifesto's content and distribution. The "Appel" was reprinted in *Les Temps modernes*, no. 186 (November 1961): 618–28, and was also reprinted in Manceron, *Textes, de l'époque*, 51–55.

42 Henri Kréa, "Le racisme est collectif, la solidarité individuelle...," *France Observateur*, October 26, 1961, 15. The reference to the 1960 Otto Preminger film, based on the 1958 novel by Leon Uris, is a curious one. The novel recounts the real story of a group of Jewish émigrés bound from Cyprus to the new State of Israel on board the *Exodus*. The novel has been criticized for its depiction of Arabs.

43 A. Delcroix, "On ne peut plus ignorer ça," *France Observateur*, October 26, 1961, 15.

also lucid about the nature of Franco-Algerian relationships, stating, "Il y a du racisme profond" (There is deep-seated racism), but also calling for solidarity, stating, "On est toujours le bicot d'un autre" (You're always sombody's wog).[44] The editorial accompanying Kréa's reportage hazards a final analysis: "La chasse à l'homme qui s'est instaurée dans la région parisienne, ce n'est même pas la chasse au FLN. C'est la chasse à l'arabe—qu'il soit tunisien, marocain ou algérien—c'est le racisme, à la fois sans honneur et sans efficacité" (The manhunt undertaken in Paris and environs is not a hunt for the FLN. They are hunting Arabs—Tunisian, Moroccan, or Algeria; this is racism, as inglorious as it is ineffective).[45]

For an event so generally held to have been "invisible," many questions and opinions were voiced in public forums by members of the political class. On October 11, 1961, fourteen Muslim deputies and senators collectively authored a manifesto that fell into the hands of the police and was reproduced for the archival record. Among the politely worded complaints about the treatment of the Algerian community in Paris, the officials sought to express their indignation before "les mesures vexatoires, discriminatoires, pour ne pas dire racistes" (these humiliating, discriminatory—not to mention racist—measures).[46] French politicians took up this issue in various official sessions, the records of which reveal a direct engagement with the nature of the police actions and violence. In a summary of a ministerial cabinet meeting published in *Libération* several weeks after the repression, the tone implicitly critiqued Papon's handling of the situation: "Considérant d'une part que de mesures de rigueur ont été prises à l'encontre de toute la population musulmane de Paris et de sa banlieue, que ses mesures ne sauraient être admises dans un pays qui s'honore d'ignorer de telles discriminations raciales" (Considering that some of the severe measures target the Muslim population of Paris and its suburbs, these are measures that could not be tolerated in a

44 Kréa, 16.

45 Delcroix, 15.

46 Police archives, HA 110/111. Letter dated October 11, 1961, from Muslim senators and deputies to Papon, titled "Manifeste publié par des sénateurs et députés musulmans." Following the Sétif uprising and massacre in 1945, the French government extended some additional rights and protections to Algerian Muslims. This included "a token opportunity for political participation in the French Assembly." See John P. Entlelis, *Algeria: The Revolution Institutionalized* (London: Routledge, 1986), 41. This letter is discussed again in Chapter 6.

country that takes pride in being above such racial discrimination).[47] One of the most pugnacious comments came from debates in the National Assembly held at the end of October. Centrist deputy Eugène Claudius-Petit cut directly to the heart of the matter:

> Il faut appeler les choses par leur nom. Chaque gardien de la paix ne pouvait plus se déterminer, à cause de l'ordre reçu et de la décision prise, autrement qu'en tenant compte de la couleur de la peau, de la qualité des vêtements ou du quartier habité. Heureux les Kabyles blonds qui ont pu échapper aux réseaux de la police! Faudra-t-il donc voir prochainement, car c'est la pente fatale, la honte du croissant jaune après avoir connu celle de l'étoile jaune?[48]

> (We must call things by their name. Because of the order they received and the decision made, the police could not possibly make determinations other than by assessing skin color, the quality of clothing, or the neighborhood where an individual lived. How lucky were the blond Kabyles who were able to escape the police dragnets! After having lived the shame of the yellow star, what is the next step—it is a slippery slope after all—the shame of the yellow crescent?)

In what is both a lucid and damning critique of the situation, Claudius-Petit recognizes the inevitable: that police orders targeting Algerians could only be enforced by casting a wide net over a perceived ethnic type. Finally, at a town-hall style meeting on November 3, Nanterre mayor Raymond Barbet pointed out that "les sévices, les brimades racistes existaient déjà depuis des mois" (racist abuse and bullying had been going on for months already).[49]

Numerous associations also rallied to decry the specifically racist nature of state policy. Even before the violence on October 17, the Mouvement contre le racisme, l'antisémitisme et pour la paix (MRAP) published a tract underscoring "le caractère raciste du communiqué publié par la préfecture de police le 5 octobre 1961" (the racist nature

---

47 "Les sévices contre les Algériens: Le Conseil de l'Ordre des Avocats apporte un démenti à MM. Frey et Papon," *Libération*, November 3, 1961.

48 Statement by Eugène Claudius-Petit before the National Assembly, October 30, 1961, 2nd session, pp. 3604–5 in official transcript, http://archives.assemblee-nationale.fr/1/cri/1961-1962-ordinaire1/037.pdf. Also archived in Police archives, HA 110/111. The question of Claudius-Petit's reference to the "yellow crescent" will be taken up more fully in Chapter 6.

49 Cited in Georges Bouvard, "Bastonnades des heures durant: Voici des preuves des sévices infligés aux Algériens," Police archives, HA 110/111.

of the communiqué published by the Prefecture of Police on October 5, 1961).[50] Jeune résistance (Young resistance), an anti-war, anticolonial group composed primarily of French deserters and *refusniks*, circulated a tract calling for full support of the FLN, and condemning "le racisme de la police," and calling on readers to "Unissez-vous à eux [les Algériens] contre une police raciste" (Unite with Algerians against a racist police).[51] Student groups organized rallies and protests in which the racially motivated actions of the police and the state were held up for specific action. The UNEF (a national student union) issued a call that began: "La répression policière à caractère raciste dont les travailleurs algériens ont été victimes ces derniers jours ne saurait être tolérée sans compromettre gravement l'avenir des relations entre le people français et le people algérien" (The racist police repression targeting Algerian workers in recent days cannot be tolerated without greviously compromising the future of Franco-Algerian relations). The manifesto ends with a call to action: "Les évènements de cette semaine nous imposent de vous appeler à manifester lundi soir votre opposition au racisme" (The events that took place this week compel us to call for a protest on Monday night to demonstrate our opposition to racism).[52]

A different student rally appears to have been infiltrated by a police informant, who wrote up his findings in a document dated October 21 (the same day as the rally). The memo recounts that a certain Professor Dresch presided over the meeting, defining its goal as "protester et manifester publiquement contre les mesures d'exception à caractère raciste prises à l'encontre des travailleurs et étudiants algériens" (to publicly protest and demonstrate against the exceptional measures, racist in nature, to which Algerian workers and students have been subjected). The informant notes that the crowd was exhorted to stand up "contre le fascisme et le racisme qui viennent officiellement d'être réinstaures en France, depuis quelques jours" (against the fascism and racism that have just been officially reinstated in France in the past few days).[53]

50 Police archives, HA 110/111; reprinted in Manceron, *Textes de l'époque*, 46.
51 Police archives, HA 110/111; untitled tract with cover memo dated October 24, 1961.
52 Police archives, HA 110/111; document titled "UNEF, Fédération des groupes d'études de lettres."
53 Dresch was a geographer and professor at the Sorbonne and at the Institut de géographie de Paris (1960–70). He specialized in arid areas (North Africa and China), but was also interested in "the human geography of colonization." Dresch was part of the resistance during World War II and a member of the Audin

The quotidian press, most notably left-leaning papers such as *L'Humanité*, *Libération*, and *Témoignage chrétien*, was especially dogged in its critique. On October 18, in an extensive editoral published in *L'Humanité*, the Communist Party's political desk opined: "Le pouvoir gaulliste [...] tend, en favorisant la discrimination et la haine raciales, à rendre la situation des Algériens travaillant en France aussi difficile et dramatique que celle de leurs compatriotes d'Alger et d'Oran" (Promoting discrimination and racial hatred, the Gaullist power [...] tends to make life for Algerians working in France as difficult and dramatic as it is for their compatriots in Algiers and Oran). They also issued a call to action, again underscoring the racist nature of the events: "Le Bureau politique appelle la classe ouvrière, l'ensemble des républicains à réagir vigoureusement contre la propagande et les mesures de discrimination raciales visant les Algériens" (The paper's political desk calls on the working class and all those who value the republic to react vigorously against the propaganda and the racial discrimination targeting Algerians).[54]

Humanité also reproduced eyewitness testimony describing incidents of racial profiling at the Gare St. Lazare: "La police en très grand nombre scrute les visages. Dès qu'ils en aperçoivent un plus basané que les autres ils se précipitaient. Papiers ou pas l'homme est entrainé au plus loin, sans management" (Massively deployed, the police examine every face. As soon as they notice one a bit darker than the others, they rush in. Documents in order or not, the man is brusquely taken aside).[55] Finally, in early November, in a headline announcing that the curfew was to be made less stringent, *Libération* declared, not without irony, "Le racisme recule d'une heure et demie" (The clock of racism gets turned back an hour and a half).[56]

Police work product adds yet another layer to the story of race and racial profiling told in the archive. The documents resulting from correspondence with constituents and investigations suggest that the

---

Committee. His speech is recorded in Police archives, HA 110/111, in a document titled "Objet: Manifestation d'étudiants," dated October 21, 1961.

54 "Déclaration du Bureau politique du Parti communiste français," *L'Humanité*, October 18, 1961; reprinted in Manceron, *Textes de l'époque*, 56–58.

55 "Pour protester contre le couvre-feu, par milliers les Algériens ont manifesté hier dans Paris," *L'Humanité*, October 18, 1961.

56 "Demi-succès d'une vague de protestation: la discrimination raciale recule d'une heure et demie," *Libération*, November 4, 1961.

police were continually navigating these choppy straits. For example, letters to Papon from the Tunisian and Moroccan Consulates, written shortly after the curfew was instated, anticipated problems for their nationals and requested reassurance from the Chief of Police.[57] Although Papon responded to each of these letters and issued orders for "identity checks" to be carried out prior to arrests, the October 20 deposition of Moroccan national Brahim Habbaz suggests that these orders were not always followed. Habbaz claimed to have been badly beaten by police officers who accosted him as he was leaving work.[58] The cruel irony of Habbaz's story is that the police considered his declaration of Moroccan nationality to be a ruse, a trick designed to make his beating look like a case of mistaken identity, thus discrediting the police and protecting himself from further harm.

In light of this abundance of contemporaneous race talk, the narrative produced in Panijel's film begins to look more ambivalent. Certainly, *Octobre à Paris* highlights the widespread use of racial profiling, but its insistence on the unerringly *anti-Algerian* nature of the practice seems to paper over the problematic ideological underpinnings of police actions and government policies. In this sense, perhaps we should simply read *Octobre à Paris* as deeply invested in the importance of collective action and the specificity of the Algerian situation (to the detriment, perhaps, of other considerations). Such an interpretation can be confirmed, in part, by certain narrative and structural choices in the film, particularly its use of reenactment and reconstructions. Perhaps the most significant of these re-creations is the FLN cell meeting. While difficult at times to understand—the sound quality is poor and the

57 In a memo issued by the office of the Prefect (reference: 4272F Cab/SD) and dated September 20, 1961, Papon claims to have been made aware of "de nombreuses doléances de la part de M. le Consul Général du Maroc et M. le Consul Général de la Tunisie, au sujet du traitement qui aurait été infligé aux ressortissants marocains et tunisiens au cours des opérations de police. [...] C'est ainsi qu'un haut fonctionnaire marocain a été l'objet récemment, rue des Pyramides, d'une interpellation et d'un contrôle dans des conditions que rien ne justifiait en un tel lieu" (the numerous complaints on the part of the Consul-Generals of Morocco and Tunisia concerning the treatment supposedly inflicted on Moroccan and Tunisian nationals during police operations. [...] This was recently the case for a high-ranking member of the Moroccan government who, on the rue des Pyramides, was subjected to unwarranted questioning and identify verification). Police archives, HA 110/111.

58 Police archives, HA 110/111. The document is a deposition taken by Maurice Thomas, commissaire adjoint.

men, who speak in both French and Arabic, are ill at ease with either the artificiality of reenacting reality or the presence of the cameras (or both)—the scene has been identified by some critics as the lynchpin of the film. In the journal *Positif,* critic Robert Benayoun identifies this reconstitution as the moment "les manifestants [...] comprirent pour la première fois en formulant leurs mots, le rôle capital de leur action envers la lutte de leurs frères sur le sol natal et le sens profond de leur combat" (the protesters [...] verbalized their experience and thus came to understand, for the first time, the major role their actions played in the liberation struggle at home and the deep meaning of their fight).[59] Panijel's emphasis on social actors *en bloc* might be seen as of a piece with the broader ethos of third-world liberation struggles, whose goals necessarily emphasized the collective over the individual.[60]

Yet we must complicate this story once again, for the film's ending seems to undo both a third-worldist reading of the film and the notion that it is mainly invested in the specificity of the Algerian situation and of October 17. The final five minutes of *Octobre à Paris* leap out of the temporal frame defined by the title to showcase footage of police violence on February 8, 1962, and testimonials of several survivors of that episode.[61] Panijel's decision not only to include, but to conclude with footage of the Charonne massacre and the testimony of French victims, produces a seemingly unwitting erasure of October 17 and the Algerian victims. The relative clarity of these moving images, coupled with the more readily understood testimonials from the French native speakers, are in sharp contrast with the earlier, more impressionistic tableaux of October 17 and the sometimes halting language of the Algerians. It is as though the final five minutes bring the film, at last, into sustained sharp

59   Robert Benayoun, "Où commence le témoignage?" *Positif* 49 (December 1962), 27–28. Benayoun concludes: "À la catharsis individuelle, narcissique des personnages de Rouch et de Morin, *Octobre à Paris* oppose la prise de conscience positive d'une collectivité" (The positive, collective awareness staged in *Octobre à Paris* is in sharp contrast to the individualistic, narcissistic catharsis of Rouch and Morin's characters). Here, Benayoun refers to Rouch and Morin's *Chronique d'un été.*
60   Indeed, we might think of *The Battle of Algiers,* made several years later (Gillo Pontecorvo, 1966), in which relatively strong individual actors (such as the anti-hero Ali la Pointe) are nonetheless depicted as bound up in the social fabric of the collective struggle. When Ali is finally located by the French military, for example, he does not die alone, but in close quarters with his co-revolutionaries.
61   See Introduction, pp. 21–22, for historical context of Charonne.

focus, suggesting that the entire project had been driving toward this galvanized, universal vision of state violence and the subjects who suffer it. Furthermore, the tighter editing and better quality of image and sound in this final sequence are overlaid with the first and only intrusion of voice-of-god narration in the film, which punctuates the images and instructs the viewer as to how to understand them, as if to say "this is what fascism looks like, this is what it does." Panijel's closing monologue is nothing short of a diatribe:

> La porte va se fermer sur l'Algérien. Mais ne partez pas ! La porte va se rouvrir. C'est sur nous qu'elle se rouvre! Sur nous qui ne sommes pas des bicots, qui n'étions pas des youpins, il y a vingt ans [...] A bas le fascisme et la guerre! disent les français. Et l'autobus n'importera plus les Algériens vers la merde et la mort. Des hommes pacifiques, comme le 17 octobre... comme le 17 octobre...il y a les autres, la même police...la même police de basse police qui conge, qui conge et que tue! Et voici le métro Charonne! La station de métro Charonne! Le métro Charonne [...]. Cet homme saoulé de coups, ne sait pas où il en est. Au fascisme simplement. C'est tellement clair...et après...on a ça...et puis ça...et ça. Qu'est-ce qu'il faut donc encore pour que tout le monde comprenne que tout le monde est un youpin, que tout le monde est un bicot...

> (The door is closing on the Algerian. But don't go! The door is going to open again, and it will open on us! On us, who aren't wogs, who weren't kikes 20 years ago. [...] Down with fascism and war, exclaim the French. And buses will no longer carry Algerians toward shit, toward death. Peaceful men, like on October 17...like on October 17...there are the others, the same police...the same lowlife police who beat, who beat and kill! And here's the Charonne metro. The metro station Charonne! Metro Charonne! [...] This man, beaten senseless, has no idea where he is. In fascism, simply. It's so clear...and after...there's that...and then that... and that. What do we still have to do for everyone to understand that everyone is a kike, everyone is a wog...)

The last line is voiced over a still photograph from October 17, which appears on screen after a series of filmed images from Charonne. As Panijel intones what will be the penultimate words of the film, the camera pans to different details of the photo; each movement is punctuated by the offscreen voice, asking: "Qu'est-ce qu'il faut donc encore (cut) pour que tout le monde comprenne que (cut) tout le monde est youpin, (cut) que tout le monde est un bicot. D'accord Kader?" (What else needs to happen for everyone to understand that we are all kikes, that we are all wogs...all of us. Right, Kader?) Here the screen cuts to black, from the depths of obscurity, Kader, the Algerian who voiced the film's introduction, responds, "Oui, c'est d'accord" (Yes, that's right).

If we understand this ending as a return to the images of victimized Algerian bodies on October 17, we might be tempted to say the film re-places the Algerian subject in the center of the frame and gives Kader the literal last word. On closer inspection, however, the ending seems to encapsulate the Algerian subject's disaffection: The final words we hear are disembodied—the body itself is resolutely removed from the visual field to leave behind a plain black screen—and Kader's voice evinces not an expression of a fully conscious political subjectivity but rather an acquiescence with the colonial voice-of-god narrator who asks for nothing more than a mimetic playback of what he has already argued: "Agreed, Kader? Agreed."

The film ultimately turns its gaze away from the specificity of the Algerian and the particularity of October 17 to proffer a universal commentary on state violence—referring not only to Charonne and the French Communist victims of the police but also, by virtue of the use of the word *youpin* (kike), evoking the anti-Semitic ideologies (and by extension, practices) of World War II. In the press coverage of the few screenings of *Octobre à Paris* that took place in 1962, not a single article fails to mention the ending, and the critics uniformly applaud the shift to Charonne, despite its contradiction with a narrative whose purported goal was to "restituer à la population algérienne le droit de parole" (give the right to speak back to the Algerians).[62] Notably, quite a few critics even take up the film's terms: *Témoignage chrétien*, for example, agreed, "On est toujours le bicot de quelqu'un" (We are always someone's wog); and in Michel Capdenac's article in *Lettres françaises*, he notes, "Pour le fascisme, on est toujours l'Algérien de quelqu'un" (Under fascism, you are always somebody's Algerian).[63]

The ending of *Octobre à Paris* thus lends itself to two seemingly opposed interpretations. From a third-worldist point of view, the final scenes—and particularly the final cut away from a wounded Algerian to a black screen—evacuate the specificity of the plight of Algerians and the anti-colonial struggle, amalgamating October 17 with generalized "state violence" and more pointedly, with fascism. Some of the final moments linger on images of men and women who are not Algerian (the

---

62 "*Octobre à Paris*, Introduction, Fiche culturelle," *Images et son* 160 (March 1963); no page numbers given.

63 Both articles cited in Fiche culturelle; no page numbers given.

white survivors of Charonne and "Jeanson"-style activists), which risks
undoing all the positive representational work the film has performed
up to that point in its staging of Algerian "actors" in the midst of their
emergence as political subjects.[64] Moreover, even though an Algerian man
(Kader) has the literal last word, the word in question—"d'accord"—is an
acquiescence to French colonial authority (here, the off-screen narrator),
which compels the Algerian to kowtow to a dominant narrative of
history. The ending thus conscripts the Algerian subject into a particular
vision of history, one that pulls October 17 away from a particularized
story and into a larger phenomenon of state violence.[65]

If I believe that Panijel's film indeed neglects the complexity of race in
the context of October 17, and if I am convinced that this is particularly
noteworthy given the film's status as the "alpha" text of the anarchive,
I cannot in good faith end the story on this note. Notwithstanding my
own abiding aversion to "intentionalist" criticism, any interpretation
of *Octobre à Paris* owes Panijel—this most unlikely of filmmakers—
at least a sidelong glance at his remarkable trajectory. A biologist by
training, he could date his political engagements to his activity in the
resistance during World War II.[66] This moment was also the occasion
for his first foray into authorship: He fictionalized his experience in the
resistance in a novel titled *La Rage*, published to tepid reviews in 1948 by
Maspero's Éditions de Minuit.[67] During the Algerian War, Panijel was
a founding member of the Audin Committee, a group that opposed the

64   See Chapter 3, n. 47.
65   Mani Sharpe's essay is one of the few to pay attention to the film's framing
technique and the relationship between images and Panijel's authorial commentary.
See Sharpe, "Visibility, Speech, and Disembodiment in Jacques Panijel's *Octobre à
Paris*," *French Cultural Studies* 28, no. 4 (2017): 360–70.
66   Panijel was a researcher at the CNRS. His only prior filmmaking experience
was as an assistant director to Jean-Paul Sassy on *La peau et les os* (1961).
67   Called "a saga of the Resistance and an experimental epic," *La Rage* was
poorly received at the time of its publication and remains nearly unknown. In 1995,
Panijel wrote, in the literary magazine *Lire*, that he had been terribly disappointed
by the novel's reception, noting that readers and critics were "sick of these stories"
(that is, stories of the resistance). He was critical of poets who thought that
publishing poetry had the same value as armed action. The Communist Party did
not like *La Rage*—they viewed the book as denouncing their own actions. See Phil
Watts, "Jacques Panijel: à l'avant-garde de l'après," in *Mémoires occupées: Fictions
française et Seconde guerre mondiale*, ed. Marc Dambre (Paris: Presses Sorbonne
Nouvelle, 2013), 167–74.

situation on the ground in Algeria, particularly the use of torture, but that was also founded in opposition to the Jeanson network.[68]

Panijel witnessed first-hand the "horror" of October 17 and immediately thought that documentary film would be the best way to expose the truth of what had happened that night.[69] Although he was not an experienced film director, he carried his ethical engagement onto the set, rejecting Jean Rouch's offer to make a "light" film (that is, with a handheld camera, in the mode of *Chronique d'un été*), and insisting that the film be shot in 35mm, in close collaboration with Algerian victims and the FLN. For six months, Panijel and his skeleton crew filmed in the Nanterre *bidonville*, in the Goutte d'Or neighborhood, and at other sites of violence in and around Paris, always accompanied by Algerians. It seems reasonable to imagine that Panijel, given his political commitments, would have understood the racial implications of the government's policies. Moreover, in light of his proximity to the Algerian community, he would likely have witnessed phenotypical bias at work.

It is critical, however, to keep in mind that Panijel had chosen "Audin" over "Jeanson"; in other words, he had opted for an intellectual community devoted to truth and democratic ideals over direct action. He described his commitment in the following terms: "J'ai expliqué que je faisais partie du comité Audin, que nous n'étions pas strictement opposés au FLN mais que cela voulait dire quand même notre désaccord avec le réseau Jeanson. Nous n'étions pas des porteurs de valises, mais des militants républicains français exempts de souvenirs algériens et n'obéissant à aucun patriotisme" (I explained that I was a member of the Audin Committee, that we weren't necessarily opposed to the FLN but that we nonetheless disagreed with the Jeanson network. We weren't "suitcase carriers," but rather French militants in the republican tradition with no particular nostalgia for Algeria and no particular patriotism).[70] Panijel was no third-worldist;

68 Unlike the Jeanson network, whose members worked actively alongside (and under the orders of) FLN cadres, the Audin Committee was against direct intervention in the conflict, preferring, instead, to investigate allegations of state torture. (See Introduction, pp. 34–35.)

69 Panijel stated: "En traversant les Champs-Élysées, je découvre l'horreur: des centaines d'Algériens assis par terre entre deux rangées de flics en uniforme" (Crossing the Champs-Élysées, I discover the horror: hundreds of Algerians sitting on the ground between two rows of cops in uniform). Panijel, interview, *Vacarme*.

70 Panijel, interview, *Vacarme*.

rather, he belonged to a category of engaged intellectuals that Pierre Vidal-Naquet would later call "anti-war intellectuals in the Dreyfusard vein," that is to say, he was a militant invested, first and foremost, in a "certain idea of France."[71] Understood in this light, the ending of *Octobre à Paris*, with its distancing from the specificity of the Algerian cause and its bid to universalize October 17 by inscribing it in a history of state violence, seems to fuse perfectly with the director's personal politics.

Layering Panijel's own story into the mix does not change the film's effects, but it does force us to live in an interpretative double bind. The film is keenly driven to leverage the anti-Algerian violence of October 17 as state-sponsored fascism, and to place it in a genealogy that links colonial violence with Nazi ideology and the politics of collaborationist France.[72] It is thus possible to read the tethering of October 17 to a grander narrative of state violence as a gesture of solidarity, and as an effort to legitimize the fight against racist violence through a process of analogy. In so doing, the film ensures that the symbolic and historical weight of October 17 is anchored to moments of recognized gravitas (World War II and Charonne) that signify more transparently and resonate in 1962 despite the *refoulement* of memories of Vichy. To borrow from Michael Rothberg and Max Silverman, we need not read this as a competitive gesture but rather as a "linking" one, a seeking—*avant la lettre*—of connections both multidirectional and palimpsestic, foregrounding "overlapping realms of history [and] memory."[73] Moreover, we should remember that Panijel's evocation of the Holocaust and Vichy is particular to this time period and, in certain ways, anticipates what Annette Wieviorka would call the "era of the witness."[74] In this regard, rather than focus

71 See Pierre Vidal-Naquet, "Une fidélité têtue. La résistance française à la guerre d'Algérie," *Vingtième siècle. Revue d'histoire* 10 (April–June 1986): 10–13.

72 So much so that even once political censorship was lifted, Panijel refused to show the film because he felt it required a preface to contextualize the events. This preface, presumably, is the one by Mehdi Lallaoui that accompanies the DVD version of the documentary released in 2011.

73 Silverman, "Violence of the Cut," 18. Rothberg's and Silverman's memory models are discussed further in Chapters 1 and 6.

74 "In those postwar years," writes Silverman, "the Holocaust was not perceived in the way that we presently understand the event." *Palimpsestic Memory*, 16. For Wieviorka, the Eichmann trial that began in late 1961 marked "the advent of the witness" (Annette Wieviorka, *The Era of the Witness*, trans. Jared Stark (Ithaca,

on the final black screen and the disembodied voice of the Algerian, we should perhaps remember the penultimate shot: the feet of an Algerian lying in the streets of Paris, surrounded by his brothers in arms, and by the Parisian police.

Yet it is also undeniable that the film's portrayal of the Algerian experience in Paris unintentionally plays into a colonial, racial logic whereby certain peoples possess visible traits that constitute a particular type, and could thus be identified and separated out. Panijel's focus on the anti-Algerian character of Octber 17—to the detriment of understanding just how pervasive and undifferentiated police hatred had become—attributes to the police a type of discretionary power they did not have, and, in so doing, reifies notions of indigenous types. Despite all that it does make visible, *Octobre à Paris* nonetheless hides the historical fact that Moroccans and Tunisians—as well as Italians, Algerian Jews, and others—were also victims of the Parisian police. In eliding this reality, furthermore, the film elides the complexity of the period and the particular character of the racism to which Algerians and others were subjected. It also allows us to code the racism of the police as a kind of circumstantial racism, or even a justifiable fear or even hatred of one's enemy.

All of this makes for a very complex opening monologue about race talk in the October 17 anarchive. As the first in what would become a long series of cultural productions, *Octobre à Paris* inaugurates a conversation about race and the events of October 17 while at the same time smoothing out some of the most interesting and problematic wrinkles. It becomes our job, then, to read these wrinkles back into the text and set it in dialog with its contemporaries.

NY: Cornell University Press, 2006), 57). The "era of the witness" began in the late 1970s, a period characterized by the systematic collection of testimonies and what Wievorka calls "an extraordinary craze for ethnological life stories" (97).

"Not Quite White, Surely Not Black": Negotiations of Visible Difference

If *Octobre à Paris* is implicitly about the vagaries of invisible difference in the context of October 17, William Gardner Smith's 1963 novel *The Stone Face* is concerned with plumbing the depths of *visible* difference. A number of superlative statements can be attributed to Smith's novel: it is the very first literary work to feature the massacre of October 17 and the only one written at the time of the events; it is the only published novel to deal with both racial politics in America *and* the Algerian question in France; and it is the first cultural production to unambiguously figure the treatment of Algerians in terms of racism. Tyler Stovall has called *The Stone Face* the most unique text of all those devoted to October 17: a work that "raises the question of the politics of displacement, and the ways in which citizenship shapes political strategies," while also "speaking to a new internationalist historiography of the civil rights movement."[75] Kristen Ross has called Smith one of the few fiction writers who "kept a trace of the event alive during the 30 years when it entered a 'black hole' of memory."[76]

Notwithstanding these superlative qualities, *The Stone Face* has received little critical attention, particularly in comparison with the abundant scholarship on Smith's contemporaries, Richard Wright and James Baldwin, and especially in the context of October 17 cultural productions. More so, perhaps, than any work from the anarchive, *The Stone Face*'s renegotiation of racial and juridical categories compels us to understand October 17 as a signal event in both history and literary representation. When the novel opens, the protagonist, a black American artist named Simeon Brown—very much an avatar of Smith in this autobiographical novel—has just arrived in Paris. It is May 1960 (not coincidentally, the very moment the Civil Rights Act of 1960 was passed into law in the US). In Paris, Simeon is just "another refugee" (12)—as a fellow black American expat describes him—a fugitive from his native Philadelphia and the racist United States. Through flashbacks, we learn of the experiences of physical and psychological racist violence that marked his life, from childhood to his stint serving in the army in World

---

75 Tyler Stovall, "Preface to *The Stone Face*," *Contemporary French and Francophone Studies* 8, no. 3 (Summer 2004): 308–9.

76 Kristin Ross, *May '68 and Its Afterlives* (Chicago: University of Chicago Press, 2002), 44.

War II. Simeon has fled not only to find a better life for himself, but also to keep from giving in to his own murderous rage and desire for revenge. He equates Paris with being at peace. In the French capital "the old tension like poison began to seep out of him"; here, "he would become a new man" (7).

Simeon's initial encounter with the Algerians who live in Paris is an ambivalent moment marked by an instinctive recognition of them as simultaneously "same" and "other":

And these men, walking toward him in a group, with crinkly hair and skin which is not quite white but surely is not black? They had sullen, unhappy, angry eyes, eyes Simeon knew from the streets of Harlem. [...] They glanced at Simeon unsmiling, and something strangely like recognition passed between him and them. They went on by him and disappeared. (4)

The implicit questions about "these men"—who they are, where they come from, where they are going—are left suspended for some 30 pages, while Simeon has experiences that begin to dislodge the interiorized racism he has imported with him from the States. Race, and how phenotype determines positionality within a given power structure, is continually reevaluated and re-coded in the novel, beginning with Simeon's own realization that his black skin signifies differently in France. At one point, after having bitterly convinced himself that his failure to seduce a white woman at a café can only be chalked up to her racism, he is stunned when her boyfriend—"a tall African, black as anthracite"—shows up to meet her (6).

In another early episode of racial resignification, a waiter and restaurant manager defend Simeon and his friend Babe from attacks by white American businessmen seated at a table next to them. The manager throws the white Americans out, offering Simeon and Babe champagne and clucking that their "compatriots behave in disagreeable ways sometimes." Being black in France clearly elicits a different set of reactions, and Simeon begins to feel "post-racial" *avant la lettre*: "He was amazed to find himself relaxed and calm. Sometimes in Paris he dreamed that he was back in Philadelphia, unable to escape. Slowly, as consciousness came, the terror faded. Yes, it was all right; he was in Paris" (35).

Unlike the expat group he frequents, whose members spend most of their time discussing American politics, Simeon is motivated to understand more about the situation in Algeria and the liberation struggle. Initially, despite witnessing incidents of police brutality and seeing firsthand the poverty of Algerian neighborhoods like la Goutte d'Or, Simeon persists in reading Algerians as white: "Their skins were white, all right. They looked like Southern Slavs" (92). He learns, however, that the Algerians, whom he codes as "white" based on their phenotype, in turn code *him* as "white" based on the rights and freedoms to which he lays claim in French society, despite the fact that he is a foreigner and they are ostensibly "French."

Simeon experiences this turnabout firsthand in an episode where he intervenes in a scene he wrongly interprets as an Algerian mugging a Dutch woman while his friends look on. When the police arrive, Simeon is treated respectfully and then released, while the Algerians—innocent bystanders, it turns out—are subjected to physical and verbal abuse, and taken into custody. Simeon is unnerved by what is clearly an injustice, but one he cannot yet parse. A few days later, he is wandering the boulevard St. Germain when a voice calls out to him, "Hey! How does it feel to be a white man?" (55) Implausibly but instinctively, Simeon understands these words are meant for him. Hossein, one of the Algerians who had witnessed the episode, beckons him to join his table, and offers an angry, precise gloss of the scene Simeon has been unable to decipher:

> I been to Philadelphia. Baltimore too. New York. Went with the Free French [...] Nice, the States. I saw how they treated people like you there, black people [...] what was the word they use? *Niggers*. That's what they called you, ain't it? Niggers! Yeah, I saw. And guess what—in the States, they considered me and people like me white! [...] Well, how do you feel now? Feel fine, huh? Over here in France, land of the free. Far away from the stuff back in the States, huh? Can go anyplace, do anything. That's great. I remember how it was back there. If a white man fought a black man, the black man was guilty, the white man was innocent. [...] How does it feel to have the roles reversed, eh? How does it feel to be the white man for a change? [...] We're the niggers here! Know what the French call us—bicot, melon, raton, nor'af. That means nigger in French. Ain't you scared we might rob you? Ain't you appalled by our unpressed clothes, our body odor? No, but seriously, I want to ask you a serious question— would you let your daughter marry one of us? (56–57)

It thus takes Hossein, an Algerian—a "black man" in France—to make the scene legible for Simeon and to school him in a new vocabulary of racism. Hossein exposes the inner logic of phenotype in this new context, jarring Simeon's perhaps complacent vision of race as a "black and white" issue and of France as a haven from discrimination.

The Stone Face, however, is not interested in representing something like pure turnabout. Even as the novel places race relations in a comparative context, it also X-rays each group in ways that make visible their internal complexities and divergences, thus thwarting essentialist representations of black Americans or Algerians. For Hossein, Simeon is a black American, and "that means he thinks like a white man" (82); Ahmed, however, an Algerian friend of Hossein's, seeks out conversation with Simeon: "I have never talked to a black American before. I felt sympathetic to you when I saw you that first time. I told Hossein: how can you talk to this man this way, he has a black skin" (82). Hossein's enmity is grounded in a particular vision of national privilege, whereby Simeon, as an American, would have access to rights that Hossein does not. Ahmed, however, experiences a sense of cross-racial empathy, instinctively seeing in Simeon not a privileged Westerner but a potential fellow traveler, his skin color a kind of shibboleth.

Similarly, within the community of black American expats, empathy for the Algerian situation is not universal, and the group does not evince the same type of analogical thinking. Simeon's friend Babe, for example, has no interest in the Algerians or their cause; ironically, however, his rejection is grounded in a rationale that is strikingly similar to Hossein's. For Babe, to sympathize with the Algerians would not only mean getting involved in a struggle that doesn't concern him, it would mean intervening on behalf of a group that, to him, looks dominant by virtue of phenotype: "Algerians are white people. They feel like white people when they are with Negroes, don't make no mistake about it. A black man's got enough trouble in the world without going about defending white people" (105).

Over the course of *The Stone Face*, Simeon is forced to revise his own concept of self in the French context and to acknowledge that Algerians, whom he reads as "whiter" than him, signify as "black" within the French context. At the same time, by the end of the novel, the limits of Simeon's putative "whiteness" in France are exposed: Notwithstanding the benefits he derives from a symbolic cultural capital that places him above the Algerians in a tacit pecking order of humanity, and apart from the idea that his American citizenship makes him "white" in the eyes of Hossein, he remains a foreigner in France, and as a foreigner, political action is unavailable to him.

Race talk in *The Stone Face* is not, however, limited to discussions between outsiders. Perhaps most telling is the conversation that ensues when Simeon asks two French students: "Is there racism in France?"

The two different responses certainly reflect two prevailing trends in thinking about race in France, then and now. The first student's response—"of course not, the French don't believe in racist theories" (62)—anticipates twenty-first-century rhetoric on the issue of race in the context of French republicanism, whereby delegitimizing race in political and public discourse (like the removal of the word "race" from the Constitution) holds the promise of eliminating racism in practice. The other student, however, voices a sentiment found in newspapers and in some political discourse of the era: "The French are racists as far as the Algerians are concerned, no doubt about it." The arguments offered up by the student who argues that France is not racist rings familiar to Simeon: "It's not racism. They're different. I wouldn't rent a room to an Arab because he'd probably rob the whole apartment while I was out. That's a fact. But it's not racism. Simeon suppressed a smile, and said nothing" (63). The young man seems to be arguing for an empirical, anecdotal basis to the dislike of Arabs, while at the same time performing a quintessentially racist discourse—articulated in terms strikingly similar to those used by the interviewees featured in Lalou's 1961 documentary "Le Racisme."

Simeon's experiences discussing and witnessing racism in France cause him to interrogate his own position in a society where he lives as "privileged," while, in his own country, others like him are fighting for their lives and their rights. Indeed, he is haunted by a story in the *Herald Tribune* about the lynching of a young girl named Lulu Belle in Little Rock, a fact that assumes particular relevance as the racial thematics coalesce in the final chapters of *The Stone Face*. In a narrativization of the October 17 massacre, Simeon not only witnesses the violence, but intervenes on behalf of an Algerian woman and her child. He thus enters a fight that is not his own and perhaps, momentarily, absolves himself of the bystander guilt he feels for "sitting out" the civil rights movement in the US. His spontaneous participation in October 17 stands in for the struggle he cannot (or will not) join, with the Algerian child serving as a metonymy for Lulu Belle.

As a result of his actions, Simeon is arrested and taken to a temporary prison alongside thousands of Algerians. His American passport draws the attention of the police, and he is released before any of the others with an admonition from the on-duty officer: "I've been reading in the newspapers about the troubles in the schools. You understand, we like Negroes here, we don't practice racism in France, it's not like the US. We can understand why you prefer to live here. We wouldn't like to have to expel you" (208). This thinly veiled threat makes visible the tenuousness of Simeon's status as a "white man"; while he may be more at ease in France, his host country is well aware of the type of protection it affords him, making threats of deportation all the more violent.

Simeon's experiences on October 17 are a catalyst for his political and existential crisis; he decides to return to the US and join the civil rights movement. In a certain way, this decision seems to signal the failure of analogical thinking, the futility of cross-racial empathy. For while it may look like an opportunity for Simeon to find coherence between his beliefs and his actions, it also implies that to live outside of one's "natural context"—even if one lives better outside of that context—is impossible. The novel's ending suggests that Simeon is in an awkward position in France and the only way to find closure is to return to the place he comes from.

Although Paul Gilroy has hotly critiqued this ending, calling it a "capitulation to the demands of a narrow vision of kinship," I would like to suggest two alternate readings in response.[77] On the one hand, Gilroy's vision of Simeon's return as capitulation seems to overlook the soul-searching our protagonist has engaged in throughout the novel, and the degree to which he has put his understanding of race, alterity, and empathy to a litmus test. After all, to stay in Paris among the privileged black expats might suggest a form of "capitulation to kinship," but Simeon's return to the US to fight for civil rights might also be understood as less about "kinship" than about the desire for political subjectivity—or at least the *potential* for it. Indeed, at the end of the novel, Simeon becomes willing to exchange certain security for an uncertain future, albeit one that holds, at the very least, the possibility for change.

My second reading of this novel's conclusion opens back onto broader questions of the racial politics of the era and William Gardner Smith's role as a stranger in France. Our understanding of the ending must necessarily be filtered through the knowledge that Simeon's departure from France was not how *The Stone Face* originally ended. In the manuscript submitted to Farrar, Straus and Giroux (FSG), Simeon Brown leaves for Africa after the October 17 massacre. The book was already in proofs when the FSG editor wrote to Smith, encouraging him to "return Simeon to the United States," arguing that

---

77 Paul Gilroy, *Against Race: Imagining Political Culture Beyond the Color Line* (Cambridge, MA: Harvard University Press, 2002), 323.

it would be "better for *The Stone Face*." This eleventh-hour change would forever cleave apart the trajectories of Simeon and his creator:[78] Smith himself moved to Ghana in 1964, only to return to Paris two years later after the 1966 military coup. He lived in France for the rest of his life, traveling back to the US just once for a brief stint to report on the race riots for Agence France-Presse (1967). *The Stone Face* was his last novel, and it marked the last time he would speak about "the Algerian question" or allude to racism in France, even in fiction. Unlike Simeon, who ultimately, we imagine, found a way to coincide with himself, Smith is emblematic of the divided self: In letters to his mother, he wrote, "I don't feel like a stranger here; I feel at home in Paris" (1961), but he also wrote, later, that he was "rotting in Paris" because he "couldn't be political" there.[79] Read against the text of Smith's life, the ending of *The Stone Face* also looks like the fantasy of a road not taken, a virtual reality posited in a novel but ultimately unattainable.

The question of whether or not to speak out about racism in France, and about the Algerian cause in particular, seems to have been an excruciating double bind that would eventually break up the entourage of black expats.[80] Like October 17, so too *The Stone Face* would find itself only intermittently visible, on both sides of the Atlantic. The novel attracted little attention in the US, where, by 1963, a novel about race in France felt too far removed from the realities of racial confrontation on the ground.[81] Curiously, the novel has never been translated into French—despite Smith's visibility in France as a journalist *engagé*. Of course, for a given novel not to be translated in French is not

78   Editor John C. Farrar's letter to Smith, 24 July 1964, is cited in Weik von Mossner, "Confronting *The Stone Face*: The Critical Cosmopolitanism of William Gardner Smith," *African American Review* 45, no. 1–2 (Spring/Summer 2012): 181–82.

79   Quoted in Michel Fabre, *From Harlem to Paris: Black American Writers in France, 1840–1980* (Champaign: University of Illinois Press, 1991), 240.

80   Indeed, the "Gibson Affair," a murky story whereby Richard Gibson and perhaps Smith purportedly wrote letters in support of Algerian independence but signed them "Ollie Harrington," created a major rift in the community of black expat writers. See Fabre, 249–50.

81   Fabre notes, "That *The Stone Face* never attracted the attention it deserved was largely due to its late publication, in 1963, when the scene of racial confrontation had shifted from France and the Algerian War to the United States and the Civil Rights Movement" (245–46).

unusual in and of itself; we know very well, however, that there was already a taste for American fiction in 1960s France, and particularly for the works of the black American expatriates. Moreover, Smith's earlier novel, *Anger at Innocence* (1950), was translated into French.[82] In this light, then, one can only wonder whether the invisibility of *The Stone Face* in France was not an innocent omission, but rather an editorial choice to avoid reproducing a narrative that probed an open wound by holding up to France a mirror in which the racist United States was reflected.

Do Facts Matter in Stories about Race and October 17?[83]

Vivre me tue, the novel that provided the opening anecdote for this chapter, has been the object of a small but significant polemic revolving around authenticity, ethnic usurpation, and the status of facts in fiction. When the novel appeared on the French literary scene in 1997, the *beur* cultural phenomenon had already achieved a kind of critical mass, so while its content no longer constituted a literary event in and of itself, the originality of *Vivre me tue* caused critics to pay attention, hailing Smaïl as elevating the genre and auguring a new wave in *beur* storytelling.[84] The revelation that Paul Smaïl was not a *beur*, but rather the native French author Jack-Alain Léger, did not dampen the enthusiasm of most critics, who saw in this authorial subterfuge little more than an inside joke.[85] French readers and critics barely registered

---

82 According to Weik Von Mossner, who has interviewed Smith's widow and entourage extensively, Smith never tried to publish *The Stone Face* in French, mostly likely because Smith was well aware that the content would have been political dynamite at the time. Email correspondence, July 13, 2019. Weik von Mossner also points out Fabre's speculation that "Smith refrained from airing his views in interviews. He would have run the risk of losing his job [at Agence France-Presse] and being expelled from the country for interfering in French politics" (248). See Chapter 1, p. 38 for more on Smith.

83 This title is a slight riff on an essay by Susan Rubin Suleiman; see Chapter 1, p. 70.

84 More than a decade after the *Marche pour l'égalité et contre le racisme*, the *beur* phenomenon was a familiar feature of the cultural and political landscape. See Chapter 1, pp. 40–42 for more on *beur* context.

85 See Brozgal, "Hostages of Authenticity," and Miller, *Imposters*.

the implications of the irony that the "great *beur* novel" of the decade would have been written by a white French man.[86]

Some years after the fact, however, the novelist Azouz Begag roundly denounced what he called Léger's "ethnic usurpation" in an essay published in the US-based academic journal *Research in African Literatures*.[87] A sociologist by training and a *beur* by virtue of both his Algerian origins and his upbringing in an immigrant neighborhood on the outskirts of Lyon, Begag was the only critic to suggest that the book's subterfuge was not only unethical, but poorly executed, and thus, ultimately, a failure. "Far from representing the triumph of a free-floating literary talent over minority ethnic bonds," Begag argued, "*Vivre me tue* founders in a sea of artistic incompetence fed by the author's inability to divest himself of a majority ethnic mindset clouded by racist prejudices."[88] To Begag, Léger's white, French fingerprints were all over the text: on its argot, its cultural and historical references, and the protagonist's attitudes. The only readers who could have been duped by *Vivre me tue* were those who knew nothing of *beur* culture; any *beur*, or any reader who really knew who the *beurs* were, how they lived, talked, and wrote, would have readily identified the novel as a fake.

In his attempt at a forensic examination of Léger's fakery, Begag marshals both linguistic and historical evidence, the latter of which is at issue here.[89] For the lynchpin of Begag's critique is Léger's representation of October 17, and while the events of 1961 are not central to the story, they are related on several occasions, with Smaïl first hinting, then ultimately revealing that his Uncle Mehdi, a Moroccan, was killed during the massacre. This detail becomes the target of Begag's surgical strike on the novel's authenticity:

> The night of 17 October 1961 was not an anti-Arab pogrom but an anti-Algerian pogrom. The confusion in the text between "Arab,"

---

86   "Smaïl" would go on to write two more novels following the peregrinations of the *beur* Paul Smaïl. The "imposture" would become more of a headline after the publication of *Ali le magnifique*, but there is no critique in the French press of Léger's "ethnic" posturing.

87   Azouz Begag, "Of Imposture and Incompetence: Paul Smaïl's *Vivre me tue*," *Research in African Literatures* 37, no. 1 (2006), 55–71. The essay was translated into English from the French by Alec Hargreaves; there is no published version of the original.

88   Begag, 56.

89   See Brozgal, "Hostages of Authenticity."

"Muslim," "Algerian" and "Moroccan" is typical of the thinking we might expect to find in the mind of a French author of Jack-Alain Léger's age, indiscriminately lumping together all North Africans in France under the label of "Arabs."[90]

In what amounts to an indictment of Léger not just as a usurper of ethnic identity and a racist, but as a historical revisionist as well, Begag accuses the French author of perpetuating retrograde ideas and essentialist categories about Arabs and the Maghreb, and of being so blind to the actual diversity of the Maghrebi immigrant community in France as to misrepresent this deadly historical episode.

Begag's own blind spot when it comes to the racial politics of October 17 is the most interesting aspect of his quarrel with Léger/Smaïl. He exudes an unimpeachable certainty in reporting that the violence on October 17 targeted Algerians exclusively; however, Begag's demonstration of Léger's putative essentialism actually tends to disprove his own argument: If a French man of Léger's age would tend to place "North Africans in France under the label of 'Arabs,'" it is plausible that, in 1961, the Parisian police might have done the same, in other words, "lumped together" all men of a certain phenotype. Moreover, Begag does not parse the possible divergence of intention and action: While the police might have indeed *meant* to target Algerians in practice, "typical thinking" (that is, racism) might have led police to act indiscriminately on October 17. In his attempt to indict Léger and reveal his clumsy misconstrual of history, Begag unwittingly puts his finger on the very phenomenon that renders Uncle Mehdi's fictional death on October 17 plausible. And history, as we have seen, is on Léger's side: Both archival documents and anecdotal evidence confirm that Moroccans were victims of police violence on October 17, thus undermining Begag's accusation that this particular detail proves the inauthenticity of *Vivre me tue* and reveals Léger's essentialist thinking.

Although Begag's mistake is clearly not a Freudian slip—there is nothing accidental about his statement—I want to entertain the possibility that this error contains analytic potential similar to that of the lapsus or the joke; in other words, that it might hold repressed content, ideas, and information.[91] The fact that Begag got it wrong is ultimately less interesting than the opportunity to construct his error

90   Begag, 62.
91   Sigmund Freud, *Jokes and their Relation to the Unconscious* (1905), trans. James Strachey (London: Vintage, 2001).

as a productive site of inquiry, a signpost in an unexpected place that prompts us to think through October 17 in terms of race, phenotype, and the various ways they are instrumentalized in both official discourse and cultural texts.

In 1997, *Vivre me tue* tapped into a reality about October 17 that would have been invisible for the many decades during which the archives were classified. Moreover, as has already been demonstrated, even the anarchive—for reasons of censorship, circulation, or content—might have been of little help on this front. The anarchive does contain multiple cultural texts that either refer to, or stage, the events of October 17 as profoundly linked to race-based policies and politics. With the exception of Nacer Kettane's *Le Sourire de Brahim* (1985) and Tassadit Imache's *Une fille sans histoire* (1989), however, most of these were produced after 2001. In many of the third-wave texts, the period in question is figured as highly charged with racist animosity; references to racism or racial types are explicit and include not only the experience of racism but also political discussions about the racist implications of government policies.

As I noted in the previous chapter, Nacer Kettane's *Le Sourire de Brahim*, along with Daeninckx's *Meurtres pour mémoire*, is one of the first French-language novels to evoke October 17 and one of two early *beur* novels to represent the repression and its erasure from history and memory. *Sourire*, we recall, devotes its first chapter to staging the October 17 protest and the brutality of the police repression. An omniscient narrator reveals the thoughts of the young protagonist Brahim, who reflects on the days leading up to this moment as he and his family join the columns of Algerians already occupying the streets of the capital:

> On les voyait de plus en plus fréquemment sillonner la ville, des groupes de quatre ou cinq personnes en cordon serré en quête de ratissage. Non seulement on les voyait venir, mais on les entendait avec leurs grosses bottes noires montant jusque dessous le genou, rappelant un autre temps où certains uniformes hantaient la France. Blouson de cuir au col relevé, crâne rasé [...] C'était une scène de chasse en banlieue revue et corrigée par les tenants d'un 'ordre nouveau.' Celui de la chasse à l'homme traqué, le frisé, le basané, le métèque, l'homme inférieur, quoi! (11–12)

> (We saw them crisscrossing the city more and more often, in tight formations of four or five, looking for trouble. Not only did we see them coming, but we could hear them with their heavy black boots that went right up to the knee—boots reminiscent of another era when certain

uniforms haunted France. Leather jackets with collars turned up, shaved heads [...] It was a hunting scene in the projects, revised and corrected by the "new guard." This time around, the prey was the nappy-haired guy, the darkie, the wog—you know, the inferior man!)

The text makes an implicit yet clear comparison with anti-Semitism and the Nazi occupation of Paris—a period when "other," similar uniforms "haunted" the country—thus creating an equivalence between the Parisian police and a fascist regime. Yet the text's leveraging of racism is not solely dependent upon a comparison with the recent past. The narrator also gestures specifically to a process of "ratissage" (literally, raking)—a word used to describe the roundup of undesirables—and to the inevitable processes of racial profiling. Multiplying adjectives that have historically been used to describe not only North Africans but other Southern Europeans and even South Americans as well (frisé, basané, métèque), the text underscores the concept of a hunt focused on visible difference.

Kettane's novel grows increasingly political as Brahim comes of age and becomes aware of certain inequalities and social injustices. Yet October 17 seems to be left behind: After the first chapter, nary a mention is made of the repression or its consequences for Brahim's family (his younger brother is killed that night). Nonetheless, the text can in fact be read as a performance of the return of the repressed. The section of the first chapter that narrates the violence on October 17 and his brother's death concludes with the line: "Le sourire de Brahim s'envola" (Brahim's smile disappeared). The titular smile thus becomes a metonymy for October 17; all subsequent mentions of Brahim's absent smile—which occur at moments of political intensity—refer back to October 17 and signal the intrusion of this repressed trauma into Brahim's everyday experiences. The novel ends with Brahim participating in the 1983 *Marche pour l'égalité et contre le racisme* (which would come to be known as *La marche des beurs*), and as he waits for a friend, the faintest notion of a smile quivers at the corner of his lips. This other march, with its explicit goal of exposing and countering racism, would indeed be a peaceful one, and perhaps the occasion for Brahim to recover the smile he lost on October 17.

After *Le Sourire de Brahim*, questions of "passing," mistaken identity, and police anxieties about them become a persistent trope in novels and films. In Tassadit Imache's novel *Une fille sans histoire* (1989), the young protagonist Lil witnesses the police reaction to her Algerian father's atypical looks when their car is pulled over: "T'es sur que c'est à toi, ça?"—Are you sure this is yours? the policeman asks as he inspects the identity card proffered by Lil's father. Turning to his men, the officer says: "Faut faire gaffe, y en a qui n'ont pas le type, des yeux clairs et blancs de peau" (30–31, You gotta watch out, some of them don't have the look, some have got blue eyes and pale skin). This episode—which may or may not be an autobiographical detail—recalls the testimony in *Octobre à Paris* in which a fair-skinned Algerian marvels at the French police's ability to root out even those Algerians who don't fit the phenotypical mold. At the same time, however, it codes the police as anxiously aware of the potential for error, as fearful of being bested by a chaotic situation in which their enemy may not be as easily identified as they might like.

In more recent works from the anarchive, representations of passing create a cacophonous discourse, one that may accurately reflect the complexities of policing the other in a context of heightened imperial anxiety, but one that also seems to reproduce the indeterminacy of race. Police paranoia is on display in Alain Tasma's 2005 docudrama *Nuit noire*: In an early sequence in the film, a police officer roughs up an elderly man who claims to be Moroccan, despite the fact that there is no reason to think the man is lying to protect himself. Conversely, in Daeninckx's graphic novel *Octobre noir* (2011), set at the time of the massacre, the main Algerian character, Mohand, lives a double life as a musician named Vincent, playing in a rock band where he sings Elvis songs and passes for French. On the night of October 17, Mohand escapes arrest not because he claims to be something other than Algerian, but because the police simply fail to recognize his ethnic origin: "Qu'est-ce que tu fous là?" they ask him. "T'es pas un raton…Alors dégage. Rentre chez toi, on n'est pas au spectacle" (42, What are you doing there? You're no wog…Get lost. Go home, we don't need any spectators).

Although no archival evidence appears to suggest that Italian nationals were caught up in the October events, they feature in two anarchival works. The aforementioned film *Nuit noire*, which culminates with the October 17 protest and the police repression, stages a scene depicting arrests made early in the evening, with the police pulling passengers off a city bus for triage. Two officers hesitate over one man, trying to decide whether or not he is Algerian. The man protests loudly, in French and Italian: "Mais je suis italien, ma non sono magrebino, non sono magrebino…je suis italien…vi lo giuro, vi lo giuro…" (But I'm Italian, I'm not Maghrebi, I'm not Maghrebi…I'm Italian…I swear it to you, I swear it to you…). The man is ultimately arrested, but the viewers are given no sense of closure: Was this indeed a case of "paranoid policing" or was the man in fact Algerian, and using his "ambiguous" appearance to avoid arrest? Italians are also the victims of mistaken identity in Didier Daeninckx's short story, "Fatima pour mémoire," in which an eyewitness recounts, "Sous nos fenêtres, un barrage de police…une rafale arrose la façade. Les deux jeunes ne se relèveront pas. Trop mats de peau…On apprendra plus tard qu'il s'agissait d'enfants d'immigrés italiens" (Right under our windows, a police blockade…the building is sprayed with bullets. Two young men remain on the ground. Too olive-skinned…We'd learn later that they were Italian immigrants).[92] Regardless of the veracity of these representations, what is of greatest interest is the way these cultural productions stitch such details into an October 17 narrative that is verisimilar: If Italians had been bothered on October 17, there might or might not have been a record of it, yet the factuality of these representations matters perhaps less than their plausibility, since they speak to the ambiguities of race and racism in France at the time and push against a narrative (such as the one produced by Panijel's film and by Begag's anlaysis) that Algerians were the sole targets and therefore, logically, the sole victims of the police.[93]

Several of the works that have critiqued October 17 as a racist episode train their focus on the politics of the curfew itself. In *Vivre au paradis*, the film adaptation of the eponymous novel about life in the Nanterre *bidonville*, one of the FLN organizers whips a crowd into a frenzy, shouting: "À bas le couvre-feu, à bas le racisme" (Down with the curfew, down with racism).[94] Other works situate their critique at the moment of policy-making rather than at the scene of its enforcement. Most of these are invested in revealing Papon's understanding of the stakes of his curfew, and on indicting Papon, however implicitly, as an enemy of the Republic, willing to run roughshod over universalist French principles in the name of "law and order." *Nuit noire* features the following exchange

92 Daeninckx, "Fatima pour mémoire," in *17 octobre 1961, 17 écrivains se souviennent* (Paris: Au nom de la mémoire, 2011), 83.

93 It is worth noting that questions of phenotype and passing are complex; while some Italians may have been taken for Algerian and thus harassed by police, there is also evidence that some Algerians eluded arrest by claiming to be Italian. See House and MacMaster, 268.

94 This episode is not present in the book by Brahim Benaïcha, *Vivre au paradis: d'une oasis à un bidonville* (Paris: Desclée De Brouwer, 1992), on which the film is based.

between Papon and Pierre Somveille (Papon's chief of staff at the time of the massacre):

> Somveille: Les musulmans d'Algérie sont français, on ne peut pas interdire une catégorie de français de sortir...
> Papon: C'est compliqué sur le plan du droit mais indispensable pour l'ordre; trouvez-moi une formule qui sauve les apparences.
> Somveille: On ne pourra appliquer cette mesure qu'en ayant recours à des critères physiques, les policiers vont arrêter tous les gens basanés—Marocains, Italiens, Espagnols...on va accuser la police de faire la chasse au faciès.

> (Somveille: The Algerian Muslims are French, we can't prohibit a category of Frenchmen from going out...
> Papon: It's legally complicated but essential for order, find me a turn of phrase that keeps up appearances.
> Somveille: We won't be able to apply this directive without using physical traits to identify people. The police will end up arresting anyone with olive skin—Moroccans, Italians, Spanish...the police will be accused of racial profiling.)

Eric Michel's historical novel *Algérie, Algérie!* (2007), meanwhile, stages a very similar conversation between Papon and a character he calls "Soville":[95]

> Soville: Maurice, ces mesures, qu'on le veuille ou non, se fondent sur un principe de discrimination raciale et confessionnelle. Ne crains-tu pas qu'on t'en fasse le reproche?
> Papon: Tu as raison de le souligner. [...] Je comprends tes inquiétudes, mais ces mesures sont concertés avec le ministre de l'Intérieur. [...] Cette mesure exclut les élus FMA, les hauts fonctionnaires sur présentation de leur carte, les agents de la RATP, les facteurs en tenue et les étudiants. [...] Et puis aussi les Marocains et les Tunisiens. Nous avons eu trop de plaintes des ambassades. (404–5)

> (Soville: Maurice, these directives, whether we like it or not, are based on racial and religious discrimination. Aren't you afraid you'll be reprimanded?
> Papon: You are right to point this out. [...] I understand your concern, but these measures were agreed upon by the Minister of the Interior. [...] This directive excludes the FMA who are elected officials, senior officials upon presentation of their IDs, RATP (public transportation) agents,

---

95 Soville is a transparent reference to Pierre Somveille, Papon's Chief of Staff.

mail-carriers in uniform, and students. [...] And also Moroccans and Tunisians. We've had too many complaints from the embassies.)

Notwithstanding the archives' inaccessibility at the time, both Tasma and Michel were able to document their fictional works by interviewing historians and reading the existing historiography on the Algerian War in general and October 17 in particular. Although the exchanges represented in these two works are largely informed by material collected by Einaudi, Stora, Vidal-Naquet, and others, they remain the stuff of speculative fiction. The archives, which were officially declassified only after both of these works were produced, do offer evidence that the wording of the curfew declaration was edited several times, yet the versions largely suggest that modifications of the curfew hours and types of establishments targeted had as much to do with economics and intelligence collection as they did with respecting the rule of law and republican principles. Factual or fictional, these episodes have the effect of producing an intentional Papon, one who was quite aware of the implications of his actions.

This brief tour of the anarchive's representation of racial profiling is certainly useful insofar as it spotlights an abundance of race talk in fictional productions at a time when the racist nature of the violence on October 17 remains a point of contention. Yet it also serves to reframe the plausibility of the account put forward in *Vivre me tue* and to contest Begag's critique of the novel. *Vivre me tue* is profoundly, albeit subtly, invested in exploring the limits of "passing"—and this investment is situated in both the diegetic content and in the backstory of Léger's "passing" as Smaïl. The novel is resolutely of the moment in which it is set (the late 1990s), and it is true that the explicit represen-tation of racism and passing refers to that time period. Paul Smaïl, the protagonist, describes his difficulty in finding work in spite of his "Christian" first name: "il y aura toujours un autre candidat moins basané que moi, le cheveu moins crépu, la peau moins grenue, le nez moins busqué. [...] Les pires sont les directeurs des ressources humaines. Ils vous repèrent tout de suite, ils vous flairent comme des chiens dressés à le faire, ils ont l'œil" (12, there will always be a lighter-skinned candidate, with straighter hair, smoother skin, a less hooked nose. [...] The worst are the human resources people. They spot you right away, they sniff you out like trained hunting dogs, they have the eye, 2). As a result, Paul explains, Maghrebis in France try to "pass" by means that are always, inevitably, foiled: "Les maghrébins qui essaient de se blanchir sont comme ces juifs allemands qui crurent s'en sortir, avant la guerre, en demeurant dans le flou. Un faux nez se voit encore mieux que le nez au milieu d'une figure" (12, The Maghrebis who try to whitewash themselves are like the German Jews who thought they could save themselves, before the war, by blending in. A false nose sticks out even more than a real nose in the middle of your face, 2). Paul's brother is one such "passeur," a gay bodybuilder who dyes his hair blond in order to look French. His brother's attempts to physically alter his body in order to render himself acceptable to society end up killing him: He dies young as a result of steroid use, returned to his original form: "[un] bicot, de vieux bicot du Rif, sec, noueux, décharné" (13, an A-rab, an old A-rab from the Rif, dry, scrawny, and bony, 2–3).

Paul himself remarks that his own phenotype is inconclusive: "Les francaouis de souche me caguaient parce qu'ils me jugeaient un peu trop sidi, les Sidis parce qu'ils me jugeaient un peu trop françaoi" (27, The trueblood born-'n'-raised Frenchies would rib me because they'd decided I was too much of a *sidi* by half, the *sidis* would rag me because they reckoned I was too much of a Frenchie by half, 15). In this context, Paul's brother and uncle represent opposite ends of a spectrum of passing: The brother dies as a result of trying to be something he is not; the uncle dies because of a dangerous resemblance to something he is not. Paul occupies a strange middle ground where he is both taken for something he is not and often made to suffer for what he is. From Smaïl/Léger's vantage point in 1997, the problem of the phenotypically ambiguous *beur* is inscribed in a longer, dastardly history.

In a novel that is sutured to its contemporaneous cultural zeitgeist through linguistic tics and musical references (lyrics from The Cure recur throughout the text), it is worth noting that October 17 is the only real historical event mentioned. The initial references to the moment are veiled, as Paul summarizes his family history in the following manner: "Un grand-père mort pour la France, un oncle assassiné par la police française aux ordres de Papon" (62, A grandfather who died for France, an uncle murdered by the French police on Papon's orders, 45). The second reference to October 17 is far more explicit, occurring at the moment when Smaïl recounts his friendship with one of his high-school teachers who, in private conversation at his own home (not, notably, in school), teaches Paul about this particular history. Finally, it is the funeral of Paul's father, and a glimpse of the *carré musulman*, or Muslim section of the cemetery, that instantly calls up the anonymous dead of October 17 and segues into one of the final chapters of the novel, a three-page historicized narrative of October 17 that feels nearly extradiegetic. The story includes several mentions of phenotype-driven discrimination: "En pleine jour, une 403 banalisée s'arrêtait à la hauteur d'un malheureux qui avait le faciès. [...] Les Arabes, Algériens ou non, vivaient dans la peur. Des Italiens, des Portugais ont été assassinés simplement parce qu'ils avaient le type" (178–79, In full daylight, an unmarked Peugeot 403 would pull up level with a poor guy who had «the features.» [...] Arabs, whether Algerian or not, lived in a state of fear. Italians and Portuguese guys were murdered simply because they looked "the type," 143–44). Smaïl goes on to qualify this as an "effroyable tuerie," as a savage killing, and to reveal that his parents hardly ever spoke of the events.

It is clear from the detail that Léger knows much of the invisible story of October 17, and is sensitive to the multiple ways in which that story was elided from both collective and personal histories. And perhaps we can read his story of Smaïl and his Uncle Mehdi as an attempt to inscribe the *beur* situation in 1997 into a longer, more complex history of racism, non-belonging, rogue attempts to fit in, and their consequences. Uncle Mehdi's death symbolizes the impossibility of escaping one's ethnic envelope. Twenty years later, Maghrebi French youth are still fighting the same battles.

In a clever reappropriation of Shylock's monologue in Shakespeare's *Merchant of Venice*—"Hath not a Jew eyes," and so on—Smaïl attempts a plea for interethnic empathy: "Je suis arabe. Un Arabe n'a-t-il pas des yeux, un Arabe n'a-t-il pas des mains, des organes, des proportions [...] n'est-il pas blessé par les mêmes armes, sujet aux mêmes maladies [...] qu'un Français de souche?" (181, I'm an Arab. Doesn't an Arab have two eyes? Doesn't an Arab have hands, organs, proportions [...]? Isn't he wounded by the same weapons, liable to have the same illnesses [...] as a born and bred Frenchman?, 146) It is not merely that the Arab here replaces Shakespeare's Jew; perhaps we should also keep in mind that all of this is filtered through a fictional *beur* whose master puppeteer is, himself, a "Français de souche." In his creation of a *beur* literary persona who is also a literary scholar, Léger appears—to Begag anyway— to be poking fun and taking advantage. Yet regardless of whether we read it that way, it is impossible to ignore the kind of empathic relationship between the author and his protagonist. Léger's vision of Paul is genuinely benevolent. Moreover, that he uses Paul's story to stage October 17 as a complex, racially motivated, hidden event is doubled by the fact that he stages it as a foundational moment, the one historical reality that penetrates this fiction and shares the same core issues as those dealt with by the protagonist.

————

Vivre me tue is clearly one in a series of works to have gestured, implicitly or explicitly, to the complex racial politics of October 17, and it remains the only text to have been taken to task for representing the events as something other than a strictly "anti-Algerian pogrom." But let us return to the notion of Begag's error as a site of inquiry, as an impetus for speculative research. What is at stake when someone like Begag—a highly educated *beur* and an individual who has held positions within conservative governments—has constructed, or been educated to believe in a vision of October 17 as a targeted attack on Algerians?[96] Without asking him directly, we cannot know for sure when or how Begag came to know about October 17. We can, however, surmise that he would not have learned about it in school, and we might also imagine that his family (like that of the fictional Smaïl but also like so many other real Algerian families), first out of fear and later out of trauma, would have avoided speaking of the event, or at the very least, would have spoken of it only in fragmentary or veiled ways. Regardless, Begag's lack of access to a complex picture of October 17 points, above all, to the existence of a powerful dominant narrative that is blind to important nuances.

One of the benefits of tracking racism diachronically is that it helps us to avoid the pitfalls of periodization and of ascribing representation to circumstance alone. In 1961 and again in 2005, Panijel and Begag, respectively, put forward a notion of October 17 as a targeted operation against Algerians, in theory and in practice. The facts do not support this vision of the events, but the facts can, at times, be beside the point. Regardless of whether they produce a correct version of the story, the works by both Panijel and Begag participate in a variegated, complex narrative of the racial politics of October 17.

Begag is absolutely correct that on October 17, and during the months surrounding the demonstration and its repression, French governmental policies and police dictates and actions were specifically anti-Algerian,

96 Begag holds a doctorate in economics and served as Minister for Equal Opportunity under Jacques Chirac (2005–07).

intended to contain and defeat the FLN. But in implementing these policies, the state knowingly opened the door for racial profiling and what are euphemistically called *bavures*, or mistakes. To recognize other victims of October 17 is not to diminish the facts of the events, nor does it dishonor the Algerian victims of the police massacre. On the contrary, by understanding the racist atmosphere and confusion of "types" that led non-Algerians to be victimized, we are able to place October 17 not just within the context of the turbulence of decolonization, but within a spirit of ethnic discrimination that still haunts France today.

CHAPTER SIX

The Entangled Stories of October 17, Vichy, the Jews, and the Holocaust

The Algerian war was not very easily placed in a politically correct vision, especially after Auschwitz.[1]
—Jean-Pierre Rioux

It would be difficult to overstate the importance of *Meurtres pour mémoire* (*Murder in Memoriam*) for the October 17 anarchive: Its publication coincided with the beginning of the two-decade-long Papon affair, and it was the first cultural production to imagine a Papon-esque character; it was the first French-language novel to narrativize October 17; its pulpy *polar* style made it highly accessible, and the structure of the detective novel dovetailed neatly with the open-ended nature of its content; and, finally, its afterlives as a made-for-TV movie, a graphic novel, and an educational tool are a testament to its staying power.[2] This rare combination of factors has made *Meurtres pour mémoire* a foundational October 17 fiction, and its author a de facto expert on both the event and its elision from history and cultural memory.[3] Yet, if *Meurtres*

---

1 Quoted in Maurice T. Maschino, "L'histoire expurgée de la guerre d'Algérie," 8.

2 For more on *Meurtres* and the genre of the *roman noir* (or the *polar engagé*), see Gorrara, "Historical investigations: Didier Daeninckx's *Meurtres pour mémoire* (1984)," in *The Roman Noir in Post-War French Culture: Dark Fictions* (Oxford: Oxford University Press, 2003), 73–89. See also Gorrara, "Reflections on Crime and Punishment: Memories of the Holocaust in Recent French Crime Fiction," *Yale French Studies*, no. 8 (2005): 131–45.

3 *Meurtres* is arguably the most successful October 17 novel, commercially and in terms of course adoptions. (See Chapter 1 for more details.) Daeninckx continues to write about World War II and its secrets (*Un salaud ordinaire*);

has remained a centerpiece in literary scholarship, it is also because of the particular nature and handling of its subject matter. In 1983, the novel speculated about a "real life" political entanglement that would captivate the nation and later be proven true: Papon's responsibility for crimes against humanity under Vichy and, later, under de Gaulle.

Like any work of literature that has attained significant attention, *Meurtres* has its champions and its detractors alike. There is no shortage of criticism of the work's literary qualities. More potent, perhaps, is that readers do not necessarily converge in their assessment of the novel's treatment of its historical material, and there is some disagreement about where its political investments lie: Is *Meurtres* a Vichy novel that uses October 17 as a mere narrative pretext, or is it an October 17 novel that uses Vichy for historical ballast?[4] Ultimately, it is not a question of whether one reads "with" or "against" the grain; the grain of the novel is itself ambivalent, allowing a reader with a particular ideological prism to invest narrative content and proportion with meaning that reinforces her own particular view. Of course, it is also possible to embrace rather than resolve the novel's ambivalence, to approach the representation of two different historical moments "multidirectionally" rather than competitively. As Michael Rothberg has suggested, *Meurtres* places October 17 and Vichy "in the same narrative frame without forcing them into a single, causal narrative."[5] Moreover, he observes, "by making the discovery of homologies between eras the point of the narrative, Daeninckx provokes an engagement with the larger problems of French complicity."[6] I find an approach that refuses to pick sides salutary in general: Allowing

colonial history (*Cannibale*, *Galadio*); and October 17 (the graphic novel *Octobre noir*, and the short story *Fatima pour mémoire*).

4   For one example of such a reading, see Stephen Steele's review essay, "Daeninckx, Quand le roman policier part en guerre," *French Studies Bulletin* 20, no. 71 (1999): 9–10.

5   Rothberg, 277. Rothberg's multidirectional analysis concludes that *Meurtres* is ultimately less about October 17 and the Shoah than about "the connection between different eras and the persistence of the unresolved past in the present. Cadin's investigation [...] provides a materialization of the missing link between different crimes and different histories" (276–77).

6   Rothberg, 277. Bringing narratives of different events into discursive and narrative proximity with one another is referred to by Rothberg as "sideshadowing," a generic convention typical of detective novels that reveals "a contingent or metonymical field of associations" (279).

the book to be about both moments is imperative to interpreting a detective story that is also a historical fiction deeply invested in foregrounding the experience of the unknown and that is, ultimately, resistant to reductive analyses.

Regardless of its putative aesthetic, historical, or political shortcomings, what is true is that, in 1983, *Meurtres* waded into waters that remain, to this day, profoundly murky, both in the French context and in terms of broader, transnational questions about representation and World War II. By virtue of its explicit staging of the potential connections between France's Vichy and colonial pasts, the novel not only anticipated the denoument of the Papon affair, but has proven itself to be deeply entangled with ethical and existential issues that have animated the second half of the twentieth century, and that continue to pulsate in contemporary France. These include questions of resistance and collaboration; debates about surfeits of memory; discourses of culpability and repentance; and, more recently, reflections on the relationship between World War II and the colonial project, and between the colonial project, its afterlives, the rise of fundamentalism, and the return of anti-Semitism. *Meurtres* also engages a thicket of issues related to the representation of the Holocaust, its comparison with other genocides, and the stakes of "the global presence of the Holocaust as a site of memory"—debates that have taken on greater urgency in the decades after the novel's publication.[7]

However much *Meurtres* functions as a signal work in the anarchive, it is only one of many cultural productions to stage connections with World War II. In a significant number of works about October 17, roles for Jews, the Vichy regime, and the Holocaust are articulated or imagined, pointing up networks of association that may be historical, apocryphal, real, or romanced. In the section that follows, I take up the question of whether Vichy and October 17 can or should be compared, that is, of whether Daeninckx (and others) produced what at least one scholar has viewed as a perilous comparison. The chapter then turns its attention to the anarchive, not to unravel, but rather to observe the cultural entanglements of October 17, Vichy, Jews, and the Holocaust. If I am interested in speculating about *why* representations of a massacre of Algerians have been, and remain, yoked to images and tropes of World War II, I am above all concerned with *how* such representations function

7   Susan R. Suleiman, *Crises of Memory and the Second World War* (Cambridge, MA: Harvard University Press, 2008), 2.

within their discrete literary worlds, and how we might speculate about the payoffs and pitfalls of such entanglements.

"Dangerous Parallels"

In his work on historical trauma, public memory, and art, Andreas Huyssen issues a helpful caveat regarding the ubiquity of the Holocaust in representations of trauma: "Although the Holocaust as a universal trope of traumatic history has migrated into other, nonrelated contexts, one must always ask whether and how the trope enhances or hinders local memory practices and struggles, or whether and how it may help and hinder at the same time."[8] This call for a judicious skepticism— particularly as Huyssen is writing about art in Argentina under the dictatorship and in New York City after 9/11 (two cases in which recourse to the Holocaust would be allusive rather than historically grounded)— appears so eminently sensible and un-contentious that I have taken it up as the scaffolding of my own readings of October 17 works, even though the Holocaust and October 17 are not, to use Huyssen's term, "unrelated contexts."

Or are they?

In an important essay on *Meurtres*, written in 1998 and thus from within the maelstrom of the end of the Papon trial, Richard J. Golsan suggested that Daeninckx's comparison of the Nazi treatment of the Jews and Papon's treatment of Algerians was a risky conflation of significantly different historical periods. The "skewed equation" whereby "Gaullism equals Vichy" is, for Golsan, "both ironic and ludicrous."[9] The end of *Meurtres*, which finds an Algerian worker in a subway station peeling away layers of posters to uncover a notice dating to the Nazi occupation, exemplifies what Golsan calls a "dangerous *parallel* between the implementation of the Final Solution in France and the excesses of *la guerre sans nom*."[10]

My interest in Golsan's assessment of historical conjecture in *Meurtres* has less to do with its accuracy than with its challenge to the

---

8   Andreas Huyssen, *Present Pasts: Urban Palimpsests and the Politics of Memory* (Stanford, CA: Stanford University Press, 2003), 16.

9   Golsan, "Memory's *bombes à retardement*," 170.

10   Golsan, "Memory's *bombes à retardement*," 169–70; emphasis in the original.

amalgam of "Gaullism" and "Vichy."[11] What is at stake when these two historical moments are conflated? Conversely, what are the implications of cleaving apart the Holocaust and the Algerian War, of configuring them as essentially "unrelated"? Answers to questions such as these are necessarily conditioned by the context in which they are asked. Indeed, in 1998, it was still too soon to articulate the lessons of the Papon trial, and the Algerian War remained a deeply contentious political issue (France would only officially recognize the war in 1999). Moreover, Golsan's argument leans quite heavily on what was, at the time, the most important study of the French grand narrative of the occupation and Vichy, Henry Rousso's *The Vichy Syndrome* (1987). In positing a model for understanding the shifting national memory of Vichy over time, the book has been fundamental to the analysis of collective memory more generally. Rousso's assessment of the links between Vichy and the Algerian War are echoed in Golsan's essay, namely in his assertion that the two historical moments bear no relation, notwithstanding a few anecdotal connections. One line from *The Vichy Syndrome* in particular seems to sum up the putative reality of the situation for Rousso: "When viewed in hindsight, and with strict objectivity, the Algerian War has only a tenuous relation to the Occupation, but contemporaries did not see it that way. In their imaginations and slogans and at times in their actions, the most prominent figures in this new *guerre franco-française* identified with the men and events of 1940."[12]

But Rousso's vision of the matter would evolve in the decades following the publication of the 1987 book. His work on memory and Vichy led

11   Moreover, Golsan's essay predates a groundswell of scholarship devoted to making visible the links between colonialism and World War II—in politics and in cultural production. See Emmanuel Blanchard, Jim House, Gérard Noirel, and Françoise Vergès. As Max Silverman argued more than a decade later, it should not surprise us that these different histories—of colonialism and of the Holocaust, but also of capitalism, the rise of the nation state, and experiments in "total domination"—come to roost together in various art forms (*Palimpsestic Memory*, 14). Note also, however, that Silverman himself doesn't view this "amalgam" as new: "This is at the core of the Dialectic of the Enlightenment in which, for Adorno and Horkheimer, capitalism, imperialism, the rise of the modern nation-state and racial theory were interconnected processes responsible for the production of 'interchangeable' victims, 'Frenchman, Negro, or Jew'" (14). (Silverman cites the Continuum edition of *The Dialectic of the Enlightenment*, reissued in 2001, pp. 171 and 183.)

12   Rousso, *Vichy Syndrome*, 75.

him to train his critical gaze on French memories of the Algerian War. Subsequently, he would revise some of his earlier conclusions about the relationship between the two periods, eventually stating that "the two events are quite linked," and that "in terms of history, there is an abiding connection between the two events."[13] Taken in 2002, this stance looks like a radical reversal, or a thoroughgoing revision, of his earlier position; however, if we look carefully at the details of *The Vichy Syndrome*, it becomes clear that in 2002, he is merely throwing wide open a door he had, in fact, already left ajar in 1987. In keeping with the medical metaphor embedded in the notion of a "syndrome," Rousso described the years of 1955–71 as a period of *refoulement*, during which memories of Vichy were repressed or rearticulated into positive narratives. Recognizing, however, that even within this nearly 20-year period, the repressed had returned sporadically, Rousso's schema sought to account for these eruptions by identifying certain moments of "accès de fièvre" (bouts of fever) or "rejeux" (replays) of memory.[14] One of these "rejeux" corresponds to 1960–62, the final two years of the Algerian War. Given that Rousso never mentions October 17 in *The Vichy Syndrome*, nor delves into the historical specificities of the Algerian War, it is all the more intriguing to observe that 1961 falls squarely into one of these moments of sudden "high fever" in Vichy memory. Clearly, part of what was repressed during the period of *refoulement* was, precisely, a sense of historical connection so troubling as to be tamped down for decades following the events.

Viewed from the late 1980s, 1961 obviously constituted a flare-up, a recurrence, a return of vaguely familiar symptoms whose origins had been left undiagnosed. And yet, even if Rousso sidestepped the

13 Rousso, "La guerre d'Algérie dans la mémoire des français" (lecture given at the conference "La guerre d'Algérie 1954–1962"), https://www.canal-u.tv/producteurs/universite_de_tous_les_savoirs/les_conferences_de_l_annee_2002/la_guerre_d_algerie_1954_a_1962. Rousso further develops this idea in the essay "Les raisins verts de la guerre d'Algérie," in *La Guerre d'Algérie (1954–1962)*, ed. Yves Michaud (Paris: Odile Jacob, 2004), 127–51. The knot composed of memories of Vichy, the Shoah, and the Algerian War is revisited yet again in Rousso's book *Face au passé* (Belin, 2016). In a chapter titled "Le double fardeau: Vichy et l'Algérie," he states that the comparison of these memories "ne relève pas simplement d'un exercice heuristique: elle est nécessaire pour comprendre ces phénomènes" (is not simply an heuristic exercise: it is necessary for our understanding of these phenomena, 131).

14 Rousso, *Vichy Syndrome*, 219–20.

events of October 17, contemporaneous archival materials make it clear that this particular episode constitutes a rupture in the period of *refoulement*. The connections and conflations articulated during this brief moment in time have implications for how we read the anarchive, but also for how we consider the historical narratives that have been set before us. Reading the police archives today, 30 years on from *The Vichy Syndrome*, our diagnostic tools may be better calibrated to read the micronarratives behind the passing yet sudden "high fever" of Vichy memory in 1961, and, of course, the contemporary context may be more propitious as well. What we are able to discern today is that, regardless of whether World War II and the Algerian War in fact constituted related contexts, in 1961 politicians, activists, professors, students, trade union representatives, and others perceived a connection between policies implemented during World War II and the contemporaneous polices being implemented by Papon. The actors on the ground were, themselves, articulating a "dangerous parallel."

Even in the weeks before the repression on October 17, a whiff of something distasteful, reminiscent of a recent yet unacknowledged past, was in the air: Papon's office had announced a "curfew" for all Algerians living in Paris and its neighboring suburbs.[15] In keeping with a kind of apparatchik double-speak, the official communiqué, issued on October 5, neither used the word "curfew" nor billed itself as an "order." Rather, Algerians were "encouraged with utmost urgency to refrain from going out between 8:30 p.m. and 5:30 a.m." Moreover, it was "strongly recommended" that Algerian men move around the city alone, rather than in groups, as groups were more likely to raise suspicion. Although Papon's internal memos to his men did explicitly use the word "curfew," he would continue to use elliptical language in external communications defending his tactics.[16] Notably, in a letter addressed to the president of the National Assembly, dated October 17, 1961, Papon wrote that "[les Français Musulmans d'Algérie] ont été

---

15   The curfew strategy had already been implemented in Algeria and tested in mainland France in 1958. See Sylvie Thénault, "Des couvre-feux à Paris en 1958 et 1961: une mesure importée d'Algérie pour mieux lutter contre le FLN?" *Politix* 84, no. 4 (2008): 167–85.

16   See "Ordre du jour du préfet de police Maurice Papon, 5 octobre 1961" and "Circulaire no. 43-61 du directeur général de la police municipale de Paris concernant la 'circulation des Français musulmans algériens,' 7 octobre 1961." Police archives, HA 110/111; see also Manceron, *Textes de l'époque*, 35 and 38, respectively.

invités à s'abstenir de circuler entre 20h30 et 5h30 du matin" ([the French Muslims of Algeria] have been invited to abstain from going out between 8:30 p.m. and 5:30 a.m.).[17]

Reactions to the curfew came swiftly from a variety of camps, and, as we saw in the previous chapter, many of these did not hesitate to point out the racism of the measure. More still were quick to notice—and name— the curfew's eerie resonances with tactics deployed in France a brief two decades earlier. Of the various social and political actors to make the historical connection to the recent past, the left was perhaps most vociferous and explicit.[18] In a letter dated October 6, addressed simply to "Monsieur" and received by the prefecture of police on October 9, the St. Denis office of the General Confederation of Labor (known in French as the CGT) called the curfew a machination against Algerian workers, as well as an insult to the French. In a sentence set apart from the rest of the letter, it warns: "[Cette mesure] rappelle étrangement les méthodes de la Gestapo sous l'occupation" ([This measure] is strangely reminiscent of the methods used by the Gestapo during the occupation).[19] Moreover, 14 Muslim deputies and senators also banded together to express their disapproval of the curfew in a manifesto published on October 11 and preserved only in the police archives. Representing a variety of parties and interests within the Algerian community in France, the signatories wrote to "exprimer solennellement leurs indignations contre les mesures vexatoires, discriminatoires, pour ne pas dire racistes, qui rappellent celles prises en d'autres temps" (solemnly express their indignation with respect to these humiliating, discriminatory—not to mention racist— measures, which are reminiscent of those enacted in times past).[20]

In addition to their timing (they predate the repression), these acknowledgments of the historical precedent are unique in their rhetoric. The Muslim senators and deputies—French politicians, after all— opt for elliptical language that banks on allusion to make its point.

17   Police archives, HA 110/111. Letter dated October 17, 1961, from Papon to the President of the National Assembly.

18   For more information on the French left, the Communist Party, and October 17, see House and MacMaster, "Fractured Protests on the Left," in *Paris 1961*, 226–32.

19   Police archives, HA 110/111. Letter dated October 6, 1961, from CGT headquarters in La Plaine St-Denis to Papon.

20   Police archives, HA 110/111. Letter dated October 11, 1961, from Muslim senators and deputies to Papon, titled "Manifeste publié par des sénateurs et députés musulmans." (See Chapter 5, n. 46.)

This allows them to suggest a connection with World War II without naming Hitler or the Gestapo, and, perhaps more importantly, without naming the collaborationist French Vichy Regime. The CGT is similarly cautious: While their letter does explicitly mention the Gestapo, it avoids implicating the French State.

In the few weeks following the October 17 massacre, however, responses evoking World War II were more frequent, strident, and specific. A call to protest organized by students underscored methods that "rapellent trop l'hitlérisme dont nous souffrions ici même il y a une vingtaine d'années" (are all too reminiscent of the Hitlerism we suffered in this very spot 20 years ago).[21] The *Lumières des Gondoles*, a communist leaflet, featured an anonymous inset that recounted the experience of an eyewitness present a few days after the massacre at the Palais des Sports: "Quand le 19 octobre je pénétrais dans cet établissement, j'ai cru rêver devant le spectacle qui s'offrait à mes yeux, je me croyais revenu aux temps de l'occupation allemande, quand des millions de juifs étaient parqué [*sic*] dans l'ancien 'Vél d'Hiv'" (When I entered the arena on October 19, the spectacle before my eyes made me think I was having a dream. It was as if I had gone back in time to the German occupation, when millions of Jews were rounded up and held in the former Vél d'Hiv).[22] Similarly, military veterans who were incarcerated at the Fresnes prison at the time made a connection with the Vél d'Hiv roundup in their manifesto: "Les représailles collectives, les Algériens parqués au Palais des Sports, à qui cela ne rappellerait-t-il les méthodes de répression nazies et le Vél d'Hiv de l'Occupation qui était l'antichambre de la déportation" (Collective retaliatory measures, Algerians held in the Palais des Sports: Who wouldn't be reminded of the Nazis' methods of repression and the Vél d'Hiv during the Occupation, which was a waiting room for deportation?)[23]

---

21   Police archives, HA 110/111. This document is a report, ostensibly commissioned by the Prefecture and written up by an observer, on a student rally held on October 21, 1961. The three-page report was issued the same day, with the title "Objet: manifestation d'étudiants."

22   Police archives, HA 110/111. The anonymous tract is typed on the Lumière des Gondoles letterhead, and mentions the "Cellule 'le Moal'"—a communist cell based in Choisy-le-Roi, southeast of Paris. Vél d'Hiv is common shorthand for the Winter Velodrome (formerly a stadium in the 15th *arrondissement*) a site that has become synonymous with the mass roundup of Jews by French police that occurred there on July 16–17, 1942. The stadium was destroyed by fire in 1959.

23   Police archives, HA 110/111. This single-page document is titled "Appel des militaires français emprisonnés à Fresnes."

Neither did the FLN hesitate to underscore the similarities between the very recent events of October 17 and the apartheid-like curfew that led up to them, and the fascism that had haunted the territory in the not-so-distant past. Indeed, the FLN had long been aware that connecting French actions in Algeria to World War II, Vichy, and Nazism was a source of great political embarrassment to the government, and the organization had already sought to exploit this link prior to 1954.[24] The day after the massacre, in a call written by the FLN leadership based in Germany and destined to be played on radios and in the French press, the FLN blatantly called upon the French people to imagine a scenario in which Algerians, like Jews all over Europe, would be marked for identification: "Pour appliquer ces mesures tout aussi odieuses que celles dont furent victimes les Juifs à une certaine époque, des discriminations sont faites selon le faciès des passants. Pour ne pas les confondre avec les Italiens, les Espagnols et autres méditerranéens ou touristes sud-américains, à quand l'étoile jaune pour les Algériens?" (To apply these measures that are just as heinous as those applied to the Jews during a certain period, a form of racial profiling is practiced in the streets. To avoid confusing them with Italians, Spaniards, other Mediterraneans, or South American tourists, why not force Algerians to wear a yellow star?)[25] The FLN, however, were hardly the only ones to observe and comment on the way Papon's curfew brought the fascist tactics of World War II to the surface. We may recall, from the previous chapter, the comments made by Eugène Claudius-Petit at the National Assembly, in which he not only denounced the racial profiling of the police but also drew a parallel with the Vichy tactics of identifying Jews, wondering whether France was destined to replay past shames, this time in the form of "the yellow crescent."[26]

24   As Jim House has observed, "throughout the war, the FLN was very skillful in addressing the French public…[They] knew metropolitan French society intimately well, and always stressed transversal themes such as antifascism, antiracism, and the right to human dignity" in "Memory and the Creation of Solidarity," 28.

25   Police archives, HA 110/111. The two-page manifesto is titled "Un Appel au Peuple Français." The notion of an Algerian yellow star was a leitmotif in FLN propaganda targeting French sentiment. In a tract dated October 24, 1961, we find the following comment: "[Le people Algérien] s'oppose tout entier aux mesures de discrimination raciales qui le frappent sous l'aspect hypocrite de «conseils.» Après le couvre-feu, à quand l'étoile jaune?" ([The Algerian people] are wholeheartedly opposed to the racial discrimination to which they are subjected under the hypocritical guise of "advice." First the curfew; next the yellow star?)

26   See Chapter 5, p. 233.

Despite the fact that Jews and Muslims are often depicted as historical enemies, the Jews of France banded together in defense of the Algerians, drawing a parallel with their own suffering. Mobilizing World War II in a statement of support, the Union des sociétés juives de France (French Union of Jewish Organizations) declared its

> inquiétude en face de ces mesures à caractère raciste décrétées par les autorités publiques ces derniers jours envers la population nord-africaine de Paris. Nous ne pouvons rester insensibles [...] à ces persécutions, comme l'ont fait certains à l'époque quand on nous imposa le port de l'étoile jaune. C'est pourquoi, nous, les victimes classiques du racisme, nous exprimons notre solidarité aux persécutés et nous demandons qu'aucune mesure de répression collective ne soit appliquée envers la population nord-africaine.[27]

> (concern with respect to the racist measures that the public authorities have decreed against the North African population in recent days. We cannot remain indifferent [...] to these persecutions, as some did during the period when the yellow star was imposed on us. This is why we, the classic victims of racism, are expressing our solidarity with those persecuted and are demanding that no acts of collective repression be applied to the North African population.)

Compelling in its expression of empathy and identification, as well as for its recognition that the measures in question would have affected a population far beyond that which they targeted, this statement by the collective Jewish organizations of France adds complexity to the picture of Judeo-Muslim solidarity in Algeria and during the war in general.[28]

Much of the above was published in internal communications, tracts, pamphlets, and manifestos that circulated from hand to hand— documents that were collected by the prefecture of police at the time, and thus constitute part of the long sought-after archival material relative to October 17 that was held incommunicado for decades. These elements demonstrate a hyper-consciousness of World War II in 1961 and an ability to apply lessons from the recent past to the contemporary moment, something we are only able to discern now that the police

---

27 Anon., "7000 Algériens encore détenus dans divers centres de la région parisienne," *L'Aurore*, October 23, 1961.

28 See House, "Memory and Creation of Solidarity," 25–27. For a longer history of Judeo-Muslim relations in Algeria, see Ethan B. Katz, *The Burdens of Brotherhood: Jews and Muslims from North Africa to France* (Cambridge, MA: Harvard University Press, 2015).

archives have been declassified. This sentiment, however, was also echoed in publications with official vectors of distribution, such as *Les Temps modernes* and the daily press.

Under the editorial supervision of Jean-Paul Sartre at the time, *Les Temps modernes* weighed in on the matter in several ways: The November 1961 issue not only republished the FLN's October 18 call, with its clear references to the yellow star, but also simultaneously circulated and published a petition calling for the immediate abrogation of all anti-Algerian measures. Signed by 229 intellectuals, including Simone de Beauvoir, Robert Antelme, Aimé Césaire, Claude Lanzmann, and Elsa Triolet, the brief call reaches its apogee in a clear reminder of where France had been not so long before:

> En restant passifs, les Français se feraient les complices des fureurs racistes dont Paris est désormais le théâtre, et qui nous ramènent aux jours les plus noirs de l'occupation nazie: entre les Algériens entassés au Palais des Sports en attendant d'être «refoulés» et les Juifs parqués à Drancy avant la déportation, nous nous refusons de faire la différence.[29]

> (By remaining passive, the French would become accomplices to the racist furor that currently reigns in Paris and that takes us back to the darkest days of the Nazi occupation: we refuse to differentiate between Algerians packed into the Palais des Sports while they await "repatriation" and the Jews rounded up at Drancy prior to deportation.)

While many of these texts might have only seen the light of day for a short time before being seized by the censors, the daily press was also explicit in its indictment of the return of World War II in Papon's strategy. Notwithstanding the censure, newspapers with massive print runs such as *L'Humanité* would have been difficult to corral without their headlines and photos, at the very least, being glimpsed by the general public. In *L'Humanité*, one interviewee stated, "Nos compatriotes, travailleurs immigrés, ont tenu à protester contre la répression de style nazi qui s'abat quotidiennement sur eux et notamment contre les mesures discriminatoires récemment renforcés" (Our compatriots, immigrant workers, insisted on protesting against the Nazi-style repression that they [the Algerians in Paris] are subjected to every day and especially against the

29   This petition for solidarity was circulated on October 18, 1961, and published in *Les Temps modernes*, no. 186 (November 1961): 624–28. Reprinted in Manceron, *Textes de l'époque*, 59–60 and in Péju, *Le 17 octobre des Algériens*, 93–97.

discriminatory measures that have recently been reinforced).[30] And in the November 3 issue of *Témoignage chrétien*, an editorial referred to the Palais des Sports as a "moderne camp de concentration pour Algériens" (a present-day concentration camp for Algerians).[31] Some of the photos published in the mainstream press at the time would have been even more acerbic in their accusations. One such snapshot, taken of a group of Algerian men as they awaited deportation on the tarmac of the Orly airport, bore the caption "Drancy, en d'autres temps" (Drancy, in other times)—a clear reference to the French transit camp north of Paris from which many Jews were deported to death camps in Eastern Europe.

The references to World War II in the October 17 archives present us with a curious discursive knot. On the one hand, while a major intellectual publication such as *Les Temps modernes* not only embraced but also made use of analogies and anecdotes that connected state tactics of the day with fascist tactics in use during *les années noires*, its competitor, *L'Esprit*, took a stand against conflating the situation of Jews in Europe during the war and that of Algerians in France under colonization.[32] On the other hand, it is difficult to deny that many venues, organizations, and individuals, ranging from Jews to communists to union organizers, and from students to elected politicians, clearly saw World War II in the rearview mirror of Papon's Algerian politics. Notwithstanding this lucidity, many of the references name the past as Hitlerism, Nazism, or the Gestapo; in other words, they point to the German occupier rather than acknowledge the complicity, authority, and autonomy of the French government in carrying out anti-Jewish measures and legislation during World War II. The few mentions that do acknowledge the French government's role tend to function metonymically, with references to the Palais des Sports as an iteration of the Vél d'Hiv, or with evocations of place names such as Drancy serving as placeholders for the horror. In only one instance—an elocution by Senator Jacques Duclos, published in a collective document put together

30 Anon., "Un porte-parole du GPRA: 'Les manifestations ne sont pas dirigées contre le peuple français mais contre le colonialisme,'" *L'Humanité*, October 19, 1961. Police archives, HA 110/111.

31 Georges Montaron, "Conclusions provisoires," *Témoignage chrétien*, November 3, 1961. Police archives, HA 110/111.

32 "Contre la barbarie," signed Le Comité directeur, *L'Esprit* 300, no. 11 (November 1961): 667–70.

by le Mouvement contre le racisme et l'antisémitisme et pour l'égalite (MRAP)—is Vichy mentioned by name:

> Les brutalités policières dont sont victimes les travailleurs algériens de Paris, et qui ont atteint une violence inouïe les 17, 18 et 19 octobre, font revivre des temps que les démocrates et les patriotes considéraient comme révolus, je veux parler de l'époque où *les hitlériens et leurs valets* régnaient sur notre sol.[33]

> (The police brutalities to which the Algerian workers have fallen victim, and that reached an unprecedented level of violence on October 17, 18, and 19, compel us to relive the times that democrats and patriots had considered long gone—I'm talking about the period when *Hitler's henchmen and their lackeys* reigned over our land.)

The uneven narratives produced by the press and other archival materials from 1961 reveal hesitations that are not only rhetorically interesting, but also demonstrate that a parallel between "Gaullism" and "Vichy" existed in public discourse. In this way, they also speak directly to Rousso's "high fever" of 1960 to 1962, or "les rejeux de la guerre d'Algérie." Clearly aware of connections both anecdotal and administrative, yet under the spell of what Rousso would later call the "myth of the good Vichy," few, if any, of these narratives seem willing to explicitly link the excesses of Papon in 1961 to the French state that governed from 1940 to 1944.[34] Moreover, most of those who made these historical imbrications visible fall into what Pierre Vidal-Naquet has defined as the "dreyfusard" strain of anti-Algerian War activists, activists motivated by an attachment to a "certain idea of France" rather than affinities with third-world liberation movements or an ideological belief in a free Algeria.[35] And yet, the mere mention of World War II and its various permutations (Drancy, the Gestapo, the Vél d'Hiv, Nazis, Hitler) does tell us that, regardless of whether or not October 17 and Vichy constituted "unrelated" contexts, at least one strand of public discourse gave voice to those connections.[36]

33 Manceron, *Textes de l'époque*, 83; my emphasis.
34 Rousso, *Vichy Syndrome*, 174.
35 Rousso, *Vichy Syndrome*, 88. See Pierre Vidal-Naquet, "Une fidélité têtue. La résistance française à la guerre d'Algérie," *Vingtième siècle. Revue d'histoire* 10 (April–June 1986): 10–13.
36 Franco-Algerian solidarity during this period, as well as links between World War II and the Algerian War, have been examined in Martin Evans, *The Memory of Resistance: French Opposition to the Algerian War (1954–1962)* (Oxford:

Jews as Litmus Test: The Sebbah Dossier

In September 1961, a few days after Yom Kippur, Moïse Sebbah, an Algerian-born Jewish plumber, was walking down the boulevard Barbès in northern Paris when he happened to pass in front of a neighborhood police station. Without provocation, a gendarme posted outside stopped Sebbah, ordered him into the station, searched him, and confiscated his personal effects. For the next two hours, the officers on duty proceeded with a violent interrogation: They accused Sebbah of sending money to the *fellaghas* (Algerian freedom fighters); they questioned his religion (If you are a Jew, they asked, why haven't you gone to Israel?); and, finally, they resorted to physical violence, even placing a revolver against his temple while threatening to execute him. Sebbah was released after spending a few hours in a cell.

Two months later, on October 19, the police again picked up Sebbah. This time, he was waiting to board the 170 bus at the "Quatre-Chemins" stop in Pantin (a suburb that borders Paris to the northeast). It was four o'clock in the afternoon and he was on his way to the St. Denis city hall to register his fourth child, born that very morning. When the paddy wagon pulled up to the bus stop, Sebbah produced his identity card—a document proving his status as an Algerian Jew (or Israelite, in the parlance of the day), and thus as a French citizen. He was nonetheless roughed up, thrown into the vehicle alongside a number of Algerian Muslims who had been arrested earlier, and driven to the police headquarters in the suburb of Aubervilliers. There, all of the Algerians were subjected to beatings; Sebbah's designation as an Israelite, however, earned him special derision from the officers on duty, who greeted him with anti-Semitic jeers and promised him a quick trip to the "four crématoire" (cremation oven).[37]

Sebbah was held in a cell with other Algerians from 4:30 to 9pm, at which point the group was transferred to a police station in Paris's 18th *arrondissement*. At the second station, the entire group was again subjected to physical and verbal violence. However, during a roll call of

---

Berg French Studies, 1997); Daniel Gordon, "Le 17 octobre 1961 et la population française. La collaboration ou la résistance?" in *La guerre d'Algérie revisitée: Nouvelles générations, nouveaux regards*, ed. Aïssa Kadri, Moula Bouaziz, and Tramor Quemeneur (Paris: Karthala, 2015), 339–50.

37   Police archives, HA 110/111. Dossier labeled "4562: Violences contre Algériens. Affaire Moïse Sebbah."

the detainees, the attending officers immediately recognized Sebbah as a Jewish name and singled him out for specifically anti-Semitic abuse. At some point after 9pm, the entire group was driven to a yet another police station near Opéra in central Paris. It was here that a commanding officer took note of Sebbah's status as an Israelite and insisted on his immediate release. The commander recommended, however, that Sebbah spend the night at the police station rather than risk being picked up again. The Jewish plumber must have felt that a night at the police station under the commander's protection was preferable to another round of abuse, and so it wasn't until the morning of October 20 that he would make his way home. Between his arrest at 4pm in Pantin and his late-night arrival at Opéra, a gauntlet that took him quite literally from the margins to the center, Sebbah had been so badly beaten that he would require medical attention and a 21-day disability leave from his job.

For an Algerian living in Paris in October 1961, Moïse Sebbah's story is perhaps an unremarkable one. What makes his story worthy of note, however, and of more than a cursory glance, is that he was not, in fact, Algerian (or an FMA), in the juridical or administrative sense of that designation. A Jew born in Massad (Djelfa commune, Algeria) in 1931, Sebbah was technically a French national: Algerians had been granted French citizenship under the Crémieux Decree.[38] The "Sebbah Affair," which can be reconstructed through documents found in the recently declassified "October 17" archives of the Paris police, is the story of an innocent individual caught in a thicket of state policy at a time when the brambles of race, ethnicity, and nationality were especially dense and unruly. The archival records of Sebbah's complaint against the police and the official response to his allegations are a unique study in the slipperiness of colonial categories, their inherent racism, and the impossibility of patrolling their boundaries while remaining faithful to republican values. More poignantly, perhaps, the police investigator's report offers a rare performance of institutional self-reflection, giving the reader tiny glimmers of self-doubt and of a collective guilty conscience. Finally, although Moïse Sebbah's is the only "Jewish story" in the archives, it is not the sole instance in which statements by and about Jews, and references to Jewish experience, roil the subconscious

---

38   The Crémieux Decree of 1870, which granted French citizenship to Algerian Jews, was abrogated in 1940 under Vichy's anti-Semitic legislation; the statute was reinstated in 1943. Sebbah voluntarily served in the French Army during the war in Indochina.

of October 17. In already turbulent waters, these eddies may have a particular significance, suggesting a place for Jewish stories in the history of an Arab massacre.

Although Sebbah had made no report after his first arrest in September, his second experience at the hands of the police prompted him to file an official complaint demanding compensation not only for his injuries, but also for a valuable wristwatch that had been willfully destroyed. Aided by his brother-in-law, a lawyer named Jacob Attia, Sebbah obtained a medical certificate detailing the nature and gravity of his injuries.[39] Attia also personally wrote to Police Commissioner Maurice Papon to explain Sebbah's status (as an Algerian Jew and a veteran of Indochina), detail the circumstances of his arrest, and request an official interview. On November 8, Papon responded personally; he would not receive Attia himself, but invited Attia and Sebbah to meet with his delegate, at their convenience, at the Prefecture. The brothers-in-law must have done so promptly, for on November 24, in a two-page letter to the Director of Internal Affairs, Papon detailed Sebbah's grievances and made an urgent demand for an official inquest, ending with the following plea: "En raison de la gravité des faits ci-dessus, je vous serais obligé de bien vouloir faire procéder à une enquête approfondie dont les résultats me seront communiqués le plus rapidement possible assortis à des propositions de sanctions que vous estimerez opportun de prendre" (Given the severity of these facts, I request that you proceed with an in-depth investigation of this matter; the results, along with your suggestions for disciplinary action, should be communicated to me as quickly as possible).[40]

The Sebbah File consists of an initial hand-written deposition, a medical certificate, correspondence between Attia and Papon's office, and a 20-page typed report detailing the complaint, the official investigation, the lead officer's analysis of the investigation, and a final summary/order written by Pierre Somveille, Papon's majordomo, articulating the official response to the complaint and ordering that damages be paid to Sebbah. The dossier stands out in the October 17 police archives as the single most copiously documented individual complaint—far more

39 The medical report is signed by Dr. Roland Blotnik, whose offices were located at 28 rue de Rivoli (in the center of Paris).
40 "Note Pour Monsieur le Directeur Inspecteur Général des Services," dated November 24, 1961, signed by Maurice Papon. Police archives, HA 110/111. Dossier "Affaire Sebbah."

substantial than that of Guy Chevalier, a French man from Brittany who was on vacation in Paris when he was caught in cross fire on the *grands boulevards* on October 17 and accidently killed by the police.

In addition to its unusual length, which would tend to suggest that the investigation was taken seriously, the Sebbah File is also remarkably different in tone from other documents in these particular archives. Papon's seemingly unquestioning recognition of the facts and the urgency of his order for an investigation—one that would be not only thorough but fast—are surprising, particularly as compared to a clear tendency (demonstrated in so many other documents contained in the archives) to dismiss victims' complaints.[41] The correspondence not only shows that Papon was quick to order an investigation, but that he did so with a certain preconceived idea that these facts—those presented in the Sebbah case—were of a "gravité" that, we presume, was never imputed to those "versions" of murders reported by the FLN. Moreover, the investigation into Sebbah's grievance was concluded and a lengthy report established within a month of Papon's order.

In addition to these various idiosyncrasies that make the Sebbah File stand out from the archival mass, it is the content and nature of the lengthy investigative report that make the dossier invaluable. Inspector Mignonneau's 20-page narrative establishes the facts of the case as presented by Sebbah and by the officers accused of violence and anti-Semitism.[42] The report then toggles back and forth between the plaintiff's version and that of the accused. In the 15 pages or so that make up this pursuit of the truth, Mignonneau does not miss opportunities to discredit Sebbah, noting for the record that he was *un oisif* (unemployed), which made him naturally suspect; that he wasn't able to identify all of his aggressors by name or by sight; that his physical condition turned out to be better than predicted by the doctor who signed the medical certificate (he started working 10 days after the arrest although the doctors report requested a sick leave of 21 days—a fact that would actually seem to disprove the qualification

41   Although numerous FMA appear to have registered or attempted to register their experiences with law enforcement, there are no dossiers devoted to their "affaires" and no evidence of any follow-up.

42   The Mignonneau report is bound with a cover note signed Le Directeur, Inspecteur Général des services, addressed to Maurice Papon and dated December 26, 1961. Police archives, HA 110/111. Numbers in parentheses refer to the page numbers of the report.

of Sebbah as "oisif"); and that he hadn't bothered to file a complaint upon his first arrest in September. Mignonneau also subtly suggests that Sebbah's decision to spend the night at the police station even after being released was a sign that he was in fact content to have a night away from his family (5).

These elements are used by Mignonneau to undergird his general conclusion that Sebbah's claims of anti-Semitism are not only exaggerated, but are in fact a form of revenge against the police for other humiliations: "Je pense plutôt que, justement indigné du traitement qu'il a subi, il se venge de cette manière sur les gardiens auxquels il eut affaire. Peut-être aussi y a-t-il de sa part l'amertume d'avoir dû passer toute une nuit dans une cellule avec des Musulmans qui, eux, ne manifestent guère de sympathies pour les Israélites" (17, I tend to think that, justly indignant at the way he'd been treated, he is trying to get back at the police officers who abused him. Perhaps he is also bitter about having to spend an entire night in a cell with Muslims, who are not, typically, well-disposed toward the Israelites). Mignonneau goes on to state that Sebbah's stories of anti-Semitic treatment lack credibility because "à l'en croire, tous nos fonctionnaires de police seraient animés de sentiments hostiles à l'égard des Israélites" (17, he makes it sound as though our entire police force were driven by hostile feelings toward Israelites).

Notwithstanding this faulty logic, what is most striking about this document are the lengths to which Mignonneau goes to in order to put questions of anti-Semitism and racism to rest, particularly given the relative lack of concern manifested by the majority of the documents in the police archives. The section in question begins with a somewhat astonishing moment of soul-searching: "Racistes, nos gardiens? Je ne le crois pas" (Could our men be racist? I think not). Mignonneau goes on to offer several types of proof that the police cannot be racist or anti-Semitic: 1) Many police live in the 4th *arrondissement*, which is also the neighborhood where many North African Jews reside, and altercations between the two groups there are rare; 2) no police officer ignores the situation in Algeria and the precarious situation of the Israelite community there, and they all know that Jews are the victims of the FLN just as the police are; and 3) during the days surrounding October 17 and the night in question, no incidents occurred between police and "individuals of the black race," who "n'ont jamais été inquiétés, et ont toujours pu circuler librement, sans même être interpellés" (17–18, have never been bothered, and have always been able to move around freely, without even being stopped).

Of course, none of these statements deny in a convincing way the racism of the police. After all, living in the 4th *arrondissement* and knowing that Jews were often victims of the FLN would not guarantee empathy (even if it were true). And the fact that no blacks were arrested or subjected to harassment during the same period only reinforces the notion of *la chasse au faciès*, since black Africans and Afro-Caribbeans generally do not share a similar phenotype with populations hailing from the Mediterranean basin. The fragility of these justifications is followed by an admission that makes Mignonneau's blithe dismissal of the problem at hand even more perplexing. He concludes, for reasons he can't delve into in the report, that the police, too often victims of FLN assassins, "éprouvaient une animosité certaine à l'égard des ressortissants d'Afrique du nord" (felt a clear animosity toward North Africans.) And he goes on to admit:

> Nos gardiens semblent bien avoir englobé dans la même réprobation tous les natifs d'Afrique du nord, qu'ils soient Algériens, Tunisiens ou Marocains, Israélites ou Musulmans. Il est significatif à cet égard—je crois devoir souligner—que les investigations nécessitées par la plainte de M. Sebbah aient été, dans l'ensemble, assez mal vues du personnel soumis à l'enquête. Pour tous, en effet, le plaignant «est un nord-africain.» (16)

> (Our men seem to have developed a generalized suspicion of all North Africans, be they Algerians, Tunisians, or Moroccans, Israelites or Muslims. It is significant to note—and I believe I must highlight this— that the personnel under investigation in Mr. Sebbah's case were generally annoyed by our questions and the tenor of the inquiry. Indeed, for them, the plaintiff "is a North African.")

This brief moment of lucidity is then drowned in a page of hypothetical, speculative language about whether or not Sebbah did actually declare himself to be Jewish (the arresting officers claim he did not), whether or not it would have been reasonable for the officers to recognize "Moïse Sebbah" as a Jewish name, and whether an identity verification would have been in order even if they had understood that he was not an FMA. Mignonneau's ultimate recommendation is that Sebbah receive compensation (of some undetermined sum); that a note be placed in the personnel file of one of the five police officers accused; and that special instructions be given regarding the interpellation of Algerian Jews. These instructions, notes Mignonneau, could be based on the same orders given in early October with respect to the treatment of Moroccan and Tunisian nationals; after all, "il est en effet parfois assez difficile de les distinguer (les juifs algériens) des autres" (18, it is indeed often fairly difficult to tell the difference between Algerian Jews and other [North Africans]).

By February 14, 1962, the investigation had been concluded and Somveille issued a memo ordering the claims division to compensate Sebbah for damages in an amount that would indemnify him materially (ostensibly for the loss of his watch) and psychologically.[43] As far as sanctions against the police officers are concerned, Somveille's conclusions are lost in a hypothetical bureaucratic double-speak: there are no clear orders to sanction any of the individuals cited in the report on the investigation. Moreover, Mignonneau's suggestion that the police commissioner issue special instructions for dealing with "North African Israelites" is rejected. In a handwritten comment in the margins, Papon (presumably) asks: "à quoi bon une note de plus? Cette affaire prouve bien que les vérifications ont été faites avec une certaine légèreté. Les instructions n'y changeront rien" (why bother with yet another memo? This case proves that the identity checks were not done rigorously. Instructions won't change anything).

Mignonneau's report on Sebbah's complaint may be the closest the October 17 archives come to offering up real detail not only about police attitudes and policies, but about their awareness of the legal and ethical minefield in which they were maneuvering. While the dossier concerns only a single individual, and not the 200 souls who were lost on October 17, it does offer incontrovertible evidence of racial profiling. Mignonneau's report is also unique in its willingness to interrogate its own bias, even if its conclusions remain ambiguous at best.

But we might also ponder why a single Jew merited a 20-page report while so many complaints by FMA were dismissed wholesale as fabrications, and while some 200 Algerian Muslims still remain lost to official history. Do Papon's urgency and Mignonneau's report in fact suggest a special attitude with respect to Jews? Is it conceivable that Papon—subconsciously haunted by his crimes during World War II while Chief of Police in Bordeaux—seeks to offer up a revisionist narrative of his own anti-Semitism? In 1961, does the Jew activate the French state's guilty conscience?

Those calling for state transparency and better access to the October 17 archives likely do not have the Sebbah File in mind. And we too should also wonder about the stakes and payoffs of foregrounding such an idiosyncratic dossier, and even of suggesting that October 17 might be fruitfully

---

43   The amount awarded is not identified in any of the documents.

read in light of its Jewish content. Yet the entanglements laid bare in Sebbah's story prompt us to contemplate the ways French colonial policy played out in Paris, and the file itself reveals a state grappling, however cautiously and clumsily, with its own contradictions. Colonial categories, as defined and policed in the colonies, were already in violent discord with republican values. Kept at a remove from the mainland, however, this aporia remained tucked away in the nation's blind spot. Brought to the *métropole* and practiced on the ground, in the capital, before the eyes of the people, such forms of discrimination could not but create a jarring dissonance within a generally accepted narrative of a color-blind republic. For all that, the Sebbah File remains a detail in the larger tableau of October 17 and the Algerian War, in its staging of an explicit negotiation between the state and an Algerian Jew, and also casts an implicit sidelong glance at the state's treatment of its Algerian Muslim subjects.

On Papon: Speculative Fiction and Revenge Fantasy

The "dangerous parallels" articulated in the anarchive did not originate with Daeninckx's *Meurtres*. We would do well to remember the similar equivalency created by Panijel in 1962, at the end of *Octobre à Paris*, when he drew a direct line between the treatment of Jews 20 years prior and the contemporary abuse of Algerians. More to the point, however rogue later anarchival productions may appear in their representation of the links between October 17 and the Vichy period, a careful reading of the archive tells us that the perilous nature of such comparisons lies not in their creation in fiction, but in their existence in fact.

Certainly, the frequency of allusions to World War II, the Holocaust, or Vichy in October 17 fiction can be partially explained by the fact that the anarchive is invested in recovering and narrativizing historical material. There are numerous ways in which the actual histories of World War II and October 17 intermingle, even if the two events share no temporal common ground. One obvious point of entanglement is the recurring role of Maurice Papon. From 1942 to 1944, Papon served as Secretary General of the Gironde region and supervisor of its Service for Jewish Questions. During this time, he was responsible for the deportation of some 1600 French Jews from Bordeaux to the transit camp at Drancy, from where most were conveyed to Auschwitz.[44] In

44   Named Secretary General of the Gironde on June 1, 1942 (the area with

1958, after occupying various positions in the colonial administration of Morocco and Algeria, Papon served as Paris Police Chief from 1958 to 1967, a period that coincided with the escalation of the Algerian War and the opening of a second front in the *métropole*. It was in this role that Papon enacted measures (including the notorious curfew) to control and monitor the Algerian population living in and around Paris.[45] As Max Silverman has observed, the "extraordinary career of Papon [...] demonstrates the ways in which the same administrative practices of surveillance, classification, round-up, deportation and violence [...] circulated freely between France and the colonies and between the Nazi and colonial eras."[46]

Papon's story, and his role as a recidivist perpetrator, would become a matter of public interest in 1981, when the French satirical newspaper *Le Canard enchaîné* published evidence of his participation in the deportation of Jews from the Gironde (with a brief mention of the October 17 repression). The article ignited two decades of episodic legal proceedings that revolved around Papon's culpability for acts committed under Vichy and would culminate in 1998 with a guilty verdict.[47] Yet it was only at the end of the trial, in 1997, that Papon's role in October 17 would enter the legal record and, to a certain extent, the court of public opinion. When historian Jean-Luc Einaudi provided testimony on Papon's actions during October 1961, the Police Chief sued the historian for slander, touching off a period of intense media and political attention, and forcing October 17 to the surface of public

---

the second highest concentration of Jews after Paris), Papon presided over the Bordeaux roundups of July 15–16, 1942. Over the course of his two years as a highly placed civil servant in the Gironde, 12 convoys would relay nearly 1600 Jews from Bordeaux to Drancy, to Auschwitz. After the war, Papon held administrative posts in North Africa, both in Morocco (1954–55) as Secretary General of the Protectorate and then in Constantine, Algeria, from 1956 to 1958—years that marked the beginning of the Algerian War of Independence. In 1958, he was named Chief of Police in Paris, a position he held until 1967, and of course the post from which he presided over a long-term repression of Algerians' rights, culminating in the violence perpetrated by his forces on October 17.

45   For a detailed study on policing during this era, see E. Blanchard, *La police parisienne et les Algériens* and Amiri, *La bataille de France*.

46   Silverman, 15. See also House and MacMaster, 34, on the failure of historians to note similarities between techniques used under Vichy and during the Algerian War.

47   See Chapter 1, pp. 40–41 and 49–51.

consciousness in a way that Papon undoubtedly had not intended. Nonetheless, up to his death in 2007, the former prefect would never be officially charged for his responsibility in the Algerian massacre.

In the anarchive, the figure of Papon has loomed large since the early 1980s. Although few of these works explicitly mention his Vichy past, Papon may be understood as the primary vehicle through which allusions to World War II, Vichy, and the Holocaust are mobilized. This is particularly salient in a number of recent works that produce detailed representations of the chief of police at the time of the October events. As we observed in the previous chapter, Alain Tasma's 2005 film *Nuit noire*, a docudrama that focuses exclusively on the events of October 1961, features an exchange between Papon and his chief of staff, Pierre Somveille, in which they discuss the ramifications of the curfew. Similarly, in Eric Michel's *Algérie, Algérie!*, we find a conversation between Papon and his right-hand man that represents the Police Chief as being aware of the racial implications of his measures. The film and the novel both situate their critique of Papon at the moment of policy making rather than at the scene of its enforcement, revealing a calculating, intentional Papon. By staging his lucidity with respect to the stakes of his curfew, these representations serve to indict him, however tacitly, for his willingness to compromise republican values.[48]

In Natacha Michel's 2013 novel *Plein présent*, also set at the time of the events in October 61, a French character named Marianne witnesses the violence on October 17. Several weeks later, her friend Romain, a history student at the Sorbonne, upbraids her for not knowing more about the aftermath of the repression:

> Je t'ai dit, il suffit de savoir lire les journaux [...] J'applique la méthode historique en temps de disette: tu te réfères aux archives, mais tu croises les pleins et les vides et même les déliés [...] Rien qu'avec ça tu peux voir qu'en s'en donnant la peine on peut savoir. Et aussi sans s'en donner la peine. Tout le monde en cause du 17 octobre [...] En tout cas Claude Bourdet [...] membre du Conseil national de la résistance [...] et élu de l'Union de la gauche socialiste au conseil de Paris, il a interpelé Papon pas plus tard que le 27 octobre [...] et pas avec des gants blancs. (183–84)

> (I told you, all you have to do is read the newspapers [...] I'm applying the historical method in an information vacuum: you check the archives, but you have to read between the lines, crosscheck everything [...] That alone shows that with a bit of effort it is possible

48   See Chapter 5, pp. 257–59.

to know. But it's also possible without effort. Everyone's talking about October 17 [...] Claude Bourdet [...] member of the National Council of the Resistance [...] and elected member of Union of the Socialists to the Paris Council, he called out Papon as early as October 27 [...] and he didn't pull any punches...

Although Papon is not embodied in this scene, Romain's knowledge of Bourdet's appeal—which is indeed a historical fact of which there exists a published record—provides a twist on the critique of Papon: the text not only suggests that his methods were questioned at the time, but by asserting that one had only to know what to read and how to read between the lines, the novel subtly inculpates a French public that would later claim ignorance.

As "classic" historical fictions in a realist mode, these three texts emphasize referentiality and the factual through their allusions to archival material and realia. Moreover, they all name Papon explicitly (which is not always the case in the anarchive). None of the aforementioned works, however, refer directly to Papon's role in the deportation of French Jews. This absence can be partially attributed to the texts' investment in historical accuracy: In late 1961, after all, Papon's actions in Bordeaux may not have been common knowledge. I would argue, however, that any representation of Papon in fictions produced after 1998 is inherently freighted with the historical, political, and cultural baggage of the *affaire Papon*. Whether we understand "Papon" as a kind of metonym for "Vichy perpetrator" or even for state violence, or whether we understand representations of his October 17 activities as implicitly dis-narrating his Vichy activities, representations of Papon are necessarily encumbered by his Vichy past. The unspoken in *Nuit noire, Algérie Algérie,* and *Plein présent* banks on the reader's capacity to activate the historical connections between the Holocaust and October 17.

Yet not all references to Papon are equally imbued with such reality effects. From the very beginning of the *affaire* and up to the present, October 17 fictions have indulged in speculation and revenge fantasy, leveraging the figure of Papon as an occasion for creative and cathartic rewritings of certain historical details. This is certainly the case for the much-discussed *Meurtres pour mémoire,* in which the fictional Papon (André Veillut) is assassinated, foreshadowing the prefect's ultimate political demise. But even after the Papon *affaire* came to an end, third-wave anarchival works such as Aziz Chouaki's *La Pomme et le couteau* (2011) continued to imagine a comeuppance for the former prefect. The play's ten brief scenes are set at the time of the October events. In the eighth scene, a journalist named Sylvie interviews Papon in his office just a few days after the signing of the curfew. Over the course of a conversation in which Papon makes unwanted sexual advances, compares Algerians to termites, and gives free quarter to his racial theories, the journalist becomes frustrated and abandons her line of inquiry. As Sylvie takes her leave, she turns to Papon to ask if he knows Martin Niemöller and the poem he wrote in Dachau in 1942. When the prefect professes his ignorance, Sylvie recites it for him, modifying the penultimate line to drive home her point:

> Quand ils sont venus chercher des communistes,
> je n'ai rien dit, je n'étais pas communiste.
> [...]
> Quand ils sont venus chercher les juifs,
> je n'ai rien dit, je n'étais pas juif
> [...]
> Quand ils sont venus chercher les Algériens,
> je n'ai rien dit, je n'étais pas Algérien.
>
> «Celui-là je l'ai rajouté.»
>
> Puis il sont venus me chercher et il restait personne pour protester.[49]
>
> (First they came for the communists,
> and I did not speak out, because I was not a communist.
> [...]

49   Chouaki, 49. The work and its author are in fact real: Martin Niemöller (1892–1984) was a Lutheran pastor and an outspoken critic of Adolf Hitler who spent seven years in concentration camps. The text in question is in fact a modified version of a poem Niemöller read at lectures, varying the content depending on his audience, inserting "Trade Unionists" or "Socialists" as the context demanded. According to Harold Marcuse, "Although Niemöller told the story behind the poetic version of this quotation many times over the years from 1946 to 1979, even after exhaustive researching I could find NO printed document indicating his exact words. In those many narrative (non-repeating, non-poetic) retellings he varied some of the groups, but he always included Communists and almost always Jews, and he always ended with 'me.' In the first documented use of the poetic version, in 1955, he included 'the Catholics,' but that was very likely a unique situation, and he never included them in any other version we know of." Harold Marcuse, "Niemoeller Quotation Page," September 12, 2000, http://www.history.ucsb.edu/faculty/marcuse/niem.htm.

Then they came for the Jews,
and I did not speak out, because I was not a Jew.
[...]
Then they came for the Algerians,
and I did not speak out, because I was not Algerian.

"I added that line."

Then they came for me, and there was no one left to speak out for me.)

A limpid plea for identification and empathy, Sylvie's appropriation of Niemöller's words adds "Algerians" to a list of historically persecuted groups, including Jews and communists. *La Pomme et le couteau* thus uses real elements (Papon and a well-known statement by a fervent anti-fascist) in a surrealist staging in order to fantasize about catharsis: The Niemöller citation highlights the common predicament of persecuted peoples, and Sylvie's citation of it boldly holds a mirror up to this fictionalized Papon, forcing him to recognize the continuity of his actions. Without explicitly mentioning Papon's past, this imagined act of retaliation reminds the reader of his role in the deportation of Jews, and inscribes October 17 in a continuum of crimes against humanity.

A final example of a third-wave reboot of the Papon story offers a twist on the genre of revenge fantasy. Rachid Bouchareb's 2010 historical fiction film *Hors-la-loi* is in many ways a continuation of the Algerian saga the director began with *Indigènes*, a historical drama about the "soldiers of the Empire"—the approximately 1.5 million African men pressed into service to liberate France during World War II. *Hors-la-loi* picks up where the first film left off. Beginning in 1945 with the Sétif massacre, concentrated in France during the Algerian War of Independence, and ending on the night of October 17, 1961, the film traces the various political engagements of three brothers who make their way from Algeria to the Nanterre *bidonville*.[50] One of the brothers, Abdelkader, emerges as a leading figure in the FF-FLN. On October 17, as he is rallying the Algerians in preparation for the peaceful protest on October 17, he tells them: "Pour un coup reçu, nous en porterons dix" (For every blow received, we will dole out ten).

---

50   Even before it opened at the 2010 Cannes Film Festival, *Hors-la-loi* was the subject of heated protest; it was labeled anti-French and accused of playing fast and loose with historical facts.

While Papon does not appear in the film, this phrase is enough—for those well versed in the history of October 17—to conjure the presence of the prefect. Papon pronounced this line publicly on October 2, 1961, in the courtyard of the Prefecture, at a ceremony to mark the death of a police officer felled by the FLN.[51] The phrase itself, in its proper context, has been amply redeployed within the anarchive, in films (such as *Nuit noire*, for example) that hew as closely as possible to historical reality. In *Hors-la-loi*, the use of the phrase by a senior FLN cadre is no historical mistake; indeed, we might call it an act of *détournement*, or appropriation. Of course, the protest on October 17 was a peaceful one. In accordance with the film's historical imperatives, it makes no sense to suggest that Algerian protesters would have been exhorted to violence, nor would retaliatory rhetoric have been the word of the day. But the recuperation of Papon's line by the aptly named FLN leader Abedelkader (Abdelkader was a nineteenth-century Algerian freedom fighter and politician, considered the symbol of the combat against French domination) has the effect of both appropriating Papon's power and reinvesting the threat with new meaning. In *Hors-la-loi*, Papon is evoked only to be symbolically eviscerated, his rhetorical flourish resignified in the mouth of his enemy.

The Holocaust Survivor as Trope

In the anarchive, Papon—functioning as both historical actor and powerful signifier—keeps Vichy and the Holocaust in play, underscoring both the factual and the ethical entanglements of these inglorious pasts. But Papon is not the only means by which October 17 fictions allude to Vichy or World War II. Works in the anarchive also imagine fictional Holocaust survivors who interact with Algerian victims on October 17 or, in one case, with descendants of Algerian victims. This inclusion might be read as a bid to create historical and ethical equivalencies between October 17 and the Shoah, and to prompt readers to consider a continuity of "state terror," but it might also be understood as a troping

---

51   At about the same time, Papon made a series of similar comments indicating to his forces that they had carte blanche in their dealings with Algerians. He is reported to have said "réglez vos affaires avec les Algériens vous-mêmes, vous êtes couverts" (deal with the Algerians as you see fit, you will be covered). Brunet, *Police contre FLN*, 89.

mechanism. In October 17 fictions, the figure of the Holocaust survivor provides a means by which to negotiate the possibility of cross-cultural and interfaith empathy. These works, ranging across the three waves of the anarchive, envision quite different outcomes for their variously staged encounters.

In the previous chapter, I discussed the trans-Atlantic entangling of black American and Algerian experiences of racism in William Gardner Smith's 1963 novel *The Stone Face*. Through the figure of Maria— Simeon's love interest, a Polish Jew, and a Holocaust survivor—the story incorporates a third history of oppression, focalized through Maria's devastating sexual abuse at the hands of a German officer and the eventual murder of her parents. Despite Simeon's attraction to Maria's "turbulent, somber passion" (44) and their shared predicament involving vision (Simeon lost an eye in a childhood fight with a racist boy; Maria's eyesight is failing and she requires an operation), Simeon had found Maria impossible to "grasp" prior to her revelation about the past. She was a woman who "did not understand him and whom he did not understand" (69). Yet her story, in all its horror, activates a deep sense of empathy in Simeon, and when she finishes recounting it, he revises his feelings: "Perhaps they could understand each other, after all" (78).

Simeon's sense of connection to Maria—notwithstanding his awareness that "many Negroes disliked Jews" (126)—alongside his burgeoning solidarity with the Algerians he meets in Paris, seems to point to the potential for a multi-directional ethnic empathy. But this happy triangulation is foiled when Maria meets Ben Youssef and Hossein (two Algerians Simeon has befriended) and the men engage in an extended anti-Semitic tirade. The scene ultimately has more to do with historical narratives of enmity between Arabs and Jews (just as Simeon's later reflections speak to a certain construction of Jews as "part of the majoritarian tradition"[52]) than with World War II or with Maria as a Holocaust survivor. Rothberg has read the Maria character as making Jewishness in *The Stone Face* an "explicit, if ambivalent presence," one that is eventually disappeared from the novel (Maria leaves Simeon to pursue an acting career in Hollywood) in a gesture that "marks the marginalization of the Nazi genocide."[53]

---

52 Bryan Cheyette, *Diasporas of the Mind: Jewish and Postcolonial Writing and the Nightmare of History* (New Haven, CT: Yale University Press, 2014), 4.
53 Rothberg, 259–61.

There is good reason to read *The Stone Face* as bracketing off the Holocaust, and perhaps Jews more generally. That Maria and Simeon are of different races and religions is never at issue in their relationship; however, even as Simeon tries to counter Hossein's anti-Semitic diatribe, telling him, "The Jews are persecuted as much as we are" (123), he also, in private reflection, explores what we might call a minor transnational anti-Semitism, noting that there was a reason why black Americans disliked Jews: "The Jews, discriminated against in the white society, were often left with the crumbs—the real estate and stores in Negro neighborhoods. They were therefore the most visible exploiters of the American Negroes, and detested by many Negroes because of this. The same must be true in North Africa. But how could he explain this to Hossein?" (126).

If it seems true that *The Stone Face* is far more interested in staging conversations that highlight trans-Atlantic solidarities and antagonisms than in a thoroughgoing exploration of how Jews fit into the picture, I am less certain that the novel's marginalization of the Holocaust constitutes an ethical or a political shortcoming. What strikes me as interesting, in a book written so soon after the events of October 1961 and, in many ways, still fairly soon after the Holocaust, is the way in which it seems to be struggling—in the figure of Simeon—with the destabilization of received ideas about oppressors and the oppressed. Simeon's "reasonable" understanding of black Americans' hatred of Jews in the United States collides with his vision of Maria, a European Jew, a victim and survivor of the Holocaust, and these opposing narratives have no logical resolution in his mind—or in the novel, for that matter. Maria's departure from Simeon's life and from the plot certainly removes the Holocaust from the story (as Rothberg has argued). Yet we might do well to marvel at its inclusion in the first place. *The Stone Face*, after all, could have completely elided this historical detail but chose instead to engage it. To focus on Maria's exit from the story may risk glossing over the important, if unresolved, work her character performs.

Regardless of how we read the treatment of Maria in *The Stone Face*, these details take on a new luster when read alongside a similar—but more narratively jarring—bracketing of the Holocaust in Nacer Kettane's 1985 novel. *Le Sourire de Brahim* is not about the relationship between October 17 and Vichy (or World War II), but neither is it a book lacking in historical consciousness. References to real moments of historical suffering and to contemporaneous political issues create a broad referential web: A brief mention of an old cobbler named Aram, for example, reminds readers of the Armenian genocide of 1915 and France's role in harboring refugees from that conflict; likewise, a series of episodes that bring Brahim into contact with pro-Palestinian activists suggests a transnational comparison between postcolonial France and the Middle East conflicts of the 1980s that would come to a head in the First Intifada (1987–93).[54]

The novel does, however, mobilize references to World War II and the Holocaust through characters and allusions, and the first reference in the text appears while Brahim is marching behind his parents on October 17, in a scene we have already examined in the context of our discussion of race and October 17 (in Chapter 5).[55] The narration draws an analogy between the profiling and terror to which Algerians had been subjected in the previous months and the occupation of France during World War II, with groups of four or five men in tight formation, wearing "leurs grosses bottes noires montant jusque dessous le genou, rappelant un autre temps où certains uniformes hantaient la France" (big black boots that went up to their knees, boots that brought to mind another time when France was haunted by certain uniforms). The image of these men, the narrator goes on to note, was tantamount to "une scène de chasse en banlieue revue et corrigée par le tenant d'un nouvel ordre" (11–12, a hunting scene in the projects, revised and corrected by the new guard). The notion of a "hunting scene in the projects" speaks more directly to the context of the novel's publication (the mid-1980s, when police violence in the French suburbs was particularly violent) than to the historical context described. As such, however, it nonetheless pulls together three historical strands: "certain uniforms" is a barely veiled reference to Nazi soldiers and the French police, which connects the fascism of World War II to the police violence of 1961 Paris, and also to that of the mid-1980s. Moreover, the third-person narration allows this historical linkage: Brahim, a young boy in 1961, would not have remembered a time when other uniforms "haunted" France, nor could he know, already, about a "hunting scene in the projects."

Just as October 17 makes no other explicit appearance in the text, neither does World War II, other than a brief mention that Brahim's father served in the French Army during World War II and had stayed

---

54 See Olivia Harrison's discussion of "Palestine as metaphor" and the transcolonial in her introduction to *Transcolonial Maghreb: Imagining Palestine in the Era of Decolonization* (Stanford, CA: Stanford University Press, 2016), 1–16.

55 See Chapter 5, pages 254–55.

on in France after being demobilized. However, the novel makes a significant bid for inter-religious empathy through the story of Brahim's love affair with Sophie Rosenberg, the daughter of Jews from Poland who had fled pogroms and been welcomed into the secular bosom of France (61). Their intense courtship, which lasts only a few pages, is focused on their shared difference in French society: both reject ham-and-cheese sandwiches; both come from immigrant families; both want to be French but without losing the connection to their origins. Sophie carries around an old Palestinian coin with Arabic and Hebrew writing on it, a keepsake her uncle gave to her mother just before he was deported to Treblinka (62); Brahim has a special *burnous,* woven by his mother in Kabylia that kept him warm as a child.

But the intense love and inter-religious identification that Brahim and Sophie enjoy—an incarnation of that old Palestinian coin—is short lived. The novel gives no indication of the actual passage of time, but just a few pages after their meeting, their idyll is shattered. In a scene that recalls the courtyard of Parisian police headquarters on October 17, 1961, where the police bludgeoned Algerian protesters under the symbolic eye of the state and far from the reproachful gaze of the street, Brahim, Sophie, and several other classmates are attacked in the courtyard of their high school by a group of neo-Nazis. Harking back to its descriptions of Nazis from the first chapter, the text details their "leather jackets" and their "shaved heads." One of their friends insults the horde, calling them "petits nazillons merdeux," shitty little Nazi-wannabes. The description of the attack also mirrors descriptions of October 17: the "nazillons continuaient à charger, tout en courant et tapaient dans tous les sens" (66, the Nazi-wannabes kept coming at us, running and hitting everything in sight).

Sophie is left paralyzed by the brutal violence. The cruel details are handled quickly in the novel and narrative time is compressed. Within a page of the attack, nearly six months have passed:

> Voilà bientôt deux saisons que Brahim emmenait Sophie dans son fauteuil roulant sur les chemins forestiers. Presque tous les weekends il la sortait et passait des heures entières à lui raconter des histoires. Mais elle lui répondait à peine, en hochant la tête. Il lui rappelait les bons moments passés ensemble. [...] Une fois il avait presque souri...(67–68)

> (For nearly two seasons now, Brahim has been taking Sophie on the forest paths, in her wheelchair. He took her out almost every weekend and spent hours telling her stories. But she barely responded, only nodding

her head. He reminded her of all the good times they'd had together. [...]
One time, he nearly smiled...)

What seems to be a narrative bid to represent interfaith tolerance and even mixity is cut short not only by the cruel deeds of the *nazillons*, but also by the narration. For this image of Sophie, voiceless and in a wheelchair, is the last image we have of her. Brahim never sees her again; she and their relationship disappear from the text altogether.

The introduction and relatively rapid deletion of Sophie from the text is somewhat reminiscent of Maria's fate in *The Stone Face*. Like Maria, Kettane's Sophie in *Le Sourire de Brahim* embodies an analogous "explicit yet ambivalent" presence. Comparatively, however, Maria's exit from *The Stone Face* is narratively motivated by the aspiring actress's departure for Hollywood, making that novel's "turn away" from her (and from Jewishness) perhaps less strange and less symbolic than the one we observe in *Le Sourire de Brahim*, in which Sophie simply evaporates from the plot with no explanation. Furthermore, because Brahim will go on to have relationships with several young women who, like him, were born in France to Algerian parents, and because these characters are portrayed as politically conscious, we might also observe that Sophie is neatly erased to make way for a certain political vision, just as Maria is "replaced" by two Algerian mujahedeen *in The Stone Face*.[56]

But a critical difference in the way the two novels treat their female Jewish characters is that Sophie is not the sole means for evoking Jewishness in *Le Sourire de Brahim*, a fact that allows the novel to produce a more complex portrait of inter-ethnic negotiations. Within a context of young love and love at first sight, the interfaith empathy experienced by Brahim and Sophie is figured as pure and innocent, the stuff of fairy tales and no match for real-world intolerance. Moreover, it is politically naïve. Just a few episodes after Brahim and Sophie meet, Brahim witnesses a heated encounter between a student named Davide (referred to by another character as "une especè de sionist," or a Zionist pig), and a pro-Palestinian student. Davide is tearing down a Palestinian flag, a gesture that provokes a tirade; "barre-toi espèce de sioniste" (fuck

---

56 Rothberg, 259–60. The notion that Maria is "replaced" by two Algerian revolutionary fighters is tenuous. It is true that Simeon is introduced to two women whose stories impress him for their bravery and their commitment to a cause. But he does not become romantically involved with either one, and neither is described in as much psychological detail as Maria.

off Zionist pig, threatens the pro-Palestinian student), "Vous êtes en train de génocider un people" (You are genociding a whole people).[57] Davide responds, "Génocide? Tu ne sais même pas de quoi tu parles. Moi oui; six millions de juifs qu'on a exterminés" (Genocide? You don't know what you're talking about. I do: six million Jews who were exterminated). The altercation provokes a reflection in Brahim:

> Brahim ne comprenait pas cette rage de certains juifs de la diaspora. Pour lui, un enfant palestinien orphelin ressemblait à tous les orphelins du monde. Rien ne pouvait justifier cette machine de guerre infernale qui tentait de faire de chaque palestinien un terroriste aux yeux de l'Occident bien-pensant, qui en d'autres temps avait réglé comme du papier à musique un autre génocide. Brahim se sentait concerné par ce non-sens de l'histoire. (76)

> (Brahim did not understand this rage in some Jews of the diaspora. For him, an orphaned Palestinian child was like all the orphans in the world. Nothing could justify this infernal war machine that tried to make every Palestinian into a terrorist in the eyes of the self-righteous West, who, in other times, had organized another genocide like clockwork. Brahim felt implicated in this non-sense of history.)

The text's overall tone of tolerance and its general bid for understanding make it difficult to read the demise of Sophie as a rejection of Jews or even as a marginalization of the Holocaust, particularly as Brahim links the situation in Palestine to the Holocaust, pointing a finger at, simply, "the West." Yet there is, just as we observed in *The Stone Face*, a bracketing of certain histories: Kettane's novel is ultimately less concerned with the past than with the present, notwithstanding the sustained haunting of the text by October 17. In light of other events that transpire in *Le Sourire de Brahim*, the turn away from—or abandonment of—Sophie reads less like a failure of empathy and more like a cautionary tale about the difficult work required to create the conditions in which empathy can survive. The novel clearly provides a vision of Jews and Muslims united in their common victimhood at the hands of state fascism, and the critiques it does evince are fairly even-handed: in his ruminations about Zionism, Brahim does not lump together all Jews in France. But the text does suggest that in the mid-1980s, at a moment when memories of the Holocaust and Vichy collaboration were beginning to "break the

57 My translation maintains the French version's non-idiomatic transformation of the word "genocide" into a verb.

mirror" (to borrow Rousso's expression for the period when repressed memories of Vichy returned in an enduring way) and the children of colonialism were just beginning to emerge in the public sphere (as their parents did on October 17), the conditions may not yet have been ripe for interfaith empathy to live out in the open.[58]

This historically and politically sited reading of *Le Sourire de Brahim* should not be understood as the ascription of a political *telos* to the representation of World War II, France's Vichy past, and empathy in October 17 fictions. Examples from the third wave of the anarchive feature Jewish characters who, even when minor, evince significantly more agency than Sophie. Moreover, these characters, all Holocaust survivors, have different reactions to October 17 and different abilities to connect their own experience with the events of the moment.

In *Les fantômes d'octobre*, a young adult novel by Algerian writer Ahmed Kalouaz (2011), the character of the Holocaust survivor is a small detail.[59] When police bullets begin to fly on October 17, an Algerian named Akli finds shelter in an apartment building and rings a doorbell at random, hoping for refuge. The door opens to reveal an elderly gentleman who immediately recognizes Akli as Algerian and understands his predicament: "Ne craignez rien," the man tells Akli. "Je m'appelle Nathanaël Zitoun, je sais ce que la police a fait de nous en juillet 1942. J'ai échappé à la rafle. Soyez la bienvenue" (97, Don't be afraid. My name is Nathanaël Zitoun, I know what the police did with us in July 1942. I escaped the roundup. You are welcome here). In this very brief sequence, the elderly Parisian Jew with the unmistakably Sephardic name articulates a connection between the anti-Jewish measures in place during World War II (which crystalized in the 1942 Vél d'Hiv roundup to which Zitoun refers) and the anti-Algerian politics of 1961, to which he bears witness. Zitoun's identification thus has clear ethical and political implications.

If identification begets empathy and even righteous action in *Les fantômes d'octobre*, in French author Michel Piquemal's "Le bon

---

58 Rousso's "broken mirror" phrase corresponds to 1972–80. See *Vichy Syndrome*, Chapter 3.

59 Kalouaz has more than 40 titles to his name, yet he is perhaps best known for another novel about a racist murder: *Point kilométrique 190* (Paris: L'Harmattan 1986) recounts the brutal murder in 1983 of Algerian tourist Habib Grimzi. Grimzi was traveling by train from Bordeaux when he was accosted by three men and thrown from the train. The crime took place during *La Marche des beurs* (the March for Equality and Against Racism) and has generally been considered a racially motivated hate crime.

samaritain" (The good Samaritan, 2011), cross-cultural connections are short-circuited and empathy fails.[60] The ten-page short story is structured as a framed tale; it opens in a confessional with a young French doctor, Henri, wracked with guilt over a professional and moral mistake. Several weeks prior, on October 17, 1961, a wounded Algerian, visibly in need of medical attention, had been left at his front door. Motivated by his professional code, the doctor treats the Algerian, Ahmid, who asks Henri to call his FLN contacts to come retrieve him. Henri's wife, Rachel, begs Henri not to get involved, pointing out that Ahmid is clearly an Algerian demonstrator, that demonstrations are forbidden, and that Henri would be preventing the police from doing their job. Henri explains Rachel's reaction to the priest:

> Il faut la comprendre. Elle est d'origine juive. Ses parents ont été raflés et menés à Drancy. Seul son père en est revenu. Depuis la fin de la guerre, Rachel n'aspire qu'à une vie tranquille. Elle n'aime pas les débordements. [...] Je n'osai pas lui rappeler que c'était cette même police française qui avait arrêté ses parents en juillet 1942... Je la savais si fragile sur ce sujet-là. Nous n'en parlions pratiquement jamais. Rachel avait décidé de tout oublier. (176, 179)

> (You have to understand her. She's of Jewish descent. Her parents were rounded up and taken to Drancy. Only her father came back. Since the end of the war, all Rachel wants is a quiet life. She doesn't like things to get out of line. [...] I didn't dare remind her that it was the same French police that had arrested her parents in July 1942... I knew it was a sensitive subject for her. We hardly ever talked about it. Rachel had decided to forget it all.)

Acquiescing before his wife's fears, Henri abandons the idea of calling the FLN contact and instead calls a superior on the Medical Board to ask for advice, evoking his deontological ethics and the biblical story of the good Samaritan. Utterly unsympathetic to both the Algerian cause and Henri's moral bind, the mentor takes matters into his own hands and sends the police to arrest Ahmid. The story returns to the present tense of the confessional, where Henri explains that he had stumbled upon a photo of Ahmid in the newspaper, with a caption stating that the Algerian had been "repêché dans la Seine [...] les

60 Piquemal is a prolific and award-winning YA writer whose work has not traditionally focused on postcolonial themes, although the fate of American Indians is a recurring theme throughout his writing. His short story appears in the commemorative volume *17 octobre 1961, 17 écrivains se souviennent*, 173–84.

mains attachés dans le dos avec du fil de fer barbelé" (182, fished out of the Seine [...], his hands tied behind his back with razor wire). Henri feels that his actions led directly to Ahmid's murder. Like the medical board mentor, however, the priest is not swayed by Henri's ethical conundrum; he gives the doctor both spiritual and political absolution: "Vous le savez, de Gaulle va bientôt signer les accords de paix. C'est une question de jours. Tout cela sera bientôt du passé. Vous n'êtes pas responsable" (182, You know that de Gaulle is about to sign the peace treaty. It's a matter of days. All this will soon be in the past. You are not responsible).

In this brief story, interfaith empathy fails at several levels. Unlike Zitoun in *Les fantômes d'octobre*, who readily sublimates his trauma, Rachel cannot identify with the Algerian running for his life. Or rather, it is a misidentification that takes place: She understands all too well what it means to be a victim of state terror, and she fears attracting the attention of the police. Henri, who sees a connection between the Vél d'Hiv roundup of Jews and the treatment of Algerians in 1961, is animated by a sense of Christian and professional duty, but ultimately decides to heed his wife's (and his mentor's) advice. Both the priest and Henri's mentor minimize the doctor's sense of moral and professional duty; their complacency serves to indict the apathetic bystanders of October 17. And the text itself is extremely critical of its titular "good Samaritan," ending on an ironic note: "Le docteur sentit dans son coeur une onde de soulagement et un étrange bien être. Il allait pouvoir tourner la page, oublier le visage tuméfié de l'Algérien...Et Dieu l'avait absous!" (183, The doctor felt a wave of relief in his heart and an odd feeling of well-being. He was going to be able to turn the page, to forget the swollen face of the Algerian...And God had given him absolution!).

Through the fictionalized figure of the Holocaust survivor, these works point up the knot of affective entanglements between the Holocaust and October 17. But such representations have dramatically different ramifications in *Fantômes* and *Le bon Samaritan*. While the former revels—however fleetingly—in the possibility of solidarity, the latter suggests how difficult such negotiations might be. And indeed, if intersubjective empathy fails in *Le bon Samaritain*, the actions of Henri's mentor and the priest's hearty absolution suggest that grave failures of empathy are also situated at the institutional level: The very establishments one might reasonably expect to value the sanctity of human life—medicine and the church (embodied by the doctor on the medical board and the priest, respectively)—are revealed as hypocritical.

The Holocaust survivor plays a leading role in *Le professeur de musique* (The Music Teacher), another young adult novel published in 1997 by the prolific Franco-Israeli writer Yaël Hassan. The drama of *Le professeur de musique* turns on the shared traumatic pasts of the titular *prof de musique*, Simon Klein, and his *beur* student, Malik Choukri.[61] Malik wants to learn to play the violin because his grandfather was an Algerian violinist who was killed during what the text vaguely represents as the repression of October 17, 1961. The family recovered the grandfather's violin, but never his body. Out of superstition, Malik's mother forbade him from learning to play the instrument, claiming "c'était le violon qui l'avait tué!" (46, it was the violin that killed him!). Malik dreams of sublimating the trauma of his grandfather's loss, and of making his instrument sing again. But when he explains his motivations to Simon, who was once a virtuoso violinist, Malik's story has the unintended consequence of reactivating Simon's own repressed trauma. We learn that Simon, like his wife Bella, had been deported from Paris to Auschwitz in 1943, and the violin plays a weighty role in his traumatic experience: As a child prodigy, he had been compelled by the Nazi officers to play the violin every day, in the central square of the camp, while around him, Jews, including his own father, were marched into gas chambers.

The leitmotif of learning to play the violin structures the novel, becoming a complicated form of emotional, and perhaps political, currency. Simon initially refuses to teach Malik, but he doesn't explain that it is because he associates the violin with the unbearable irony of being forced to produce beautiful music in "l'endroit le plus immonde de la terre" (113, the most wretched place on Earth). Unaware of Simon's past and thus unable to understand his strong reaction to a seemingly simple request, Malik seeks out lessons with another teacher. Then, in a series of reversals vaguely reminiscent of "The gift of the Magi," Simon, whose repressed past has returned thanks to Malik's story, decides to confront his ghosts: He performs the cathartic gesture of telling his story to his students and colleagues at the college where he teaches. Working through this repressed material frees Simon, who—eager to reconnect with the violin, now re-signified as survival rather than abjection—proposes to give Malik lessons. At this point, however, Malik has heard the tale of the violinist of Auschwitz, and cannot bear

61 *Le professeur de musique* won the French Chronos Prize for YA literature in 2002.

the thought of compelling Simon to play. This benevolent cat-and-mouse game culminates on the last day of school, when Malik, having learned enough of the rudiments of the violin to play at the school recital, surprises Simon by playing "an old Jewish melody." In a made-for-Hollywood ending, as an emotional Simon looks on from the wings, someone hands him a violin and gently propels the old teacher to join his pupil on stage: "le vieil homme et l'enfant jouèrent de concert et côte à côte. Dans la salle l'émotion était à son comble. Car tous connaissaient à présent l'histoire de la rencontre de ce vieux prof de musique juif et du petit garçon musulman" (138, the old man and the child played in unison, side by side. Emotions ran high in the theatre, as everyone knew by then the story of the meeting of the old Jewish music teacher and the little Muslim boy).

Unlike "Le bon Samaritain," both YA novels articulate positive outcomes for encounters between Holocaust survivors and Algerians affected by the repression on October 17, even if, in the case of *Le professeur de musique*, Malik's connection to this traumatic past is best understood through Marianne Hirsch's concept of postmemory.[62] But if Kalouaz and Hassan similarly stage interfaith empathy as not only possible but highly salutary, their engagements with the historical material of their narratives are quite different. Wholly devoted to representing October 17, *Les fantômes d'octobre* is followed by a 15-page dossier comprised of an interview with Didier Daeninckx and a testimony by a police officer who participated in the repression. Written for roughly the same age group, Hassan's novel contains no such paratextual material, and is decidedly less interested in narrativizing October 17. Although *Le professeur de musique* narrates, via Simon's fictionalized personal account, the experience of deportation and Auschwitz, the novel plays fast and loose with the facts of the Algerian massacre. The text never mentions October 17 directly; rather, Malik explains to Simon, "Quand il y a eu la guerre d'Algérie, les Arabes n'ont plus eu le droit de sortir, à cause du couvre-feu, on ne pouvait plus aller dehors à partir d'une certaine heure. [...] Pourtant, un soir, Baba n'est pas rentré" (42, During the Algerian War, Arabs couldn't go out, because of the curfew, we couldn't go out after a certain time. [...] But one night, Baba didn't come home). A footnote here informs young readers that "le 5 octobre 1961, suite à de violentes manifestations à Paris, un couvre-feu fut imposé aux Algériens de France" (on October 5, 1961, following violent protests in

---

62 See Chapter 4, n. 43.

Paris, a curfew was imposed on the Algerians of France). This is the text's first error: The curfew was indeed decreed on October 5, but it was not a response to violent manifestations (moreover, the violence that would take place during the demonstration would emanate from the police). Second, when Malik describes his family going out to search for Baba in the streets of Paris—"Quand ils sont arrives près du métro Charonne, ils ont vu qu'il y avait eu du grabuge. Il y avait plein de CRS partout et des ambulances, aussi" (43, When they got close to the Charonne metro, they saw that things had gotten messy. There were tons of riot police everywhere and ambulances, too)—he commits a now-classic error. Malik's reference to the Charonne metro conflates October 17, 1961, and February 8, 1962, the date on which nine French anti-war protesters were killed by police at the Charonne metro station, an event that, unlike October 17, has been enshrined in French political history. (See Introduction, pp. 21–22.)

While the message of empathy contained in *Le professeur de musique* is certainly the most optimistic one of the works discussed in this context, and while mistakes can often be important sites for meaning making, in a text destined for such young readers, perpetuating misinformation is not only regrettable, but also makes Hassan's use of October 17 look opportunistic. At the same time, the last line of the novel seems to point in a different direction: By referring, for the first time, to Simon and Malik as "le juif et le musulman," *Le professeur de musique* may be subconsciously gesturing to the historically embattled binary of "Jew and Muslim," that is, to an imagined solidarity beyond the Holocaust and October 17.

Multidirectional Memory and its Limits

In this project based on a historical event, nowhere has my impulse to bracket historical indexicality come under more intense self-scrutiny than in the present chapter. For reasons undoubtedly related to the politically charged nature of the material and the impact of ambient discourses of comparison, competitive memory, and claims to "uniqueness," I have often found myself wrestling with the urge to justify the "troping" of the Holocaust in fictional texts, to find a way to substantiate the move historically. I have found myself worried about engaging in "dangerous parallels." Yet, through this particular exploration of the anarchive, it should be obvious that the Holocaust is thematized in October 17 cultural productions, and that its manifestations and significations are neither uniform nor univalent. It should also be obvious that it is impossible to reduce representations of the Holocaust, Vichy, or Jews to mere historical indices. Numerous contemporary cultural productions, for example, do feature Papon in an indexical fashion, but the mechanisms of this representation can be ambivalent, leaving the historical record incomplete while also hypothesizing about history.

The figure of the Holocaust survivor—a character who has some plausible yet fictional interaction with Algerians on October 17 or in its aftermath—provokes a kind of eruption of the past into the present tense of the narration. While the presence of the survivor encodes an analogous episode of state violence and trauma, it also gestures to different outcomes for cross-cultural empathy. These moments of intersubjective recognition may, as I suggested in my reading of *Le professeur de musique*, say as much about future hopes as they do about past dreams. Various micro-interpretations can be drawn from the ways Holocaust, Vichy, and World War II symbols are mobilized throughout the anarchive. Recognizing this diversity is constructive, as it helps us to answer some of the bigger, and often thorny, questions that arise whenever representations of the Holocaust are invoked. So, it is worth working through some of the broader stakes of engaging the question of the representation of the Holocaust in the October 17 corpus.

Some may see this operation as inherently risky. Returning to Golsan's charge that *Meurtres pour mémoire* draws a "dangerous parallel" between the Vichy regime and de Gaulle's presidency, and risks blurring "the specificity of the final solution,"[63] I can't help but wonder if my sustained attention to the representation of the Holocaust in the October 17 anarchive also risks "blurring specificity" and instantiating an infelicitous parallel between Vichy and de Gaulle. Golsan's comment also invokes, however tacitly, the tenets of the "uniqueness discourse," which holds the Holocaust to be a "novum," an unparalleled historical event whose comparison to other episodes of genocide or state violence risks universalizing the murder of the Jews and detracting from its own exceptionality.[64]

---

63   Richard J. Golsan, *Vichy's Afterlife: History and Counterhistory in Postwar France* (Lincoln: University of Nebraska Press, 2000), 21.
64   The notion of the Holocaust as novum is articulated in Emil L. Fackenheim, *To Mend the World: Foundations of Post-Holocaust Jewish Thought* (Bloomington: Indiana University Press, 1982).

I in no way wish to delegitimize Golsan's concerns, but if we move from that singular example to a wide-angle view of the anarchive as a whole, one cannot deny that such "dangerous parallels" are indeed a major pattern, insofar as all the works discussed here, through processes of analogy and metaphor, create an implicit parallel between Vichy and the early years of the Fifth Republic. Thus, regardless of how a given reader might view such "comparisons," we should not simply ignore the fact of their existence in cultural productions. And, of course, the creation of links between the Holocaust and colonialism, more broadly, is not the sole purview of the anarchive. We might think of more recent fiction that seems to have anticipated the critical turn toward understanding memory as "multidirectional" or "palimpsestic," works such as the Algerian novels *Le Village de l'Allemand* (2008) and *Le fils du Shéol* (2015), or the Mauritian novel *Le dernier frère* (2007).

But perhaps part of the issue lies in the use of the word "comparison." One of the reasons I have insisted on the word "entanglement" to describe this phenomenon in the anarchive is because it recognizes co-presence without assigning a dominant status to one element over the other. At the same time, it does not necessarily invite a "compare and contrast" methodology. To name the connections between the Holocaust and October 17 as *entangled* allows us instead to recognize the interaction as unruly, impossible to hierarchize, as perhaps without a coherent origin or genesis story. This stance is indeed not far from Michael Rothberg's, who proposed "multidirectional memory" as a corrective to forms of competitive memory—of which the uniqueness discourse is one example. For Rothberg, the co-presence of October 17 and Vichy in *Meurtres pour mémoire*, for example, can be read fruitfully through the prism of "multidirectionality," which prompts us "to see memory as subject to ongoing negotiation, cross-referencing and borrowing, as productive and not privative" (3). "Entanglement" also shares some conceptual DNA with Max Silverman's "palimpsestic memory," a model that de-hierarchizes memories and events, recognizing that "the relationship between present and past takes the form of a superimposition and interaction of different temporal traces to constitute a sort of composite structure [...] so that one layer of traces can be seen through, and transformed by, another" (3).

Rothberg, Silverman, their critical forbears (such as Paul Gilroy), their contemporaries (Debarati Sanyal, with whom they edited the *Yale French Studies*' special issue *Noeuds de mémoire*), and other proponents of globalized Holocaust memory, cosmopolitan memory—and I would add myself to this list—have all sought ways out of the impasse of the uniqueness discourse and competitive memory more generally. Their work has been immensely helpful insofar as it names particular habits of discourse and points up how they foreclose discussion. But my path diverges slightly from this august company, and particularly from Rothberg, one of the few scholars to have devoted sustained attention to October 17 fictions. Notwithstanding a genuine, deep-seated ethical concern with his objects of study, and a goal of "uncovering historical relatedness," it is impossible not to notice that, for Rothberg, the Holocaust remains both subject and object. *Multidirectional Memory*'s subtitle is "Remembering the Holocaust in the Age of Decolonization," and the book "takes the remembrance of the Holocaust as its paradigmatic object of concern" (6). Thus, memories such as those of October 17 are necessarily derivative of, and subordinated to, memories of the Holocaust; decolonization is a setting, not a leading actor. And so, when Rothberg imagines October 17, 1961, as "a site of Holocaust memory," I cannot help but wonder whether we have unwittingly ended up in a unilateral, rather than multidirectional, situation.

More to the point, the cultural productions in question do not always lend themselves so readily to "multidirectional" reading. While I agree that competitive memory discourse hampers the possibilities of reconciliation, it also seems important to recognize, rather than evacuate, the manifestations of competitive memory in literature. To borrow an example from a work discussed in a previous chapter, in Sebbar's novel *La Seine était rouge*, the Algerian refugee journalist Omer spray-paints statements about Algerian history on numerous monuments to World War II, an act that has been held up by Rothberg as a demonstration of multidirectional memory.[65] However, while these aspects of *La Seine* do lend themselves to such a reading, to attach the qualifier "multidirectional" to Omer's rogue historiography is to evacuate the *necessarily competitive* nature of his gesture. Omer, after all, is competing, and self-consciously so—for space, for attention, for readability—with histories and memoires whose inscriptions are profoundly anchored in the Parisian memorialscape. Even closer to the particular concerns of this chapter, let us return for a moment to *Nuit noire* and *Algérie! Algérie!*, works that don't explicitly mention Papon's Vichy past. We

---

65 Rothberg, 299. "*La Seine* does not engage in competitive memory and instead follows *Meurtres* in employing metonymical means: Omer's messages never cover over other sites, but rather take their place *alongside* them."

can, as I suggested earlier, read Papon as a signifier for Vichy and the Holocaust; but we could also imagine that writing Vichy out of the story is a way of claiming an Algerian specificity for Papon's story, and offering October 17 its own narrative space, elevating it to a subject of memory and an object of study in its own right, rather than a mere setting for Holocaust memory. To insist on this might seem "competitive," but it might also be closer to the texts' intentions. Similarly, but with a quite different outcome, if we think back on Hassan's *Le professeur de musique*, we might also see her historical gaffe as the worst kind of instrumentalization: an Arab story, used poorly and counterfactually, in service of a Holocaust survivor's catharsis.[66]

Of the various stakes of reading the anarchive's entangled stories of October 17 and the Holocaust, certainly we can point to a productive engagement with both older and newer memory models. We might even want to mull over the question of *memory* versus *representation*—how do we pull these two apart when it comes to works of fiction, works in which any memory is necessarily a representation? But attending to these entanglements *as* entanglements reveals other, related paths of inquiry that we might have otherwise overlooked. First, it prompts us to recognize that the anarchive in fact mobilizes a broader, transnational network of historical connections. Indeed, reading the anarchive for its representations of the Holocaust can produce an unexpected, against the grain observation: while the Holocaust is the historical event *most often* pressed into service in October 17 fictions, it is not the *only* one. Indeed, several works in the corpus make reference to US apartheid (*The Stone Face*), the conflict in the Middle East (*Le Sourire de Brahim*; plays by Mohamed Rouabhi), and in one case, the Argentinian Dirty War of the 1980s (*Bastille Tango*, by French novelist Jean-François Vilar). The anarchive is thus fundamentally relational, seeking connections with oppressions above and beyond those that are historically related to October 17, thus cracking open October 17 and figuring it as site of global import, rather than simply an isolated episode of a larger conflict.

Thinking through entanglements in the anarchive also leads us back to the archive itself, and offers some new lessons on how to read it.

66 For a similar engagement with multidirectional memory, one that recognizes the concept's inherent value while remaining attentive to the "collisions and conflations" that can occur when representations of memory are multivalent, see Debarati Sanyal, *Memory and Complicity: Migrations of Holocaust Remembrance* (New York: Fordham University Press, 2015), 6–7.

If we return to the police archives with these entanglements in mind, it becomes readily apparent that, in October 1961, after the signing of the curfew and after the repression on the 17th, numerous French citizens, union bosses, politicians, and associations—including Jewish ones—wrote to express their dismay at the "reenactment" of Vichy to which they bore witness. In a pure chronology, of course, the archive predates the anarchive. However, reading sequence matters, and given the archive's 50 years of invisibility, its position with respect to the anarchive is distinctly belated. Moreover, however random or orderly a given consignment of documents, the archive does not classify by "trope." Thus, it is through the lens of the anarchive that we can assign meaning to the texts of the archive. And here, perhaps, it would be fruitful to take note: The "dangerous parallel" between Vichy and de Gaulle's early Fifth Republic was always, already there.

Epilogue

The Ends of the Anarchive

As of this writing, it has been five years since the multi-sited terrorist attacks in Paris. In the days following November 13, 2015, the French and international press used a variety of superlative expressions in an attempt to contextualize the unfathomable. These were the "deadliest attacks in France since World War II"; they constituted "the deadliest violence to strike France since World War II"; "the worst bloodshed in France since World War II"; and "the bloodiest day in France since World War II." Recourse to World War II as a point of comparison offers a measure of the historical span between two episodes of national trauma and emphasizes their exceptionality. At the same time, the diachronic comparison has the effect of bookending the intervening period, marking off the era from 1945 to 2015 as a time of relative peace and distinguishing it from these violent episodes. Beyond their capacity to periodize, these references to World War II form—particularly by virtue of their repetition—an evocative trope, one that activates multiple layers of collective and individual memory, and conjures, in the general imagination, multiple sites and types of horror. The comparison is remarkably efficient in plotting November 13 along a graph of historical violence, and even foreshadowing its political weight and potential post-traumatic aftereffects.

The link drawn between these two moments creates a powerful implicit narrative that is, of course, incorrect. One can only posit November 13 as the bloodiest, most violent, deadliest day in France since World War II if one ignores that on October 17, 1961, on a Tuesday evening, in bustling neighborhoods of central Paris, with a Gabin film playing at the Berlitz and the Shah of Iran in town on an official state visit, 200 Algerians were massacred by the Parisian police.

As I have argued at several points in this book, any error is a potential site of meaning.[1] Its historical inaccuracy notwithstanding, this mistake nonetheless suggests that the superlative relationship between World War II and the 2015 terror attacks functions as *true* in the national imaginary. In other words, the massacre committed on October 17, 1961, has not only been erased from historical discourse, the erasure in and of itself is utterly unremarkable. October 17, the actual bloodiest, most violent day in France prior to 2015, continues to fail to signify, to produce meaning, to participate in a national narrative.

To brandish this anecdote as a closing salvo is admittedly somewhat unfair. While those newspaper accounts would tend to suggest that nothing has changed in more than 50 years of French political and cultural memory—in other words, that October 17 remains invisible, there is, in fact, plenty of evidence to suggest otherwise. The police archives have been declassified and relocated to a facility better adapted for research; a president has recognized and admitted a measure of responsibility in Algerian deaths; multiple historical accounts have been published; activist work and memorial activities at the local level proliferate. Médine's "17 octobre" rap has been included in the "Algerian War" section of a major history textbook for high-school seniors—perhaps the most literal sign that October 17 has entered "history."[2] And the amount of information available about October 17 on the internet has multiplied exponentially in the last 15 years: When I first attempted to Google the event in 2005, it had almost no web presence at all. Today, for what it is worth, a search for "17 octobre 1961" yields about 1,730,000 results. However imperfect it may be to invoke internet search results as "evidence," the obvious change over time cannot be summarily dismissed.

Moreover, the anarchive continues to log new entries. *Nos richesses* (2017), a novel by Algerian author Kaouther Adimi, weaves together a rich historical narrative based on the notebooks of the Algerian-born French editor and publisher Edmond Charlot and features important

---

1   One freelance journalist did pick up on this mistake. Iranian-American journalist Alex Shams issued a correction via Twitter: "(November 13) was not the bloodiest day in Paris since WWII," wrote Shams. "It was in 1961, when police killed 200 Algerian protesters."

2   In 2012 the rap was selected for inclusion in the history textbook geared for graduating seniors in the "ES" stream (*sciences économiques et sociales*, or economy and social sciences), published by Éditions Nathan. It bears mentioning that the rap was excerpted, and only approximately one-third of the lyrics are made available to students.

events such as the massacre in Sétif and October 17. The Franco-Romanian dramaturge Alexandra Badea premiered the second volume of her trilogy *Points de non-retour* at the 2019 Avignon Theatre Festival, where *Quais de Seine*—a multigenerational story about the Algerian War and October 17's impact on a family—ran for seven nights to sold-out crowds. A "hip hop ballet" titled "Les Disparus"—performed in 2011 and again in 2016—begins in the world of Algerian factory workers, only to re-create the demonstration, its repression, and even the experience of drowning.[3] In the era of the anarchive's third wave, every anniversary is an occasion for a new site-specific commemorative performance, a new work of art.

In addition to the perceptible (if not always unanimous) shifts in public awareness and the clear sign that the anarchive is far from sealed, the nature of my own questions has changed since I began this project. Whereas I was originally most interested in the forces that had conspired to render October 17 invisible and in uncovering the ways in which cultural texts had formed a discreet yet present bulwark against the obliteration of this memory, today I find myself wondering: When will Algerian and French individuals and families, activist associations, and scholars decide that October 17 no longer constitutes a blind spot in French history and memory? At what point might we be able to say that October 17 has been inscribed in the *roman national*? What will it take for recognition itself to be recognized?

———

Whither the anarchive now, after 2012 and the declassification of the police archives, and well into what Henry Rousso has called the "obsessional" phase of memory? The accessibility of the police archives is no reason for the rate of cultural production to decline—writers and artists may even be interested in mobilizing the archives in creative ways. But the definition of the anarchive may indeed require retooling: Initially understood as a corpus that emerged during a long period of archival inaccessibility that produced a rogue form of historiography during a

3 The "hip hop ballet" was imagined and choreographed by Mehdi Slimani, director of La Compagnie No MaD (based in Seine-Saint-Denis). His artist statement can be found on the company's site: http://www.cienomad.com/choregraphies-2/les-disparus-2011/.

time of censure, the anarchive cannot continue to exist as such once the gap it pointed up has been officially filled. Perhaps, then, "anarchive 2.0," or a putative fourth wave, will reconfigure itself to include works produced in the presence of the archive that nonetheless recognize the archive's inherent incompleteness and continue to poke holes in totalizing notions of archival plenitude.

The speed and instantaneousness that have come to characterize our postmodern condition in general are also at work on the anarchive. Just as the internet now abounds with historical and political information, it has also become a repository for actual archival material. Various letters, documents, and photos previously held by the Parisian police and subject to censure, have been available on the internet since before 2012. While the entirety of the archives has certainly not been digitized—it has hardly been catalogued—the type of access provided now by the internet almost (but not quite) obviates the need for a trip to the actual archives.

It is also true that the anarchive itself now resides, at least in part, on the internet. Many of the films, even some of the obscure documentary shorts, are housed on special sites (such as Guène's documentary, for example, archived on the site of *Les Engraineurs*), and one of course does not need a special cable package in order to be able to view the videos by Médine or Têtes Raides. Numerous anarchival texts are also available online and, of course, for those that are not, with a few clicks one lands on a site through which the texts can be purchased. Even from outside France, I encountered only one text that could not be ordered and paid for by internet (and an email directly to the bookseller was all it took to acquire it). Moreover, the rhizomatic structure of the web makes it possible to chase down leads in ways that would have either taken a long time or been nearly impossible in the analog world. And, of course, the digitally interactive web-based works put the experiences of October 17 quite literally at the fingertips of the user.

A question thus naturally emerges: Can the anarchive be archived? If it is contained, fully digitized, and made available on the internet, can it still properly be called an anarchive? Once these works are consigned, do they cease to create an oppositional force to the archive? Is it possible to imagine that the official archives and the anarchive might one day reside together, on a single platform? That in the future, the reader of the digital version of *Meurtres pour mémoire* might be just a hyperlink away from the digitized versions of the actual archives, press clippings, and film footage referred to in that fictional text? Or that the viewer of

Octobre à Paris may be able to zoom in on a recreation of the Nanterre *bidonville*, or use virtual reality glasses to join the column of protesters as they make their way into the city center?

While aspects of the anarchive as I define it are unique to the conditions that produced October 17 and its in/visibility, the concept itself is portable. Perhaps readers will explore the possibility that at other dark moments, in different places, when governments have papered over their crimes and scripted national narratives to make their egregious acts "invisible," literature and culture have been busily making history. We can imagine the existence of anarchives of the Argentinian Dirty War, the Ukrainian Holodomor—the great famine of the 1930s, and the Armenian genocide, perhaps, even if those events are relatively better known than October 17. While cultural productions related to the Holocaust have received much scholarly attention, we might think of the smaller corpus of texts and films that represent epiphenomenal experiences of the Shoah—the Tunisian cultural productions that wrestle with both colonialism and the experience of German occupation, for example—as a type of anarchive. Perhaps we would do well to attend to the various present-day injustices, both visible and invisible, that may be in the process of producing their own anarchives?

In a book that has been primarily about culture, I have nonetheless argued for the consideration of October 17, 1961, as a signal event, as a foundational episode for thinking about contemporary, multiethnic, multicultural France. The violence of October 17 may indeed have been "secondary" insofar as it did not impede the goal of ending the Algerian War; however, its continued failure to signify within certain spheres of political and public discourse is echoed in the status of populations today who are the direct inheritors of the legacy of October 17. As I suggested above, in the aftermath of November 13, 2015, no news outlet recognized that it was the bloodiest day in Paris since October 1961. The work ahead of us is to create the conditions wherein this true statement can become a significant one.

And so I would like to conclude with a brief reflection on what might be a kind of anarchival apotheosis: In 2017 the Ivry-based eclectic "Mediterranean rap" group Zik Zitoun released a video of its new, ironically titled single "On a appris à nager" (We've learned to swim).[4]

---

4 The video can be viewed at: https://www.youtube.com/watch?v=gvpYCwP8d Pc&feature=youtu.be. Additional information provided by Brahim (alias Mess B) and Zik Zitoun, email correspondence dated January 20, 2020.

The lyrics and images combine to exemplify the fundamentally relational nature of the anarchive, particularly in its contemporary phase. Drawing on earlier anarchival works, the mise-en-scène and montage layer past and present: the video opens with the photo of the 1961 "Ici on noie les Algériens" graffiti, which slowly dissolves into a present-day, sepia-toned aerial shot of the Seine. A lone trumpet plays a mournful line, punctuated by the names of the victims, which are intoned by the signers and accompanied by the mention "disparu" (disappeared) or "explusé" (deported). After several seconds, testimonial images from Panijel's *Octobre à Paris* are layered into the mix, visually and sonically. When the litany of the dead comes to an end after 30 seconds, the visual field is replaced by a montage of archival images and footage (including images that re-enact the painting of the graffiti), and the trumpet hands off the solo to a single *oud*, whose minor melody is overlain with the singers' recitation of Kateb's 1962 poem "Dans la gueule du loup."[5] After posing Kateb's haunting questions— "Maintenant vas-tu parler? Maintenant vas-tu te taire?" (Now will you speak? Now will you be silent?)—the band marks a single beat of silence before the rap takes off in earnest. Now electrified, the *oud* is joined by a darbouka and other percussion to ground the opening lyrics that pick up where the very earliest "writing" about the massacre left off:

> Ici, on noie les Algériens,
> Comme le poisson après l'affaire,
> Inimaginable,
> Nager, oui j'ai appris à le faire…
>
> (Here's where they drown Algerians
> Like fish after the fact,
> Unthinkable,
> Now I can swim it's not an act…)[6]

The lyrics are rapped but the music is *chaâbi*, a traditional form of popular Algerian music. Together with the imagery, they converge in

---

5   The graffiti re-enactment is taken from a documentary short titled "Événement du 17 Octobre 1961, témoignage d'un soldat français: Ici on noie les algériens," available only on YouTube (no director given): https://www.youtube.com/watch?v=gvpYCwP8dPc&feature=youtu.be. According to the credits, some of the footage in the video is also borrowed from Tasma's *Nuit noire*.

6   The last line reads, "Yes now I know how to swim" (or, more literally, "To swim, yes now I've learned") I've allowed myself some poetic license in the translation in order to respect the original's rhyme scheme.

Fig. 16. "On a appris à nager" (We've learned to swim).
Final image of music video by Zik Zitoun (2017).

what I believe to be the best example of sublimation in the anarchive: the refrain, however ironic or "on the nose," articulates a new subject position for Algerians in France, responding to the tacit question: What has changed for Algerians in France since 1961? The images pay homage to the past but look to the future by recuperating the graffiti—the first textual and visual representation of the massacre—and editing it: While the video opens with the photo of the graffiti indicating "where Algerians were drowned," it closes on the same photo, the slogan now revised as a declaration of defiance and a warning that the state's weapons of yesterday will no longer work on today's "Algerians": "On a appris à nager" (we've learned to swim). Finally, it is the melody itself that inflects a tragic story with a note of hope. The chorus repeats the line "On a appris à nager" eight times. The first four rounds are sung in a quasi-monotone and a minor key, but in the second set of four lines, the last note ascends a halftone, resolving into a bright, major key. From performances of drowning, of falling below the surface—of the Seine, of history—to a performance of resurfacing: melodically and symbolically, the music *lifts up*, pulling the reaching hand of the drowning Algerian up out of the Seine and onto the world stage.

Bibliography

The Anarchive—Primary Sources

Film and Media

Adi, Yasmina. *Ici on noie les Algériens*. Agat Films/INA, 2011. 35mm. Documentary.

Akika, Ali. *Les Enfants d'octobre*. Les Productions de la lanterne, Images plus, 2000. Documentary.

Bouchareb, Rachid. *Hors-la-loi*. StudioCanal, 2010. 35mm.

Brooks, Philip, and Alan Hayling. *Drowning By Bullets (17 Octobre 1961: une journée portée disparue)*. Point du Jour, BBC 4, France 3, 1992. Documentary.

Corre, Florence, and Aure. *Octobre noir ou Malec, Saïd, Karim et les autres*. Animated short film, 2011.

Delahautemaison, Virginie. *17 Octobre 1961, retour de mémoire*. 2001. Documentary.

———. *Mémoire du fleuve*. 1997. Documentary short.

Denis, Agnès, and Mehdi Lallaoui. *Le silence du fleuve*. Mémoire vive production, 1991. Documentary.

Guène, Faïza, and Bernard Richard. *Mémoires du 17 octobre*. Les Engraineurs, 2002. Documentary short.

Guerdjou, Bourlem. *Vivre au paradis*. Tadrart Films, 1998. 35mm.

Haneke, Michael. *Caché*. Les Films du Losange, 2005.

Heynemann, Laurent. *Meurtres pour mémoire*. 1985.

Krief, Jean-Pierre. *Les années Kagan*. 1989. Documentary.

Kupferstein, Daniel. *17 octobre 1961: dissimulation d'un massacre*. CNC, 2001. Documentary.

———. *Mourir à Charonne, pourquoi?* TVM/Télé bocal, 2010. Documentary.

Lallaoui, Mehdi. "À propos d'octobre." Preface to *Octobre à Paris* (directed by Jacques Panijel). Included on DVD, *Octobre à Paris*. Les films de l'Atalante, 2011. Documentary short.

Lévy, Denis. *Mémoire en blanc.* 1981. Short film.

Panijel, Jacques. *Octobre à Paris.* Le Comité Audin and Vérité-Liberté, 1962. 35mm. Documentary. Les films de l'Atalante, 2011. DVD.

——. "*Octobre à Paris,* introduction, fiche culturelle." *Images et son* 160 (March 1963): n. p.

Pascot, Sébastian. "17 octobre 1961." Included on DVD, *Octobre à Paris.* Les films de l'Atalante, 2011. Documentary.

——. *Témoignage d'octobre.* Documentary short, 2002. http://www. dailymotion.com/video/xmflp_temoignages-d-octobre-massacre-d-et_ news (accessed August 27, 2020).

RaspouTeam. "17.10.61." Webdoc. Accessed January 23, 2020. http://www.ina. fr/medias/webdocs/17oct/home.html (accessed August 27, 2020).

Tasma, Alain. *Nuit noire, 17 octobre 1961.* 2004. Docudrama.

Touita, Okacha. *Les sacrifiés.* 1982. http://www.fabriquedesens.fr/index. php?title=Les_sacrifi%C3%A9s (accessed August 27, 2020).

Touly, Aude. *La Guerre sans nom dans Paris: une nuit d'octobre 1961.* 2001. Documentary.

Graphic Novels and Illustrations

Abbas-Kebir, Benyoucef. *17 octobre 1961, 17 bulles: Tragédie-sur-Seine.* Algiers: Éditions Dalimen, 2011.

Daeninckx, Didier. *Octobre noir.* Anthy-sur-Léman: Ad Libris, 2011.

Daeninckx, Didier, and Jeanne Puchol. *Meurtres pour mémoire.* Paris: Futuropolis-Gallimard, 1991.

Maffre, Laurent, and Monique Hervo. *Demain, demain: Nanterre, bidonville de la folie, 1962–1966.* Arles: Actes Sud BD, 2012.

Stora, Benjamin, Anne Tristan, and Mehdi Lallaoui. *17 octobre 1961: 17 illustrateurs.* Bezons: Au nom de la mémoire, 1999.

Novels

Adimi, Kaouther. *Nos richesses.* Paris: Éditions des Points, 2017.

Aït-Taleb, Hamid. *De grâce.* Paris: Lattès, 2008.

Bachi, Salim. *Amours et aventures de Sindbad le Marin.* Paris: Gallimard, 2010.

Benaïcha, Brahim. *Vivre au paradis: d'une oasis à un bidonville.* Paris: Desclée De Brouwer, 1992.

Bertina, Arno. *Le dehors ou la migration des truites.* Arles: Actes Sud, 2001.

Daeninckx, Didier. *Meurtres pour mémoire.* Paris: Gallimard, 1983.

Djemaï, Abdelkader. *Gare du nord.* Paris: Seuil, 2003.

Ernaux, Annie. *Les années.* Paris: Gallimard, 2008.

Hassan, Yaël. *Le professeur de musique.* Paris: Casterman, 2016.

Huston, Nancy. *L'empreinte de l'ange.* Arles: Actes Sud; Montreal: Leméac, 1998.

Imache, Tassadit. *Presque un frère: conte du temps présent*. Arles: Actes Sud, 2000.

———. *Une fille sans histoire*. Paris: Calmann-Lévy, 1989.

Kalouaz, Ahmed. *Les fantômes d'octobre: 17 octobre 1961*. Paris: Oskar Éditions, 2011.

Kettane, Nacer. *Le Sourire de Brahim*. Paris: Denoël, 1985.

Lallaoui, Mehdi. *Les Beurs de Seine*. Paris: Éditions de L'Arcantère, 1986.

———. *Une nuit d'octobre*. Paris: Éditions Alternatives, 2001.

Le Bourhis, Michel. *Les yeux de Moktar*. Paris: Syros Jeunesse, 2004.

Michel, Éric. *Algérie! Algérie!* Paris: Presses de la Renaissance, 2007.

Michel, Natacha. *Plein présent*. Lagrasse: Verdier, 2013.

Mounsi, Mohand. *Territoire d'outre-ville*. Paris: Stock, 1995.

Rémy, Pierre-Jean. *Algérie, bords de Seine*. Paris: Albin Michel, 1992.

Saloff, Michel, and Jean-François Vilar. *Paris la nuit*. Paris: ACE, 1982.

Sebbar, Leïla. *La Seine était rouge*. Paris: Thierry Magnier, 1999.

Smaïl, Paul. *Vivre me tue*. Paris: Balland, 2003. Translated by Simon Pleasance and Fronza Woods as *Smile* (London: Serpent's Tail, 2000).

Smith, William Gardner. *The Stone Face*. New York: Farrar, Straus and Giroux, 1963.

Streiff, Gérard. *Les caves de la Goutte d'or*. Paris: Baleine, 2001.

Vilar, Jean-François. *Bastille tango*. Arles: Actes Sud; Montreal: Leméac, 1998.

Short Stories

17 octobre 1961: 17 écrivains se souviennent, edited by Mustapha Harzoune and Samia Messaoudi. Montigny-lès-Cormeilles: Au nom de la mémoire, 2011. (Collection of 17 short stories and personal accounts, including works by Didier Daeninckx, Tassadit Imache, Mehdi Lallaoui, and Leïla Sebbar.)

Bachi, Salim. *Le grand frère*. Paris: Éditions du Moteur, 2010.

Sebbar, Leïla. "Octobre 2001, Solférino: L'Algérien." In *Métro: Instantanés*. Monaco: Éditions du Rocher, 2007.

Poetry

Janvier, Ludovic. "Du nouveau sous les ponts." In *La mer à boire*. Paris: Gallimard, 1987.

Yacine, Kateb. "Dans la gueule du loup." *Jeune Afrique* 90 (June 25, 1962): 22–23.

Theatre

Badea, Alexandra. *Points de non-retour [Quais de Seine]*. Paris: L'Arche, 2019. Premiered at Avignon Theatre Festival, July 4, 2019.

Boudiaf, Mounya. *Née un 17 Octobre*. Based on script by Rachid Benzine. Premiered at Maison Folie Wazemmes (Lille), October 6, 2018. Performed at Avignon Theatre Festival, « Off », July 4, 2019. Unpublished.

Chouaki, Aziz. *La pomme et le couteau*. Paris: Les Cygnes, 2011. Staged reading at the festival La Mousson d'été in Pont-à-Mousson, August 25, 2011. Recording aired on France Culture, October 16, 2011.

Granouillet, Gilles. *Nuit d'automne à Paris*. Commissioned and directed by Guy Rétoré. Premiered at Théâtre de l'est parisien, March 7–April 2, 2000. Paris: Avant-scène théâtre, 2002.

Lallaoui, Mehdi. *Monique H., Nanterre 1961*. Montigny-lès-Cormeilles: Au nom de la mémoire, 2014.

Méliani, Hamma. *Lamento pour Paris: chroniques parisiennes sur le massacre des Algériens les 17 et 18 octobre 1961*. Paris: La Marsa, 2011. Directed by Myriam Allal. Performed October 11, 2011, at the Espace Jemmapes in Paris and October 20–21, 2001, at "La cave à Théâtre" in Colombes.

Prati-Belmokhtar, Marie-Christine. *C'était un 17 octobre*. Paris: Marsa Éditions, 2009.

Rouabhi, Mohamed. *El menfi/L'exilé*. Unpublished play staged by Nadine Varoutsikos in Ramallah, Palestine, July 21, 2000. Unpublished.

———. *Requiem Opus 61: une prière pour les morts*. Unpublished play premiered in Epinay, France, 2001. Unpublished.

Performance and Dance

Compagnie de la Pierre noire. Untitled commemorative performance. Bobigny, October 17, 2011. http://www.pierrenoire.org/?page_id=465 (accessed August 27, 2020).

Compagnie No MaD. "Les Disparus." Dance/Hip Hop. Multiple performances. 2011. http://www.cienomad.com/choregraphies-2/les-disparus-2011/ (accessed August 27, 2020).

Komplex Kapharnaüm. "Memento." Performed at multiple venues. 2009. http://www.komplex-kapharnaum.net/en/projets/memento-2009 (accessed August 27, 2020).

Music and Music Video

Fils du béton. "17 octobre 1961." Video, 3:59. https://youtu.be/TRCOibmb5Tw (accessed August 27, 2020).

grand.B. "11'30 contre les lois racistes." 2008. Video, 11:35. https://dai.ly/x3pya7 (accessed August 27, 2020).

Médine. "17 octobre." Track 6 on *Table d'écoute*. Din Records, 2006. Video, 5:53. https://youtu.be/oXAIHLNEcOo (accessed August 27, 2020).

Mounsi, Mohand. "Bâtard." Track 1, *Seconde génération*. Les Disques Motors, 1984. Vinyl.

Têtes Raides. "Dans la gueule du loup." Track 9, *Chamboultou*. 1998. BMG Rights Management France SARL. MP3. Amazon Music (accessed August 27, 2020).

———. "Dans la gueule du loup." July 16, 2007. Video, 2:18. https://youtu.be/lNWLEAXdSqw (accessed August 27, 2020).

Zik Zitoun. "On a appris à nager." 2017. Tracks 9 and 10, *Ça va huiler*. Video, 5:46. https://youtu.be/7SzJ3cLhzxc (accessed August 27, 2020).

Images

Einaudi, Jean-Luc, and Élie Kagan. *17 octobre 1961*. Arles: Actes Sud, 2001.

Tristan, Anne. *Le silence du fleuve, octobre 1961*. Bezons: Éditions Au nom de la mémoire, 1991.

Bibliography—Selected Secondary Sources

"À la mémoire des algériens." *Libération*, October 18, 2001.

Abdallah, Mogniss. "Le 17 octobre 1961 et les médias: de la couverture de l'histoire immédiate au 'travail de mémoire.'" *Hommes et migrations* 1228 (December 2000): 125–33.

Agamben, Giorgio. "We Refugees." Translated by Michael Rocke. *Symposium* 49, no. 2 (1995): 114–19.

Ageron, Charles-Robert. "L'Opinion française devant la guerre d'Algérie." *Revue française d'histoire d'outre-mer* 63, no. 231 (1976): 256–85.

Amine, Laïla. "Double Exposure: The Family Album and Alternate Memories in Leïla Sebbar's *The Seine Was Red*." *Culture, Theory and Critique* 53, no. 2 (2012): 181–98.

Amiri, Linda. *La Bataille de France. La guerre d'Algérie en métropole*. Paris: Robert Laffont, 2004.

Anonymous. "7000 Algériens encore détenus dans divers centres de la région parisienne." *L'Aurore*, October 23, 1961.

Anonymous. "Un Porte-parole du GPRA: 'Les manifestations ne sont pas dirigées contre le peuple français mais contre le Colonialisme." *L'Humanité*, October 19, 1961. Police archives HA110/111.

Arendt, Hannah. "Race-Thinking Before Racism." *Review of Politics* 6, no. 1 (January 1944): 36–73.

Atack, Margaret. "From *Meurtres pour mémoire* to Missak: Literature and Historiography in Dialogue." *French Cultural Studies* 25, no. 3–4 (2014): 271–80.

Barakat, Sidi Mohammed. *Corps d'exception: les artifices du pouvoir colonial et la destruction de la vie*. Paris: Éditions Amsterdam, 2005.

———. "Corps et État." In "Corps en guerre: imaginaires, idéologies, destructions." Special issue, *Quasimodo* 9 (Spring 2006): 153–62.

Barclay, Fiona. *Writing Postcolonial France: Haunting, Literature, and the Maghreb*. Lanham, MD: Lexington Books, 2011.

Beauchemin, Cris, Christelle Hamel, and Patrick Simon. *Trajectoires et origines. Enquête sur la diversité des populations en France*. Paris: INED, 2015.

Beck, Robert. *Histoire du dimanche, de 1700 à nos jours*. Paris: Éditions Ouvrières, 1997.

Begag, Azouz. "Of Imposture and Incompetence: Paul Smaïl's *Vivre me tue*." Translated by Alec Hargreaves. *Research in African Literatures* 31, no. 1 (2006): 55–71.

Benayoun, Robert. "Où commence le témoignage?" *Positif* 49 (November 1962): 23–28.

Berlière, Jean-Marc. "Archives de police/historiens policés?" *Revue d'histoire moderne et contemporaine* 48, no. 4b (2001): 58–59.

———. "On risque de ne trouver dans les dossiers que des coupures de presse." Interview by Annette Lévy-Willaiard. *Libération*, October 18, 1997.

Bernard, Philippe, and Christine Garin. "Le massacre du 17 octobre 1961 obtient un début de reconnaissance officielle." *Le Monde*, October 17, 2001.

Birnbaum, Jean. "Le goût de l'anarchive." *Le Monde*, October 18, 2012.

Blanchard, Emmanuel. "Encadrer des 'citoyens diminués'. La Police des Algériens en région parisienne (1944–1962)." Doctoral thesis, Université de Bourgogne, 2008.

———. *La Police parisienne et les Algériens: 1944–1962*. Paris: Nouveau Monde éditions, 2011.

———. "Monique Hervo, une vie avec les Algériens et les mal-logés." *Plein Droit* 4, no. 91 (2011): 36–40.

———. "'Montrer à de Gaulle que nous voulons notre indépendance, s'il faut crever,' Algériens et Algériennes dans les manifestations d'octobre 1961." In *La Ville en ébullition. Sociétés urbaines à l'épreuve*, edited by Pierre Bergel and Vincent Milliot, 205–36. Rennes: Presses universitaires de Rennes, 2014.

Bleich, Eric. "Anti-Racism Without Races: Politics and Policy in a 'Color-Blind' State." In *Race in France: Interdisciplinary Perspectives on the Politics of Difference*, edited by Herrick Chapman and Laura L. Frader, 162–88. New York: Berghahn Books, 2004.

Brand, Philippe. "Des nœuds dans le web: la commémoration du 17 octobre 1961 sur internet." *Entrelacs*, no. 12 (January 10, 2016).

Brimo, Nicolas. "Papon, aide de camps: quand un ministre de Giscard faisait déporter des Juifs." *Le Canard enchaîné*, May 6, 1981.

Brozgal, Lia. "Gros plan sur le 17 octobre 1961: Violence coloniale, cinéma documentaire et le sujet algérien." In *Représentations de la guerre d'indépendance algérienne*, edited by Maya Boutaghou, 99–114. Paris: Classiques Garnier, 2019.

———. "Hostages of Authenticity: Paul Smaïl, Azouz Begag and the Invention of the *Beur* Author." *French Forum* 34, no. 2 (Spring 2009): 113–30.

Brunet, Jean-Paul. "Le Racisme dans la répression policière des manifestations algériennes à Paris en 1961." *Cahiers de la Méditerranée* 61, no. 1 (2000): 69–89.

———. *Police contre FLN.* Paris: Flammarion, 1999.

Burton, Antoinette, ed. *Archive Stories: Facts, Fictions, and the Writing of History.* Durham, NC: Duke University Press, 2006.

Buzenet, Julien. "Manifestation du 17 octobre 1961 à Paris: l'oubli pour mémoire collective d'une violente répression policière." *Conserveries Mémorielles* 10 (2011). https://cm.revues.org/899 (accessed August 27, 2020).

Cau, Jean. "Jean Cau chez les ratons." *L'Express*, October 27, 1961.

Celik, Ipek A. "'I Wanted You to Be Present': Guilt and History of Violence in Michael Haneke's *Hidden*." *Cinema Journal* 50, no. 1 (Fall 2010): 59–80.

Chambers-Samadi, Chadia. *Répréssion des manifestants algériens: la nuit meurtrière du 17 octobre.* Paris: L'Harmattan, 2015.

Cheyette, Bryan. *Diasporas of the Mind: Jewish and Postcolonial Writing and the Nightmare of History.* New Haven, CT: Yale University Press, 2013.

Cohen, Ronald L. "Silencing Objections: Social Constructions of Indifference." *Journal of Human Rights* 1, no. 2 (June 2002): 187–206.

Cole, Josh. "Entering History: The Memory of Police Violence in Paris, October 1961." In *Algeria & France 1800–2000: Identity, Memory, Nostalgia*, edited by Patricia M.E. Lorcin, 117–34. Syracuse, NY: Syracuse University Press, 2006.

Combe, Sonia. *Archives interdites. L'Histoire confisquée.* Paris: La Découverte, 2001.

Conan, Eric, and Henry Rousso. *Vichy: un passé qui ne passe pas.* Paris: Fayard, 1994. Translated by Nathan Bracher as *Vichy, An Ever-Present Past* (Lebanon, NH: University Press of New England, 1998).

Connelly, Matthew James. *A Diplomatic Revolution: Algeria's Fight for Independence and the Origins of the Post-Cold War Era.* Oxford: Oxford University Press, 2002.

"Contre La Barbarie." *L'Esprit* 300, no. 11 (November 1961): 667–70. Editorial.

Crapanzo, Vincent. *The Harkis: The Wound That Never Heals.* Chicago: University of Chicago Press, 2011.

Crowley, Patrick. "When Forgetting Is Remembering: Haneke's *Caché* and the Events of October 17, 1961." In *On Michael Haneke*, edited by Brian Price and John David Rhodes, 266–79. Detroit: Wayne State University Press, 2010.

Cusack, Tricia. "Bourgeois Leisure on the Seine: Impressionism, Forgetting and National Identity in the French Third Republic." *National Identities* 9, no. 2 (June 2007): 163–82.

———. *Riverscapes and National Identities.* Syracuse, NY: Syracuse University Press, 2010.

Daeninckx, Didier. "Délphine pour mémoire." In "Hommage et témoignages." Special issue, *Actualité de l'émigration* 59 (October 1986): 30–31.

———. "Je la connais, mon histoire des massacres, jeune homme." Interview by Françoise Kerleroux, June 16, 2014. http://editions-verdier.fr/2014/06/16/entretien-avec-francoise-kerleroux/ (accessed August 27, 2020).

Dana, Catherine. "Les Enfants Antigone." *French Forum* 29, no. 1 (Winter 2004): 113–25.

Dassarre, Ève. "La Marche du désespoir." *France Observateur*, October 26, 1961.

Daumay, Jean-Michel. "Les Heures noires de la France resurgissent à Bordeaux." *Le Monde*, October 17, 1997.

Debord, Guy. "La Théorie de la dérive." *Les Lèvres nues* 9 (December 1956). https://www.larevuedesressources.org/theorie-de-la-derive,038.html (accessed August 27, 2020).

Delacroix, A. "On ne peut plus ignorer ça." *France Observateur*, October 26, 1961.

Derrida, Jacques. *Archive Fever: A Freudian Impression.* Translated by Eric Prenowitz. Chicago: University of Chicago Press, 1996.

Donadey, Anne. "Anamnesis and National Reconciliation: Re-Membering October 17, 1961." In *Immigrant Narratives in Contemporary France*, edited by Susan Ireland and Patrice J. Proulx, 47–56. Contributions to the Study of World Literature, no. 106. Westport, CT: Greenwood Press, 2001.

———. "Retour sur mémoire: *La Seine était rouge* de Leïla Sebbar." In *Leïla Sebbar*, edited by Michel Laronde, 187–98. Paris: L'Harmattan, 2003.

———. "'Une certaine idée de la France': The Algeria Syndrome and Struggles over 'French' Identity." In *Identity Papers: Contested Nationhood in Twentieth-Century France*, edited by Steven Ungar and Tom Conley, 215–32. Minneapolis: University of Minnesota Press, 1996.

Einaudi, Jean-Luc. *La Bataille de Paris, 17 octobre 1961.* 2nd ed. Paris: Seuil, 2001.

———. *Scènes de la guerre d'Algérie en France: Automne 1961.* Paris: Le Cherche midi, 2009.

Entlelis, John P. *Algeria: The Revolution Institutionalized.* New York: Routledge, 1986.

Evans, Martin. *Algeria: France's Undeclared War.* Oxford: Oxford University Press, 2012.

———. *The Memory of Resistance: French Opposition to the Algerian War (1954–1962).* Berg French Studies Series. Oxford: Bloomsbury, 1997.

Fabre, Michel. *From Harlem to Paris: Black American Writers in France, 1840–1980.* Urbana: University of Illinois Press, 1991.

Fanon, Frantz. *Les Damnés de la terre*. Paris: Maspero, 1961. Translated by Richard Philcox as *The Wretched of the Earth* (New York: Grove Press, 2005).

Farge, Arlette. *Le Goût de l'archive*. Paris: Seuil, 1989. Translated by Thomas Scott-Railton as *The Allure of the Archives* (New Haven, CT: Yale University Press, 2015).

Ferry, Jules. "Speech Before the French Chamber of Deputies, March 28, 1884." In *Discours et opinions de Jules Ferry*, edited by Paul Robiquet. Paris: Armand Colin, 1897. Translated and quoted by Ruth Kleinman in *Brooklyn College Core Four Sourcebook*, http://sourcebooks.fordham.edu/halsall/mod/1884ferry.asp (accessed August 27, 2020).

Flinn, Margaret. "Documentary and Realism." In *Directory of World Cinema: France*, edited by Tim Palmer and Charlie Michael, 31–38. Chicago, University of Chicago Press, 2013.

Flood, Maria. "Brutal Visibility: Framing Majid's Suicide in Michael Haneke's *Caché* (2005)." *Nottingham French Studies* 56, no. 1 (March 2017): 82–97.

———. *France, Algeria, and the Moving Image: Screening Histories of Violence (1962–2010)*. Oxford: Legenda, 2017.

———. "(Un)Familiar Fictions: Documentary Aesthetics and the 17th October 1961 Massacre in Jacques Panijel's *Octobre à Paris* (1962)." *Forum for Modern Language Studies* 54, no. 2 (2018): 157–75.

Forsdick, Charles. "'Ceci n'est pas un conte, mais une histoire de chair et de sang': Representing the Colonial Massacre in Francophone Literature and Culture." In *Postcolonial Violence, Culture, and Identity in Francophone African and the Antilles*, edited by Lorna Milne, 31–57. Bern: Peter Lang, 2007.

Foucault, Michel. *L'Archéologie du savoir*. Paris: Gallimard, 1969. Translated by A.M. Sheridan Smith as *The Archaeology of Knowledge* (New York: Pantheon Books, 1972).

Freshwater, Helen. "The Allure of the Archive." *Poetics Today* 24, no. 4 (2003): 729–58.

Fulton, Dawn. "Elsewhere in Paris: Creolised Geographies in Leïla Sebbar's *La Seine Était Rouge*." *Culture, Theory and Critique* 48, no. 1 (2007): 25–38.

Galissot, René. "Secret des archives et raison d'état." In *Le 17 octobre, un crime d'état à Paris*, edited by Olivier Le Cour Grandmaison, 103–12. Paris: La Dispute, 2001.

Gallagher, Brianne. "Policing Paris: Private Publics and Architectural Media in Michael Haneke's *Caché*." *Journal for Cultural Research* 12, no. 1 (2008): 19–38.

Gilroy, Paul. *Against Race: Imagining Political Culture Beyond the Color Line*. Cambridge, MA: Harvard University Press, 2000.

———. "Shooting Crabs in a Barrel." *Screen* 48, no. 2 (2006): 233–35.

Giradet, Raoul. *L'Idée coloniale en France de 1871 à 1962*. Paris: Hachette, 1972.

Golsan, Richard J. "Memory's *bombes à retardement*: Maurice Papon, Crimes Against Humanity, and 17 October 1961." *Journal of European Studies* 28, no. 1 (1998): 153–72.

———. *Vichy's Afterlife: History and Counterhistory in Postwar France*. Lincoln: University of Nebraska Press, 2000.

Gordon, Daniel. "Le 17 octobre 1961 et la population française. La collaboration ou la résistance?" In *La Guerre d'Algérie revisitée: nouvelles générations, nouveaux regards*, edited by Aïssa Kadri and Moula Bouaziz, translated by Tramor Quemeneur, 339–50. Paris: Karthala, 2015.

Gorrara, Claire. "Black October: Comics, Memory and Cultural Representations of October 17, 1961." *French Politics, Culture and Society* 36, no. 1 (Spring 2018): 128–47.

———. "Historical Investigations: Didier Daeninckx's *Meurtres Pour Mémoire* (1984)." In *The Roman Noir in Post-War French Culture: Dark Fictions*, 73–89. Oxford: Oxford University Press, 2003.

———. "Reflections on Crime and Punishment: Memories of the Holocaust in Recent French Crime Fiction." *Yale French Studies* no. 108 (2005): 131–45.

Green, Nancy. "Le Melting-Pot: Made in America, Produced in France." *Journal of American History* 86, no. 3 (December 1999): 1188–208.

Gronstad, Asborn. *Screening the Unwatchable: Spaces of Negation in Post-Millennial Art Cinema*. New York: Palgrave Macmillan, 2012.

Hamilton, Carolyn, Verne Harris, Michèle Pickover, Graeme Reid, Razia Saleh, and Jane Taylor, eds. *Refiguring the Archive*. Dordrecht: Kluwer Academic Publishers, 2002.

Hamon, Hervé, and Patrick Rotman. *Les Porteurs de Valises*. Paris: Albin Michel, 1979.

Haneke, Michael. Interview by Karin Schiefer, May 2005. http://www.austrianfilms.com/news/en/bodymichael_haneke_talks_about_cachbody (accessed August 27, 2020).

Harbi, Mohammed, and Benjamin Stora. *La guerre d'Algérie*. Paris: Fayard, 2010.

Hargreaves, Alec G. *Voices from the North African Immigrant Community in France: Immigration and Identity in Beur Fiction*. Berg French Studies Series. New York: Bloomsbury, 1991.

Haroun, Ali. *La 7e wilaya: la guerre du FLN en France, 1954–1962*. Paris: Seuil, 1986.

Harrison, Olivia C. *Transcolonial Maghreb: Imagining Palestine in the Era of Decolonization*. Cultural Memory in the Present. Stanford, CA: Stanford University Press, 2016.

Hiddleston, Jane. "Cultural Memory and Amnesia: The Algerian War and 'Second-Generation' Immigrant Literature in France." *Journal of Romance Studies* 3, no. 1 (2003): 59–71.

Hirsch, Marianne. *The Generation of Postmemory: Writing and Visual Culture after the Holocaust*. New York: Columbia University Press, 2012.

Horne, Alistair. *A Savage War of Peace: Algeria 1954–1962*. 2nd ed. New York: NYRB, 2006. First published in 1977 by Macmillan (New York).

Hosseini, Melahat, and Ron Wakkary. "Influences of Concepts and Structure of Documentary Cinema on Documentary Practices in the Internet." Papers: Museums and the Web, 2004. https://www.museumsandtheweb.com/mw2004/papers/hosseini/hosseini.html (accessed August 27, 2020).

House, Jim. "Anti-Racism in France, 1898–1962: Modernity and Beyond." In *Rethinking Anti-Racisms: From Theory to Practice*, edited by Floya Anthias and Cathie Lloyd, 111–27. New York: Routledge, 2005.

———. "Memory and the Creation of Solidarity during the Decolonization of Algeria." In *Nœuds de Mémoire: Multidirectional Memory in Postwar French and Francophone Culture*, edited by Michael Rothberg, Debarati Sanyal, and Maxim Silverman. Yale French Studies, nos 118/119. New Haven, CT: Yale University Press, 2010.

———. "October 17: On the Past and Its Presence." *Bulletin of Francophone Postcolonial Studies* 3, no. 2 (Autumn 2012): 2–9.

House, Jim, and Neil MacMaster. *Paris 1961. Algerians, State Terror and Memory*. Oxford: Oxford University Press, 2006.

Huyssen, Andreas. *Present Pasts: Urban Palimpsests and the Politics of Memory*. Cultural Memory in the Present. Stanford, CA: Stanford University Press, 2003.

Jaccomard, Hélène. "The Algerian War on French Soil: The Paris Massacre of 17 October, 1961." In *Theatres of Violence: Massacre, Mass Violence and Atrocity throughout History*, edited by Philip G. Dwyer and Lyndall Ryan, 258–70. New York: Berghahn Books, 2012.

Johnson, Barbara. "The Critical Difference: BartheS/BalZac." In *The Critical Difference: Essays in the Contemporary Rhetoric of Reading*, 3–12. Baltimore, MD: Johns Hopkins University Press, 1978.

Jones, Kathryn N. "'Les fantômes d'une mémoire meurtrie': Representing and Remembering La Bataille de Paris in Novels by Nacer Kettane, Mehdi Lallaoui and Tassadit Imache." *Romance Studies* 24, no. 2 (2006): 91–104.

Kaplan, Alice. "Working in the Archives." *Yale French Studies* 77 (1990): 103–16.

Katz, Ethan B. *The Burdens of Brotherhood: Jews and Muslims from North Africa to France*. Cambridge, MA: Harvard University Press, 2015.

Keen, Suzanne. *Romances of the Archive in Contemporary British Fiction.* Toronto: University of Toronto Press, 2001.

Kleppinger, Kathryn. *Branding the 'Beur' Author: Minority Writing and the Media in France.* Liverpool: Liverpool University Press, 2015.

Knox, Katelyn. "Rapping Postmemory, Sampling the Archive: Reimagining 17 October 1961." *Modern and Contemporary France* 22, no. 3 (2014): 381–97.

Kréa, Henri. "Le Racisme est collectif, la solidarité individuelle..." *France Observateur*, October 26, 1961.

Kwon, Miwon. *One Place After Another: Site-Specific Art and Locational Identity.* Cambridge, MA: MIT Press, 2002.

"La manifestation du FLN à Paris le 17 octobre 1961: Le témoignage du lieutenant-colonel Montaner." *Guerres mondiales et conflits contemporains* 206, no. 2 (2002): 87.

Laronde, Michel. "Effets d'histoire. Représenter l'histoire coloniale forclose." *International Journal of Francophone Studies* 10, no. 1–2 (March 2007): 139–55.

Le Roux, Thomas. "Une Rivière industrielle avant l'industrialisation: La Bièvre et le fardeau de la prédestination, 1670–1830." *Géocarrefour* 85, no. 3 (2010): 193–207.

Lebas, Clotilde. "Au fil de nos souvenirs: le 17 octobre 1961, emblème des violences policières." *Revue des mondes musulmans et de la Méditerranée* 119–20 (November 2007): 233–48.

Lemire, Vincent, and Yann Potin. "'Ici on noie les Algériens': Fabriques documentaires, avatars politiques et mémoires partagées d'une icône militante (1961–2001)." *Genèses* 49 (December 2002): 140–62.

Lewis, Jonathan. "Filling in the Blanks: Memories of 17 October 1961 in Leïla Sebbar's *La Seine était rouge*." *Modern & Contemporary France* 20, no. 3 (2012): 307–22.

———. *The Algerian War in French/Algerian Writing: Literary Sites of Memory.* Cardiff: University of Wales Press, 2018.

Liauzu, Claude. "Les Archives bâillonnées de la guerre d'Algérie." *Le Monde diplomatique*, February 1999.

———. "Notes sur les archives de la guerre d'Algérie." *Revue d'histoire moderne et contemporaine* 5, no. 48–4bis (2001): 54–56.

———. "Voyage à travers la mémoire et l'amnésie: le 17 octobre 1961." *Hommes et migrations* 1219 (May–June 1999): 56–61.

Lloyd, Catherine. *Discourses of Antiracism in France.* Research in Ethnic Relations Series. Aldershot, UK: Ashgate, 1998.

Maillot, Agnès. "La presse française et le 17 octobre 1961." *Irish Journal of French Studies*, 25–35, no. 1 (2001): 25–35.

Malberg, Henri. "On a sous-estimé la portée du 17 octobre 1961." Interview by Sébastian Crepel. *L'Humanité*, October 16, 2011.

Manceron, Gilles. "La Triple occultation d'un massacre." In *Le 17 octobre des Algériens*, edited by Marcel Péju and Paulette Péju, 111–85. Paris: La Découverte, 2011.

Manceron, Gilles, and Sortir du colonialisme. *Le 17 octobre 1961 par les textes de l'époque*. With an afterword by Henri Pouillot. Paris: Les Petits matins, 2011.

Mandelbaum, Jacques. "*Octobre à Paris* et *Ici on noie les Algériens*: le 17 octobre 1961, la justice se noya dans la Seine." *Le Monde*, October 14, 2011.

Maschino, Maurice T. "L'histoire expurgée de la guerre d'Algérie." *Le Monde diplomatique*, February 2001.

Massumi, Brian. "Working Principles." In *The Go-To How-To Book of Anarchiving*, edited by Andrew Murphie, 6–8. Montreal: SenseLab, 2016.

Mbembe, Achille. "The Power of the Archive and Its Limits." In *Refiguring the Archive*, edited by Carolyn Hamilton, Verne Harris, Michèle Pickover, Graeme Reid, Razia Saleh, and Jane Taylor, 19–26. Dordrecht: Kluwer Academic Publishers, 2002.

Miller, Christopher. *Imposters: Literary Hoaxes and Cultural Authenticity*. Chicago: University of Chicago Press, 2018.

Milligan, Jennifer. "'What Is an Archive?' In the History of Modern France." In *Archive Stories: Facts, Fiction, and the Writing of History*, edited by Antoinette Burton, 159–83. Durham, NC: Duke University Press, 2006.

Mills-Affif, Edouard. "Le Racisme: la malédiction des immigrés." In *Filmer les immigrés: les représentations audiovisuelles de l'immigration à la télévision française, 1960–1986*, 73–94. Brussels: De Boeck, 2004.

Mognin, Olivier. *La Condition urbaine, la ville à l'heure de la mondialisation*. Paris: Seuil, 2005 [2007].

Morrison, Toni. "On the Backs of Blacks." *Time*, December 2, 1993.

———, ed. *Race-Ing Justice, En-Gendering Power: Essays on Anita Hill, Clarence Thomas, and the Social Construction of Reality*. New York: Random House, 1992.

Mortimer, Mildred. "Probing the Past: Leïla Sebbar, *La Seine était rouge/The Seine Was Red*." *French Review* 82, no. 6 (May 2010): 1246–56.

Myers, Kristen A. *Racetalk: Racism Hiding in Plain Sight*. Lanham, MD: Rowman & Littlefield Publishers, 2005.

Noirel, Gerard. "French and Foreigners." In *Realms of Memory: The Construction of the French Past*, edited by Pierre Nora, translated by Arthur Goldhammer, vol. 1, Conflicts and Divisions, edited by Lawrence D. Kritzman, 145–78. New York: Columbia University Press, 1996.

Nora, Pierre. "Algérie fantôme." *L'Histoire* 43 (March 1982): 9.

———. "Between Memory and History." In *Realms of Memory: The Construction of the French Past*, edited by Pierre Nora, vol. 1, *Conflicts and Divisions*, edited by Lawrence Kritzman, 1–20. New York: Columbia University Press, 1996.

———. *Les Lieux de Mémoire.* 7 vols. Paris: Gallimard, 1984.

———. "Les Lieux de Mémoire (Interview)." By Pierre Kerleroux and Hubert Tison. *Historiens et géographes* 340 (June 1993): 355–66.

Nordmann, Charlotte, and Jérôme Vidal. "La Politique de la mémoire." In *Le 17 octobre, un crime d'état à Paris*, edited by Olivier Le Cour Grandmaison, 171–81. Paris: La Dispute, 2001.

Papastmakou, Sophia. "Le 17 octobre 1961: le silence des affiches." *Matériaux pour l'histoire de notre temps* 106, no. 2 (2012): 60–62.

Péju, Marcel, and Paulette Péju. *Le 17 octobre des Algériens.* Paris: La Découverte, 2011.

Péju, Paulette. *Ratonnades à Paris. Précédé de Les harkis à Paris.* With a preface by Pierre Vidal-Naquet, an introduction by Marcel Péju, and an afterword by François Maspero. Paris: La Découverte, 2000.

Pratt, Mary Louise. *Imperial Eyes: Travel Writing and Transculturation.* 2nd edition. New York: Routledge, 2008.

Rancière, Jacques. "The Cause of the Other." *Parallax* 4, no. 2 (1998): 25–33.

———. *Figures de l'histoire.* Paris: Presses universitaires de France, 2012. Translated by Julie Rose as *Figures of History* (New York: John Wiley and Sons, 2014).

———. *The Politics of Aesthetics.* Translated by Gabriel Rockhill. London: Continuum, 2004.

Reeck, Laura. *Writerly Identities in Beur Fiction and Beyond.* Lanham, MD: Lexington Books, 2011.

Renan, Ernest. "'Qu'est-ce qu'une nation?' Lecture delivered at the Sorbonne, Paris, March 11, 1882." In *Qu'est-ce qu'une nation?: et autres essais politiques*, edited by Joël Roman. Paris: Presses Pocket, 1992. Translated by Ethan Rundell as "What is a Nation?" (http://ucparis.fr/files/9313/6549/9943/What_is_a_Nation.pdf, accessed August 27, 2020).

Renouard, Jean-Philippe, and Isabelle Saint-Saëns. "Festivals d'un film maudit: entretien avec Jacques Panijel." *Vacarme* 13 (Fall 2000).

Rice, Alison. "Rehearsing October 17, 1961: The Role of Fiction in Remembering the Battle of Paris." *L'Esprit Créateur* 54, no. 4 (2014): 90–102.

Riceputi, Fabrice. *La Bataille d'Einaudi, ou comment la mémoire du 17 octobre 1961 revint à la république.* Paris: Le Passager clandestin, 2015.

Rigouste, Mathieux. *L'ennemi intérieur: la généalogie coloniale et militaire de l'ordre sécuritaire dans la France contemporaine.* Paris: La Découverte, 2009.

Rioux, Jean-Pierre. "Torture: L'état coupable mais amnistié." *Libération*, December 11, 2000.

Rosello, Mireille. "Remembering the Incomprehensible: Hélène Cixous, Leïla Sebbar, Yamina Benguigui, and the War of Algeria." In *Remembering Africa*, edited by Elisabeth Mudimbé-Boyi, 187–205. Portsmouth, NH: Heinemann, 2002.

Ross, Kristin. *Fast Cars, Clean Bodies*. Cambridge, MA: MIT Press, 1995.

———. *May '68 and Its Afterlives*. Chicago: University of Chicago Press, 2002.

Rothberg, Michael. *Multidirectional Memory: Remembering the Holocaust in the Age of Decolonization*. Stanford, CA: Stanford University Press, 2009.

Rousso, Henry. *Face au passé*. Paris: Belin, 2016.

———. "La Guerre d'Algérie dans la mémoire des Français." Lecture presented at the La guerre d'Algérie 1954–1962, n.d. https://www.canal-u.tv/producteurs/universite_de_tous_les_savoirs/les_conferences_de_l_annee_2002/la_guerre_d_algerie_1954_a_1962 (accessed August 27, 2020).

———. "Les Raisins verts de la guerre d'Algérie." In *La guerre d'Algérie (1954–1962)*, edited by Yves Michaud, 127–51. Paris: Odile Jacob, 2004.

———. *Le Syndrome de Vichy: 1944 à nos jours*. XXe Siècle. Paris: Seuil, 1987. Translated by Arthur Goldhammer as *The Vichy Syndrome. History and Memory in France Since 1944* (Cambridge, MA: Harvard University Press, 1994).

Sanyal, Debarati. *Memory and Complicity: Migrations of Holocaust Remembrance*. New York: Fordham University Press, 2015.

Saranga, Karen. "Le Jeune homme qui suivait le FN." *L'Express*, April 10, 1998.

Schaefer, Joy C. "The Spatial-Affective Economy of (Post)Colonial Paris: Reading Haneke's *Caché* (2005) through *Octobre à Paris* (1962)." *Studies in European Cinema* 14, no. 1 (2017): 48–65.

Schatz, Adam. "'How does it feel to be a white man?': William Gardner Smith's Exile in Paris." *New Yorker*, August 11, 2019, https://www.newyorker.com/books/page-turner/how-does-it-feel-to-be-a-white-man-william-gardner-smiths-exile-in-paris (accessed August 27, 2020).

Schneider, Rebecca. "Performance Remains." In *Perform, Repeat, Record: Live in Art History*, edited by Amelia Jones and Adrian Heathfield, 137–50. Bristol: Intellect, 2012.

Schor, Naomi. "The Crisis of French Universalism." *Yale French Studies* 100 (2001): 43–64.

Schwerdtner, Karin. "Enquête, transmission et désordre dans *La Seine était rouge* de Leïla Sebbar." *Temps zéro. Revue d'étude des écritures contemporaines* 5 (2012). http://tempszero.contemporain.info/document727 (accessed August 27, 2020).

Sharpe, Mani. "Visibility, Speech, and Disembodiment in Jacques Panijel's *Octobre à Paris*." *French Cultural Studies* 28, no. 4 (2017): 360–70.

Shepard, Todd. *The Invention of Decolonization: The Algerian War and the Remaking of France*. Ithaca, NY: Cornell University Press, 2006.

Silverman, Max. *Palimpsestic Memory: The Holocaust and Colonialism in French and Francophone Fiction and Film*. New York: Berghahn Books, 2013.

——. "The Violence of the Cut: Michael Haneke's *Caché* and Cultural Memory." *French Cultural Studies* 21, no. 1 (February 2010): 57–65.

Steele, Stephen. "Daeninckx, quand le roman policier part en guerre." *French Studies Bulletin* 20, no. 71 (9–10): 1999.

Stoler, Ann Laura. *Along the Archival Grain: Epistemic Anxieties and Colonial Common Sense*. Princeton, NJ: Princeton University Press, 2010.

——. "Colonial Aphasia: Race and Disabled Histories in France." *Public Culture* 23, no. 1 (January 1, 2011): 121–56.

——. "Colonial Archives and the Arts of Governance." *Archival Sciences* 2 (2002): 87–109.

Stora, Benjamin. "Guerre d'Algérie, France, la mémoire retrouvée." *Hommes et migrations* 1158 (October 1992): 10–14.

——. *Les Guerres sans fin: un historien, la France et l'Algérie*. Paris: Stock, 2008.

Stovall, Tyler. "Preface to *The Stone Face*." *Contemporary French and Francophone Studies* 8, no. 3 (June 2004): 305–27.

Sue, Derald Wing. *Race Talk and the Conspiracy of Silence: Understanding and Facilitating Difficult Dialogues about Race*. Hoboken, NJ: John Wiley and Sons, 2015.

Suleiman, Susan Rubin. *Crises of Memory and the Second World War*. Cambridge, MA: Harvard University Press, 2008.

——. "Do Facts Matter in Holocaust Memoirs? Wilkomirski/Wiesel." In *Obliged by Memory: Literature, Religion, Ethics*, edited by Steven T. Katz and Alan Rosen, 21–42. Syracuse, NY: Syracuse University Press, 2006.

Tevanian, Pierre. "Hommage à Brahim Bouarram: Retour sur un crime raciste et son effacement." *Les mots sont importants*, May 1, 2020. https://lmsi.net/Hommage-a-Brahim-Bouarram (accessed August 27, 2020).

——. "Le 'corps d'exception' et ses métamorphoses. Réflexions sur la construction et la destruction de 'l'immigré' et eu 'jeune' issu de l'immigration coloniale et post-coloniale." *Quasimodo* 9 (Spring 2006): 163–80.

Thénault, Sylvie. "Des Couvre-feux à Paris en 1958 et 1961: une mesure importée d'Algérie pour mieux lutter contre le FLN?" *Politix* 84, no. 4 (2008): 167–85.

———. "Le Fantasme du secret d'état autour du 17 octobre 1961." *Matériaux pour l'histoire de notre temps* 58 (2000): 73.

Thibaud, Paul. "Le 17 octobre 1961: un moment de notre histoire." *Esprit* 11, no. 278 (November 2001): 6–19.

Valat, Rémy. *Les Calots bleus et la bataille de Paris: une force de police auxiliaire pendant la guerre d'Algérie.* Paris: Éditions Michalon, 2007.

Vallaeys, Béatrice. "17 octobre 1961: des archives parlent." *Libération,* October 22, 1997.

Vidal-Naquet, Pierre. *La Torture dans la république: Essai d'histoire et de politique contemporaine (1954–1962).* Paris: Éditions de Minuit, 1972.

———. "Une Fidélité têtue. La résistance française à la guerre d'Algérie." *Vingtième siècle. Revue d'histoire* 10 (June 1986): 10–13.

Vince, Natalya. "Transgressing Boundaries: Gender, Race, Religion and 'Françaises Musulmanes' during the Algerian War for Independence." *French Historical Studies* 33, no. 3 (2010): 445–74.

Watts, Phil. "Jacques Panijel: à l'avant-garde de l'après." In *Mémoires occupées: Fictions françaises et Seconde Guerre Mondiale,* edited by Marc Dambre, 167–74. Paris: Presses Sorbonne Nouvelle, 2013.

Weik von Mossner, Alexa. "Confronting *The Stone Face*: The Critical Cosmopolitanism of William Gardner Smith." *African American Review* 45, no. 1–2 (Spring/Summer 2012): 167–82.

———. "Cosmopolitan Sensitivities: Bystander Guilt and Interracial Solidarity in the Work of William Gardner Smith." In *Cosmopolitan Minds: Literature, Emotion and the Transnational Imagination,* 89–119. Austin: University of Texas Press, 2014.

Weil, Patrick. "Le Statut des musulmans en Algérie coloniale: une nationalité française dénaturée." In *La Justice En Algérie, 1830–1962,* 95–109. Paris: La Documentation française, 2005.

———. *Qu'est-ce qu'un Français? Histoire de la nationalité française depuis la révolution.* Paris: Grasset, 2002.

Index

All numbers referring to figures are in **boldface**.
Titles are listed under the names of authors and directors.

17 octobre 1961, 17 illustrators 53–54
Le 17 octobre contre l'oubli *see under*
    associations (activist)

Abbas-Kebir, Benyoucef
    17 octobre 1961, 17 bulles:
      Tragédie-sur-Seine 53, 55
Abu Ghraib torture trials 206
Actualité de l'émigration
    25th-anniversary issue (1986) 36,
      48, 52n55, 174
Adi, Yasmina
    Ici on noie les Algériens (film)
      10n22, 37, 57, 126n26, 132–36,
      134, 150, 154n56, 197–99, **199**
Adimi, Kaouther
    Nos Richesses 312–13
affaire Papon (Papon affair) *see under*
    Papon, Maurice
Agence France-Presse 250, 251n82
Algerian Civil War (1991–2001)
    17–18n38, 146, 148n50
Algerian community in France 12, 40,
    41–42, 50, 87, 111, 138, 232,
    241, 245–46, 272
    Jews 7, 230, 243, 279, 280n38, 281,
      284–86
    Muslims 8, 50, 81, 96, 100–1,
      166–67, 222–23, 232n46, 258,
      279, 285–86

    rank-and-file 9, 19n40, 35–36n7, 90,
      174–75, 231
    see also FMA
    see also Sebbah, Moïse
    see also the names of individual
      suburbs
Algerian War of Independence 6–7,
    12, 15, 17–18n38, 22, 41,
    56, 65, 221, 265, 269, 286,
    315
    50th anniversary of 13, 68
    and anarchives 67, 259
    and archives 19–20, 75, 81–82, 84
    and French memory 13, 34–35,
      49–50, 270, 271, 312
    and racism 225–26, 250n81
    anti-war activists/protestors 21, 51,
      234, 242, 278, 303–4
    Évian Accords 12, 68
    second front in mainland France
      7–8, 46, 90, 287
    use of torture 182, 227n34
    see also Michel, Eric, *Algérie!*
      Algérie!
    see also Pontecorvo, Gillo, *The*
      Battle of Algiers
anamnesis 34n3, 65
anarchive
    and the internet 29, 30, 60–61, 112,
      181, 312, 314

definition 24–27
Octobre à Paris as ur-text 230
other uses of term 24–25, 26n58
periodization 33, 49, 68–69, 262 *see
    also* wave, first; wave, second;
    wave, third
see also Derrida, Jacques
see also Massumi, Brian
see also SenseLab
anti-Semitism 239
    and the police 279–86 *see also*
        Sebbah, Moïse
    in literature 255, 267, 293–94
    Vichy legislation 221, 274, 280n38
Arab Spring 157
archive stories 74–75, 85, 90, 105, 114
archives
    access and legislation 76, 77, 78, 80,
        82, 84–85
    alternative archives 98, 101, 107, 114
    and activists 72–73, 82–83
    and *mal d'archive* (archive sickness)
        76
    archival politics 79, 80, 83
    in literature 71, 92–93, 95, 98, 100,
        101, 103, 104–5, 106, 109, 114,
        195
    theories of 24–25, 59, 73–74, 76–77,
        84
    see also anarchive
    see also archivists
    see also October 17 police
        archives
archivists 51, 77–78, 84, 85, 101
    in literature 71, 94–95, 101, 103–4,
        107, 108
Argenteuil 138
    in literature 176, 193, 195
Argentinian Dirty War 46, 308, 315
Armenian genocide 47n42, 295, 315
Arnold, Georges 99
associations (activist)
    Au nom de la mémoire 48–49,
        53–54, 58n65, 80n27, 82–83,
        112, 192n41

Le 17 octobre contre l'oubli 49, 82,
    154n56
Le Mouvement des jeunes
    communistes de France 154
MRAP (Mouvement contre le
    racisme) 83n36, 233–34, 277–78
Union nationale des étudiants de
    France (UNEF) 234
Union des sociétés juives de France
    275
Assouline, David 80
Au nom de la mémoire *see under*
    associations (activist)
Aubervilliers 121, 122, 125, 167–68,
    279
    Place du 17 octobre 119, 123n21
Audin Committee 34–35, 52,
    234–35n53, 240–41
Audin, Maurice 34
Augé, Marc
    on *non-lieux* 158
Auschwitz 43, 265, 286–87
    in literature 106, 302–3
Avant Garde 154
Avignon Theatre Festival *see under*
    theatre (venues and festivals)
Azenstarck, Georges
    see under photography

Badea, Alexandra
    *Points de non-retour: Quais de
        Seine* 5, 313
Baldwin, James 38, 244
banlieue 121, 124–25, 128, 131n38, 132,
    181n29, 232–33
    in literature 58, 136–37, 138, 142,
        176, 254–55, 295
Barbet, Raymond 233
Barthes, Roland
    city-text 116–18
    lisible vs. *scriptible* 116–17, 122–23,
        151
Bédar, Fatima 39
    Fatima Bédar Park (Saint-Denis)
        119, 123n21

Begag, Azouz
  critique of Léger's *Vivre me tue*
    69–70, 89n42, 252–54, 257, 259,
    261–63
Belkebla, Fadila 121n18
Benaïcha, Brahim
  Vivre au paradis 46–47, 257n94
Benayoun, Robert 186n34, 237
Berlière, Jean-Marc 80, 83–84n38
les beurs
  beur characters 45, 302
  beur cinema 44n35
  beur literature 43, 45, 214
  beur movement 41, 44, 48, 178n26
  beur novel 44–46, 56, 66, 131, 191,
    214, 251–54
  beur rap 60
  scholarship on 42n28, 44n35, 45
beurs' march *see* March for equality
  and against racism (*La marche
  des beurs*)
Bezons 100–1, 168, 176
  October 17 memorial 121, 122,
    200
bidonville see also under Nanterre
  in film 46, 227, 229, 241, 257, 291,
    315
  in literature 99, 132n39, 141
  in theatre 160
Bièvre River 207–8
Blanchard, Emmanuel 9n19, 14n31,
  32n2, 99, 126n17, 128, 165n9,
  223n26, 269, 287n45
Blanchard, Pascal 13n29, 15
Borvo, Senator Nicole 81–82
Bouarram, Brahim 163–66
Bouchareb, Rachid
  Hors-la-loi 51, 57, 66–67, 69–70,
    291–92
Boudjellel, Farid
  political cartoons 48
Bourdet, Claude 288–89
Boutadjine, Mustapha
  17 octobre 1961 (poster) 61, 63,
    200

Brel, Jacques 2, 97
Brooks, Philip, and Alan Hayling
  Drowning by Bullets 10n22, 47, 99,
    202n50
Brunet, Jean-Paul
  Police contre FLN 10n22, 48, 80,
    90n43, 133n40, 292n51

canal de l'Ourcq 167, 212
canal Saint-Denis 39, 167
Le Canard enchaîné 41, 50, 287
Cannes Film Festival
  Caché (*Hidden*) 202n49
  Hors-la-loi 57, 291n51
  Octobre à Paris 36
Capdenac, Michel
  Lettres françaises 239
Cau, Jean (*L'Express*) 128
Le cave se rebiffe (The Counterfeiters
  of Paris) 2
cemeteries
  le carré musulman (Muslim
    section) 260–61
  Père Lachaise 21
  Thiais Cemetery 50
censorship 19, 30, 40, 115, 254, 314
  of archives 112, 112n31
  of cinema 34, 36, 242n72
  of press 124n25, 224, 224n31, 276
Césaire, Aimé 222, 276
CGT (General Confederation of
  Labor) 272–73
Chambers-Samadi, Chadia
  *Répréssion des manifestants
  Algériens* 66
Charef, Mehdi
  Le thé au harem d'Archi Ahmed 44
Charles, Ray 2
Charlie Hebdo 54n56
Charonne massacre 20n42, 21–22, 42,
  69, 237–40, 242, 304
  la chasse au faciès 223, 258, 284
  see also racial profiling
Cherfaoui, Affif
  "Les enfants d'octobre" 61

Chevalier, Guy 3n6, 282
Chevènement, Jean-Pierre 79
Chirac, Jacques 13n30, 164, 262n96
Chouaki, Aziz 51, 55, 58, 209–10, 289
    La Pomme et le couteau 51, 190–91, 289–91
cinema
    censorship of 34, 36–37, 242n72
    see also individual authors and titles
cinema (venues)
    Action ciné-club 36
    Berlitz 2, 139, 311
    Grand Rex 2, 3, 139–40
    Saint-Michel 183
    Studio Bertrand 36
civil rights movement 35, 38, 248, 249
    Civil Rights Act of 1960 244
Claudius-Petit, Eugène 233, 274
Clichy-la-Garenne 121
Colombes 121, 168
colonialism 6, 15, 119, 299, 306, 315
    and the Holocaust 64, 224, 296n11
    and republican values 286
    as product of violence 130
    Fanonian prophecy 127, 128–30
comics/comix *see under* graphic novel
commemorative activities/ performances 13, 313
    "Memento" 158–61 *see also* Komplex Kapharnaüm
    Pierre noire 59, 159n64
    subway station 119–20 *see also* Slimani, Mourad
commemorative plaques 116, 119
    Aubervilliers 121–22
    Bezons 121, 122
    Fontenay-sous-Bois 122
    in literature 149–53
    pont Saint-Michel 121–22, 154
    Saint-Denis 122–23
    Saint-Michel fountain 153

commemorative posters 63n77, 166, 199–201, 209, 211
    Boutadjine, Mustapha 61, 63, 63n76
    Kerzazi, Miloud 199–200
commemorative stamp
    Day of Emigration 22–23, 24n54
Communist Party *see* French Communist Party (PCF)
Communists 9, 277, 290, 291
    see also Lumières des Gondoles
Compagnies Républicaines de Sécurité (CRS) 139–40, 304
Coty, René 108
La Courneuve 63, 120
Crémieux Decree 7n11, 127, 280
Critical Race Theory 218
critique génétique 86
curfew 9–10, 123, 225, 271, 287
    critiques of racism 223, 231–36
    in literature 215, 257, 259, 288, 290, 303–4
    reactions to 219–20, 235, 272, 274, 309
    references to commemorative plaques 122n20, 123
    revisions to 86–87, 259

D'Agraives, Jean
    France is an Empire 128–29, 131
Dachau 290
Daeninckx, Didier 5, 29, 42, 43, 46, 51–53, 55, 66, 70, 98, 105, 121, 268, 286, 303
    "Delphine pour mémoire" 39n20, 48
    "Fatima pour mémoire" 257
    Meurtres pour mémoire 29, 48, 51, 71, 101, 106, 114, 289, 305, 306, 314
    and city as text 139–45, 158
    as archive romance 92–98
    illustrated version of 43, 53
    significance of 42–44, 64, 92, 216, 254, 265–69
    TV adaptation of 43, 47

Octobre noir 39, 53, 256–57, 266
on the *polar* 43
Dark Decade
   see Algerian Civil War
Day of Emigration 22, 23–24n54 *see also* commemorative stamp
de Beauvoir, Simone 276
Debord, Guy 148n51
   Guide psychogéographique de Paris 130–31
   Naked City 130–31
de Certeau, Michel 116
decolonization 6, 7, 14, 15, 130, 263, 307
   narrative of 196n44
La Défense 117, 126, 147, 149, 151
de Gaulle, Charles 4, 11–12, 111, 127n28, 152, 224n31, 266, 301, 305, 309
Delahautemaison, Virginie
   Mémoire du fleuve 47
Delanoë, Bertrand 21n45, 121, 154
deportation 249, 273, 276, 277, 287, 289, 291, 303
   from Bordeaux/Gironde 41, 88, 287
   from France 249
   represented in *Meurtres pour mémoire* 43, 93–94
Derrida, Jacques 24–25, 29
Diên Biên Phu 12n26, 14
Djemaï, Abedelkader
   Gare du nord 66
documentary *see under* film
Drancy 276, 277, 278, 286, 287
   in literature 43, 93–94, 114, 300
Drew, Richard
   "The Falling Man" 201n47
Dreyfus affair 221
Drowning by Bullets see under Brooks, Philip
Dumas, Alexandre
   La tour de Nesle 171, 184
Duvivier, Julien
   Pépé le moko 2

Éditions de Minuit 240
8 May 1945 *see* Sétif and Guelma massacre
Einaudi, Jean-Luc 32, 50, 51, 98, 259, 287
   as Renucci 191
   La Bataille de Paris 3n6, 4n7, 48, 77
   La Bataille de Paris reissue 80
   L'Humanité interview (2001) 3
   Papon libel suit 50–51, 78, 98–101, 109, 191
   preface to Kagan's *17 octobre 1961* 19n39
Elkabbach, Jean-Pierre 58
Les Engraineurs 45–46, 131n38, 314
Enlightenment 15n33, 220n15, 269n11
entanglements 6, 13, 266–67, 268, 292–93, 301, 306, 308–9
   Moïse Sebbah story 286
   Papon, Maurice 286
era of the witness 242–43, 243n74
erasure of October 17, 24, 29, 32, 34, 52, 237, 312
Ernaux, Annie 56
Évian Accords *see under* Algerian War of Independence
exceptional bodies *see under* Seine, La
Exodus (film by Otto Preminger, 1960) 231
Exodus (novel by Leon Uris, 1958) 231n42

Faire face see under television
Fanon, Frantz 127–28, 130, 136, 222
Farrar, Straus and Giroux 35, 249
Feldman, Hannah 14, 68
   From a Nation Torn 67, 124n23, 128n30, 131
fellaghas (Algerian freedom fighters) 279
Ferry, Jules 222
FF-FLN (FLN French Federation)
   see FLN (National Liberation Front)

film
   Caché 5, 51, 56–57, 66–67, 202–10
   Chronique d'un été 223–24, 237, 241
   documentary 4, 28, 31, 33, 37, 46–48, 67, 314
   Mémoires du 17 octobre 45
   nouvelle vague 36
   Silence du fleuve 48
   see also Ici on noie les Algériens
   see also Haneke, Michael
   see also Hors-la-loi
   see also Panijel, Jacques
FLN (National Liberation Front)/
   FF-FLN (FLN French
   Federation)
   accused of October 17 deaths 3
   and Algerian national politics 22
   and Jews 283–84
   and Jacques Panijel 35n5, 241–42
   and the Paris police 11n23, 227, 262–63, 271, 274, 292
   and race talk 230–32
   and second front in France 223, 230
   archival narratives of 79–80, 87–88
   criticism of 36, 174–75
   depicted in literature 99, 300
   depicted in film 69, 71, 106, 205, 291–92
   filmic recreation 108, 113, 227, 236–37, 257
   October 17 demonstration plans 2, 9–10, 19n40, 128
   October 18 call, *Un Appel au Peuple Français* 231n41, 274, 276
   revolutionary activity in France 7–10, 20, 123–24, 230
   tracts/manifestos 86, 108, 113, 231, 232
   see also Brunet, Jean-Paul
   see also Haroun, Ali
FMA (Français musulmans d'Algérie)
   8n15, 88–89, 100–1, 167, 258, 280, 282n41, 284, 285

France is an Empire 128–29, **129**, 131
France Observateur 19n40, 107–8, **108**, 229n39
France-Soir 124–30, **125**
Franco-Prussian War 169, 170
French Association of Archivists 78
French Communist Party (PCF) 81, 83, 121n17
French Jews 41, 223, 275, 277, 286, 289
French Muslims 127, 209, 271–72
   see also FMA
   see also under Algerian community in France
French National Archives 77, 103–4
French Republic 75–76
   and foundational myth 220–21, 225
   and universalism 15, 220–23
   civilizing mission of 222
   French Republican principles 9, 42, 75
Frey, Roger 10–11, 20, **125**
Front de libération nationale (National Liberation Front) *see* FLN

Gabin, Jean 2, 139, 311
   La belle équipe 181n29
Gaullism 268–69, 278
genres
   autoethnography 45
   docudrama 51, 89, 111, 256–57, 288
   graphic novel 39, 43, 53–55, 256
   music video 4, 29, 39, 57, 181, 317
   photography 67
   poetry 35–36, 170, 172–78, 179, 181, 290, 316
   polar 43, 53–54, 91–92, 105, 265
   posters 61, 63, 166, 199, 200–1
   pulp fiction 39, 43, 46, 53, 91, 196, 209
   theatre 49, 55, 57–59, 190, 313
   webdoc 60–61
   see also film; graphic novel; novels; young adult literature
   see also under les beurs, beur novel

German occupation *see under* Nazism, Nazi occupation
Gilroy, Paul 38, 306
    on *Caché* 204–6
    on *The Stone Face* 249
Gironde 88, 93, 286, 287
    Gironde prefecture 41
"Glorious Thirty" 41, 156
Gobineau, Joseph Arthur de 221, 226n33
Golsan, Richard J. 268–69, 305
graffiti 28, 115, 167
    and the anarchive 118, 145, 151, 154, 158–59, 161
    and the scriptable city 116, 118, 148–49, 150–52, 154
    and Texier's photo 18, 48, 67–68, 154–56, 317
    as alternative history 150–51
    as genre 29, 154
    denunciatory 3, 17, 155
    in literature 65, 97, 143–47, 148–51, 153, 156
    in performance 158–61, 161, 315–17, 316
    map of October 17 graffiti 155
    see also "Ici on noie les Algériens" (graffito)
    see also Sebbar, Leïla
    see also Texier, Jean
    see also Zik Zitoun
Grand, Philippe *see* archivists
Granouillet, Gilles 55
    Nuit d'automne à Paris 58
graphic novel 53–55
    17 octobre 1961, 17 bulles: Tragédie-sur-seine 53
    17 octobre 1961, 17 illustrators 53–54
    Meurtres pour mémoire 43, 265
    Octobre noir 39, 256
Greenaway, Peter
    Death in the Seine 170n18
Grimzi, Habib 299n59
"A Group Declares..." 109–13

"Un group de policiers républicains declare..." *see* "A Group Declares..."
Guedj, Boualerm
    Vivre au paradis 46
Guène, Faïza 46, 314
    Kiffe kiffe demain 45, 66
    Mémoires du 17 octobre (film) 45, 131–32, 133
guillotine 152

Habbaz, Brahim 236
Hadj, Messali 3n6 *see also* MNA
Hai Phong 97, 144
Haneke, Michael
    Caché (Hidden) 5, 29, 51, 56–57, 64, 65, 66–67, 202–9, 210
Harki 9, 71, 106, 183, 149, 227–28
Haroun, Ali 48
    La 7e wilaya 108
Hassan, Yaël 54, 69, 70
    Le professeur de musique 54, 302–5, 308
Haussmann, Baron 168n11, 207
Hayling, Alan *see* Brooks, Philip
Herald Tribune 248
Hervo, Monique 131–32
    as Monique Devaux 99
Heynemann, Laurent 46, 47
    Meurtres pour mémoire (docudrama) 43
Hidalgo, Anne 212
high culture 55, 209
Himes, Chester 38
Hirsch, Marianne
    The Generation of Postmemory 194n43
HLM 42
Holiday, Billie
    "Strange Fruit" 189–90
Hollande, François 68–69n89, 72
    official recognition of October 17 83
Holocaust, the
    and the anarchive 265, 267, 286–89, 292–93, 299, 304–6, 308, 315

and "comparative discourse" 88
and "dangerous parallels" 268–69,
    304, 305
and error as site of meaning 70
and memory studies 64–65, 201,
    268, 306–7
and Maurice Papon 264–65,
    286–92, 305, 307–8
and witness deferral 76
depicted by Jacques Panijel 242–43
entanglements of 306–8
in literature 28, 223–24, 267,
    288–304
marginalization of 293–99
Holocaust survivors
in literature 293, 299, 301, 305
Hôpital Sainte-Anne 151–52
Hôtel de Crillon 151, 152, 153
House, Jim
    Paris 1961 82, 84–85
Hugo, Victor
    L'Année terrible 170–71
Human Genome Project 218
L'Humanité 16n34, 124, 276–77
    Humanité Dimanche 112
    on racial profiling 235
    publishes Texier photo 48
Huyssen, Andreas 116, 268
hypermnésie 49–50, 68–69
hypervisibility 209–12

"Ici on noie les Algériens" (graffito) 3,
    17, 48, 115, 118, 144–45, 153,
    167, 198–99, 316
    see also Adi, Yasmina
    see also Texier, Jean
Île de France 138, 168, 192n42
Île de la Cité 139, 154, 168
Île St Louis 168
Imache, Tassadit 44, 45
    Une fille sans histoire 254–56
indigènes 127, 130, 165–66
    Indigènes (film) 291
    Indigènes de la République 13n29,
        199

Indochina 12n26, 14, 97, 144, 281
Institut de France 18, 154
Insitut du monde arabe 178n26
Intifada, First 178n26, 295
Iraq War 206

Janvier, Ludovic
    "Du nouveau sous le pont" 175–78,
        209
Jeanson network (porteurs de valise)
    106, 146n47, 239–41
Jeune Afrique 36
Jeune résistance 234
Johnson, Barbara 117

Kabyles/Kabylia 28, 45, 213, 233,
    296
Kagan, Élie
    see under photography
    see also Krief, Jean-Pierre
Kalouaz, Ahmed
    Les fantômes d'octobre 32, 44n33,
        299, 303
    Point kilométrique 299
Kaplan, Alice
    on peritextuality 73
Kassovitz, Mathieu
    La Haine (film) 142n45, 164
Kerzazi, Miloud
    commemorative posters 199–200,
        200
Kettane, Nacer 45, 66, 118
    Le Sourire de Brahim 44, 45, 56,
        136–39, 158, 179–80, 189n37,
        254–55, 294–99, 308
Komplex Kapharnaüm 58–59, 158, 161
    "Memento" 158–61
Kréa, Henri
    interviews 231–32
Krief, Jean-Pierre
    Les années Kagan 47
Kwon, Miwon 158

L'Express 128
Lainé, Brigitte *see* archivists

Lallaoui, Mehdi 38, 52, 53–54, 66, 82,
    109, 121n18
    Le silence du fleuve 47, 48–49,
        192n41
    Les Beurs de Seine 44, 45, 118,
        138–39, 141, 143, 158, 191–92,
        209
    Monique H., Nanterre 1961 58,
        99n53
    preface to *Octobre à Paris* (Panijel)
        37, 242n72
    Une nuit d'octobre 51, 71, 98–102,
        105, 110, 191
    see also under associations
        (activist) Au nom de la mémoire
Lalou, Étienne
    "Le Racisme" (television) 213,
        224–25, 248
Lanzmann, Claude 276
Laronde, Michel 65, 67
Latin Quarter 2, 154
Laurent, Pierre 83
Le Bourhis, Michel *Les yeux de
    Moktar* 54
Left Front 218n10
Léger, Jack-Alain (Smaïl, Paul)
    Vivre me tue 213–16, 251–54,
        259–62
Leibowitch, Mauricette
    Le cœur a sa mémoire 181n28
Leon Blum Square 160
Les Engraineurs 45–46n39, 131n38, 314
les renseignements généraux (les RG)
    132–33, **134**, 135
Lévine, Michael
    Les ratonnades d'octobre 48
Lévy, Denis
    Mémoire en blanc 46
Liauzu, Claude 82
Libération 19, 232–33, 235
    "The Archives Speak" 79–80
lieux de mémoire 28, 115, 119, 158
    see also memorialscapes
    see also Nora, Pierre
Le Louvre 117

Lumières des Gondoles 273
Lyon 158, 160
    immigrant communities of 252

M'Bowolé, Makomé 164n7
MacMaster, Neal
    Paris 1961 82, 84–85
made-for-TV movie see under genres,
    docudrama
Mandelkern
    Commission 51n52, 79, 80
    Report 11n24, 100
Mandelkern, Dieudonné 79n24
Mangier, Thierry 52, 54
maps of October 17
    France is an Empire 128–31, **129**
    France-Soir map 124–28, **125**,
        130–31, 132
    graffiti map **155**
    Hervo eyewitness map 131–32, **133**
    in literature 138, 140, 145, 147–50,
        156
    RG maps 132–36, **134**
maps of Paris 124, 135, 136, 155–56,
    206
    clickable 61
    in literature 143, 145, 150
    see also under La Seine
    see also maps of October 17
March for equality and against racism
    (*La marche des beurs*) 42
    in literature 255
Marianne statues 149, 199
Marker, Chris 37
    La Jetée 135
    Le Joli mai 21n46
Marseille 160–61
massacres
    Camp de Thiaroye, Sénégal 12n26,
        66
    see also Charonne massacre
    see also Sétif and Guelma massacre
Massumi, Brian 25, 31
Mattei, Georges 19n40
May '68 6, 21–22, 200–1

Mbembe, Achille 76–77, 84, 89, 114
Mecca 147, 157
Mechkour, Larbi
    political cartoons 48
Médine 60, 190n30, 314
    17 octobre (rap) 51, 55, 186–90,
        191, 209, 210, 312
Mélani, Hamma
    Lamento pour Paris 61–62
Memmi, Albert 222
memorial 149, 150, 151, 152, 153, 156,
        159, 160
    practices 68, 138
    productions 197
    sites 61, 63, 65, 201
memorialscape 28, 147, 150, 151, 155,
        156, 307
    codes 122
    Parisian 119
    representation of October 17 118
memory
    collective 4, 82, 118, 269, 311
    competitive 304, 306–7
    Holocaust as site of 267, 268, 308
    lieu(x) de mémoire 118, 119, 158
    of the Algerian War 13, 34, 34n3,
        49–50, 269–71
    of Vichy 6, 68, 221, 242, 269–71
memory studies 64–65
    multidirectional 64, 151, 242,
        266n5, 306–7
    palimpsestic 65, 151, 242, 306, 307
    postmemory 194n43, 216, 303
    screen memory 20n42, 22
Messaoudi, Samia 48–49
métro 17 octobre 1961 *see under*
        commemorative activities/
        performances, subway station
métropole 7, 41, 130, 147n49, 226n33,
        286
    second front 287
Michel, Eric
    Algérie! Algérie! 51, 56, 71, 106–9,
        111, 112, 114, 258–59, 288,
        307–8

Michel, Natacha
    Plein présent 51, 56, 288–89
Mignonneau, Inspector 282–85
Mitterrand, François 164–65
MNA (le Mouvement national
        algérien) 3n6, 78–79n23
Le Monde 10n22, 35n5, 112
    coverage of Papon trial 50–51
    La nuit oubliée (webdoc) 60–61
Le Monde diplomatique 13–14n30, 82
Mongin, Olivier 116
Morin, Edgar 223–24, 237n59
Moroccans
    as victims of police violence
        229–30, 236, 243, 252–53, 256,
        258–59, 284–85
Morocco 7, 129–30, 229n39, 236n57,
        286–87
Morrison, Toni 217
Mossner, Alexa Weik von 38, 251n82
Mounsi, Mohand 44–45n36, 45, 163
    Territoire d'outre-ville 44
multidirectional memory *see under*
        Rothberg, Michael
music 29, 57
    chaâbi 316
    The Cure 260
    Mediterranean rap 315
    rap 51, 186–90, 189
    see also Médine
    see also Têtes raides

Nanterre 58, 125, 126, 148, 175, 190n40
    bidonville 8, 10, 46–47, 99, 132n39,
        138, 141, 147, 227, 229, 241, 257,
        291, 314–15
    see also Barbet, Raymond
National Assembly 7n10, 230, 233, 271, 274
National Front 163–64
National Liberation Front *see* FLN
Nazism 277, 293
    Nazi occupation 110n67, 152–53,
        219–21, 255, 268–69, 272, 273,
        276, 295, 315
    and October 17 219–21

Neuilly bridge 126, 149, 194
Neuilly-sur-Seine 2
Niemöller, Martin 290–91
non-lieux
    defined 158
Nora, Pierre 40, 113, 119, 158
North African Jews 283
North African Surveillance Team 223
North Africans 7, 89, 165, 275, 284,
    285
Notre-Dame de Paris 137
novels *see also under les beurs* (*beur
    novel*)
    see individual authors and titles
November 13, 2015, terror attacks 168,
    312, 315
Nuit noire (docudrama) *see under*
    Tasma, Alain
La nuit oubliée (webdoc) 60–61

OAS (Organisation armée secrète) 108
occupation *see under* Nazism, Nazi
    occupation
October 17 anniversaries
    25th anniversary 174
    30th anniversary 77
    40th anniversary 121, 199
    50th anniversary 68, 72, 121n17,
        166, 199
    52nd anniversary 83
    effect of 69
    occasions for new works of art 313
October 17 police archives
    accessibility 82
    and Jospin government
        investigation 78
    declassification 68, 74, 75, 82, 83
    Pré-Saint-Gervais 73
    see also under Mandelkern
        (Report)
Octobre à Paris see under Panijel,
    Jacques
Octobre noir see under Daeninckx,
    Didier
"On a appris à nager" *see* Zik Zitoun

Paillard, Didier 123
Palais des Sports 1, 273, 276–77
palimpsest 65, 151, 156, 242
    in film 198–99, 208
    Paris as 116
Panijel, Jacques 34–35, 37
    and the Audin Committee 34–35,
        240–41
    La Rage 240, 240n67
    Octobre à Paris 17, 19n39, 37, 67,
        118, 182–86, 187, 188, 197,
        226–43
    on racism 241, 257, 262
Pantin 45, 279, 280
Papon, Maurice
    affaire Papon (Papon affair) 40–41,
        44, 50, 79, 265, 268, 269,
        286–88
    and Bordeaux (Gironde) 41, 50, 88,
        285, 286, 287, 289
    and Einaudi libel trial 50–51,
        77–78, 79, 109, 287–88
    as Chief of Police (Paris) 2, 9,
        11, 20, 80, 90, 125, 271, 274,
        281–83, 292
    as colonial administrator 286n44,
        287
    death of 49
    deportation of Jews 41, 88, 286–87,
        289
    guilty verdict 41, 287
    in film 69, 205, 257–58, 291–92
    in literature 43, 92–92, 98–99, 101,
        104, 107, 149, 153, 258–59, 260,
        265–66, 288
    in music 187–88
    in theatre 289–91
    interview with Elkabbach 58
    Service for Jewish Questions 286
paraliterary 53, 54, 91
    see also under genres, pulp fiction
Paris
    Algerians deported from (1961–62)
        11, 277
    Algerian population in 8, 90, 287

as Lutèce 168
as symbolic site 8, 14–15, 118, 140,
    167, 168
axe historique 117
banlieue of 121, 124–25, 126, 128,
    232
banlieue represented in the
    anarchive 132, 137, 138, 142,
    176, 254, 295
Commune 117, 169, 170, 172–73,
    188
city as text 116
lisible/scriptible 116–18
mayors of 78n21, 121, 212
rue de Goutte d'Or 9n19, 246
see also maps of Paris
see also memorialscapes
see also La Seine
*see also the names of individual
    suburbs*
Paris archives 101
    see October 17 police archives
Péju, Marcel 8, 18, 19
Péju, Paulette 8, 18, 19, 123
Le Pen, Jean-Marie 163
phenotype 89, 228–29, 245–47, 253,
    254, 257n93, 260, 261, 284
photography 17–18, 47, 66–67
    Azenstarck, Georges 18–19, 97n48,
        102n57
    Kagan, Élie 17, 18–19, 47, 48, 52,
        67, 97, 139
    Texier, Jean 18, 154–56
pieds noirs 7, 213n1
Piquemal, Michel
    "Le bon samaritain" 299–301
polar 53–54, 91–92, 265
    as hypothesis about reality 43,
        70–71
    Polarchives series 106
    see also under genres, *polar*
Pontecorvo, Gillo
    The Battle of Algiers 12, 237
Porte de Versailles 1, 86, 128
porteurs de valise *see* Jeanson network

Portzer, Emile 112
Positif 186n34, 237
postmemory 194, 216, 303
    see also Hirsch, Marianne
    see also memory studies
Pour! 112
Prati-Belkmokhtar, Marie-Christine
    58
    C'était un 17 octobre 61
Préfecture de Paris 139, 156
pulp fiction *see under* genres

Quai de Conti 18, 154
Quai Saint-Michel 154

race talk
    definition 217
    in *Chronique d'un été* 223–24
    in *Faire face* 224–25
race-ing 216, 216n5, 220
racial profiling 19n40, 28, 70, 88–89,
    215–16, 255, 263
    and the Sebbah dossier 279–86
    reported in the press 235
    represented in *Octobre à Paris*
        228–30
racism
    and colonialism 218, 221–22, 226,
        226n33
    beur protests against 42
    in contemporaneous media 231–35
    in FLN materials 230–31
    in police archives 88–89, 219–23,
        236
    of the "curfew" 257–59, 271–75
radio
    RadioBeur (BeurFM) 45
    TNZ 1 133
Ralite, Jack 121
Rancière, Jacques 1, 16–17, 67
rap *see under* music
Raspouteam-*17.10.61* 61
ratonnade 20, 20n43, 217–18n8, 226
RATP (Régie Autonome des
    Transports Parisiens) 119, 258

refoulement (repression) *see under*
    Rousso, Henry
Rémy, Pierre-Jean
    Algérie, bords de Seine 46
Renan, Ernst 169, 226n33
Renoir, Jean
    Boudu sauvé des eaux
       (*Boudu Saved from Drowning*)
       184
Renucci (fictional avatar) 191
    see under Einaudi, Jean-Luc
représentation décomplexée 51
Republic, Third 7n10, 170
Republic, Fifth 13, 306, 309
Resnais, Alain 37
Richard, Bernard 131n38
rights of man 10, 15
    Declaration of the Rights of Man
       and Citizen 220
roman policier *see polar*
romance of the archive 92, 106
    typology of 91
Rothberg, Michael
    Multidirectional Memory 64–65,
       306, 307
    multidirectional memory, concept
       151, 306, 308n67
    on *Chronicle of a Summer* 224
    on Jewishness in *The Stone Face*
       293–94
Rotman, Patrick 57
Rouabhi, Mohamed 55, 58, 308
Rouch, Jean 35, 37, 241
    Chronicle of a Summer 223, 224,
       237n59
Rousso, Henry 34, 49, 50, 269
    broken mirror phase 298–99
    obsessional memory 313
    refoulement (repression) 221, 242,
       270–71
    rejeux (high fever) 270, 278
    Vichy Syndrome 221, 269–70
Rwandan genocide 201n48

Sanyal, Debarati 306–7, 308n66

Sarkozy, Nicolas
    and October 17 police archives 20,
       68, 72, 83
Sartre, Jean-Paul 19n39
    Les Temps modernes 38, 231n41,
       276–77
Screen 66–67
Sebbah, Moïse 279–86
    as "archive story" 88–89
Sebbar, Leïla
    "La Seine était rouge" (essay) 48, 174
    La Seine était rouge (novel) 48,
       52–55, 64–65, 89, 102n58, 108,
       145–57, 207, 216
    "L'île Seguin, le retour" 156–57
    Shérazade trilogy 146n48
La Seine
    and culture of the *guinguettes*
       181–82, 185, 188, 211–12
    and French Impressionism 169–70
    as mass burial site 166–68, 170–71,
       172, 178, 186, 201, 209
    Brahim Bourram 163–65
    geography of 124, 156, 168, 209
    history and politics of 138, 168–71,
       194n42, 211–12
    in the press (1961) 198n46
    map of (in *Caché*) 209
SenseLab 1, 25, 31
Sétif and Guelma massacre 12n26, 14,
    22, 35–37n7, 37n13, 232n46
    in literature 138–39, 291, 313
Shah of Iran (Mohammad Reza
    Pahlavi) 1, 311
Shams, Alex 312
shantytown 8, 10, 42
    see also bidonville; Nanterre
Shoah 55, 70, 266, 270, 292, 315
    see also Holocaust, the
Silverman, Max 65, 67n86, 203n51,
    206, 242, 269, 287
    palimpsestic memory 65, 151, 306
Situationists 67, 97
    Guy Debord 130–31, 158
    psychogeography 148–49

Slimani, Mehdi 313n3
Slimani, Mourad 119–20
Smaïl, Paul *see* Léger, Jack-Alain
Smith, William Gardner
  Anger at Innocence 38, 251
  The Stone Face 4, 29, 35, 244, 293
Socialist Party 82
Somveille, Pierre 257–59, 258n95, 281, 285
La Sorbonne 288
SOS Racisme 137n42
Le Sourire de Brahim see under Kettane, Nacer
Spiegelman, Art
  Maus series 55
St. Bartholomew's Day Massacre 170
Star of David (yellow star) 201, 231, 233, 274, 275, 276
Stierle, Karlheinz 116
Stora, Benjamin 6n9, 13n29, 17n38, 49, 54, 259
Stovall, Tyler 38, 244
Streiff, Gérard
  Les caves de la Goutte d'or 29, 53, 71, 103–6, 108, 109, 111, 112, 114
Suleiman, Susan Rubin 70, 251n83, 267

Tahrir Square 157
Tasma, Alain
  Nuit noire (TV) 29, 55, 57, 89, 111, 288, 289, 292, 307
television
  ARTE 47, 202n50
  BBC 99, 202n50
  BBC Four 47, 47n42
  BeurTV 45
  Canal+ 57
  Faire face (series) 213n1, 224–25 *see also* Lalou, Étienne
  France 2, 75
  France 3, 47, 80, 111, 319
  RTF 225
  TF1 47n41
Témoignage chrétien 186n34, 235, 239, 277

Les Temps modernes 19n39, 38n16, 231n41, 276, 277
Têtes Raides 39, 180–82, 188, 314
Tevanian, Pierre 164n5, 165n8
Texier, Jean *see under* photography
theatre (groups)
  Komplex Kapharnaüm 58–59, 158–61
  Les Oranges 13n29, 58n65, 190n40
  Pierre noire 59, 159n63
theatre (venues and festivals)
  Avignon Theatre Festival 5, 57–58, 313
  Le TEP—Théâtre de l'Est parisien 58
  Le Théâtre des Quartiers d'Ivry 190n40
Thiaroye *see under* massacres
Tibéri, Jean 78n21
Touabti, Hocine
  L'Amour quand-même 44n35
Touita, Okacha
  Les Sacrifiés 46
La Tour de Nesle
  Dumas play 171n21, 184
  legend of 171, 178
Trautmann, Catherine 79, 82
Tristan, Anne 54
  Le Silence du fleuve 47
Truffaut, François 35
Tunisia 7
Tunisians
  as victims of police violence 230, 232, 236n57, 243, 284

United Nations General Assembly 10
universalism 15n33, 220, 221–22

Vautier, René
  Avoir vingt ans dans les Aurès 36–37
  hunger strike 242n72
Vélodrome d'hiver 1
  Vél d'Hiv roundup (1942) 273, 277, 278, 299, 301

Venice Film Festival
  Octobre à Paris 36
Vichy 6, 28, 50, 88, 270, 278, 305, 306,
    307, 308, 309
  in literature 43, 92, 94, 266–68,
    286–89, 292, 299
  myth of the good 278
Vidal-Naquet, Pierre 34, 241–42, 259,
    278
  surveillance of 86
Vilar, Jean-François
  Bastille tango 22n51, 46, 109, 308
Le Village de l'Allemand 306
La Villette 139–40, 212
Vincennes 9
Vivre au paradis 47, 121
Vivre me tue 44, 69, 214–16
  Begag's critique of 89n42, 252–54
  racial profiling 89, 228, 230

wave, first (of the anarchive; 1961–63)
    34–40
  ambivalence of 36, 39–40
  and censorship 36–37, 40
  chronology of 32, 34, 40
  "Dans la gueule du loup" 35–36,
    172
  defined 34
  links between October 17 and
    Vichy 43
  Octobre à Paris 34–35
  The Stone Face 35, 38
wave, second (of the anarchive;
    1983–99) 40–49
  and sited representation of
    October 17 118, 136
  as referencing the anarchive 109
  catalyzed by the *beurs* 44–46, 213
  films in 46–48
  historiography 48
  memory activism 40, 48–49

novels in 42–46
Papon affair 40–41, 42, 44
  see also Brooks, Philip, and Alan
    Hayling, *Drowning by Bullets*
wave, third (of the anarchive; 1999–)
    49–56
  and "A Group Declares..." 109–13
  and anarchiving 59–60
  and racism 254
  defined 49–50
  genres 53–55, 57–61
  memorialist activity 68–69, 313
  narrative proportion 55–56, 201
  novels 51, 145
  Papon libel trial 49–52, 289–92
  scholarship 64, 66–68
  see also under Holocaust survivors,
    in literature
World War II 34, 88, 146, 242, 267,
    271–73, 307
  and racial profiling 223
  fascism of 295
  hyperconsciousness of 275
  in literature 138, 151–52, 286, 288,
    292, 295, 299, 305
  specter of (in 1961) 275–78, 285
  specter of (in 2015) 311–12
Wright, Richard 38, 244
Wuillaume Report 108

Yacine, Kateb
  "Dans la gueule du loup" 4n8,
    12–13n28, 22, 35–36, 39, 48,
    172–76, 180–82, 188, 316
young adult literature (YA) 29, 49, 52,
    53, 54, 299, 302–3

Zik Zitoun
  "On a appris à nager" (2017) 4,
    315–17, **317**